The Big Spring on Court Square, as in Former Days

MEN OF MARK
AND REPRESENTATIVE CITIZENS

of

HARRISONBURG

AND

ROCKINGHAM COUNTY

VIRGINIA

PORTRAITS AND BIOGRAPHIES OF MEN AND WOMEN

EDITOR-IN-CHIEF
JOHN W. WAYLAND

CLEARFIELD

Originally published
Staunton, Virginia, 1943

Reprinted for
Clearfield Company, Inc. by
Genealogical Publishing Co., Inc.
Baltimore, Maryland
1999, 2002

International Standard Book Number: 0-8063-4834-8

Made in the United States of America

FOREWORD

THE purpose of this book is three-fold: First, to pay a deserved tribute to merit and achievement; second, to stimulate the young people of the county and city to worthy effort; and, third, to preserve in a permanent and accessible record many personal and historical facts that will be of interest and value to students, historians, and genealogists. The value of such records is always enhanced by time—future generations will appraise them more justly than we who are now living can do.

Most of the men and women who are presented herein are natives of Rockingham County; those not natives have become identified with the county or the City of Harrisonburg by a considerable period of residence—some by an honorable career of many years. At the same time many sons and daughters of Rockingham have gone out to other fields, some to distant lands, where they have won honor or wrought valiantly. These we have attempted to follow; some of them appear in the following pages; concerning others we lack information.

It will be observed that the subjects of the following portrayals are not restricted to any narrow limits—they represent a wide range of occupations, achievements, and interests: there are farmers, business men, teachers, educators, preachers, doctors, nurses, lawyers, jurists, statesmen, soldiers, writers, musicians, civil officials, stockmen, fruit-growers, and philanthropists: men and women. They have been nominated by a number of well-informed persons who have endeavored to consider all claims without partiality. All selections for inclusion have been based upon a consensus, and not merely upon the judgment of a single individual. It has not been possible in one small volume to include the portraits and biographies, or even brief sketches, of all persons worthy of such recognition—there are many others who are amply qualified to be given a place, concerning whom the public is well entitled to information.

The work is presented in two divisions: Part I and Part II. In the former are the more extended biographical sketches, with accompanying portraits; in the latter are brief chronicles, without portraits, concerning persons of distinction, the majority of whom are not now living.

DEDICATION

This book is dedicated to our Sponsors, men and women of public spirit, whose generous and patriotic cooperation has made the publication possible, and who thereby have enabled us to assemble a permanent and accessible record of facts concerning individuals, families, and local history that is of interest in the present and will be of value in the future.

ROSTER —— PART ONE

PORTRAITS AND BIOGRAPHIES

	Page
Acker, D. C.	24
Barglebaugh, C. E.	26
Bauserman, James E.	28
Beahm, Isaac N. H.	30
Beard, J. Owen	32
Biedler, John M.	34
Bloom, I. Mortimer	36
Blosser, Emanuel	38
Blosser, Gabriel	40
Bowman, Floyd M.	42
Bowman, George L.	44
Bowman, Paul H.	46
Bowman, Warren D.	48
Bowman, Rufus D.	50
Bradley, Schuyler	52
Bradley, Schuyler B.	54
Bradley, Bennett L.	56
Breneman, J. R.	58
Brunk, Oliver C.	60
Burke, John P.	62
Byers, Ashby C.	64
Byers, F. LeRoy	66
Byrd, William H.	68
Callender, Sam H.	70
Carver, Perry A.	72
Cleveland, Miss E. P.	74

ROSTER —— PART ONE

PORTRAITS AND BIOGRAPHIES

	Page
Cline, Justus H.	76
Cline, Solomon G.	78
Cline, S. Glenn	80
Clougherty, Hugh E.	82
Coffman, F. Wilmer	84
Conrad, Charles E.	86
Conrad, Laird L.	88
Converse, Henry A.	90
Cover, Jesse R.	92
Cox, Samuel M.	94
Crown, John R.	96
Dean, William	98
Dechert, Wilmer L.	100
Denton, J. S.	102
Denton, E. Warren	104
Denton, Bernard T.	106
Devier, D. Clint	108
Devier, Charles W.	110
Devier, Sheffey L.	112
Dewey, Charles N.	114
Deyerle, James H.	116
Dorsey, LeRoy H.	118
Duke, Samuel P.	120
Earman, D. Wampler	122
Estep, Charles S.	124
Fahrney, Welty B.	126

ROSTER — PART ONE
PORTRAITS AND BIOGRAPHIES

	Page
Fallis, William S.	128
Farver, Mrs. Mary V.	130
Flory, Isaac L.	132
Flory, Walter S., Sr.	134
Foley, O. F.	136
Forrer, Henry	138
Fry, James A.	140
Gambill, J. R.	142
Garber, F. Barth	144
Garber, Harry J.	146
Garber, J. A.	148
Garber, Minor W.	150
Garber, Paul N.	152
Garrison, J. Silor	154
Glick, J. Paul	156
Goeckerman, Mrs. W. H.	158
Good, Carter V.	160
Hall, J. H.	162
Hanley, Claude W.	164
Harman, James A.	166
Harnsberger, C. G.	168
Harnsberger, Thos. K.	170
Harpine, J. P.	172
Harrison, J. Houston	174
Harrison, Michael H.	176
Hartman, Dan	178

ROSTER —— PART ONE

PORTRAITS AND BIOGRAPHIES

	Page
Heatwole, Frank H.	180
Hedrick, Bayard M.	182
Henry, J. Maurice	184
Higgs, Kenneth M.	186
Hollar, Herman L.	188
Hoover, David H.	190
Hoover, John H.	192
Hoover, Lester D.	194
Hoover, Lawrence H.	196
Hoover, S. Beery	198
Hopkins, Abner K.	200
Huffman, C. Herbert	202
Jackson, Z. Davis	204
Johnston, James C.	206
Jordan, Elmer A.	208
Joseph, William M.	210
Kavanaugh, James M.	212
Kaylor, Quincy G.	214
Kaylor, William J.	216
Keezell, Nat H.	218
Keister, William H.	220
Keller, George W.	222
Kelley, Mrs. Hanora F.	224
Klingstein, E. L.	226
Koontz, W. Clyde	228
Kyger, W. H.	230

ROSTER —— PART ONE

PORTRAITS AND BIOGRAPHIES

	Page
Lewis, D. S., Sr.	232
Lineweaver, Ernest R.	234
Lineweaver, Ethel Irwin	236
Lineweaver, J. Reherd	238
Lineweaver, Goodrich W.	240
Logan, Conrad T.	242
Long, Luther E.	244
McGahey, Calvert R.	246
McGuffin, Mrs. Holmes	248
Menefee, William M.	250
Menefee, Wade W.	252
Miller, Ernest B.	254
Miller, John D.	256
Miller, E. R.	258
Miller, Minor C.	260
Miler, M. Oliver	262
Miller, O. L.	264
Monger, R. S.	266
Moore, K. C.	268
Mowbray, W. O.	270
Mundy, Charles S.	272
Myers, Fred P.	274
Myers, John C.	276
Neff, John H.	278
Ney, Baruch	280
Ney, Henry	282

ROSTER —— PART ONE

PORTRAITS AND BIOGRAPHIES

	Page
Ney, Albert H.	284
Nicholas, John J.	286
Palmer, Mrs. Charles E.	288
Price, C. Grattan	290
Prichard, Samuel J.	292
Riddel, James A.	294
Riddel, C. T., Sr.	296
Roller, John E.	298
Rosenberger, A. R.	300
Ruebush, Ephraim	302
Ruebush, Joseph K.	304
Ruebush, Glenn W.	306
Sanger, William T.	308
Scruggs, James T.	310
Shadwell, Lemuel R.	312
Shank, David E.	314
Shenk, Jacob A.	316
Showalter, David R.	318
Showalter, J. Henry	320
Sipe, William H.	322
Slaven, H. Bruce	324
Smith, Claude V.	326
Snapp, Herbert P.	328
Stickley, James O.	330
Strickler, R. E. L.	332
Strickler, Harry M.	334

ROSTER —— PART ONE

PORTRAITS AND BIOGRAPHIES

	Page
Sublett, Frank L.	336
Swank, Ward	338
Swartz, William P., Jr.	340
Switzer, Walter C.	342
Switzer, J. Robert	344
Thomas, Peter S.	346
Thompson, Mrs. Frances Calvert	348
Tucker, Mrs. Mercye Childress	350
Wampler, Fred C.	352
Weaver, Hershey H.	354
Weaver, Marion R.	356
Weaver, Russell M.	358
Wenger, Clement D.	360
Wetsel, Daniel M.	362
Wetsel, Arnold W.	364
Wilson, Benjamin F.	366
Wine, John E.	368
Wine, William E.	370
Wright, Joseph L.	372
Wyant, Herbert W.	374
Yancey, Burbridge S.	376
Yancey, Charles L.	378
Yancey, Philo B.	380
Yancey, Edward B.	382
Zigler, Howard S.	384

ROSTER — PART TWO
BIOGRAPHICAL SKETCHES

	Page
Acker, John	388
Aldhizer, George S.	388
Alexander, R. Glen	388
Allemong, J. W. F.	388
Avis, James L.	389
Barbee, Gabriel T.	389
Bassford, Kirby T.	389
Baugh, Miss Ada E.	390
Baxter, George A.	390
Bennett, Jesse	390
Bradley, Philo	391
Brown, Edward T.	391
Brown, John	391
Bryan, Daniel	392
Bryan, Mrs. Emma L.	392
Carr, Mrs. Maria G.	392
Carr, C. C. C.	393
Chrisman, George	393
Colvin, Robert M.	393
Compton, George F.	393
Conrad, George O.	394
Conrad, Edward S.	394
Conrad, George N.	395
Conrad, Miss Mary L.	395
Cootes, Samuel	395
Cox, Samuel K.	395
Cravens, William	396

ROSTER — PART TWO

BIOGRAPHICAL SKETCHES

	Page
Davis, Miss Jennie Y.	396
Davisson, Ananias	396
Devier, Giles	396
Dingledine, William J.	397
Dwyer, James H.	397
Early, Henry C.	398
Flory, George W.	398
Flory, John S.	398
Funk, Joseph	399
Funkhouser, Abram P.	399
Funkhouser, Jacob	399
Gay, Samuel	400
Gibbons, A. S.	400
Gibbons, Simeon B.	400
Gilbert, Felix	401
Gilmer, Thomas M.	401
Graham, John	401
Grattan, George G.	402
Grattan, Peachy R.	402
Gray, Robert	402
Gray, Algernon S.	402
Gwin, David W.	402
Haas, Talfourd N.	402
Hardesty, J. R. L.	403
Harris, John T.	403
Harrison, Gessner	403
Harrison, Thomas	403

ROSTER — PART TWO
BIOGRAPHICAL SKETCHES

	Page
Hart, Silas	404
Hawse, Jasper	404
Hay, James, Jr.	404
Hays, Daniel	404
Heatwole, Lewis J.	404
Heatwole, Cornelius J.	405
Heneberger, Lucien G.	405
Henry, Arthur L.	405
Herring, William	406
Hog, Peter	406
Hooke, Robert	406
Houck, Joseph P.	407
Hulvey, George H.	407
Jeffries, T. Fayette	407
Jones, Gabriel	408
Jones, John R.	408
Jones, T. O.	408
Kaylor, Peter C.	409
Keezell, George B.	409
Kemper, Albert S.	409
Kemper, Charles E.	410
Kenney, James	410
Kieffer, Aldine S.	410
Kilmer, Willis S.	410
Kimler, Abram C.	411
Kline, John	411
Koontz, John	411

ROSTER —— PART TWO
BIOGRAPHICAL SKETCHES

	Page
Kyle, David	412
Lanahan, John	412
Leake, William G.	412
Leedy, Robert F.	412
Lewis, Charles H.	412
Lewis, John F.	413
Lewis, Thomas	413
Liggett, Jacob N.	413
Lilly, Gordon W.	413
Lincoln, Abraham (1)	414
Lincoln, Jacob	414
Lincoln, Abraham (2)	414
Lincoln, John E.	414
Logan, Joseph T.	415
Long, Isaac	415
Lowman, Miss Fannie	416
Lupton, James R.	416
McMullen, Edgar W.	416
Madison, James	417
Maphis, Charles G.	417
Marshall, James W.	417
Martz, D. H. Lee	418
Massey, John E.	418
Mauzy, Richard	418
May, George E.	419
Miller, Adam	419
Moffett, Anderson	420

ROSTER — PART TWO

BIOGRAPHICAL SKETCHES

	Page
Moffett, S. H.	420
Myers, Joseph G.	420
Nalle, William	421
Neff, John H., Sr.	421
Ney, Isaac	421
Ney, Joseph	422
O'Ferrall, Charles T.	422
Ott, Lewis P.	422
Palmer, John W.	423
Paul, John, Sr.	423
Pennybacker, Isaac S.	423
Pennybacker, Miss Kate	424
Price, James R.	424
Price, Joseph	424
Reed, Lemuel S.	425
Reherd, James E.	425
Roller, Oliver B.	425
Rosenberger, George W.	425
Ruebush, George	426
Ruffner, William H.	426
Salyards, Joseph	426
Scholl, Peter	427
Scott, Thomas	427
Sevier, John	427
Shacklett, Samuel	428
Showalter, Anthony J.	428
Showalter, William J.	428

ROSTER — PART TWO

BIOGRAPHICAL SKETCHES

	Page
Sipe, Emanuel	429
Slater, Verne R.	429
Smith, Abraham	429
Smith, Daniel	430
Snapp, Robert J.	430
Snyder, Adolph H.	430
Snyder, Robert H.	431
Spiro, Morris	431
Sprinkel, Charles A.	432
Staples, Junius C.	432
Strayer, Mrs. Juliet L.	432
Taylor, David A.	433
Taylor, John W.	433
Tutwiler, Henry	433
Wampler, Isaac S.	434
Wartmann, Lawrence	434
Waterman, Asher	435
Waterman, A. G.	435
Wayland, John W.	435
Whitmore, Peter	436
Wilson, Benjamin F.	436
Wilton, Joshua	437
Winfield, John Q.	437
Winfield, Miss Paulina S.	437
Yancey, William B.	437
Yancey, Charles A.	438
Yancey, William L.	438
Yount, Walter B.	439

PART ONE

D. C. ACKER

FARMER, BUSINESS MAN, AND TRAVELER

Born October 11, 1869, near Broadway; educated in local schools, Bridgewater College, and Dunsmore Business College; farmer and stock-raiser; president of the First National Bank of Broadway; president of Rockingham Farm Bureau; vice-president of the Mutual Cold Storage Co. and chairman of directors; secretary-treasurer of the Rockingham Mutual Telephone & Telegraph Co.; director of Virginia Farm Bureau Federation; member of Agricultural Advisory Council of Rockingham County; etc.

Mr. Acker is a son of Isaac Acker (1832-1908) and his wife, Sallie V. Shoup, married November 11, 1868. She, born Sallie V. Shirkey, was the widow of Captain J. C. Shoup. Isaac Acker, son of Peter III (1808-1873), had an interesting career in the early West. He walked from Texas home to join the Brock's Gap Rifles under Captain John Q. Winfield. Later he was orderly sergeant in Co. B, 7th Va. Cavalry, under Generals Turner Ashby and Thomas L. Rosser, and was typical of the daring and resolute men who gave character and fame to the "Laurel Brigade." Peter III was a son of Peter II (1765-1852), who came to the Shenandoah Valley from Codorus Township, York County, Pa. His father, Peter I, was an early settler in Lancaster County, Pa. In Europe the Ackers lived in Lorraine. The family has been prominent in Rockingham for generations. Six of D. C. Acker's seven uncles served in the Confederate army. From 1888 to 1891 John Acker, prominent livestock dealer and brother of Isaac Acker, was a member of the Virginia Senate.

The Rockingham Farm Bureau, of which Mr. Acker is president, with a membership of 3100 farmers and doing an annual business of two and a half million dollars, has set standards for similar organizations in many parts of the country. The other enterprises, mentioned on the preceding page, with which Mr. Acker is associated, are successful and well known. Besides those mentioned, there are others, the Rockingham Petroleum Company, the Harrisonburg Telephone Company, etc., with which he is officially connected. He has been secretary-treasurer of the Rockingham Mutual Telephone & Telegraph Company for 35 years, and has been a notary public for over 40 years. He is also a member of the National Re-employment Committee for the Rockingham County board. He is typical of the men who have made the name of Rockingham a synonym for thrift and enterprise.

On April 6, 1906, Mr. Acker married Miss Martha M. B. Sellers, daughter of the late J. S. Sellers, a prominent farmer and stock dealer and an extensive landowner of the Smith Creek section of the county. Mr. and Mrs. Acker have three sons: Isaac J., born April 19, 1907, who in January, 1932, married Miss A. Lillian Bowen of Washington, D. C.; D. Clarence, born October 11, 1912; and E. D. Acker, born October 18, 1913.

Mr. D. C. Acker, while carrying on stock-raising and diversified farming, and participating actively in various business enterprises, as already indicated, has found time to follow out his inclinations towards educational and cultural activities. He has been an extensive traveler in Europe and America, and has been in all the states of the American Union except two. The farm which he owns and on which he resides is located on Linville Creek about three miles south of Broadway. The old Acker homestead, where his father was born, is also on Linville Creek, about three miles north of Edom, adjoining the lands where "Virginia John" Lincoln and his sons located in or about 1768.

CHARLES EDGAR BARGLEBAUGH
EDUCATOR AND CHURCHMAN

Born January 31, 1852, near Cootes's Store; a student in Oakland Academy and an honor graduate of Richmond College; founder of the Broadway High School; principal of Harrisonburg High School and Oak Hill Academy at McGaheysville; professor in Shenandoah Institute and Southside Female Institute; pioneer in normal school work; a charter member of the Broadway Baptist Church; died at Broadway, March 25, 1939.

Professor Barglebaugh, the eldest son of John Michael and Rebecca Bowman Barglebaugh, was born in the "White House" across the river from Cootes's Store. Having received his early education in Oakland Academy, he attended Richmond College for six years, graduating with high honors. On February 12, 1878, in Grace Street Baptist Church, Richmond, he married Miss Emma Gunn Greenhow Tyree, youngest daughter of Josiah Samuel and Elizabeth Gunn Tyree. Returning to the Shenandoah Valley, he founded the Broadway High School and was its principal for seven years. There, on May 1, 1940, with appropriate exercises, a marker was erected in his honor. As high-school principal in Harrisonburg and McGaheysville and as professor of Latin, Greek, and mathematics in Shenandoah Institute and in Southside Female Institute, Nottoway County, Va., he continued his work as a successful teacher. A pioneer in normal school work, he taught in summer normals for teachers for thirteen years. He regarded literary societies as a valuable aid in student development, and organized such societies in all of his schools. His students, many of whom have attained wide usefulness and high accomplishment, testify to his mastery in teaching and his wholesome influence. He was endowed with a keen and constructive intellect, a remarkable memory, and exercised a marked degree of gentleness and patience.

In addition to his intellectual endowments, Professor Barglebaugh was sincerely and thoroughly religious. He was a member of the Second Baptist Church in Richmond and was one of the charter members of the Baptist Church in Broadway. He was an untiring student of the Bible, a thoroughly consecrated Christian gentlemen, and cherished a life-long desire to go abroad as a missionary. His special interest was directed towards the mission fields of Persia.

Although his dream of a missionary career in foreign fields was never realized, Professor Barglebaugh rendered an important service in his home church and in the councils of his denomination. His piety and the wisdom born of long experience were of incalculable value to his associates in church work.

Mrs. Barglebaugh died on September 17, 1933. Professor Barglebaugh passed away on March 25, 1939, at the advanced age of 87. He is survived by his only daughter, Mrs. Randolph Tucker Montague, and four grandchildren: John Tyree Montague of Westport, Connecticut; Miss Renee Montague of New York City; Miss Emma Tyree Montague also of New York City; and Randolph Tucker Montague, Jr., of Broadway, Va. There are also two great-grandchildren: Landa Tyree Montague and Peter Gunn Montague of Westport, Connecticut.

Some of Professor Barglebaugh's associates in summer normal school work in Harrisonburg around 1890 were Supt. George H. Hulvey, Professor Charles G. Maphis, and Miss Belle Hannah (later Mrs. George B. Keezell).

JAMES EDWARD BAUSERMAN
TEACHER AND SCHOOL SUPERVISOR

Born Sept. 29, 1906, at McGaheysville; valedictorian McGaheysville H. S., class of 1925; B. S. in Elementary Education, Madison College, 1936; graduate student William and Mary and G. W. Univ.; teacher and principal in Rockingham and Fairfax Co.; supervisor of elementary education in Fairfax since 1940; vice-pres. and pres. Fairfax Co. Educa. Assn.; pres. State Elem. Principals Assn.; a director Fairfax Rotary Club; sec'y-treas. Va. Guidance Assn.; member Curriculum Group, State Dept. of Education, and committee on international relations, Natl. Education Assn.

Mr. Bauserman, though a young man, has already had a notable career in civic and educational service. He is a son of Frank S. and Nora Demma Gillespie Bauserman of Rockingham; his grandfathers were James Edward Bauserman and James Roderick Gillespie; his grandmothers, Eliza Shaver (daughter of Levie and Mary Carpenter Shaver) and Elmira Lee Cross. At intervals while continuing his studies at Madison College he taught at Mt. Pleasant and McGaheysville in Rockingham County, and was principal in Fairfax County at Centerville, Groveton, and Fairfax C. H., of elementary schools, the field of his specialty. In 1940 he was appointed to his present position of supervisor of elementary education in Fairfax County. His advanced studies have been carried on at the College of William and Mary and George Washington University. At the same time he has been active in civic, social, religious, and educational bodies. He has served as vice-president and two terms as president of the Fairfax County Education Assn.; organizer and two terms as president of the Elementary Principals Assn. of the county; organizer and twice president of the Elementary Principals Assn. of District H; president two terms Dept. of Elementary Principals of the Va. Education Assn.; vice-president one year of the Northern Va. Supervisors; eight years vice-president of Fairfax County Federation of P. T. A.; and was a member of the curriculum group that prepared, under direction of the State Department of Education, the Handbook for Parents and the Teacher's Study Bulletin at Madison College. He worked at William and Mary as one of the curriculum group that prepared illustrative material issued by the State Department. He is now president of the Supervisors' Assn. of Northern Virginia, sec'y-treas. Virginia Guidance Assn., member of the committee on international relations of N. E. A., a member of the F. E. A., V. E. A., N. E. A., and the Department of Supervisors, and Director of Instruction. Under the curriculum that he has introduced into Fairfax elementary schools, upper grades, three C's—citizenship, character, and culture—replace the three R's. The pupils work together and like it; they participate more largely in planning activities and develop leadership in carrying them out.

Mr. Bauersman has worked with the Boy Scouts, teaches in Sunday-school, is adviser to the Jr. Red Cross, is a member of the Young Democrats, aids in drives for the community chest, is treasurer of the county chamber of commerce, and participates in other community enterprises. His hobby is collecting minerals and studying birds in their natural haunts. In reading he prefers educational literature and historical novels.

On December 26, 1929, Mr. Bauserman married Miss Cora Elizabeth Fisher of Manassas, born March 15, 1908, daughter of Charles E. (deceased) and Mary E. Brown Fisher.

I. N. H. BEAHM

TEACHER, PREACHER, TRAVELER, LECTURER

Born near Good's Mill, Rockingham, May 14, 1859; B. E., Bridgewater College, 1887; teacher there, 1888-90; one of the founders of Daleville College, and principal 1890-94; evangelist, 1894-96; one of the founders of Prince Wm. Normal School, and principal 1896-99—school moved from Brentsville to Nokesville in 1909; president of Lordsburg College, 1899-1900; of Elizabethtown College, 1903-09; traveler in Europe and Bible lands; chautauqua lecturer; pastor and evangelist; author of several books.

Mr. Beahm, one of Rockingham's most distinguished sons, modestly hides his honors, and among his various names and titles prefers "Brother." His father, Henry A. Beahm, was a teacher and preacher; his mother, born Anne Showalter, he describes as "a jewel of intuition and devotion." His father's parents were Abram and Mary Baughman Beahm; his mother's, Peter (b. Feb. 22, 1802) and Fanny Baker Showalter. I. N. H., a freckled, sensitive youth, like the famous old Greek, overcame his stammering to become a real orator, his voice, as one has said, "clear as a silver bell with a golden clapper." After some years as farmer, shoemaker, and wheelwright, he entered upon his life work in education and religion, as already indicated. In 1931 he celebrated his ministerial jubilee, traveling 200 miles and preaching 20 half-hour sermons in one day. Leonard Lane of Richmond sent a printed schedule to Ripley and won a prize. He has always been a dynamo of energy and enthusiasm. His unusual ability as instructor was early in evidence. His classes in mathematics, elocution, psychology, and rhetoric partook of his contagious zeal and emulated his skill. His efficiency as an organizer and school administrator have been repeatedly demonstrated; and even now he is still busy answering calls to preach in different states. The institutions served have been given a vital religious character, in keeping with his devotion to high moral and spiritual values. With wide acquaintance among influential men and churches in the United States, he has enlarged his view and extended his information by travel abroad. On his desk in 1908 he and four others outlined "Two Centuries of the Church of the Brethren," a valuable book of 398 pages. He has several book manuscripts ready for publication. His hobby is hygienic living since his severe neurasthenia. He reads extensively in history, philosophy, and Bible, as well as in general literature. He is too sincere and independent to be political or diplomatic and yet a good mixer and tactful.

On March 23, 1890, Mr. Beahm married Miss Mary Bucher of Pa., daughter of Eld. Geo., and sister of Eld. R. P. Bucher. Of this marriage were born: R. Goodwin, Jan. 31, 1891, who died in infancy; Anna (Mrs. Baxter Mow), July 31, 1893, missionary in India and now teacher in Bethany Seminary, Chicago; Sara (Mrs. C. O. Miller), Jan. 15, 1895, for some time mission teacher in Asia Minor, now in Milwaukee, Wis.; William M., Nov. 4, 1896, missionary to Africa, now teacher in Bethany Seminary; Esther (Mrs. John L. Hoff), Oct. 25, 1898, now in Chicago where her husband is statistician in publishing work; Mary (Mrs. Robert Baber), Sept. 6, 1904, now in California; and Lois (Mrs. Walter Eyles), Jan. 15, 1909, who is now resident in Washington, D. C.

For the past 30 years Brother Beahm has made his home at Nokesville, Va., the scene of some of his important earlier labors. In his letter-writing, as in his public speaking, his style is incisive, dynamic, and straight from the shoulder. His conversation, out of rich experience, is instructive and inspiring.

JOSEPH OWEN BEARD

EDUCATOR, FARMER, LEGISLATOR

Born January 1, 1883, near Edom; attended local school, West Central Academy at Mt. Clinton, and a business school in Harrisonburg; B. S., Virginia Polytechnic Institute, 1911; instructor in agriculture, high-school teacher and principal in Rockingham County and Frederick; member of Va. House of Delegates, 1932-33 and 1934-35; operator of dairy farm; president of Linville Creek Light & Power Co.; president of Virginia Holstein Club; member of precinct and county Democratic committees; on county school board; chairman of Rockingham County Selective Service Board.

Mr. Beard is a son of Jacob S. (1853-1885) and Barbara A. Geil (1855-1941) Beard. His paternal grandparents were Silas Beard (1824-1888) and Maria Allebaugh (1830-1909); his mother's parents were Jacob Geil (1828-1917) and Mary Wenger (1836-1909). He was born and reared and now lives on the homestead of his maternal great-grandparents. At V. P. I. he was a cadet officer and also held offices in the Y. M. C. A. and other organizations. For three years following his graduation he was instructor in agriculture in the 7th Va. Congressional District. From 1914 to 1916 he taught in the Linville-Edom High School, the next year in Harrisonburg High School. A volunteer in World War I, he was taking officers' training in field artillery at Camp Taylor, Louisville, Ky., when the war ended in 1918. From 1921 to 1926 he was principal and instructor in agriculture, Middletown, Va., High School. He was a member of the Rockingham County School Board, 1928-32, and in 1940 was again elected on the same board. In Harrisonburg, from 1930 to 1935, he operated the Homestead Farms Dairy, Inc. He is now a director and vice-president of the Virginia State Dairyman's Association and president of the Virginia Holstein Club. Since 1911 he has operated a dairy farm at his birthplace near Edom, where he now owns a herd of 50 registered Holsteins.

Since young manhood Mr. Beard has been a member of the Presbyterian Church, and was elder and clerk of session in the Edom Presbyterian Church during its organization, 1911-1942. He now holds his membership in Harrisonburg. He is president of the Linville Creek Light & Power Co. and also of the Edom Telephone Co. He is a charter member of the Linville-Edom Ruritan Club and served as its first president. His hobby he declares to be his work in breeding high producing dairy cows, in which he has certainly made a notable success. He likes athletics, especially baseball, in which he has been a fan in recent years. His reading preferences are given to biography and history, and he is much interested in everything relating to neighborhood history and tradition.

On August 31, 1921, Mr. Beard married Miss Pauline Elizabeth Fawley, born May 15, 1897, at Broadway, daughter of Daniel C. and Rebecca Shoemaker Fawley. She in 1920 received the B. A. degree at Randolph-Macon Woman's College in Lynchburg, and was a teacher of mathematics and Latin from 1920 to 1924. Mr. and Mrs. Beard have four children: Joseph Owen, Jr., born September 25, 1928; Priscilla May, born January 30, 1930; Daniel Jacob, born April 7, 1931; and Mary Virginia, born July 15, 1937. These young people enjoy unusual advantages by reason of their family inheritance and the fact that they live within easy reach of the Linville-Edom School, which has for years been one of the most progressive in the county. The Edom community is rich in traditions of thrift and prosperity.

JOHN MORGAN BIEDLER, M. D.

PHYSICIAN AND SURGEON

Born December 24, 1873, in Rockingham County; early education under a governess at home and in New Market Polytechnic Institute; diploma from West Central Academy at Mt. Clinton, 1897; principal Tenth Legion Graded School, 1897-99; graduate University College of Medicine, Richmond, now the Medical College of Virginia, 1903; practiced at Shepherdstown, W. Va., and Bridgewater, Va., 1903-04; located in Harrisonburg in the fall of 1904, where he has since carried on a general practice, though specializing to some extent in obstetrics.

Dr. Biedler, one of the five children of Daniel U. Biedler, a veteran of Stonewall Jackson's army, and Mary Rosenberger Biedler, grew up near the historic village of Tenth Legion, which commemorates Thomas Jefferson's reference to Rockingham as the "Tenth Legion of Democracy." His grandfathers, Morgan Biedler of Page County and Edward Rosenberger of Rockingham, represented well-known families of Northern Virginia.

Dr. Biedler inaugurated the medical inspection of school children in Rockingham, the inspection of dairies supplying milk to the city, and the keeping of vital statistics, while serving as county health officer. In World War I President Wilson appointed him on the Medical Advisory Board of Rockingham. This position and that of county health officer he resigned to enter the U. S. Army, October 1, 1918. He held responsible positions as a health and medical officer in West Virginia and Virginia and was honorably discharged March 31, 1919. For 15 years he was coroner of Rockingham, and for an equal period was city physician to the poor by election of the council. He was substitute surgeon at Harrisonburg for the B. & O. Railroad for about 10 years; is chief medical examiner in the city for four of the largest life insurance companies, and is a member of the Southern and the American Medical Associations, as well as of local and state associations. He was a charter member of the Rockingham Memorial Hospital, and served on the board of trustees and the building committee. He is now on its staff, serving in internal medicine, minor surgery, and obstetrics.

While sojourning in Florida, Dr. Biedler was licensed by the State Medical Board, being one of six in a class of 175 to pass the examination. For the past several years he has been on the Board of Examiners and is examining physician for the local draft board, and has a certificate signed by President Roosevelt. He is an outstanding Kiwanian and has been a lieutenant-governor of the Capital District; has attended all conventions for years; and has a perfect attendance record for 11 years; and has served on the District and International Alliance committees. He is a charter and also a life member of the Rockingham Public Library Association, and is a member of the city-county chamber of commerce.

In 1903 Dr. Biedler married Miss Ina Esther Long of Mt. Clinton, who died in 1908, leaving two daughters: Frances Loraine, now Mrs. Dillard R. Monsees of Arlington, Va., and Janet Esther, now Mrs. Thomas L. Yancey, Jr., of Harrisonburg. There are five grandchildren. In 1911 he married Miss Bertha Grace Tyerman of Winchester, a daughter of Ambrose S. and Elsie D. Clinger Tyerman, natives of Pennsylvania. There are no children of this marriage. Dr. and Mrs. Biedler are devoted members of the Presbyterian Church.

IRVING MORTIMER BLOOM

RABBI AND SOCIAL ORGANIZER

Born August 10, 1889, in Bellaire, Ohio; attended New Cumberland, W. Va., public schools, 1895-1900; in Harrisonburg public schools, 1900-05; graduate of Harrisonburg High School, 1905; B. A., Columbia University, 1908; B. D., Hebrew Union College, Cincinnati, 1913; Ph. D., Columbia University, 1943; rabbi in Brooklyn, Springfield, Ill., and New York City from 1914 to the present; author of dramas and other works; Mason; active in social and philanthropic conferences and organizations.

Rabbi Bloom, by reason of his schooling here, the long residence of his father, his frequent visits, and his distinguished career in education, religious work, and social betterment, is well and favorably known in Harrisonburg. He is a son of Bernard and Anna (Levy) Bloom. Bernard Bloom was for many years a leading merchant in Harrisonburg, and since his retirement from active business life has continued to make his home in this city. Mortimer Bloom, after his early boyhood in Ohio and five years in the public schools of New Cumberland, W. Va., came with his parents to Harrisonburg where he continued his education in the public schools, graduating from the Harrisonburg High School in 1905. During the next three years he was a student in Columbia University, New York City, where he was awarded the B. A. degree in 1908. From 1908 to 1913 he pursued theological courses in the Hebrew Union College of Cincinnati, graduating in 1913 with the B. D. degree. During the next two years, 1914-16, he was rabbi in the city of Brooklyn. Going then to Springfield, Ill., he was rabbi in that city from 1916 to 1919. Since the year last named he has been located in New York City, where he has continued his work in important charges as rabbi (1919-20) of the Free Synagogue, the Hebrew Tabernacle (1920-33), the Temple Oheb Sholom (1933-40), and the Congregation Beth Israel, since 1940.

As a hobby, or diversion, Dr. Bloom gives much attention to the theater. He is the author of numerous playlets and radio sketches. He has written also two volumes entitled "A History of Jewish Rationalism" and "A Study of the Words 'God' and 'Religion,' " which are soon to be published. His greatest activity has been in fraternal organizations and in fostering good will between Christians and Jews, and in this work he has occupied many Christian pulpits. He is an enthusiastic Mason, affiliated with the Knights of Pythias, the Eastern Star, the Golden Chain, the Pythian Sisters, and B'nai B'rith. He is a chaplain of the Free Sons of Israel; active in the National Association for the Advancement of Colored People, the Central Conference of Reform Rabbis, and the Council for American Indians. The fitness of and need for such humanizing activities is certainly emphasized by the present distress of the world, which is due in such great measure to racial and religious antagonisms. In his work Dr. Bloom combines the skill and tact developed from long training with unusual natural powers. As a public speaker he enhances the weight of fact with logic and eloquence. Some years ago, while sojourning in Harrisonburg, he delivered an address at Madison College, which, in the opinion of one of the older faculty members, was the most effective and finished address he had heard there over a considerable period of years.

On Dec. 18, 1934, Dr. Bloom married Miss Evelyn E. Handler, daughter of Adolph and Dora Handler, of N. Y. City. She is an officer in educational and philanthropic societies and lectures on interior decorating.

EMANUEL BLOSSER

BUSINESS-BUILDER AND BANKER

Born near Harrisonburg, October 28, 1877; educated on a farm and in the neighborhood school; one of the organizers of the City Produce Exchange in 1908; a director of the National Bank; a director and the treasurer of the Harrisonburg Loan & Thrift Corporation; vice-president of the Harrisonburg Grocery Company; president of the Harrisonburg Kiwanis Club; president of the City Produce Exchange.

The Blossers, many of whom have been prominent Mennonites, have been in Virginia for more than a century and a half, and in 1812 Peter Blosser and his sons became landowners in Rockingham County.

Henry Blosser, born in Rockingham on August 21, 1853, was a son of Abraham and Sarah Brunk Blosser. He married Sophia Showalter, also a native of Rockingham, who was born January 17, 1852, a daughter of Henry J. Showalter and his wife, Elizabeth Rhodes. Henry and Sophia Blosser lived on a farm three miles west of Harrisonburg, about midway between Garber's Church and Dale Enterprise, and there Emanuel and their other children were born.

Emanuel Blosser attended a two-room school that used to stand near Weaver's Church, and he recalls the teachers there as John R. Suter, Lewis J. Heatwole, John Floyd, Charles Kagey, Randolph Mauck, and Miss Fannie Hammond. The wholesome and thrifty life on the farm was made profitable in various ways. For one thing, Emanuel, with his father, did a small-scale business raising and dressing poultry, and in 1908 Emanuel, his brother Gabriel, and Hershey H. Weaver organized the City Produce Exchange in Harrisonburg, which has grown into one of the most extensive and successful enterprises of its kind in the United States. Eggs, chickens, and turkeys are collected from a large area by means of trucks which make daily circuits over the country-side, and at the same time the farmers bring in thousands of birds from their flocks and eggs in great quantites. The fowls are fattened and dressed for shipping in accordance with the most approved methods and processes. Since 1930 shipments to the cities have been made chiefly in capacious auto vans. Over 7500 chickens are processed daily; the annual shipments of dressed poultry aggregate several thousand tons, and the firm's yearly disbursement is two and a half million dollars. Large branch houses are operated in Elkton and Staunton.

In 1901 Mr. Blosser married Miss Mary Garber, a daughter of Daniel Garber, a neighboring farmer. She died in 1922. There were no children of this marriage. On January 31, 1924, Mr. Blosser married Miss Leona Branum, a daughter of Samuel and Julia Branum. Of this union there are two children: Julia Nelle Blosser, born August 11, 1925, and Henry Gabriel Blosser, born March 16, 1928.

Though a busy man with many important interests, Mr. Blosser is a genial companion and an all-round good fellow. He is a charter member of the Harrisonburg Kiwanis Club and is now (1942) serving as its president. Like many of his forebears, he is a member of the Mennonite Church. In politics he is a Democrat. In the selection of his reading he naturally shows a preference for commercial and news magazines. He does not claim to have any hobbies—perhaps he should have some. He no doubt finds some diversion in his variety of interests, for in addition to being president of the City Produce Exchange he is an active participant in other business and financial enterprises of the city.

GABRIEL BLOSSER
POULTRY EXPERT AND BUSINESS MANAGER

Born October 23, 1879, on a Rockingham County farm; attended the Weaver's Church public school; entered the produce business in Harrisonburg at the age of 28; vice-president of the City Produce Exchange, Inc., and manager of the Staunton branch; deacon and elder of the Staunton Lutheran Church; member of the Executive Council, Lutheran Synod of Virginia.

The Blosser family, of which Gabriel Blosser is a member, is widely distributed in various parts of the United States and has supplied a number of prominent leaders in the Mennonite Church, in business, and in other fields of activity. Some years ago Hon. Boutwell Dunlap of San Francisco compiled a sketch of the Blossers in this country, from which the items immediately following are selected.

Peter Blosser, born in Switzerland in 1752, settled first, on coming to America, in York County, Pa. In 1776 he came to what is now Page County, Va. Blosserville took its name from the family, and a house that they erected there was still standing a few years ago. Peter and his sons, in 1812, came to Rockingham and bought farms from the Harrisons, Whitmores, and others. Peter Blosser returned to York County. Pa., where he died and was buried in the Blasser graveyard. In Pennsylvania the family name has been spelled Blasser. One of Peter's sons was Jonas, born in 1791. Jonas built a stone house two miles southwest of Harrisonburg, which, with a number of other buildings, was burned in October 1864, by order of General Sheridan, but the walls were used in rebuilding the next year. Jonas married Margaret Burkholder, eldest child of Bishop Peter Burkholder and his wife, Elizabeth Coffman. Abraham, a son of Jonas, translated his grandfather's "Treatise on Baptism and the Lord's Supper" and operated a printing shop at Dale Enterprise, where, around 1880, he published *The Watchful Pilgrim*, which circulated among the Mennonites of the United States and Canada. His grandson, Perry J. Blosser, is, or was a few years ago, a Mennonite minister at South English, Iowa. One of Abraham's sons, Henry Blosser, born August 21, 1853, married Sophia Showalter and was the father of Emanuel Blosser and Gabriel Blosser, whose biographies are here presented.

Gabriel Blosser grew up on his father's farm between Garber's Church and Dale Enterprise and, with his brother Emanuel, attended the school near Weaver's Church. He, in 1908, joined with his brother Emanuel and Hershey H. Weaver in establishing the City Produce Exchange in Harrisonburg, with which he is still connected. This business enterprise has grown into one of the largest of its kind in the United States. It centers in Harrisonburg, but large branches are operated also at Elkton and Staunton. Gabriel Blosser is vice-president of the Corporation and since 1915 for a number of years has been the manager in charge of the branch in Staunton.

Gabriel Blosser is a member of the Christ Lutheran Church of Staunton, serving as deacon and elder, and has been on the Executive Council of the Lutheran Synod of Virginia. His wife was Miss Effie R. Fansler of Mt. Clifton, Shenandoah County, born March 15, 1887; married March 1, 1915, in Staunton, where they reside. Mr. Blosser is not addicted to any hobbies, so far as he admits, and does not express any particular preferences in his reading, but we may be certain that he keeps abreast of the times in the world of business, especially in those departments that relate to his own work and interests.

FLOYD MELANCTHON BOWMAN
ORCHARDIST AND BUSINESS MAN

Born July 9, 1886, near Timberville, Va.; began the study of telegraphy at fifteen; operator at New Market and Timberville; station agent at Timberville, 1907-17; successful dealer in eggs and poultry; extensive fruit-grower and shipper of choice fruit; twice vice-president of the Virginia Horticultural Society; director of the Farmers & Merchants Bank of Timberville; leader in Sundayschool and church; died at Johns Hopkins Hospital, Baltimore, February 14, 1926.

Mr. Bowman, a son of David and Catherine Arehart Bowman, represented two well-known families of Rockingham and the Shenandoah Valley. The Bowmans have been numerous and influential since colonial times not only in Rockingham, but also in Shenandoah and Frederick. Floyd Bowman very early in life began to show unusual business qualities. He was one of the first to see the possibilities of the produce business, and began buying eggs and poultry from the merchants, grading the eggs carefully, fattening the poultry, and shipping in carload lots. His genial personality, honesty, and energy contributed largely to his success. He bought up poultry and eggs from the retail merchants in the adjoining county of Shenandoah as well as in Rockingham, making his shipments from Timberville. Later he opened a branch office and storeroom in Broadway, and at the time of his death the volume of his trade was perhaps the largest of its kind in the Valley outside the city of Harrisonburg.

Along with his produce business, Mr. Bowman became an extensive and successful grower of apples and peaches, developing one planting after another until he had three large orchards in fine bearing condition. With the sites carefully selected and the trees expertly cared for, his fruit was of excellent quality, and in every place to which it was shipped it was always received with confidence. The label on every lot or package could always be relied upon.

In religious life and public affairs Mr. Bowman proved himself a good man and a good citizen. For a number of years he served as a member of the town council of Timberville; he was a valued member of the Kiwanis Club of Harrisonburg, and an active office-holder in the Horticultural Society of the State. His wholesome leadership in religious life was shown effectively as superintendent of the Sundayschool of Rader's Evangelical Lutheran Church, near Timberville, and for a considerable period he was the efficient chairman of the church council.

Mr. Bowman was twice married. His first wife, Miss Helen Middleton, of Herndon, Va., married in 1908, died in 1910, leaving two children: Catherine Elizabeth and Pasco Middleton. The former is now Mrs. Donald H. Myers of Cincinnati, Ohio. She has a son, George Dalton Myers. Pasco Bowman married Kathryn Lohr of Timberville. He died April 19, 1933, leaving a son, Pasco Bowman, Jr.

In 1915 Mr. Bowman married Miss Annie E. Garber of Timberville. Of this union were born three children: Leona Virginia, now instructor of public health nurses at Johns Hopkins Hospital, where she graduated in 1939; James Garber, who graduated from Augusta Military Academy in 1941 and is now a student at William and Mary College; and Anna LaMar, now a senior in the Timberville High School. He was survived also by two sisters, Mrs. Alice Beam and Mrs. Nettie Smith, both of Baltimore, and two brothers, Charles D. Bowman of Timberville and Dr. Rufus Bowman of Massillon, Ohio.

GEORGE LYNN BOWMAN
LAWYER AND LEGISLATOR

Born October 9, 1874, near Harrisonburg; educated in county and city schools, Western College, Iowa, and Drake University; located in Kingfisher, Okla., 1899; admitted to the bar, 1900; president board of trustees of Kingfisher College 18 years; Democratic national committeeman for Oklahoma four years; on board of regents of the University of Oklahoma 14 years; chairman of the Democratic state committee of Oklahoma, 1920-24; director of the Oklahoma State Historical Society; member of the Oklahoma State Senate.

Mr. Bowman is a son of William Harpine Bowman, born August 26, 1833, in Shenandoah County, and his wife, Emily Frances Huffman, born January 25, 1837, at Harrisonburg. His first Bowman ancestor in Virginia was George Bowman, a son-in-law of Jost Hite. George Bowman's sons, who were distinguished with George Rogers Clark in the conquest of the Northwest and other important events of the Revolution, were born at the old Bowman homestead on Cedar Creek, near Strasburg, where the stone house built by their father about 1751 is well known as Fort Bowman or Harmony Hall. In 1746 George Bowman of Frederick County, Va., purchased 500 acres of land from William Linvill on Linvill Creek, then in Augusta County, and in 1772, 260 acres in the Forest, on the Fairfax Line, now the dividing line between Rockingham and Shenandoah. In the latter transaction George Bowman is spoken of as of Augusta County, possibly because he owned land in Augusta. It may be that both these purchases were made by the pioneer George Bowman of Cedar Creek. He and his sons acquired lands in many parts of the country.

At the age of 19 George Lynn Bowman went with Rev. A. P. Funkhouser and family to Toledo, Iowa, where Mr. Funkhouser was president of Western College. This school Mr. Bowman attended for four years. In 1898 he went to Drake University in Des Moines, where he studied in the law school. In 1902, after locating in Kingfisher, Okla., he was elected attorney of Kingfisher County, then in the territory of Oklahoma, and served in this office five years. Since then he has been active and prominent in various civic, political, fraternal, and educational duties, as indicated on the preceding page. Besides, he has served as president of the Society of the Sons of the American Revolution in Oklahoma, and president of the State Bar of Oklahoma. He was a delegate at large to the national convention in Baltimore in 1912 that first nominated Woodrow Wilson for President. He was a delegate from his state to the Democratic national convention in San Francisco (1920), Chicago (1932), and Chicago again (1936). For 30 years he was a national officer in the Modern Woodmen of America, for eight years of the time a director. In 1940 he was elected to the State Senate of Oklahoma, to serve from 1941 to 1945. His biography appears in "Who's Who in America," as well as in several standard biographical and historical publications of Oklahoma.

On July 25, 1940, Mr. Bowman, in Oklahoma City, married Miss Edna Hoffman of Kingfisher. He is a member of the Congregational Church, the Rotary Club, the local chamber of commerce, and the Masonic lodge. In recent years he has been an ardent traveler, touring the United States from coast to coast, and visiting Canada, Alaska, Mexico, and Hawaii. He says: "My hobby is collecting intricate little figurines for my 'what not.' My reading preference is for government, history, and biography."

Mr. Bowman is a brother of Miss Orra Bowman and Mrs. A. L. Minnick, and an uncle of Miss Vada, Frank, and Lynnwood Whitesel, all living now in Harrisonburg.

PAUL HAYNES BOWMAN
PRESIDENT OF BRIDGEWATER COLLEGE

Born near Johnson City, Tenn., July 5, 1887; grew up on his father's farm; attended local schools and Boone's Creek Seminary in Tennessee and Bridgewater College, Va.; B.A., Bridgewater, 1910; B.D., Crozer Theological Seminary, Chester, Pa., and M.A., Univ. of Pa., 1913; D.D., Blue Ridge College, Md., 1918, and Juniata College, Pa., 1925; LL.D., Roanoke College, 1941; pastor Bethany Church of Brethren, Phila., 1910-15; president Blue Ridge College, 1915-17; professor in Bridgewater College, 1918-19; president since 1919; member Va. Academy of Science, Tau Kappa Alpha, Rotary Club, Gen. Education Board Church of the Brethren, etc.

President Bowman is a native of the historic Watauga country of East Tennessee, where his ancestors have lived for more than a century. His father, Dr. Samuel J. Bowman, born in 1858, was a son of Joseph B. and Susana Arnold Bowman; his mother, Susan Virginia Bowman, born in 1859, was the daughter of George C. Bowman and Ann Hylton. Both these Bowman families, related distantly if at all, moved to Tennessee from the Valley of Virginia about 1802. Paul grew up on Boone's Creek, named for the famous hunter and explorer, in the Watauga Settlement, the first made by white pioneers so far south on waters of the Tennessee. Most of his ancestors in this region were substantial farmers and several were faithful ministers in the Church of the Brethren. In the critical years of 1861-65 they were loyal to the Union.

Though still a comparatively young man, President Bowman has an unusual record as an educator, religious leader, and an active participant in civic and philanthropic enterprises. As a director of the Rockingham Library Association and the Rockingham Memorial Hospital, as well as in other capacities, he has been intimately identified with worthy local organizations; as a member of the General Education Board of the Church of the Brethren, as moderator of the annual conferences of the denomination, and otherwise, he has had a part in movements that are nation-wide and world-wide. He is a speaker of unusual ability and is much sought after as a preacher and lecturer not only in churches of his own faith, but in others as well. During the 24 years that he has been president of Bridgewater College the institution has made substantial progress in buildings and equipment, in progressive development of curricula, and in recognition accorded it by other colleges and universities. Many interesting details of the work at Bridgewater and related institutions in which Dr. Bowman has been an inspiring leader are set forth in the semi-centennial history of the college that was published in 1930. Biographical sketches appear in "Who's Who in America" and other works of like character.

On August 12, 1913, Dr. Bowman married Miss Flora Hoover, daughter of Mr. and Mrs. John H. Hoover of Timberville. Dr. and Mrs. Bowman are the parents of four children: Paul Hoover, Grace, John Evans, and Rebecca Gene. Paul, Jr., born June 20, 1914, B.A., Bridgewater College, 1934, B.D., Crozer Theological Seminary, and M.A., Univ. of Pa., 1937, was Relief Administrator for Spain and France, and is now engaged similarly in Ecuador. Grace, born October 8, 1917, B.A., Bridgewater College, 1939, high school teacher 1939-40, has been director of religious education in the Hagerstown (Md.) Church of the Brethren since 1941. John Evans, born April 23, 1920, B.A., Bridgewater College, 1941, M.A., Univ. of Pa., 1942, has been in C. P. S. camp since 1942. Rebecca Gene, born January 1, 1925, is a sophomore in Bridgewater College.

WARREN DANIEL BOWMAN
EDUCATOR AND MINISTER

Born April 9, 1894, near Dayton; grew up on his father's farm; graduate of Bridgewater High School, 1913; A. B., Bridgewater College, 1920; M. A., University of Chicago, 1922, and Ph. D., 1930; associate professor of education, Farmville State Teachers College, 1923-30; head department of education and psychology, Juniata College, 1930-37; pastor of the Washington City Church of the Brethren since 1937.

Dr. Bowman's father, Benjamin Franklin Bowman, was born at Dayton; his mother, born Mary Elizabeth Miller, was a native of the Bridgewater community. Both families, the Bowmans and the Millers, have been well represented in Rockingham for generations. Warren D. is an older brother of Dr. Rufus D. Bowman whose biographical sketch appears in this volume, in which connection the names of the brothers' grandparents are given.

At the University of Chicago, where both his degrees were taken in the school of education, Dr. Bowman's specialties were indicated. With prior teaching experience in Noble Center Elementary School and as principal of the McGaheysville High School, he was associate professor of education and psychology in the State Teachers College at Farmville for seven years, and from 1923 to 1926 he served as principal of the training school along with his teaching in the college. At Juniata College, 1930-37, he was head of the department of education and psychology, and for five years was dean of men. At intervals from 1923 to 1937 he taught in different summer schools: George Peabody College for Teachers, 1923 and 1924; Emory University, 1925; Virginia Polytechnic Institute, 1927; University of Virginia, 1930; Duke University (Lake Junaluska branch of the summer session), 1936 and 1937. All this time he felt an insistent urge toward a somewhat different field. He says: "When a young boy my cherished dream was to be a minister. I ran away from it, but could never get entirely away from a field of work that seemed to be incessantly calling me." In September, 1937, he became pastor of the Washington City Church of the Brethren, where he has ever since found a congenial place of service with his congregation of 1000 members. In 1940-41 he was a member of the National Christian Mission Team to the large cities of the United States, and the next year to the smaller cities of 25,000 to 100,000 population. He has conducted numerous courses for youth on Christian ideals of love and marriage and delivered many lectures on marriage and home-making before youth groups in churches and colleges. He is the author of a book for youth entitled "Home-Builders of Tomorrow," which has been widely used throughout the nation, and has contributed related articles to religious magazines. He is a member of the Phi Delta Kappa Fraternity.

On June 11, 1925, Dr. Bowman married Miss Olive Murrann Smith of Columbus, Ga. She received her B. S. degree at Farmville in 1926, and was valedictorian of her class. Of this marriage have been born four children: Warren Daniel, Jr., January 4, 1930; Helen Elizabeth, August 20, 1932; Ruth Elaine, September 15, 1937; and Jean Eleanor, May 1, 1940. All were born in the Johnston-Willis Hospital, Richmond, and so are native Virginians, though their parents were not all the time living in Virginia.

RUFUS DAVID BOWMAN
MINISTER AND EDUCATOR

Born January 23, 1899, near Dayton; grew up on his father's farm; graduate of Bridgewater High School, 1917; A. B., Bridgewater College, 1923; B. D., Yale Divinity School, 1926; graduate student in the Catholic University of America and Northwestern University; D. D., Bridgewater College, 1937; pastor of churches in Roanoke and Washington City; member of the Gen. Mission Board, Church of the Brethren, since 1935; president of Bethany Biblical Seminary since 1937.

Dr. Bowman's parents were Benjamin F. and Mary E. Miller Bowman, who lived between Dayton and Bridgewater. He is a brother to Dr. Warren D. Bowman, who appears herein. His grandfather, Daniel Bowman, lived at Silver Lake, Dayton, and owned the mill there. His mother's parents were Elder Martin P. Miller and his wife, Rebecca Heatwole. All were active in church work, and Elder Miller was one of the first trustees of Bridgewater College. Dr. Bowman says that he grew up on a farm, "the place for a boy." He was an honor graduate of Bridgewater and since moving to Chicago has completed residence requirements for the Ph. D. degree at Northwestern. He, like his brother Warren, is a member of Phi Delta Kappa, professional honorary fraternity sponsored by schools of education.

From 1926 to 1929, while Dr. Bowman was pastor of the First Church of the Brethren in Roanoke, the membership increased by about 100 each year. The next five years he was general secretary of the Board of Christian Education, Church of the Brethren, promoting a program for the church schools of his denomination. While he was pastor of the Washington City Church of the Brethren, 1934-37, he did grduate work at the Catholic University of America. In the summer of 1936 he and Mrs. Bowman attended the World's Sunday School Convention at Oslo, Norway, and toured in Norway, Sweden, Denmark, Germany, France, Switzerland, and England. At Geneva and Cambridge they attended peace conferences. In Washington, 1934-37, he was on the executive committee of the city Federation of Churches. From 1935 to 1940 he was chairman of the Brethren Peace Committee; he was moderator of the Annual Conference, Church of the Brethren, 1939-40; since 1935 he has been on the General Mission Board (chairman since 1940) and a director of the Brethren Publishing House. He has served in other important capacities in the activities of his denomination, and in 1937 and 1939, with others, was in conferences with President Roosevelt. He has preached and lectured extensively before district and national church assemblies and in colleges, as well as in local churches, and has served on the program of the International Council of Religious Education and the American Association of Theological Schools. In 1937 he was elected to the presidency of Bethany Biblical Seminary, Chicago, his present position.

On June 16, 1925, Dr. Bowman married Miss Eva Craun, born February 5, 1901, daughter of Mr. and Mrs. Wm. A. Craun of Bridgewater. She, like her husband, grew up on a farm; attended Centerville School and Bridgewater College, graduating at B. C. in 1923, with Mr. Bowman. He was president of the class, she was secretary. In 1925 she graduated M. A. from the Boston University School of Religious Education. Dr. and Mrs. Bowman have three children: Mack Daniel and Jane Esther, twins, born October 8, 1930; and Judith Margaret, born October 1, 1937. Dr. Bowman's favorite reading is in the fields of religion, biography, and international relationships. His hobby is playing with his children.

SCHUYLER BRADLEY

CHURCHMAN AND IRON FOUNDER

Born in Harrisonburg, November 27, 1860; educated in the public and private schools of Harrisonburg; entered the foundry business with his father, Philo Bradley, and his brother, John S. Bradley; with his brother, took over management of the foundry in 1893; was president of the firm from 1918 until his death, February 6, 1939; also engaged in farming; was an active member and an official of the Methodist Church; served for some time on the town council of Harrisonburg.

Mr. Bradley was a son of Philo Bradley (1829-1908), a native of Cayuga County, N. Y., and his wife, Frances Slater. Philo Bradley came to Virginia about 1854 and to Harrisonburg in 1855, where he soon thereafter established the foundry which he and members of his family have ever since operated. When his sons grew up they were associated in the business with him, and in 1893 Schuyler and his brother, John S. Bradley, took over the active management of the industry. From 1918 until his death in 1939 Schuyler Bradley was president and general manager of the firm of P. Bradley & Sons. The foundry is now the oldest enterprise in Harrisonburg that has been carried on continuously to the present time, and the firm of P. Bradley & Sons is now composed of grandsons and a great-grandson of the founder. The main buildings of the Bradley Foundry are located on both sides of South High Street of the city, which is a part of the old Harrisonburg and Warm Springs Turnpike, laid out in 1831. The first location of the foundry, it is said, was somewhat farther southeast, nearer to Black's Run, and at that time the site was on the outskirts of the town. During the more than three-quarters of a century that have elapsed since the enterprise was started the name of West Street has been changed to High Street and buildings have been erected for a half-mile or more westward beyond the foundry.

Schuyler Bradley was for many years one of the outstanding citizens of Harrisonburg, not only a successful business man but also active in the civic and religious life of the community. For two terms he served as a member of the town council. He was a devoted member of the Methodist Church, which he served in various official capacities. As one of the trustees and a member of the building committee he was largely instrumental in the erection of the splendid house of worship on South Main Street, the cornerstone of which was laid on September 1, 1911, with appropriate ceremonies by the Masonic lodge, the reading of an historical sketch by the pastor, Rev. H. H. Sherman, and a masterful address on "The House of God" by Rev. M. D. Mitchell. In national politics Mr. Bradley was a Republican, though an independent voter in local elections. He was very liberal to needy individuals and to charitable organizations whose work commended them to his confidence. He carried on farming as a hobby or an avocation. Although his schooling had not been extended to college courses, he was interested in all cultural activities and kept abreast of the times by the reading of history, current events, and general literature.

On June 17, 1885, Mr. Bradley married Miss Mary Lyne Burns of near Charles Town, Jefferson County, W. Va. Of the marriage were born two sons: Schuyler Burns Bradley, July 13, 1887, and Bennett Locke Bradley, April 10, 1893, of whom biographies follow in this work. At the time of his death, February 6, 1939, he was survived by Mrs. Bradley, his two sons, and two sisters: Mrs. John G. Yancey of Harrisonburg and Mrs. Nannie W. Thomasson of Washington, D. C.

SCHUYLER BURNS BRADLEY

PRESIDENT, P. BRADLEY AND SONS

Born July 13, 1887, in Harrisonburg; attended Harrisonburg Graded School and High School; student in Randolph-Macon Academy, Front Royal, 1906-07; started work in the P. Bradley & Sons Foundry at age 20; president and manager of the company since March 21, 1939; member of the Methodist Church; was a charter member of the Kiwanis Club of Harrisonburg; finds recreation in reading current events, histories, and biographies.

Mr. Burns Bradley is the older son of the late Schuyler Bradley (1860-1939) and his wife, who was Miss Mary Lyne Burns, born April 26, 1865, near Charles Town, the historic county-seat of Jefferson County, W. Va. The Lynes and the Burnses have been well known in this county, distinguished as the home of numerous prominent families, for more than one hundred years. Charles Town was laid out on the lands of Charles Washington and named for him. A number of other Washington homes are in the neighborhood. William Lyne Wilson, appointed Postmaster General by President Cleveland in 1895, and later president of Washington and Lee University, was born only a few miles northwest of Charles Town. Schuyler Bradley, whose biography appears on the preceding pages, was one of the sons of Philo and Frances Slater Bradley.

When Schuyler Burns Bradley, as a small boy, started to school in Harrisonburg there were, in addition to the public school, a number of excellent private schools in the town. Some of these were continued for a number of years, but gradually, especially after William H. Keister, in 1894, became principal of the public schools, the private schools were discontinued, and the boys and girls of the town gravitated to the public schools. It is a matter of interest that Mr. Bradley's grandfather, Philo Bradley, was one of the original public school trustees of Harrisonburg, some of his colleagues on the board being Benjamin Long, W. S. Lurty, Geo. S. Christie, Jasper Hawse, Geo. G. Grattan, and Gen. J. R. Jones. After Burns Bradley attended the Harrisonburg High School for three years, he spent a year in Randolph-Macon Academy at Front Royal, and then went to work in the foundry which his grandfather had established in Harrisonburg many years earlier and which was then being operated by his father, Schuyler Bradley, and his uncle, John S. Bradley. In this enterprise he has ever since been actively engaged, and since the death of his father, February 6, 1939, he has been president and manager. He is, as was his father, a member of the Methodist Church; and when the Kiwanis Club was organized in Harrisonburg 20 years ago he was one of the charter members, though not a member at present.

On June 1, 1911, Mr. Bradley married Miss Caroline Lee Newman, who was born March 24, 1890, near New Market, daughter of Charles Edward (born May 14, 1854) and Eva Watkins Newman. The latter was born March 13, 1855, near Gordonsville. The Newmans have been prominent in Rockingham and Shenandoah for 200 years, the first of the name here having been probably Samuel Newman and his wife Martha, who came from Philadelphia County, Pennsylvania, in or about 1744. Mr. and Mrs. Bradley have two children: Caroline Lee, born in Harrisonburg on May 18, 1912, and Schuyler II, also a native of Harrisonburg, born May 8, 1913.

BENNETT LOCKE BRADLEY
FIRST VICE-PRESIDENT, P. BRADLEY AND SONS

Born April 10, 1893, in Harrisonburg; attended Harrisonburg High School; V. P. I., 1911-12; University of Virginia, 1912-14; graduated in chemistry, U. Va.; worked for Duponts at Chester, Pa., Gibbstown, N. J., and Louviers, Colo., 1914-19; at the Bradley Foundry, 1919-22; with the Davis Canning Co., Laurel, Del., 18 months, then with Duponts again until the fall of 1932; since then in Harrisonburg with the Bradley Foundry; first vice-president and secretary and treasurer, P. Bradley & Sons; Methodist; scout leader, etc.

Bennett Bradley is the younger son of Schuyler and Mary Lyne Burns Bradley. Biographies of his father and older brother, Schuyler Burns Bradley, appear on preceding pages of this work. Items concerning his grandfather, Philo Bradley, may be found in Part Two, following. After attending the high school of Harrisonburg for three years, he studied for a year (1911-12) in Virginia Polytechnic Institute at Blacksburg, Va., and then entered the University of Virginia where he studied two sessions, graduating in chemistry in 1914. For the next five years he was employed by the Dupont Company of Wilmington, Delaware; then for the three years following he was engaged with his father, uncle, and older brother in the Bradley Foundry in his native city. Going again to Deleware, he was connected for a year and a half with a manufacturing enterprise, after which he spent another extended period with the Duponts at various places. Returning to Harrisonburg in the fall of 1932, he has since been actively engaged with the family firm of P. Bradley & Sons, in which he holds the position of first vice-president, also that of secretary and treasurer.

Reference has already been made on preceding pages to the long and continuous operation of the Bradley Foundry in Harrisonburg, which is the oldest industrial business in the city. For four generations it has been carried on by members of the same family, Schuyler Bradley II, a great-grandson of the founder, now taking part in the management, and it has won a place of merited confidence over a wide area in which the output of the plant has been distributed. Among its products of general utility have been stoves, firebacks, cooking utensils, plows, plow repairs, sash weights, and other builders' supplies. On a small farm in Shenandoah County the writer saw a Bradley plow before he ever saw Harrisonburg. No doubt many other persons in many other places have had their bonds of contact with Harrisonburg strengthened through a use of products of the Bradley Foundry.

In early life (about 1907) Bennett Bradley was a member of the local company of National Guards. He is a member of the Methodist Church and was for some time affiliated with the Rotary Club. In politics he is generally an independent voter. He has been interested in the work of the Boy Scouts and other progressive organizations. For recreation he plays golf; reads extensively in current events and works of a scientific character; and is very fond of flowers.

On June 10, 1922, Mr. Bradley married Miss Frances Davis of Laurel, Delaware, daughter of Curtis E. Davis and his wife, who was Frances Riggin before marriage. Mr. and Mrs. Bradley have one son, Curtis Schuyler Bradley, born February 19, 1925, in Philadelphia, who is now a student at the University of Virginia.

JACOB RALPH BRENEMAN

BUSINESS MAN AND LEGISLATOR

Born August 7, 1872, near Broadway; attended high schools at Linville and Broadway; also Shenandoah College; a teacher four years; farmer and stock-raiser; dealer in lumber and real estate; bank director; trustee of Shenandoah College; on board of West Rockingham Mutual Fire Insurance Company; member of Virginia House of Delegates.

Mr. Breneman, representing several old Valley of Virginia families, is typical of the thrifty and versatile farmers and business men of Rockingham and adjacent counties. His father, Abraham Breneman, and his grandfather of the same name, lived in the neighborhood of Edom, on Linville Creek. His mother, Mary Hoover Breneman, was born at or near Cootes's Store, the daughter of Abraham and Hannah Roadcap Hoover. Not very far from the place of their residence is the site of old Fort Hoover, which was probably erected and fortified in early days by members of the same family. After his training in local schools and Shenandoah Collegiate Institute at Dayton, now Shenandoah College, J. R. Breneman taught school four sessions near Broadway. Since then he has engaged extensively in farming, the raising of livestock, lumbering, and related industries. He has acquired much real estate, which he has bought and sold to some extent in connection with the handling of cattle, farm crops, and forest products. Some of his lands are in the Northwest, North Dakota and South Dakota, on which the growing of wheat has been a specialty.

Along with his own personal business, Mr. Breneman has participated in various civic, financial, and political activities. He is a director in the Farmers and Merchants Bank at Timberville, is a member of the board of trustees of his alma mater, Shenandoah College, is on the board of directors of the West Rockingham Mutual Fire Insurance Company, and is an associate member on the Advisory Board of Rockingham County. For 12 years he served as deputy commissioner of revenue for Plains District of the county. He is an active and honored member of the United Brethren Church. In politics he is a Democrat, and has served four full sessions and two extra sessions in the House of Delegates in Richmond. In the course of his legislative duties he has been appointed on the committees of Finance, Roads, Currency and Commerce, Agriculture, and House Expenses. His quiet manner and regular habits have earned for him the respect and confidence of his colleagues in the legislature and have given him a well established place in the esteem of his constituents at home.

On May 21, 1896, Mr. Breneman married Miss Dorcas Aubrey of Fulk's Run, the marriage taking place in Broadway. Mr. and Mrs. Breneman live at the historic Hevener homestead. They have one child, a daughter, Mae Z. Breneman, who is the wife of Robert D. Liskey of Harrisonburg. Mr. and Mrs. Liskey have two sons: Aubrey Ralph and Robert Leon. Mrs. Liskey, like her father, takes a keen interest in matters civic and educational.

Mrs. Breneman's father, George W. Aubrey, whose home was at Maysville, now West Virginia, was a captain in the Union army. He was captured and died in Libby Prison, Richmond.

OLIVER CURRY BRUNK, M. D.
PHYSICIAN

Born September 13, 1878, near Harrisonburg; student in local schools and West Central Academy; member of the Dale Enterprise Literary Society; M. D., University of Virginia, 1903; interne in the Central State Hospital, Petersburg; special course at Harvard; first assistant surgeon in Central State Hospital, Petersburg; superintendent Eastern State Hospital, Williamsburg, 1907-11; in New York hospitals and Johns Hopkins; located in Richmond since 1912; surgeon in World War I.

Dr. Brunk's father, Christian H. Brunk (1849-1921), was for many years a familiar figure in the court house at Harrisonburg, where he was deputy clerk and later clerk of the county court, and after 1902 deputy clerk of the circuit court. Many of the records are in his careful script, and much of his time was devoted to restoring the old records that were partly burned by the troops of the Federal general, David Hunter, in 1864. In his young manhood he taught in the public schools. He was a devout Christian, and was always interested in the education and advancement of the youth of the community. His wife, Elizabeth Ralston, was born in Rockingham in 1852. He had six children: Nora, who died at age 18; Lillie, now Mrs. Hershey Weaver of Harrisonburg; Oliver C.; John, who died at the age of six years; Talfourd, who died when three years old; and Grace, who lives in Harrisonburg. John Brunk, Christian Brunk's father, married Ann Weaver. He died in Rockingham, his native county, in 1885.

Dr. Brunk, in early life, was one of the younger members of the celbrated Dale Enterprise Literary Society, and on August 15, 1934, attended the reunion at Dale Enterprise, when Dr. C. J. Heatwole, J. S. H. Good, Charles A. Hammer, William P. Swartz, Otho W. Thomas, and other distinguished members of the old society were present. His interest in things literary and educational, and especially in the field of his profession, has been keen and unflagging. During the summer of 1903, following his graduation in medicine at the University of Virginia, he took special courses at Harvard. In 1911 he spent three months in the Nursery and Child Hospital of New York City, specializing in children's diseases and obstetrics, following this with work in Johns Hopkins University for a like period in internal medicine. For some time he was interne in the Johnston-Willis Hospital in Richmond. Other periods of service have already been indicated on the preceding page. After the outbreak of World War I he helped to organize an ambulance company composed largely of Richmond boys. This company was ordered to Camp Lee and was absorbed by the 80th Division. After 10 months in training the division moved to France, served one year in France, and then returned to Camp Dix, New Jersey. Dr. Brunk was discharged from Camp Dix on June 9, 1919, with the rank of captain. He then resumed his practice in Richmond, where he has been notably successful. He is a Mason; holds membership in the medical fraternities Pi Mu and Nu Sigma Nu; also in the Richmond Academy of Medicine and Surgery, the Virginia State Medical Society, and the American Medical Association. He is a member of the Presbyterian Church.

On October 25, 1921, Dr. Brunk married Miss Bernice Hall, who is a daughter of Walker W. and Sarah Shackelford Hall of the city of Lynchburg.

JOHN PURCELL BURKE

BUSINESS MAN AND OPERATOR IN REAL ESTATE

Born October 14, 1861, in New Market; finished his education in the New Market Polytechnic Institute; came to Harrisonburg at the age of 18 and worked for the Wilton Hardware Co. 15 years; bookkeeper for the First National Bank; hardware merchant for years; promoter of local industries; president of the Harrisonburg Rotary Club and prominent in the Masonic lodge; senior member of the insurance firm of Burke & Price; died July 25, 1940.

Mr. Burke, when a boy in New Market, had an ambition to be a successful business man, a dream which he fully realized. He made a beginning by carrying sheaves in the harvest field at 25 cents a day. His father, John H. Burke (June 18, 1816—September 22, 1875), married Sarah Miles (April 3, 1848—February 28, 1887), a lady from eastern Virginia. His grandfather, John Burke, was born March 11, 1776, and died in Edinburg on January 21, 1872. The latter's wife was Mary Carrier, born February 1, 1791; she died on July 9, 1857, also in Edinburg. His great-grandfather, also named John Burke, came to this country from Ireland and located first on Hawksbill Creek in what is now Page County, Va. He then for a time sojourned in Powell's Fort. Later he went into western Pennsylvania, to the locality of the present city of Pittsburgh, where he was shot and killed by an Indian who was hidden behind a tree outside his house.

In 1879 Mr. Burke came to Harrisonburg where he spent the remainder of his life, engaged in various lines of business and handling much real estate. After a long term of apprenticeship in Wilton's hardware store and in the First National Bank, he purchased the hardware store of Henry Shacklett and went into business for himself. This store, which was located on the site now occupied by the J. C. Penney Store, he sold after ten years to Nicholas & Lemley, and became agent for the Equitable Life Insurance Company, later establishing the firm of Burke & Price. For many years he was president of the Bridgewater Plow Corporation; for some time he was manager of the Newtown Giant Incubator Corporation; he was an early president of the Harrisonburg Hatchery, and was one of the organizers of Virginia Craftsmen, Inc. He owned valuable real estate in different parts of Harrisonburg and in suburban sections. Among the latter was a large acreage north of the Waterman School, and one of his later transactions was the sale of land for the Hartman Airport.

On December 19, 1889, Mr. Burke married Miss Katie Ragan of Harrisonburg, who died on September 9, 1928. For some years prior to his death, Mr. Burke's sister, Mrs. S. G. Good, made her home with him. She is now the only surviving member of their family.

Mr. Burke served for many years as a vestryman of Emmanuel Episcopal Church of Harrisonburg. In Rockingham Union Lodge No. 27, A. F. & A. M., his career was unusual. In 1889, when the lodge celebrated its 100th anniversary, he was master of the lodge; and in 1939, when the sesquicentennial was celebrated, he was one of the oldest living members and was appointed to prepare the history of the organization which was published at that time. Although he was not well at the time, he paid a visit to the lodge room and was present when his portrait was given an honored place among others that adorn the walls.

ASHBY CLIFFORD BYERS, M.D.

PHYSICIAN AND SURGEON

Born June 27, 1875, at Burketown, Augusta County; attended public schools of Augusta until 1888, then Augusta Military Academy, graduating in 1893; read medicine under Dr. J. S. Sellers two years; entered medical department of University of Maryland, 1896; graduated, M.D., 1901; practiced with Dr. E. D. Davis at Lacey Spring, 1901-10; located in Harrisonburg, 1910; charter member staff of Rockingham Memorial Hospital; in general practice and hospital instructor; member and official of medical societies; city health officer and coroner; member of school board; Rotarian, B. P. O. E., Methodist.

Dr. Byers for many years has been one of the well-known physicians of Harrisonburg and Rockingham County, and has held various civic and professional offices. His parents were Samuel Byers, Jr. (1836-1915) and wife, Katherine Cline (1849-1882). His paternal grandparents were Samuel C. and Nancy Patterson Byers. After attending public schools in Augusta County until the age of 13, he entered Augusta Military Academy where he was a student until 1893. Then, having read medicine with Dr. J. S. Sellers of Weyers Cave for two years, he entered the medical department of the University of Maryland, and from that institution received the degree of M.D. on June 2, 1901. At the University he was elected a member of the Rush Club, an organization in the medical school to which men were chosen on competitive scholastic merit. Upon graduation he established a medical partnership with Dr. E. D. Davis at Lacey Spring, continuing there until February, 1910, when he located in Harrisonburg where he has since been successfully engaged in general practice, with special work in different lines. He is one of the original staff of Rockingham Memorial Hospital, and has served from time to time as instructor in dermatology, therapeutics, and obstetrics in the hospital nursing school. He has also served as health officer for the city and coroner for the city and county. He is a member of the Medical Society of Virginia, the Southern Medical Association, the Rockingham County Medical Society, of which he has been president a number of times, and the Shenandoah Valley Medical Society, of which he was vice-president in 1938-39.

In addition to his professional work and relations, Dr. Byers has been active in civic, educational, and fraternal organizations. He is a charter member of the local Rotary Club, a life member and past exalted ruler B. P. O. E.; has served on the city school board; was president of the Rockingham Fair Association four years; has been a director of the Rockingham Turkey Festival and served as chief marshal in the mammoth parades. He is a member of the Methodist Church; in politics a Democrat. His hobby is horseback riding, and he takes a keen interest in horse shows, horticulture, and sports, such as football, baseball, and swimming.

On October 15, 1901, Dr. Byers married Miss Daisy Graichen Sherman, born July 20, 1877, daughter of John Wise (1838-1914) and Nancy Henkel (1839-1903) Sherman of Mt. Crawford. Dr. and Mrs. Byers have seven children: Katherine Sherman (Mrs. L. D. Horner, Jr., Lynchburg), Dr. Francis LeRoy, Harrisonburg, Charlotte Henkel (Mrs. John B. Acker, Harrisonburg), Ashby Clifford, Jr., Harrisonburg, Dr. Carl Cline, Harrisonburg, Nancy Graichen, Fort Belvoir, Va., and Dorothy Elizabeth (Mrs. J. E. Lee, Jr., Harrisonburg). The residence of Dr. and Mrs. Byers is located on South Main Street, Harrisonburg.

FRANCIS LEROY BYERS, M.D.

PHYSICIAN AND SURGEON

Born July 18, 1904, at Lacey Spring; attended primary school, grammar and high school in Harrisonburg, graduating from Harrisonburg High School in 1923; pre-medical course at the University of Virginia, 1923-25; entered U. Va. School of Medicine fall of 1925, graduating M.D. in June, 1929; interne Norwood Clinic, Birmingham, Ala., 1929-30; at U. Va. for additional interneship and resident work in gynecology and obstetrics; has practiced in Harrisonburg since 1931, majoring in gynecology and obstetrics; city health officer two years; county and city coroner 12 years; medical examiner Selective Service.

Dr. Byers holds an honored place among the younger physicians of Harrisonburg and Rockingham County, and is serving acceptably in various official positions. He is the eldest son of Dr. Ashby Clifford Byers of Harrisonburg, whose biography appears on preceding pages, and in that connection will be found additional items concerning his ancestors, the Byerses, Shermans, Clines, and Pattersons, families which have been numerous and well known in Rockingham and Augusta for generations. He was born at the historic village of Lacey Spring, nine miles northeast of Harrisonburg, where his father practiced from 1901 to 1910, and where he received his first schooling. After the family located in Harrisonburg in 1910 he entered the grammar grades and proceeded through them and the high school, from which he was graduated in 1923. The following autumn he began his pre-medical course in the University of Virginia, continuing therein two years; after which he pursued the regular medical course, covering four years, graduating with the degree of M.D. in June, 1929.

Following his graduation at the University, Dr. Byers was received as interne in the Norwood Clinic, in the city of Birmingham, Ala., in which he served for a year; then returned to the University of Virginia for additional internship and resident work in gynecology and obstetrics. After completing this work he, in September, 1931, entered upon the general practice of medicine in Harrisonburg, where he has since been successfully engaged, directing his chief attention to gynecology and obstetrics. For two years he was city health officer, and for the past 12 years he has been coroner for the city and county. At present he is a member of the local selective service board. He belongs to the Phi Beta Pi Fraternity, American Medical Association, Southern Medical Society, Shenandoah Valley Medical Society, State Medical Society, and the medical society of Rockingham County; is a member of the staff of Rockingham Memorial Hospital; a charter member of the city Lions Club; belongs to the Elks; and in the foregoing has held various offices. He is a member of the Harrisonburg Methodist Church. In his reading he naturally gives preference to medical literature, but is interested also in popular writings. Since boyhood he has been fond of athletics and all outdoor sports. In high school he played football and was a member of the relay track team that won the state championship in 1923. At the University he was a member of the track team and played in the University band for two years. He finds enjoyable recreation in hunting and takes much interest in gardening.

In 1935 Dr. Byers married Miss Anne Conrad, daughter of Mr. and Mrs. Albert Thomas Conrad of Fort Seybert, W. Va. Dr. and Mrs. Byers have two children: Charles Conrad, born January 5, 1938, and Frances Anne, born October 2, 1940.

WILLIAM HARRISON BYRD

CASHIER OF THE FIRST NATIONAL BANK

Born November 10, 1892, in Harrisonburg; attended schools at Mt. Clinton and in Harrisonburg; began work as runner for the First National Bank of Harrisonburg in 1910; April 28, 1917, volunteered for U. S. Army; served until February, 1919; secretary and treasurer of the Merchants Grocery & Hardware Co., 1919-23; since then cashier of the First National Bank; two years chairman of Group Three, Va. Bankers Association; Mason; past commander of American Legion; was a charter member of the local Rotary Club; director Merchants Grocery & Hardware Co., Harrisonburg Warehouse Corp., Chesapeake-Western Railway, the Harrisonburg Milk Board, and Chamber of Commerce.

Mr. Byrd is a son of Joseph C. and Nannie Harrison Byrd. His paternal grandfather was William Perry Byrd, whose wife, before marriage, was Catherine C. Burkholder. His mother's parents were John Harrison and his wife, Barbara K. Hollingsworth. The Byrds were early residents at Craney Island and neighboring places on Smith Creek; the Harrisons were numerous in the region to the southwest, including Harrisonburg and Dayton; the Hollingsworths were some of the first settlers in the vicinity of Winchester; the Burkholders have been numerous in West Rockingham for generations. Many interesting items concerning all these families (and others) are to be found in J. Houston Harrison's "Settlers by the Long Grey Trail."

After attending school at Mt. Clinton and finishing three years in the Harrisonburg High School, William H. Byrd began his business career as runner for the First National Bank of Harrisonburg, of which he has been the efficient cashier since the summer of 1923. Prior to 1923 his service with the bank was not continuous. Having been employed as runner, later as bookkeeper, for the bank from January 10, 1910, to June, 1917, he then volunteered for the armed service of the nation and continued in that service, with a period of duty overseas, until discharged in February, 1919. For the next four years he was connected officially, as already indicated, with the Merchants Grocery & Hardware Company of Harrisonburg, resigning this work to become cashier of the First National Bank on July 1, 1923.

In the army Mr. Byrd was sergeant in Battery B, 60th Artillery, C. A. C., 1st Army, serving for the period already indicated. He was for nearly 12 months in France, and saw action for 67 days without relief on the St. Mihiel front and in the Meuse-Argonne offensive. In civil life since the war he has participated in various fraternal, benevolent, and business activities as a charter member of the Harrisonburg Rotary Club, in Masonic bodies, the Red Cross, etc. He is a member and a trustee of the Harrisonburg Presbyterian Church; a director of the Merchants Grocery & Hardware Co., the Harrisonburg Warehouse Corp., the Chesapeake-Western Railway Co.; treasurer of the Good Fellows Fund, an active charity organization fostered by the late John R. Crown; a director and the treasurer of the Richmond-Harrisonburg Freight Line, Inc.; active in the local organization of the American Legion (Past Commander), and has been an official in the Va. Bankers Assn., of which he is a member. He is treasurer of the Veterans Service Organization, formed seven years ago by the county supervisors and the city council to work with the Red Cross for needy veterans of World War I and their families. He mentions "home" and "business" as his hobbies; in his reading he keeps abreast of the times in public and commercial affairs. His continuous service for 20 years as cashier of the oldest banking institution of the city and county invests him with an enviable business record.

On November 8, 1919, Mr. Byrd married Miss Clyde Sebrell, born at Courtland, Va., daughter of Mr. Thos. E. and Mrs. Ella Prince Sebrell.

SAMUEL HIRAM CALLENDER
FARMER, BUSINESS MAN, AND COUNTY OFFICER

Born September 16, 1889, at Pleasant Valley, Rockingham County; received his elementary education in Pleasant Valley schools; attended high school in Harrisonburg and at Remington, Va.; college training in Virginia Polytechnic Institute, Blacksburg; farmer and raiser of livestock; member of Rockingham County Board of Supervisors, 1932-40; sheriff of the county since 1940; member of the Elks, Odd Fellows, and the Reformed Church.

Mr. Callender is one of several sons of the late C. T. Callender of Pleasant Valley and his wife, whose maiden name was Laura Wise. He has two sisters, Pauline and Elizabeth. His mother was a daughter of Lieut. W. H. Wise and his wife, Mary E. Lago Wise. His father, C. T. Callender, was a successful farmer and business man, who took much interest in the schools and related institutions in the county and state. For some time he was secretary and treasurer of the Rockingham Home Mutual Fire Insurance Company of Cross Keys. He was also active in the Masonic fraternity, and for two years, 1903 and 1904, was master of Rockingham Union Lodge, No. 27, A. F. & A. M. C. T. Callender's father, Rev. Samuel N. Callender, D. D., was an outstanding minister and leader in the Reformed Church. He was born at Harrisburg, Pa., April 16, 1820; graduated from Allegheny College at Meadville, Pa., in 1841, and finished his theological course at Mercersburg in the same state in 1845. After holding several important pastorates in Pennsylvania, including the Old Zion's Reformed Church at Chambersburg, he came in 1870 to Rockingham County, Va. Here he served the Mt. Crawford Charge (Trinity and St. Michael's) for twenty years. In 1890 he was elected secretary of the Board of Foreign Missions, from which he retired in 1902. He died at Mechanicsburg, Pa., May 5, 1904. Rev. J. Silor Garrison, D. D., the church historian, who has supplied the foregoing facts, says: "Dr. Callender was a great scholar and preacher, and a prince of a man. General Roller frequently said to me that he was the most scholarly and eloquent preacher in the history of Rockingham County."

Samuel H. Callender grew up on his father's farm near the village of Pleasant Valley, and participated in the agricultural and stock-raising operations of the family in Rockingham County and eastern Virginia. His courses of study and training at Virginia Polytechnic Institute were in keeping with his rural experience and interests. For eight years, 1932 to 1940, he served as a member of the board of supervisors of Rockingham County, in which capacity he was afforded opportunities to give practical expression his progressive and constructive ideas. In 1940 he was elected sheriff of the county and is now discharging the duties of that office with fidelity and efficiency. He is a member of the Reformed Church and is connected with the Benevolent and Protective Order of Elks and the Independent Order of Odd Fellows. His busy life does not allow him much time for hobbies and sports, but in his reading he gives preference to information on current events and questions of public interest.

On July 25, 1931, Mr. Callender married Miss Isabel Crowder, who was born at Clarksville, Va., in 1904, daughter of A. B. and Sarah Catherine Humphreys Crowder. Mrs. Callender is a graduate of Clarksville High School and of the State Teachers College at Farmville. Prior to her marriage she was a teacher for several years in different parts of Virginia.

PERRY A. CARVER

FARM OPERATOR AND PRODUCE DEALER

Born June 8, 1889, in Rockingham County; attended local schools and Dayton High School; grew up on a farm; worked in a harness factory; employed in Harrisonburg in 1914 by J. G. Haldeman & Bro.; manager for this firm, 1918-29; in 1932 he and his brother started in produce business for themselves; now operating the Carver Produce Co. and a number of farms.

Mr. Carver is another young Rockinghamer who has remained at home and has thereby been instrumental in developing local resources in a large way. His parents were Joseph S. and Barbara A. Carver, also natives of Rockingham County. The first school he attended was one in a single room at Cross Roads, near Peach Grove; the next, another one-room school at Mt. Carmel, near Dayton; then he was a student in the Dayton High School. After living and working on a farm near Dayton until the age of 22, he went to work in a harness factory and continued in this for three years or so. Coming to Harrisonburg in 1914, he entered the employment of J. G. Haldeman & Brother, who operated a wholesale produce house in this city. In 1918 he became manager for the Haldemans and continued in that capacity until 1929 when they sold out to the Philadelphia Produce Co. In July, 1932, he and his brother, R. F. Carver, started in business for themselves, forming the Carver Produce Company, dealing in poultry and eggs.

Between 1938 and 1941 Mr. Carver and his brother acquired four valuable Rockingham County farms, by purchase, to wit: one near Harrisonburg known as the old Burkholder farm, in 1938; the second, known as the Rhodes farm, one mile from Harrisonburg, in 1939; the third, the Clark farm adjoining the Burkholder farm, in 1940; and the fourth, the old J. B. Shoemaker farm near Singers' Glen, in 1941. These farms the Carver brothers are operating, devoting them especially to the raising of large numbers of turkeys as well as cattle and hogs. The management of the farms is carried on under the name of the Carver Brothers and the business in Harrisonburg goes under the firm name of the Carver Produce Company. They raise and purchase around one million pounds of turkeys each year which they dress and ship to northern markets.

Along with his exacting business concerns, Mr. Carver has found time to participate actively in various civic, fraternal, and philanthropic organizations. For twenty years he has been a member of the Kiwanis Club in Harrisonburg. He is also a member of the Benevolent and Protective Order of Elks, the Modern Woodmen, and the United Commercial Travelers. He is a member of the Presbyterian Church in Dayton. In politics he is a staunch Republican.

Mr. Carver's wife before marriage was Miss Bessie V. Blair of Hagerstown, Maryland. They had one child, Lena Catherine, who died in 1921 at the age of seven years.

For recreation and sports, Mr. Carver is fond of boxing, wrestling, horse-racing, and motion pictures. He is known familiarly among his friends by the nickname of Dick, the origin of which is a bit of history. His father employed on his farm a man by the name of Dick, who became a familiar figure, so much so that when the boy came along and took his place he too was called Dick; and, like most nicknames acquired in boyhood, it has stuck.

ELIZABETH PENDLETON CLEVELAND

TEACHER AND WRITER

Born January 20, 1867, in Fluvanna County, Va.; A. B., Hollins College, 1889; M. A., University of Virginia, 1927; teacher in Hollins College, 1888-90; teacher of Latin and mathematics, Ouachita College, Ark., 1890-91, and head of the Latin department, 1891-93; principal, Palmyra, Va., High School, 1893-95; head of Latin department, Central College, Ark., 1895-97, and 1897-99 of the English department; teacher of English, Hollins College, 1899-1909; head of the English department, 1909-19, and since of the French department, Madison College; member of various educational organizations, contributor to periodicals, and co-author of "Practice Leaves in English Fundamentals," a series of four.

Miss Cleveland is typical and not the least eminent of the educational and religious leaders for whom Fluvanna County is famous. Of her father an old Confederate comrade said, "Tom Cleveland wasn't afraid of anything but doing wrong." Her grandfather Cleveland was Jeremiah. Colonel Ben, who in the division of spoils at King's Mountain drew Ferguson's white horse, was a relative. In Yorkshire, England, the Clevelands fought against William the Conqueror and in consequence lost their lands to the Bruces. Her mother was born Mary Elizabeth Perkins, daughter of Col. Joseph Stephen (Aug. 15, 1792—Nov. 26, 1873), whose wife was Nancy Shepherd (Oct. 10,1794— April 12, 1872). Jeremiah Cleveland's wife was Elizabeth Moon. Of this family was Lottie Moon, celebrated for her work as a missionary in China.

When Miss Annie Cleveland started to college, Betty, aged three, announced her purpose to become a teacher, "like Sister," a resolution she has well justified. Some of her first efforts at "bending the twig" were made under her sister in Inglewood Seminary, at the home of Gen. William McComb, near Gordonsville; later she and Miss Annie each taught at Hollins; and in 1909 they both came as teachers on the original faculty of the State Normal School, now Madison College, at Harrisonburg, where Miss Annie taught French until the year of her death, 1916.

All these years at Harrisonburg Miss Cleveland has been the patron saint of "The Schoolma'm," the college annual. It was due to her foresight and initiative that it was launched the very first session, on time and out of debt. The two-day Shakespeare pageant in 1916 owed much to her. To evaluate adequately her services to the college these 33 years is too much to undertake here. In addition to her college work, she has been one of the mainstays of the Harrisonburg Baptist Church. From 1910 to 1916 she was secretary of the Virginia Association of Colleges and Schools for Girls. She is a member of the Modern Language Association of Virginia, the American Association of Teachers of French, the American Association of University Women, Daughters of the Confederacy, D. A. R., and W. C. T. U. By inheritance she is a Democrat in politics, but exercises freedom in trying to support the best candidates. Her hobby is animals and birds, and in reading she prefers the great English and Scottish poets. She has been a frequent contributor to the *Virginia Teacher*, the *Virginia Journal of Education*, the *Religious Herald*, and other magazines. Her M. A. thesis at the University of Virginia was "Northumbria: The Persistence of Her Tradition." With Margaret V. Hoffman and Conrad T. Logan, she is the author of "Practice Leaves in English Fundamentals," a series of four volumes, brought out by D. C. Heath & Company, first in 1925.

In 1912 Miss Cleveland spent the summer traveling in England, finding special interest in the Lake Country and at Warwick Castle, with its traditions of a doughty ancestor.

JUSTUS H. CLINE

SCIENTIST AND CONSERVATIONIST

Born October 14, 1875, at Timberville; attended public and private schools and Virginia Normal School; B. A., Bridgewater College, 1899; student at the University of Michigan; M. A., Northwestern University, 1910; teacher in Lordsburg College, Bridgewater College, University of Virginia, and Northwestern University; mining and oil geologist in U. S. and Alaska; director at large of the National Wildlife Federation; promoter of wildlife conservation.

Mr. Cline, a native of Rockingham, after a wide and varied experience in many parts of the country, retired from business in 1929 and settled on his farm near Stuart's Draft, where he now lives. His parents were John P. Cline and wife, Mary Ann Spitler. His paternal grandparents were David (born in 1804) and Susan Wine Cline. Mr. Cline's wife was Miss Grace Snively of Lanark, Ill. The Snivelys are of Maryland stock.

From 1899 to 1901 Mr. Cline was professor of Latin and Greek in Lordsburg College, California; then from 1902 to 1910 he taught geology and biology in Bridgewater College, with an interval of one year as fellow in geology at Northwestern University. Following his work at Bridgewater, he went to the University of Virginia where he was assistant state geologist, instructor, and adjunct professor of geology until 1917. From 1917 to 1929 he was engaged as geologist in mining and oil operations in the western parts of the United States and Alaska, as chief of exploration parties for the Shell Oil Company and chief geologist for the Derby Oil Company.

Since his retirement from active business Mr. Cline has devoted himself energetically and effectively to the conservation and development of wildlife. From 1936 to 1941 he was a director at large of the National Wildlife Federation. In 1939 a granite monument with bronze plaque was erected in the Big Levels Wildlife Refuge, George Washington National Forest, and dedicated to him, Congressman Robertson making the dedicatory address. This tribute was sponsored by the U. S. Biological Survey, the U. S. Forest Service, the Virginia Game Department, and the Virginia Wildlife Federation. In 1941 he received a diploma of merit at V. P. I. for his conservation activities. He is a member of Sigma Xi, the Raven Society, and is on the Long Range Planning Committee and the James River Project Committee of the Virginia Academy of Science. He is the author of numerous papers on the geology of Virginia and related subjects; many articles on conservation of wildlife, including "Conservation Sermonettes," which has gone through its second printing and has been widely circulated. These sermonettes have been reprinted in conservation journals throughout the United States. He has delivered numberless addresses in various parts of the country.

Mr. Cline, in the words of Dr. Samuel Johnson, is a "clubable man." He has held membership in the Westmoreland Club of Richmond, the Colonnade Club of the University of Virginia, the Wichita Club, Wichita, Kansas, and the Elks Club. He has been president of the Kansas Geological Society, and has been a member of the American Association of Petroleum Geologists, the American Institute of Mining Engineers, and the American Wildlife Institute. He is an honorary member of the Waynesboro Rotary Club and is president of the Waynesboro and East Augusta Democratic Club.

SOLOMON GARBER CLINE

TEACHER AND DEALER IN MUSICAL INSTRUMENTS

Born December 4, 1864, at Broadway; attended primary and grade schools at Broadway; studied music at Shenandoah College and in Philadelphia under Professor B. C. Unseld; taught music four years in West Central Academy; traveled for Bridgewater College; taught music classes and gave private lessons in homes; founder of the Cline Music Co. in Harrisonburg; president of the same in Staunton; one of the founders of the Church of the Brethren in Harrisonburg; died at his home on Thornrose Ave. in Staunton, October 28, 1939.

Mr. Cline for many years was a prominent figure among Rockingham musicians and teachers of music and in the work of the Church of the Brethren, of which he was a faithful member. He was a son of Joseph and Mary Flory Cline of Broadway, and grew up in that community. After courses in music at Shenandoah Collegiate Institute in Dayton, now Shenandoah College, and advanced training in Philadelphia under Benjamin C. Unseld, a distinguished teacher and composer, he entered upon his own career as a teacher of singing classes and as an instructor in intrumental music. After teaching music four years in West Central Academy at Mt. Clinton, he became field agent for Bridgewater College about 1901, and traveled over the country in a horse-drawn buggy, interviewing prospective students for the college. At the same time he taught singing classes here and there and gave private lessons in homes to instrumental pupils. In connection with his teaching he began selling organs in the homes of his pupils, and in 1905 opened music store in Harrisonburg. About this time he was one of the associates of Elder P. S. Thomas in building a church for his denomination in Harrisonburg where he gave efficient service as director of the congregational singing.

With the growth of business, Mr. Cline associated his son, S. Glen Cline, with him in the music store in Harrisonburg, and about 1924 they moved to the city of Staunton, where the Cline Music Company was incorporated in 1925, and where the business has grown to large proportions, with expansions in other related lines. Mr. Cline was president of the company and active in the work until his health failed about a year and a half before his death.

On June 22, 1890, Mr. Cline married Miss Elizabeth Virginia Senger, born at Dale Enterprise in 1863, daughter of Samuel and Mary Jane Smith Senger. Of this marriage were born five children: Tenney (Mrs. Wolfrey) born March 22, 1891, who died in March, 1936; Solomon Glenn, born July 28, 1893, whose biography appears on the following pages of this book; Marjorie Elizabeth (Mrs. D. A. Snyder), born July 21, 1895; Edith Virginia (Mrs. A. L. Garber), born July 23, 1903; and Mary Jane (Mrs. John F. Stoddard Jr.,) born June 16, 1905.

Mr. Cline's hobbies were music and farming. He owned a farm near Harrisonburg and another near Staunton, though he had his residence in the city. He enjoyed traveling and toured many parts of the United States from coast to coast and from Florida to Canada. His funeral was held on October 29, 1939, from the Church of the Brethren in Harrisonburg and interment was made in the cemetery at Bridgewater. In the services Professor Nelson T. Huffman sang as a solo "Good Night and Good Morning," and the choir rendered one of Mr. Cline's favorite hymns, "My Faith Looks Up to Thee."

S. GLENN CLINE, JR.

MUSIC MERCHANT AND DEALER IN REAL ESTATE

Born July 28, 1893, at Good's Mill, Va.; graduate of Harrisonburg High School; attended Shenandoah College two years; in 1919 joined his father in the firm of the Cline Music Company, with headquarters in Staunton; dealer in real estate; has farming as an avocation; member and a past director of the Staunton Chamber of Commerce; vice-president of the Merchants and Business Men's Association; deputy chief air raid warden for the city of Staunton.

Mr. Cline's father, Solomon G. Cline, Sr., born December 4, 1864, near Broadway, was a son of Joseph E. Cline, native of the same locality, born December 30, 1823. Joseph Cline's wife, born Mary Flory, October 25, 1827, was also of the Broadway community. Solomon G. Cline, Sr., married Elizabeth V. Senger, born at Dale Enterprise, February 22, 1863, a daughter of Samuel Senger, Jr., born at at Silver Lake, Dayton, October 10, 1828, and his wife, Mary J. Smith, who was born at Churchville, Augusta County, on January 8, 1832. S. G. Cline, Sr., was a pioneer in teaching music and handling musical instruments in Harrisonburg, starting there with a small store in 1899. His natural aptitude for making friends and creating good will enabled him to build up a good trade in and around the city, and the present Cline Music Company, with its large assets and real estate holdings in Staunton are the outcome of his original efforts forty years ago.

S. Glenn Cline, Jr., after attending school and college as indicated on the preceding page, acquired an interest with his father in the Cline Music Company in 1919. The business was incorporated in 1925, and at present handles pianos and all kinds of home furniture, radios, and electrical appliances. It owns and occupies a three-story building on West Beverley Street in Staunton, with 8,400 square feet of floor space devoted to the sale and display of merchandise. Business and good will are extended by means of newspaper advertising, information by mail service to more than 2,000 regular recipients, and by free music lessons. The Cline salesmen are instructed never to make a promise that the firm cannot carry out.

In 1917 Mr. Cline married Miss E. Pauline Thomas, born November 21, 1892, a daughter of Rev. and Mrs. P. S. Thomas of Harrisonburg. Mr. and Mrs. Cline have three children: Janet L., born in Harrisonburg in 1918; Elizabeth Joyce, born in 1922 in Staunton; and S. G. Cline III, also a native of Staunton, born in 1923. Both daughters attended Stuart Hall in Staunton; later graduated from Robert E. Lee High School in the same city, and attended Mary Baldwin College. Janet received her degree from Mary Baldwin in 1941, and holds a responsible position with the Metropolitan Life Insurance Company in Staunton. On February 5, 1943, she married William B. Harman of Waynesboro. Betty holds a secretarial position with a prominent insurance company of Richmond. The son, S. G. Cline III, graduated from the Robert E. Lee High School and is now a pre-medical student at the University of Virginia.

S. Glenn Cline, Jr., is a member of the Staunton Baptist Church. He participates in civic activities as already indicated and operates several farms as a hobby. He owns Camp Riverview at Van Ike where he finds relaxation from office duties in boating, swimming, and fishing. He also enjoys golf, hunting, and deep-sea fishing.

HUGH E. CLOUGHERTY

STATION AGENT AND INSURANCE REPRESENTATIVE

Born May 10, 1893, in Cincinnati; brought to Strasburg at age of two years; grew up in Strasburg and attended schools there; worked for the Southern Railway Co.; student of the International Correspondence School of Scranton, Pa.; telegrapher for the Southern Railway; soldier in France, 1918-19; agent at New Market and Timberville; representative for the State Farm Mutual Auto Insurance Co. of Bloomington, Ill., and other companies.

Mr. Clougherty's father, H. J. Clougherty, now living at 97 years of age, was born in Galway, Ireland, as was his wife, Mary T. Cook, who is about 20 years her husband's junior. Leaving school at Strasburg, Mr. Clougherty at 16 years of age went to work as a section hand on the Southern Railway, but later took a commercial course with the International Correspondence School. After a year as section hand, he was caller and trucker at the freight station in Strasburg until September 5, 1913, when he passed his examination as a telegrapher. For the next four years he was relief agent-operator from Alexandria to Lynchburg and from Manassas to Harrisonburg. On February 13, 1917, he was appointed agent at New Market and worked there until inducted into the army, October 25, 1917. In France he was in the Somme and Meuse-Argonne offensives and in the Artois defensive sector. On June 3, 1919, he was honorably discharged at Camp Lee. He is a member of the V. F. W. Returning to New Market, he was station agent there until May 10, 1921, when he was appointed agent at Timberville, his present position.

On October 1, 1930, Mr. Clougherty became an agent for the State Farm Mutual Auto Insurance Company of Bloomington, Ill., and although the Annual Marathon was then a month under way he won fourth place among all the agents in the United States and first place among the agents in Virginia. This record was indicative of his subsequent successes, in which he has repeatedly been distinguished. In 1932 he won top honors, leading the whole agency force of the country. From September, 1932, to February 1, 1933, he again won the Marathon, and was put on the program both days of the annual convention. Since then he has kept up his record and has several times been put on the annual program. At the same time he has represented other insurance companies and held on to his seniority standing in the railway service.

In politics Mr. Clougherty is a Democrat and a member of the Democratic County Committee; he is a member of the Timberville local school committee, president of the Plains District Ruritan Club, and has been a member of the Order of Railroad Telegraphers for over 25 years. He is a member of the Blessed Sacrament Catholic Church of Harrisonburg, and is active in the various church organizations. Among periodicals, Mr. Clougherty prefers the *American Magazine* and the *Reader's Digest*.

On March 4, 1924, Mr. Clougherty married Miss Mary Irene Fisher, who was born near Strasburg on March 26, 1897, daughter of Mr. and Mrs. Charles Fisher. She is a graduate of Strasburg High School and the George Washington University Hospital. She has been a teacher and a registered nurse, and is a member of the United Brethren Church. She is the mother of two children: Mary E. ("Bette"), born January 16, 1925, now a student in Madison College, and Hugh E., Jr. ("Bud"), born August 14, 1926, who is a senior in the Timberville High School.

FLOYD WILMER COFFMAN
BUSINESS MAN AND CITY OFFICIAL

Born at East Point, Rockingham County; General Manager and Treasurer of Sisler Brothers Monument Company; author of three books; served in United States Army Air Corps in World War I; active in American Legion, church, and civic affairs; member of the Harrisonburg City Council, Chamber of Commerce, Red Cross, and other community groups.

Mr. Coffman's father was Edwin Elone Coffman (1853-1919), born in Page County, Va., farmer, magistrate, chairman of school board and member of road board in Stonewall District, Rockingham; a son of William C. Coffman, farmer, pottery manufacturer and C. S. A. officer. His first Kaufmann ancestor in America was Rev. Isaac of Berne, Switzerland, who came to America to escape religious persecution. Wm. C. Coffman's wife was Louisa DeBard (1818-58), daughter of Elijah and Winifred Massey DeBard of Louisa, Va. F. Wilmer's mother was Columbia Frances Stover (1856-1941), daughter of David H. (1827-61), member of Co. I, 10th Va. Vol. Inf., C. S. A., and Mary Ann Conrad, daughter of John and Anna Maria Nicholas Conrad. John was the eldest son of Stephen Conrad, captain of Co. 15, Rockingham militia, in and after the Revolution.

After leaving school Mr. Coffman served a five-year apprenticeship in the Dean Studio of Harrisonburg, then owing to chemical poisoning left this work and bought an interest in the Wm. B. Dutrow store. He disposed of this interest in 1925 and joined the Sisler Monument Co. as treasurer. In World War I he entered the army on Aug. 8, 1917, and served for two years. During that time he graduated from the Aerial Photo and Observation School at Langley Field, Va., and served as an observation instructor in the Cadet School at Love Field, Texas, before going to France. Overseas he served with the 16th Aerial Photo Section, 2d Army Day Bombing Group, and after the armistice with the 16th Section and the 1st Air Squadron, stationed at Weissenthurm, Germany. In June, 1919, as a member of the staff of Asst. Sec'y of War for Aviation, Gen. Benedict Crowell, he visited all American Air Service units in Germany, Belgium, and northern France. He was discharged Aug. 10, 1919, as sergeant 1st class, with recommendation for 2d lieutenant.

Since 1919 Mr. Coffman has been active in veteran work. He has been Adjutant, Commander, and Service Officer for 22 years of Rockingham Post No. 27, American Legion. In 1933 he was appointed by President Roosevelt on Virginia's special review board on questionable war service claims. In 1934 he was elected Dept. Vice Commander of the American Legion in Virginia. He organized the Veterans Service and Red Cross Office in Harrisonburg in 1936 and is chairman of its governing board. He has been secretary, treasurer, and a director of the local chamber of commerce, and a member of the board of finance and endowment of Shenandoah College. In 1940 he was director of the Rockingham Turkey Festival. He is a member of the United Brethren Church, the Masonic lodge, and from 1938 to 1942 was on the Harrisonburg City Council. He has written three books: "Our Fledging Air Corps" (1926), "Rockingham County in the World War" (1931), and "The Conrad Clan" (1939).

On Nov. 19, 1941, Mr. Coffman married Miss Mona Lucille Lyon, of Madison College faculty, daughter of Edwin Bruce and Louisa Lyon of Harrison, Neb. Her father was formerly sheriff and treasurer of Sioux County, Neb. Her ancestors on both sides were early settlers of the West.

CHARLES EDWARD CONRAD, M. D.
PHYSICIAN; SPECIALIST IN PEDIATRICS

Born July 20, 1879, in Harrisonburg; attended Harrisonburg schools and Randolph-Macon Academy, Front Royal; University of Virginia, 1901-05; M. D., U. Va., 1905; interne, Kings County Hospital, Brooklyn; Nursery and Childs and Babies Hospitals, New York City; special course in Childrens Hospital, St. Louis; member of national, state, and local professional associations; author of numerous papers in the field of his specialty; instructor of nurses in pediatrics and head of Pedriatic Service, Rockingham Memorial Hospital, Harrisonburg.

Dr. Conrad, a distinguished child specialist, is a son of Edward Smith Conrad (July 24, 1853—August 21, 1916), a prominent lawyer, and his wife, Virginia Smith Irick (May 26, 1855—August 28, 1933), of Harrisonburg. At the University of Virginia he was a member of Pi Kappa Alpha and Nu Sigma Nu (medical fraternity), and was chapter representative one year on the staff of *Corks and Curls*. Since graduation he has practiced in Harrisonburg, where he is a member of the hospital staff. He is a past president of the Rockingham County Medical Society, the Valley of Virginia Medical Society, and the Virginia Pediatric Society. For one year he was chairman of the Pediatric Section of the Southern Medical Association. He served as the first chairman of the Rockingham Chapter, American Red Cross, and was a delegate to the White House Conference on Child Health and Protection. In 1931 he was on the program of the Va. State Conference on Childhood and Youth. He has served as chairman of the Rockingham Chapter, Boy Scouts of America, and in 1938 received the Silver Beaver Award from the Stonewall Jackson Chapter, Boy Scouts of America. He is a past president of the local Rotary Club; a steward and trustee of the Harrisonburg Methodist Church.

Among Dr. Conrad's numerous contributions to medical publications, the following may be mentioned: "Congenitally Acquired Pyelitis," in the *American Journal of Diseases of Children;* "Encephalitis Secondary to Chickenpox," in the *Archives of Pediatrics;* in the *Virginia Medical Monthly,* "Intraperitoneal Transfusions with Report of Cases," "Examthem Occurring in Infants with Unusual Symptomathology," and "Acrodynia"; in the *Southern Medical Journal,* "Tetany in Breast-Fed Baby with Decided Increase in Convulsions after Giving Saline Hypodermoclysis," "Urinary Findings in the New-Born, Reporting Three Cases of Neonatal Nephritis," and "A Review of the Literature of Congenital Tuberculosis with Report of a Case"; and "Essentials of Nutrition," in the *Virginia Teacher.* Before the Governor's Conference in Richmond, in 1931, he presented a paper on "The Home and the Sick Child."

On September 29, 1914, Dr. Conrad married Miss Annie Gilliam of Lynchburg, born October 22, 1889, daughter of James Richard Gilliam and Jessie Belfield Johnson. She attended Randolph-Macon Woman's College, of her native city. Dr. and Mrs. Conrad are the parents of two children: James Gilliam, born September 5, 1915, who holds the degrees of B.S. and LL. B. from University of Virginia, and is now a lieutenant (j. g.), on active duty, in the U. S. Naval Reserves; and Virginia Laird, born June 19, 1919, who was graduated from Gunston Hall, Washington, D. C., and Madison College. On September 27, 1941, she married Richard A. Jackson, who is an ensign in the U. S. Navy, and now in active service. Prior to his enlistment he was a lawyer in Harrisonburg.

LAIRD LEWIS CONRAD
ATTORNEY AT LAW

Born June 16, 1884, in Harrisonburg; graduate of Harrisonburg High School; A. M., Randolph-Macon College, 1904; member of the faculty of Randolph-Macon Academy, Bedford, Va., 1904-05; LL. B., University of Virginia, 1907; lawyer in Harrisonburg since 1907; General Receiver for the circuit court of Rockingham County since 1918; a commissioner in chancery for the same court; a trustee of the Rockingham Memorial Hospital and of the Rockingham Library Association; president of the Harrisonburg Loan & Thrift Corporation and a director of the Rockingham National Bank of Harrisonburg.

Mr. Conrad is a brother to Dr. Charles E. Conrad, whose biography appears on the preceding pages. His father, Edward Smith Conrad, and his uncle, George N. Conrad, were both distinguished lawyers, and several younger members of the family are engaged in the same profession. His mother's maiden name was Virginia Smith Irick, a daughter of Andrew Baer Irick and his wife, Margaret Jane Laird. His paternal grandparents were George Oliver and Diana Smith (Yancey) Conrad. The latter (Diana Smith Yancey), born September 15, 1831, was the eldest child of Col. William Burbridge Yancey (1803-1858) and his first wife, Mary K. Smith, of the Smithland family. Col. Wm. B. Yancey was a son of Layton, whose wife was Frances Lewis, 10th child and 7th daughter of Thomas Lewis, first surveyor of Rockingham County, and his wife, Jane Strother. Thus it will be seen, and otherwise it may be shown, that Mr. Conrad's lineage runs back to Revolutionary and colonial families through his several lines of ancestry.

He, after an extended course of training in Randolph-Macon College and a year's experience as a teacher, entered upon his law course at the University of Virginia, which he completed in June, 1907. Returning to his native city, he began a practice which has been notably successful. He has devoted his attention to civil practice, beginning in the circuit courts of Rockingham and adjoining counties and extending to the Supreme Court of Appeals of Virginia, the U. S. District Court for the Western District of Virginia, and the U. S. Circuit Court of Appeals for the 4th judicial circuit. As general receiver for the circuit court of Rockingham County, a position which he has held since 1918, and as a commisssioner of chancery in the same court, his duties have been extended and varied and of a responsible character. In addition to his business relations already indicated, he is a director of the Harrisonburg Building & Supply Co., Inc., the Spotswood Orchards, Inc., and the Shenandoah Apartments, Inc. He is a member of the Methodist Church, a Democrat in politics, and belongs to the Rockingham Union Lodge No. 27, A. F. & A. M. He has served as president of the Harrisonburg Bar Association and the local Kiwanis Club. At present he is county chairman for Rockingham of the War Service Committee of the Virginia State Bar.

On August 10, 1927, Mr. Conrad married Miss Margaret Davis, daughter of Richard Sale and Ida Melville (Biscoe) Davis of Biscoe, King and Queen County, Va. Before marriage Mrs. Conrad was a teacher in the Harrisonburg High School and is now a member of the city school board. She is a member of the Episcopal Church, the Daughters of the American Revolution, the Colonial Daughters of the Seventeenth Century, and the Colonial Dames, and is actively affiliated with the Garden Club of Virginia. Mr. and Mrs. Conrad are both keenly interested in civic, philanthropic, and educational enterprises.

HENRY AUGUSTUS CONVERSE

PROFESSOR OF MATHEMATICS, FORMER REGISTRAR, MADISON COLLEGE

Born June 3, 1875, in Louisville, Ky.; attended public and private schools in Rockingham County and Harrisonburg; A. B., Hampden-Sydney College, 1893; Ph. D., Johns Hopkins University, 1903; taught six years in Shenandoah Valley Academy, Winchester; head department of mathematics, Baltimore Polytechnic Institute, ten years; registrar and head of mathematics department, Madison College, 1919-39; since then, professor of mathematics; Episcopalian, Democrat, Kiwanian; Kappa Sigma, Phi Beta Kappa; active in work with Boy Scouts.

Dr. Converse, widely and popularly known as an educator and a leader in fraternal, religious, and civic enterprises, is a son of Henry A. and Margaret Bear Converse. His paternal grandfather, Rev. Amasa Converse, was born in Connecticut and married Flavia Booth, a native of Massachusetts. Their son, Dr. Converse's father, was born in Philadelphia. Margaret Bear Converse was a daughter of David and Maria Anderson Bear. David's father, Andrew Bear, settled in Rockingham County, near the site of Mt. Clinton, about 1798. Maria was the daughter of David Anderson and was born at his home near Hinton, in this country, not far from the Bear home.

Henry A. Converse, Sr., lawyer, journalist, and well known as the compiler of "Converse's Index," a legal work, came to Harrisonburg in 1878 and practiced law here until his death, December 5, 1880. His son, the subject of this sketch, attended private and public schools in the county and city and then entered Hampden-Sydney College where he graduated in 1893. After teaching six years in the historic Shenandoah Valley Academy in Winchester, ne became a graduate student in Johns Hopkins University, where he received his Ph. D. degree in 1903. For ten years he headed the department of mathematics in the Baltimore Polytechnic Institute of Baltimore, Md. In 1919 he returned to Harrisonburg where he has since resided, having spent the summers here from 1912. For 20 years he was registrar and head of the mathematics department in Madison (formerly State Teachers) College, and since giving up the work of registrar in 1939 has continued as professor of mathematics.

Dr. Converse, with his infectious humor, companionable manner, and talents for leadership, has a notable record in social and fraternal activities. As scout master, member of the Court of Honor and the Council in the Stonewall Jackson area, his service has been untiring. He was awarded the Silver Beaver in 1942. A charter member of the local Kiwanis Club, he was president in 1927, lieutenant-governor of the Capital District in 1929, and district governor in 1932. Since 1934 he has been district historian, and for the past 16 years has a perfect attendance record. His hobbies are stamp-collecting, bridge whist, and golf; in reading he prefers biography and mystery stories.

On November 25, 1908, Dr. Converse married Miss Caroline McCaw Lay, of Richmond, Va., born in Florida, March 31, 1880, daughter of David M. and Nannie Marsh Lay, and granddaughter of Judge John Fitzhugh Lay of Richmond. Dr. and Mrs. Converse have two sons: Henry A. III and John Lay; a daughter, Caroline Lay, died in infancy. Henry A. III was born in Richmond, Aug. 28, 1909; is a graduate of Virginia Polytechnic Institute and is now district traffic manager, C. & P. Telephone Co., residing in Lynchburg. John Lay was born in Baltimore, Oct. 18, 1912; graduated from V. P. I. and at present is an inspector of dairies and food stores in the Department of Health, Arlington County, Va.

JESSE REESE COVER

BUSINESS MAN AND MANUFACTURER

Born August 1, 1858, at Linganore, Md.; attended school in Elkton, Va.; owner and operator of large tanneries; one of the organizers of the Rockingham National Bank of Harrisonburg; an active participant in helpful community enterprises; a large contributor to the growth and prosperity of the town of Elkton.

Mr. Cover's father was John Cover; his mother's maiden name was Mary Beal. The Cover homestead, where Mr. Cover was born, is at or near the village of Linganore, which is located in the fertile valley of Linganore Creek, in the eastern part of Frederick County, Maryland. The region is celebrated not only for the fertility of its soil and its historic associations, but also for the thrift and progressive spirit of its people. The Cover family, or at least the subject of this sketch and his father, must have located at Elkton, Virginia, about 1871, for in that year John Cover, the father, built a tannery in Elkton, and there Jesse Reese Cover attended three short sessions of the public school. In course of time the latter took up and expanded the tanning business that his father had established at Elkton, constructing larger buildings, providing modern equipment, and introducing the most approved methods in the various processes of tanning. In 1912 the Cover tannery at Elkton was turning out 220 sides of heavy sole leather daily. No doubt this output was much exceeded in later years. The extensive business of this establishment gave employment to many persons of the community and contributed materially to the growth and prosperity of the town.

At the same time that Mr. Cover was carrying on business at Elkton, he was the owner and operator of another large tannery at Augusta Springs, in the western part of Augusta County, Virginia. The products of his tanneries were famous for their quality, sold readily and widely and, in natural course, brought him large returns, making him wealthy. One who knew him well says of him: "He was a famous tanner, a wonderful financier, a self-made man." He did not aspire to hold public office, but devoted himself to business and took part in all progressive movements for the good of his community. In 1899 he was one of the organizers of the Rockingham National Bank in Harrisonburg, and served on the first board of directors of that institution, with Andrew M. Newman, Jr., George G. Grattan, Aaron H. Wilson, and Jacob Funkhouser. Mr. Cover in his religious convictions was a Methodist. In politics he was a Republican, and he was a member of the Masonic fraternity.

Mr. Cover's wife was Miss Roberta Brown of Carroll County, Maryland, born January 18, 1862. The marriage took place at Harper's Ferry, W. Va. Mr. and Mrs. Cover were the parents of five children: Herbert L., born November 22, 1878, now retired and living in Elkton; his wife was Miss Fanny Wolfe; Arthur B., born January 25, 1880, now handling real estate and insurance in Elkton; he married Miss Elsie Carter; Jessie Mae, born June 9, 1882, who died in June, 1906; Resse L., born February 12, 1885, now a farmer of Elkton; his wife was Miss Annie Palmer; and E. Russell, born December 4, 1887, now in the insurance business in Staunton; he married Miss Maud Miller.

Jesse Reese Cover died on November 30, 1932.

SAMUEL MONTREVILLE COX
RURAL LIFE LEADER

Born Aug. 17, 1897, near Independence, Va.; attended Grayson County schools; entered Virginia Polytechnic Institute, 1916; in Tank Corps of U. S. Army, March, 1918, to May 22, 1919, with overseas service, rising to 2d lieut.; at V. P. I. again at various times; also at Washington and Lee University; assistant county agent in Grayson and Rockbridge; county agent in Rockingham 15 years; promoter of soil conservation, diversified farming, livestock and poultry industry, the Triple-A Program, and rural electrification; District Extension Agent of 20 northern Virginia counties since May, 1942.

Mr. Cox believes that upon enlightened agriculture rests the welfare of the nation and all classes of its people, and his life work justifies his conviction. He is the son of Capt. M. B. Cox, Co. C, 45th Va. Inf., C. S. A., and wife, Martha Fulton, daughter of Capt. Samuel M. Fulton, conspicuous in the political and social development of Grayson County. His great-uncle, Creed Fulton, was an educational leader of S. W. Virginia, and the founder of Emory and Henry College. A paternal ancestor was Capt. John Cox, commander of a company of Regulators in the battle of King's Mountain, Oct. 7, 1780. He is a brother to Gen. Creed Fulton Cox, former chief of the U. S. Bureau of Insular Affairs, and later adviser to President Quezon of the Philippines. Another brother was the late Justice Joseph W. Cox of the Federal Court, D. C.

After service in World War I and work as assistant county agent in Grayson and Rockbridge, Mr. Cox came to Rockingham where as county agent for 15 years he did a notable work. With the great expansion of poultry raising, he and others launched an advertising campaign which culminated in the Turkey Festivals, which attracted national recognition. To balance the vast poultry industry with adequate outlets, he took a leading part in founding the Rockingham Poultry Coöperative, which, in its second year, marketed over 11 million pounds of poultry from Rockingham and adjoining counties. In connection with livestock, he forwarded the program for lamb improvement through better sires and otherwise. He advanced all phases of agriculture through improved methods and management and the opening of better markets. He was one of the first to see the possibilities in rural electrification, when first fostered by the Federal Government, and directed the attention of our rural population to its advantages. Today, largely as a result of his foresight and effort, the Shenandoah Valley Electric Coöperative serves over 3300 families in Rockingham, Augusta, and Shenandoah. When the farmers of northern Rockingham were confronted with a labor shortage he was a prime mover in securing a labor camp at Timberville to meet the need.

In May, 1942, Mr. Cox was appointed District Extension Agent for 20 counties of Northern Virginia, succeeding W. C. Shackelford, deceased. He still maintains an office in Harrisonburg. Long before his appointment to his present position the results of his outstanding work as county agent in Rockingham were felt and recognized in many of the counties now included in his district. His favorite forms of recreation are fishing and hunting, in natural keeping with his love of outdoor life. He is a member of the Methodist Church, the Elks, the Keezletown Ruritan Club, and Epsilon Sigma Phi, national fraternity for extension workers who have rendered 10 years or more of meritorious service.

In 1925 Mr. Cox married Miss Ruth Boyd Spring, daughter of Rev. and Mrs. J. E. Spring of Tennessee and S. W. Virginia. Mr. and Mrs. Cox have four children: Jane Beverly, born Nov. 6, 1926; Martha Fulton, born July 22, 1928; Samuel Montreville, Jr., born Jan. 21, 1932; and James Boyd, born Feb. 13,1934.

JOHN RANDOLPH CROWN
JOURNALIST, EDITOR, AND PUBLICIST

Born May 12, 1879, in Berryville; educated in Shenandoah University School, Berryville; in 1896 began his career as a journalist with his father. on the *Clarke Courier;* worked on papers in Omaha, Augusta, Ga., Norfolk, Washington, and other cities; a frequent attendant upon state and national political conventions; came to Harrisonburg in 1923 as editor of the *Daily News-Record;* promoter of Shenandoah Valley, Inc., Shenandoah National Park, good roads, and good government; secretary of the C.-W. Railway Co.; died in Harrisonburg, November 14, 1940.

No man in northern Virginia was more widely known and more generally loved than John R. Crown, who spent the last 17 years of a notable career as editor of the Harrisonburg *Daily News-Record*. His father was John O. Crown (1838-99), born at Smithburg, Md.; a C. S. A. veteran, and for many years owner and editor of the *Clarke Courier* at Berryville. His mother was Sarah Jane Smith (1848-1916), member of an old Clarke Co. family. His paternal grandfather, Frederick Crown, came to Maryland from Wales. An earlier ancestor, Col. Wm. Crowne, was created a Rouge Dragon by Lord Howard, Earl of Arundel, in 1630. As state editor of the Omaha *Bee*, news editor of the Augusta *Herald*, city editor of the Norfolk *Virginian-Pilot*, and correspondent eight years in Washington for the *Baltimore Sun*, Mr. Crown had a rich and varied experience. Measured in Washington with J. Fred Essary, Frank R. Kent, H. L. Mencken, and other brilliant writers, he was ranked as one of the leading correspondents. With a keen scent for news, ability to analyze a political situation, and remarkable accuracy in forecasting elections, he was a valued counselor and a trusted commentator. At the Democratic Natl. Convention in Baltimore in 1912, he had inside information of how Bryan would throw his support to Wilson. He was the first to "scoop" and publish that President Wilson would break precedent and attend the Versailles peace conference. The most interesting incident in his newspaper career, he said, was his visit to Hillsville, following the courthouse tragedy staged there by the Allens. He enjoyed the friendship of Senators Glass and Byrd, C. Bascom Slemp, M. C., Va. Highway Comsr. Shirley, and many others of high standing and influence in both political parties. His long and effcient service as editor of the *Daily News-Record* fully justified the choice of Senator Byrd in 1923. His editorials in his own paper and his columns in the metropolitan press were always discerning, fair, and constructive. He was a member of the Natl. Press Club, Kiwanis Club, Elks, chamber of commerce, and the Episcopal Church, a vestryman at Berryville.

Mr. Crown married Miss Elizabeth Lipscomb, daughter of Wm. S. Lipscomb and granddaughter of Judge Henry S. Lipscomb of Mississippi. Her mother, who died in 1939, was Miss Jimmie Andrews of Mississippi. Mr. and Mrs. Crown had three children: John Randolph, Jr., born July 5, 1916; a U. of Va. graduate, now manager C. & P. Telephone Co. at Vienna, Va.; his wife Miss Marilyn Stallard of St. Paul, Va.; James Andrews, born Feb. 14, 1920, student of U. Va. and Detroit College of Applied Science, now an engineer in a Detroit defense plant; unmarried; and Caroline Vaughan, born Oct. 29, 1921, now in school in Richmond. Martha Ann, daughter of John and Marilyn, was born Nov. 13, 1942.

Of the many tributes paid Mr. Crown, none was finer than that of Hon. R. Gray Williams of Winchester, who declared that he was a true democrat in his appreciation of the dignity of every individual, and that his kindly tongue was free from bitterness. He radiated public spirit.

WILLIAM DEAN
BUSINESS MAN, PROMINENT MASON, AND RELIGIOUS LEADER

Born February 24, 1863, near Ferrisburg, Vermont; grew up on his father's farm; graduate of Haverford College and student of photography in Philadelphia; leading photographer in Harrisonburg from 1887 to 1925; member of Harrisonburg school board and treasurer of the board 21 years; master of the Harrisonburg Masonic lodge; steward of the Methodist Church; founder of the men's Bible class in the Methodist Church, now named for him; died in Harrisonburg, December 24, 1925.

William Dean was an excellent business man, but much more. He was one of the outstanding civic and religious leaders of Harrisonburg, where he was an honored resident for nearly 40 years. After finishing high school in his native Vermont town, he attended a college preparatory school near Glens Falls, N. Y., and then entered Haverford College, where he graduated. After a course of training in a school of photography in Philadelphia, he came to Harrisonburg in 1887 and opened a studio in the L. H. Ott building on South Main Street, where he built up a substantial business, with a patronage extending throughout the state. He received four medals and first prizes from photographic conventions.

The Dean family has long been prominent in New England. Thomas Dean, born in South Chard, Somerset County, England, came to Massachusetts in 1634 and settled at Concord. His children and their descendants have lived in Massachusetts, New Hampshire, and Vermont. William Dean's grandfather, of the same name, was a Quaker minister. William's father, William Lindley Dean of Vermont, was a graduate of Brown University and taught Latin in that institution for some years. He married Mary Houghton Paige of Weare, N. H., and had children: Anna (Mrs. Sweet of Muncie, Ind.); William, of Harrisonburg; and Joshua Judson, of Andover, Mass.

On November 12, 1889, in Roanoke, Mr. Dean married Miss Martha Bower, daughter of James R. Bower, of Bedford County and Roanoke, and his wife, Mary Scott Shands of Harrisonburg. Of the marriage there are eight children: William Shands, Rockport, Mass.; Mary Rives (Mrs. Willis), Cape Charles, Va.; James Lindley, Andover, Mass.; Anna Martha (Mrs. Clarence Crist), Harrisonburg; Henry Bower, Glendale, Calif.; Edward Paige, Andover, Mass.; Virginia Mitchell (Mrs. Hague), Wilmington, Del.; and Sarah Rives (Mrs. Farley), Cranford, N. J.

Mr. Dean was a member of the Harrisonburg Rotary Club and exemplified the highest ideals and practices of that organization. He was a 32d degree Mason and a Knight Templar. Twice, in 1897 and 1898, he was Master of Rockingham Union Lodge No. 27, A. F. & A. M., and filled all the chairs of the order with distinction. He was ardently devoted to service to his country, his home, and his fellowmen. On the Harrisonburg school board with Dr. John H. Neff, Dr. T. O. Jones, Captain James L. Avis, Mr. George O. Conrad, and others, Mr. Dean gave the community diligent and efficient service. For 21 years he was treasurer of the board. He was an active and devoted member of the Methodist Church and for years served on the board of stewards. One of his special interests in the church was the Brotherhood Bible Class, which he built up from a few men to several hundred. His good teaching and his inspiring influence were given a fine response in the love and loyalty of the men under him, who have honored his memory by adopting the name, "The William Dean Bible Class."

WILMER LEE DECHERT

BANKER AND INSURANCE AUTHORITY

Born June 20, 1866, in Hagerstown, Md.; brought to Rockingham when a small child; after finishing school, worked in his father's printing office in Harrisonburg; at age of 21 launched his insurance agency; member of the county board of supervisors; director and president of the First National Bank; member of the school board; Harrisonburg postmaster; died in Harrisonburg, April 20, 1935.

Wilmer Lee Dechert, founder of the well-known W. L. Dechert Insurance Corporation, and its efficient head until his death, was for many years one of the outstanding business men of Harrisonburg and Rockingham County. He was a son of Daniel Dechert, a native of Franklin County, Pa., and his wife, Laura Parran Miller, of Shepherdstown. Prior to 1861, Daniel Dechert edited a newspaper in Charles Town, Jefferson County, now West Virginia; during the war he published a paper in Hagerstown, Md. In or about 1866 he moved to Rockingham and for a time engaged in farming. For a time he resided in Danville; then in 1878 he established the *Spirit of the Valley* in Harrisonburg, which he published for a number of years.

After finishing school Wilmer L. Dechert worked for some years in his father's printing office; then, at 21 years of age, he established his insurance agency in Harrisonburg which he developed into one of the largest and most efficient in the country. At the same time he participated actively in the civic, educational, and business operations of the city and county. For eight years he was a member of the county board of supervisors and in that capacity was instrumental in building the new court house in 1896-97. He served on the local school board, which profited greatly by reason of his business experience and sound judgement. In 1908 he was made a director of the First National Bank of Harrisonburg; nine years later he became vice-president of the institution, and from January 15, 1920, until October, 1933, he was its efficient president. In 1911 he was appointed postmaster for Harrisonburg and held that office for four or five years. Always keenly alive to affairs in the world at large, he read extensively in newspapers, magazines, and general literature, and traveled in Europe as well as in America. In politics he was a Republican, but numbered his friends in both great parties. He was a member of the Presbyterian Church and served as a deacon. When the Kiwanis Club was established in Harrisonburg twenty years ago he was one of the charter members.

On October 17, 1888, Mr. Dechert married Miss Anna Catherine Greenwood, daughter of W. C. Greenwood of Baltimore, who survives him. Mr. and Mrs. Dechert had two children: Lillian Ann, born June 14, 1889, and Harry Lee, born April 29, 1895. Lillian married Henry A. W. Happer. She died May 9, 1919, leaving a son, Henry Happer, who is now at the Naval Officers' Training School at Northwestern University, Evanston, Ill. Harry Lee graduated from Woodberry Forest School and attended the University of Virginia, where he was a member of the Delta Kappa Epsilon fraternity. He then entered the insurance business with his father. On April 30, 1917, he married Miss Laura Ward Wise of Staunton. He died on April 12, 1934, leaving two children: Wilmer Lee II, who is now at home at "Stone Lodge," Hinton, Va., and Anne Stith, who married Richard B. Yancey, and with her husband lives a few miles east of Harrisonburg.

J. S. DENTON
PIONEER FURNITURE MERCHANT

Born May 9, 1855, near Rushville, Rockingham County; attended public schools, Valley Normal at Bridgewater, and a business school in Highland County; became a skilled cabinet-maker; in Ohio several years; about 1878 returned to Virginia and opened a furniture store in Bridgewater, with one in Basic City during the early "Boom" days; located in Harrisonburg in 1905 and opened a second-hand furniture store, expanded in 1911; other expansions and his sons associated in the business; present commodious building erected in 1922-23.

Mr. Denton was devout in religion, active in fraternal organizations, and achieved a remarkable success in building up a large business from small beginnings. He was of English ancestry, a son of Wesley and Sarah Denton, whose forebears were among early Valley settlers. Left an orphan at seven years, he rose to success and usefulness through habits of thrift and industry. Having worked as a skilled craftsman in his home community and Ohio, he returned to his native state and at Bridgewater, about 1878, opened one of the first furniture stores in this section. He also conducted an undertaking business, continuing in connection his work as a cabinet-maker. In the early 1890's, when "booms" hit the Valley, he operated for some time in Basic City, returning to Bridgewater for a period before coming to Harrisonburg in 1905. Here he opened a small second-hand furniture store in the old Paul Building on W. Market Street, in a room about 15 by 20 feet. This business grew under his experienced guidance and his growing reputation for reliability, and in 1911 he took up larger quarters, 25 by 60 feet, on the same street. Within this period, in 1909, he associated his elder son, E. Warren Denton, as a partner, with the firm name of J. S. Denton & Son.

In 1915, to meet the needs of the growing business, the storerooms were doubled in size. By this time second-hand furniture had become a side line, with the major part of the business in new furniture. In 1917 two additional store rooms were required, and the next year a metal warehouse and workshop were erected in the rear of the store. Soon balconies were built in the store to provide additional facilities. In June, 1919, a second son, Bernard T. Denton, back from the war in Europe, was made a partner and the business was incorporated under the name of J. S. Denton & Sons. In 1922-23 the present large building, with modern equipment, was erected on the lot at the west corner of Court Square, long familiar as the residence in former years of Judge James Kenney. This building, home of a great establishment, is a fitting monument to Mr. Denton's energy and progressive methods, and the good will he built up.

On June 29, 1881, Mr. Denton married Miss Virginia Jenkins of Bridgewater, who died December 26, 1899. In 1902 he married Miss Laura Ott of Augusta County. He died on June 21, 1930, survived by his second wife and four children of the first marriage: E. Warren and Bernard T. Denton, who carry on the business of the firm under the well-established traditions, and two daughters: Mrs. T. R. Lokey of Harrisonburg and Mrs. Herbert Prince of Philadelphia. Mr. Denton was a member of the Methodist Church from childhood and for many years served as a steward and in other official capacities. He was also an influential Odd Fellow, and active in various civic enterprises. As a member of the old Sparkling Springs Co., he enjoyed occasional brief respites from business at the company's summer resort.

E. WARREN DENTON
PRESIDENT AND MANAGER OF J. S. DENTON & SONS

Born October 16, 1889, in Bridgewater; attended public schools in Bridgewater and Harrisonburg; located in Harrisonburg in 1903; worked in various positions; joined his father in the furniture business in 1907, and in 1909 became a partner; now president and manager of the J. S. Denton & Sons corporation; a charter member of the Harrisonburg-Rockingham Kiwanis Club; a member of the Methodist Church and on the official board; affiliated with the Elks, etc.

Mr. Denton, though still a comparatively young man, has had a long and profitable business experience, dating from the time when he, in 1907, joined his father in the furniture store that the latter opened in Harrisonburg. Indeed, prior to that time he had no doubt received valuable training and experience in connection with his father's work and business in Bridgewater, his native town. His father, Jefferson Simon Denton, whose portrait and biography appear on preceding pages, was qualified by character and habits to exert a wholesome and stimulating influence upon his sons and others in close association with him. His mother, Virginia Jenkins Denton, died when Warren was 10 years of age.

Coming to Harrisonburg in 1903, at the age of 14, Warren Denton worked in various positions of employment for several years and then, as already indicated, entered his father's furniture store. At the age of 20 he became a partner in the store and has been actively engaged in the growing business ever since. By 1922, after numerous successive expansions, the firm decided to erect a commodious building of their own, and in May of that year the old Kenney homestead at the west corner of Court Square was purchased. In June of 1923 business was opened in the new five-story brick structure which provided 35,000 square feet of space, to house the largest furniture and floor-covering establishment in the Shenandoah Valley between Roanoke and Washington. On September 28, 1938, to celebrate more than 30 years of continuous service, the *Daily News-Record* of Harrisonburg carried a special four-page supplement devoted to the Denton store. In this it was stated that the firm for more than three decades had made a specialty of furnishing carpet for churches of the Shenandoah Valley and bordering counties of West Virginia, and took credit for inaugurating the first out-of-town delivery service offered by a Harrisonburg business firm. In this supplement were pictures of the Denton brothers, Warren and Bernard, the store building, and one of the long-distance moving vans operated by the company.

Like his father, Warren Denton is a member of the Harrisonburg Methodist Church, and serves in official capacities. He is past president and secretary of the large Brotherhood Bible Class. He holds charter membership in the local Kiwanis Club and is also affiliated with the Benevolent and Protective Order of Elks, taking an active interest in movements for civic welfare. By reason of his companionable disposition and hearty manner he enjoys a wide popularity.

On August 12, 1912, Mr. Denton married Miss Lola Swisher of New Creek, W. Va. Mr. and Mrs. Denton have one son, Edgar Warren Denton, Jr., born June 26, 1926.

BERNARD T. ("JACK") DENTON
MERCHANT, WAR VETERAN, AND CIVIL OFFICIAL

Born Feb. 16, 1896, in Bridgewater; educated in Harrisonburg schools and in business experience with his father; on June 2, 1917, enlisted in Co. D, 2d Va. Regt.; later in 116th Inf., 29th (Blue and Gray) Division; transferred to 35th Engineers and sailed for France, March 10, 1918; sergeant in active service with 19th Engineers on various fronts in France for more than a year; returned to U. S. A. and discharged at Camp Meade, April 14, 1919; in firm of J. S. Denton & Sons; active in V. F. W. organizations and work; president two terms of Chamber of Commerce; member of City Council and War Price and Rationing Board.

Mr. Denton, the younger son of J. S. and Virginia Jenkins Denton, has had an unusually active and honorable career in civil and military service as well as in business. In France, in World War I, his record as a non-commissioned officer won for him the commendation of his superior officers. Following his discharge from the army, he entered the firm of J. S. Denton & Son which then became J. S. Denton & Sons, Inc., with him as secretary. Since the death of his father in 1930 he has been secretary and treasurer. In February, 1921, he took part in forming the Rion-Bowman Post 632, V. F. W., and became a charter member. After filling other offices in the Post he was chosen its commander in January, 1927, and rendered effective service in advancing its activities and objectives. His ability and zeal in behalf of veteran welfare caused him to be chosen for various department offices and assignments, including membership on the Department Council of Administration for a number of years. His efforts towards the establishment of a Virginia Cottage at the V. F. W. National Home for widows and orphans at Eaton Rapids, Mich., and the raising of funds for its construction were notable. He took a leading part in the formation of a number of new posts of the organization. Along with the expansion of his firm's business he was a leader in promoting the city's retail trade resources and advantages, and aided in a number of "Good Neighbor" motorcades to adjacent areas of West Virginia, thus developing closer commercial and social relations with those communities. His public and community spirit was recognized by his election in 1937 as a director of the Chamber of Commerce. Three years later he was made vice-president and, in 1941, president, being re-elected in 1942. During his two administrations the Chamber's membership reached its peak, and in his second term all facilities and services were mobilized for wartime duty on the home front.

In 1939 Mr. Denton was appointed to the City Zoning Board of Appeals and in June, 1940, he was elected to the City Council, leading his ticket on the west side. He is chairman of two important committees, those of Law Enforcement and Finance. He has attended every regular meeting of the Council since his election. In June, 1941, he organized the city and county Aircraft Warning Service and directed it until August, 1942. On December 1 (1942) he was made a member of the local War Price and Rationing Board He is a member of the Methodist Church; has held various offices in the William Dean Bible Class, of which he is now president; is a member of the Elks, U. C. T., and the American Legion, Post No. 27.

On June 15, 1921, Mr. Denton married Miss Maida Virginia Custer of Harrisonburg, and has a son, Bernard T. Denton, Jr., aged three years. On preceding pages of this work may be found biographies of his father, J. S. Denton, his brother, E. Warren Denton, with references to other members of the family.

DEWITT CLINTON DEVIER
JEWELER AND CIVIC LEADER

Born September 6, 1870, in West Rockingham; attended public schools of the county and city; studied the jewelry business with John W. Taliaferro; opened a jewelry store of his own in Harrisonburg about 1899; member of the Presbyterian Church, the Elks, and the Rotary Club; served for some time on the city council; was active in connection with Shenandoah Camp for Boys, and in working with the boys of Harrisonburg; died April 17, 1924.

Mr. Devier was for many years a prominent business man of Harrisonburg, active in civic affairs and in fraternal organizations, and much interested in promoting the welfare of the under-privileged boys of the city. The founder of his branch of the family, it is said, came from Georgia, where Deviers had resided for years; however, it is true that Deviers lived in Rockingham County from an early date. In 1784 James Deviers proposed to build a tobacco warehouse in Harrisonburg, and he, with Hugh, John, and William Deviers, signed a petition, along with 95 other men, praying the General Assembly of the state for leave to establish the said warehouse. This petition is now on file in the archives department of the State Library in Richmond. DeWitt Clinton Devier's grandparents were Allen and Nancy Devier; his great-grandfather was also named Allen Devier and the latter's wife was Nancy Turley, married August 18, 1813. Turleytown was probably founded by Giles Turley who settled in the county in 1804, or about that time. On June 9 of that year he presented his letter from the Little River Church in Loudoun County to the Linville Creek Baptist Church. For many years Giles Devier was a prominent citizen of Rockingham. These several items indicate a close connection between the Deviers and the Turleys.

Early in life DeWitt Clinton Devier studied and worked with John W. Taliaferro, who operated a jewelry store in connection with his shop for repairing clocks and watches in Harrisonburg, and about the year 1899 he set up in business for himself in the same line of work. He was successfully engaged in this field until a comparatively short time before his death, having in the meantime associated his sons Charles and Amiss with himself in his business. At the same time he participated in the civic, fraternal, and religious life of the community as a member of the Presbyterian Church, the Rotary Club, the Benevolent and Protective Order of Elks, and the city council. He devoted much time, along with others, to the camp for boys on the Shenandoah River. One of his associates said of him: "Clint Devier had as big a heart as God ever gave a man—generous to a fault." He was a Democrat in politics. For diversion and recreation he enjoyed hunting and fishing, and was a lover of nature.

On July 29, 1895, Mr. Devier married Miss Ida F. Bell, a native of the county, born April 2, 1875, a sister of Henry Bell. The Bells were from Pennsylvania. Mr. and Mrs. Devier had four children: Charles Wallings, born September 4, 1896; Sheffey Lewis, born March 21, 1898; Amiss Clinton, born November 13, 1900; a jeweler until his death in January, 1941; and Edythe Virginia, born December 16, 1904, now Mrs. R. E. Heatwole. Mrs. Devier, still living, is a resident of Harrisonburg. Biographies of the sons, Charles W. and Sheffey L., appear on the following pages of this book.

CHARLES WALLINGS DEVIER

OPTOMETRIST

Born September 4, 1896, in Harrisonburg; student in Harrisonburg schools—graduate of high school in 1915; student in Northern Illinois College of Opthalmology—graduated in June, 1919; passed Virginia State Board of Examiners in optometry and began practice in Harrisonburg, 1920; on executive committee of the State Association of Optometrists since 1930; chairman of executive committee, 1938; vice-president, 1939; president, 1940-41; Kiwanian, Mason, Methodist; active in organizing and directing the Harrisonburg Municipal Band.

In professional service, as a talented musician, and as a member of fraternal organizations, Dr. Devier has been an active and influential participant in helpful community enterprises for a number of years. In this respect he and his brothers have worthily maintained the traditions passed on to them by their father, the late DeWitt Clinton Devier, who was a member of the city council and a generous worker in various welfare agencies of the city and county. He is the eldest son of D. Clinton Devier and his wife, who, before her marriage, was Miss Ida Florence Bell, both natives of Rockingham County.

Having gone through the elementary schools of the city, Dr. Devier entered the high school from which he was graduated in 1915. To fit himself for work in his chosen profession, he then matriculated in the Northern Illinois College of Opthalmology and graduated from that institution in 1919. After passing the examinations required by the Virginia State Board of Examiners, he began the practice of optometry in Harrisonburg in the year 1920 and has since been successfully engaged in his profession. He has received notable recognition in the State Association of Optometrists over a period of more than twelve years. He became a member of the organization in 1925. In 1930 he was elected a member of the executive committee and was chairman of the committee in 1938. The next year he served as vice-president, and in 1940 he held the office of president. In 1941 he was re-elected to the executive committee and still continues in that capacity. He maintains offices in The National Bank Building of Harrisonburg, Rooms 207-209.

Dr. Devier is a member of the Methodist Church, the Masonic Blue Lodge and Royal Arch Chapter, and the Kiwanis Club—has been a Kiwanian for the past 21 years. In politics he is a Democrat. He is a dog fancier and devotes much time to hunting and fishing. His most notable contribution to community life and service has been made through local musical organizations. For 20 years he has been active in promoting and directing the municipal band, which, under his leadership, has won merited recognition and approval. A skilled musician himself, he has been able to inspire others with ambition and earnest effort to excellence.

On February 18, 1922, Dr. Devier married Miss Helen Margaret Miller, who was born in Baltimore, Md., on September 15, 1898, the daughter of Christopher and Ella Duvall Miller. Dr. and Mrs. Devier are the parents of three sons: Charles Wallings, Jr., born June 30, 1924; Clint M., born April 12, 1926; and Christopher D., born July 2, 1936. Charles, Jr., is a student in the University of Virginia, having been in attendance there since June, 1942. In October of the same year he enlisted in the U. S. Naval Reserve. He entered the University as a pre-med student and will continue his course unless called into active service.

SHEFFEY LEWIS DEVIER
CITY COMMISSIONER OF REVENUE

Born March 21, 1898, in Harrisonburg; attended the city public schools and graduated from the high school in 1917; studied law at the University of Virginia, 1917-20; began the practice of law in Harrisonburg in 1920; justice of the peace, 1922-26; mayor of the city, 1924-28; judge of juvenile and domestic relations court, 1924-32; commissioner of revenue for the city of Harrisonburg since 1933; formerly secretary and one term president of the Kiwanis Club; official in the Presbyterian Church.

Mr. Devier is the second son of the late DeWitt Clinton Devier and his wife, Ida Florence Bell. Biographies of his father and his older brother, Dr. Charles W. Devier, appear on preceding pages. A native of Harrisonburg, he grew up here and attended the city public schools, graduating from the high school in June, 1917. The following autumn he entered the law department of the University of Virginia, where he was a student for three years. In June, 1920, he passed the state bar examinations and opened an office for the practice of his profession in Harrisonburg. From 1922 to 1926 he was a justice of the peace, and in 1924 was elected mayor of the city, serving a regular four-year term. At the same time he served as judge (from 1924) of the juvenile and domestic relations court for Rockingham County, continuing in this office until 1932. In 1933 he was appointed commissioner of revenue to finish the term of R. Lee Woodson, who died; and in the fall of 1933 he was elected to the same office, in which he continues at the present, having been re-elected in 1937 and 1941.

When the local Kiwanis Club was organized about 1922 Mr. Devier became one of the charter members. Later, for several years, he served the club as its secretary, and for one term was president. For some time he was also a member of the Benevolent and Protective Order of Elks. He is a member of the Presbyterian Church, and for a number of years has been on the board of deacons. The duties of his office as commissioner of revenue for the city do not allow him much time for diversion or recreation, though he is fond of fishing and hunting and indulges these inclinations occasionally as he has opportunity. His reading is limited mostly to topics of the times in current periodicals.

On July 26, 1921, Mr. Devier married Miss Maisie Lavinia Morgan of Brunswick, Georgia, the marriage taking place in that city. Mrs. Devier is a daughter of Lemuel T. Morgan and his wife, a native of Indiana, whose name before marriage was Livia Allen Crozier. Mr. Morgan was a civil engineer and served as superintendent of public construction in the city of Brunswick. Mrs. Devier attended Converse College, Spartanburg, S. C., and later the State Teachers (now Madison) College in Harrisonburg, graduating from this institution in June, 1921. Mr. and Mrs. Devier are the parents of four children: Mary Morgan, born August 12, 1922; Sheffey Lewis, Jr., born April 15, 1925; Jane Morgan, born December 14, 1927; and Richard Morgan, born December 13, 1930. Mary Morgan graduated from Harrisonburg High School, attended Madison College, the Pan-American School in Richmond, and is now employed at Jacksonville, Fla. Sheffey, Jr., is a student in Harrisonburg High School and expects to be inducted into the U. S. Army in the near future. The two younger children are also students in Harrisonburg High School.

CHARLES N. DEWEY, N. D.
DIRECTOR OF BETTER HEALTH INSTITUTE

Born April 1, 1877, in Mercer County, Pa.; graduate of Utica (Pa.) High School; attended Allegheny College, Meadville, Pa; ordained a minister in the Church of Christ; held successful pastorates in Penna. and Virginia; in missionary work in S. E. Virginia; student of natural health science; in 1918 graduated in mechano-therapy and chiropractic, American College, Chicago; 1922, in electro-therapeutics and osteopathy, Natl. College, Chicago; 1930, in naturopathy, Natl. School of Naturopathy, Chicago; in 1941 received the P. H. degree, honorary, from the Indianapolis College of Physio-Therapy; president Va. State Society of Naturopathic Physicians.

Dr. Dewey is a son of Samuel I. Dewey and wife, who before her marriage was Lusetta Brest, daughter of James Brest. His father, Samuel I. Dewey, a second-cousin of Admiral George Dewey, was a son of Horace Andrew Dewey, whose wife was Elizabeth Lytle. Both were of Mercer County, Pa. Horace Andrew Dewey was a Federal veteran of the Civil War, and was honorably discharged from service at Falmouth, Va. He was a farmer, school teacher, and for some time a mail carrier. Mercer County, in northwestern Pennsylvania, Dr. Dewey's birthplace, and the residing place of his ancestors, adjoins on the east that part of Ohio which is known as the Western Reserve. This region, which was reserved by the state of Connecticut from its western lands, was settled largely at an early date by people from New England, where the Deweys were numerous.

Most of Dr. Dewey's early life was spent in Meadville, Pa. He has always been devoutly religious and for a number of years was a minister and missionary. Having been ordained in the Church of Christ, he, on February 25, 1913, took charge of a church in Kingston, Pa. After successful pastorates there and elsewhere in Pennsylvania, he came to Virginia to do missionary work in the southeastern part of the state. Being interested in the science of natural health, he devoted his study increasingly to this subject. He attended National College in Chicago and in 1922 graduated from that institution in electro-therapeutics and related branches. Locating in Harrisonburg the same year he engaged in practice and has built up a large clientele. In the meantime he has continued his studies in various institutions, as already indicated. During his residence here he has been active in religious work and for the past 18 years has taught a Sundayschool class in the United Brethren Church. He is a member of the Virginia Temperance Foundation Board and has preached occasionally in most of the churches of the city and county. For 14 years he has been president of the local Business Men's Evangelistic Club and has served for three years as president of the state organization. This organization has for its motto text: "Ye shall be witnesses unto me." For six years he has been president of the Virginia State Society of Naturopathic Physicians. He is director and proprietor of the Better Health Institute in Harrisonburg. For recreation, he enjoys hunting and fishing, and in his reading gives preference to history, fiction, and current events.

On May 5, 1897, Dr. Dewey married Miss Genevieve Cooper, daughter of Robert Cooper of Cochranton, Penna. Dr. and Mrs. Dewey have three children: Kenneth A., who holds a position in the U. S. Agricultural Department in Washington; Bernard W., who is engaged in the hardware business in Arlington, Va.; and Helen B., a talented musician, who is active in religious and social work. A grandson, now in national service, has recently been assigned work in the medical corps.

JAMES HENRY DEYERLE, M.D.
PHYSICIAN AND SURGEON

Born January 4, 1876, near Rocky Mount, Va.; grew up on his father's farm; attended local schools and Glade Spring Military Academy; A.B., Roanoke College, 1896; medical student, University of Virginia and the Medical College of Virginia; M.D., Medical College of Virginia, 1901; interne in the Virginia Hospital, Richmond, two years; in general practice four years at Harding, W. Va.; superintendent of Roanoke City Hospital, 1907-09; located in Harrisonburg in 1909; devoted almost exclusively to surgery since 1920; member of local, state, and national medical associations.

Dr. Deyerle, since locating at Harrisonburg 33 years ago, has won an enviable place in his profession, has participated actively in the civic, social, and religious life of the community, and has successfully carried on horticulture as an avocation. He is a son of Henry Shaver Deyerle, who was born in Roanoke County, Va., in 1848, and his wife, whose maiden name was Sallie Price. His paternal grandparents were Benjamin and Susan Shaver Deyerle; his mother's parents were Cyrus and Elizabeth Boone Price. Cyrus Price had five sons in the Confederate army, two of whom gave their lives in that service. Henry S. Deyerle also was a Confederate soldier. After the war he devoted himself to farming, but also served on the local school board and as a county supervisor. Benjamin Deyerle, though left an orphan at an early age and deprived of ordinary school advantages, became an owner of valuable lands and engaged extensively as a contractor and builder. Many of the substantial brick dwelling houses in his section of Roanoke County remain as his appropriate monuments.

After a wholesome boyhood on his father's farm near Rocky Mount, in Franklin County, Va., and attending the neighborhood schools and a military school at Glade Spring in Washington County (1890-91), James H. Deyerle entered Roanoke College at Salem, where he was graduated A.B. in 1896. For the next two years he had valuable experience as a pharmacist at Havre, Montana. He then returned to his native state and entered the medical school of the University of Virginia, transferring later to the Medical College of Virginia in Richmond, where he graduated in 1901. Serving a two-year internship in Richmond, and practicing four years in West Virginia, he was for two years superintendent of the city hospital in Roanoke. He then located (1909) in Harrisonburg where, for some years, he engaged in general practice, with increasing attention to surgery, to which he has devoted himself almost exclusively for the past twenty years or more. In this field he has been notably successful. He has held official positions in the local medical societies and is a member of the Virginia Medical Society and the American Medical Association. He is an Episcopalian, an honorary member of the city-county Rotary Club, and finds diversion in looking after his fruit farms on Chestnut Ridge. For some time he was local health officer and physician to Madison College.

On December 22, 1902, Dr. Deyerle married Miss Mary Byrd Warwick of Richmond, daughter of Corbin and Sarah M. Warwick. Dr. and Mrs. Deyerle have had three children: Henry Warwick, born in 1903, who died in 1905; Evelyn Byrd, who, among her other accomplishments, is a talented artist; and Henry Price, who graduated in medicine at the University of Virginia in 1942, and is now an interne in Roper Hospital in Charleston, S. C.

LEROY HOWARD DORSEY

BUSINESS MAN, FARMER, SPORTSMAN, AND TRAVELER

Born January, 19, 1887, near Logansport Ind.; student in Indiana District Schools and Harrisonburg High School; started as a salesman in the portrait business at Harrisonburg, 1904; later district manager, division manager, and director of the Chicago Portrait Company, Chicago; president of the Company since March 30, 1931; in 1923 he founded the Fine Arts Assn., of which he has been president since 1931.

Mr. Dorsey has shown the same energy and persistence in tracing his lineage that have given him notable distinction in other fields. His father was Daniel Howard Dorsey (January 28, 1862—March 5, 1926), born near Logansport, Indiana, who, on February 17, 1884, married Martha Elizabeth Umbarger (July 20, 1856—December 22, 1904), a native of Bristol, Va. Daniel Howard Dorsey was a son of Eli (January 9, 1826—November 8, 1877), born near Frederick, Md., son of Thomas Worthington Dorsey and grandson of Captain Eli Dorsey, a descendant of the English gentleman Edward Dorsey of Anne Arundel County, Md., emigrant of 1651. Edward was a direct descendant of the Earl of Essex, whose coat of arms is shown and who fought under William the Conqueror. Martha Elizabeth Umbarger was a daughter of Jonas (March 19, 1822—February 17, 1899), born in Wythe County, Va., who, on October 7, 1841, married Eliza Ann Smith (May 1, 1818—March 12, 1885), a native of Sullivan County, Tenn., and a descendant of the Smiths of Virginia.

Upon leaving Harrisonburg High School, Mr. Dorsey became a salesman for a well-known portrait firm of Chicago and he has been president of the Chicago Portrait Company since 1931. During the first World War he was affiliated with the Federal Bureau of Investigation of the U. S. Department of Justice, later serving in the Field Artillery, Officers Training School. For 25 years he has been a member of the American Legion. On November 10, 1923, he established the Fine Arts Association, of which he has been president since 1931. Since 1932 he has been president of the American Fine Arts Studios, and since 1931 a director of the Empire Art Company Pty. Ltd., of Sydney, Australia. He has been president of Corn Belt Farms, Inc., of Indiana, since 1936. He owns and operates the Dorsey Farms, Kentland and Chalmers, Indiana, consisting of eight grain farms totaling 3078 acres.

Along with his numerous business interests, Mr. Dorsey has found time for civic duties, wide travel, and for participation in various forms of sport and recreation. He is a member of the Chicago Chamber of Commerce, the Illinois Manufacturers Association, the Indiana Society of Chicago, the Sportsman's Club of Chicago, the American Geographical Society, and the Lansden Hunting Club, and is honorary president of the Tampico Tarpon Rodeo of Tampico, Mexico; also a member of the Sea Anglers Club of Colombo, Ceylon. He is a Flying Colonel C. & S., and is chairman of the Army Aviation Cadet Procurement Committee of the Air Force Sponsors of Chicago, Inc. He is a member of the Methodist Church, a 32d Degree Mason, a Knight Templar, and a Shriner. He is an enthusiastic sportsman and a proficient deep-sea angler. His home is at 5236 Lake Park Avenue, Chicago, and his office address is 509 South Wabash Avenue in the same city.

Opposite is shown the coat of arms of the Earl of Essex, who fought under William the Conqueror.

SAMUEL PAGE DUKE
PRESIDENT OF MADISON COLLEGE

Born September 5, 1885, at Ferrum, Va.; attended rural schools and Randolph-Macon Academy at Bedford; A.B., Randolph-Macon College, 1906; A. M., Columbia University, 1913; LL. D., Hampden-Sydney, 1931; teacher and school principal in Oklahoma and Virginia, 1906-14; Head Dept. of Education and Director of Training School, State Teachers College, Farmville, 1914-18; Supervisor of Va. High Schools, 1918-19; President of Madison College (formerly State Teachers College), Harrisonburg, since 1919; active in civic, educational, religious, and philanthropic organizations; member board of trustees, Randolph-Macon System of Colleges.

President Duke is a son of Rev. Thomas Page Duke (b. 1852), a well-known Methodist minister, and his wife, Jennie Gray Ward (1861-1941). In Randolph-Macon Academy at Bedford and Randolph-Macon College at Ashland he was distinguished in both literary and athletic activities. He was business manager of the college magazine and in 1906 was a contestant in public speaking. He was a member of the Franklin Literary Society, the Kappa Apha Fraternity, the varsity baseball, football, and track teams; at both the academy and the college he won the medal as best all-round athlete. Following his graduation in 1906, he was instructor in Willie Halsell College, Okla., and in 1907, at the age of 21, was elected vice-president of the same college. From 1908 to 1910 he was principal of Chase City (Va.) High School and in 1908 established the Chase City Institute for Teachers. From 1910 to 1914 he was principal of Richmond City schools, with an intermission of one year in Columbia University, where he was awarded the A. M. degree in June, 1913. From 1914 to 1918 he was head of the department of education and director of the training school in the State Teachers College at Farmville; then, after a year as supervisor of Virginia high schools, he was elected (1919) to the presidency of Madison College (formerly State Teachers), at Harrisonburg, where his work has been notably successful. Under his direction the college has added splendid buildings and improved equipment, attracted a large student body, increased its faculty, and expanded its curricula in keeping with sound educational development and the special needs of critical times, such as the present. Among his associates of the college he is fittingly termed the "Builder."

As a charter member and past president of the Rotary Club and the Chamber of Commerce, president of the board of trustees of Rockingham Memorial Hospital, a member of the official board of the Methodist Church, and a Sundayschool teacher for 20 years, President Duke has been active in community affairs. He is a Mason, a member of the Va. Education Assn., in which he has been a vice-president and a director; a life member of N. E. A.; Kappa Alpha, Phi Delta Kappa, Kappa Delta Pi, Phi Beta Kappa. In 1931 he was honored by Hampden-Sydney College with the degree of LL. D.

On August 26, 1908, President Duke married Miss Lucile Campbell of Georgetown, Texas. Children: Samuel Page, Jr., Sept. 24, 1909; Julia Lois, April 27, 1911; Robert Campbell, Sept. 11, 1917; and Marshall Ward, Jan. 8, 1920. Page attended Emory and Henry and Randolph-Macon College, and is now in business in Newport News; Julia, B.S. of Madison and M.A. of George Peabody College, is head of the dept. of physical education for women at Louisiana Polytechnic Institute; Robert, LL. B., University of Virginia, is a lieutenant in the U. S. Navy; Marshall, B. S., Virginia Polytechnic Institute, is a research chemist for the Celanese Corporation.

DAVID WAMPLER EARMAN
LAWYER; FORMER COMMONWEALTH'S ATTORNEY

Born July 19, 1884, on Cub Run, at Penn Laird; attended Keezletown public school and Harrisonburg High School; LL. B., Washington and Lee University, 1910; actively engaged in the practice of law in Harrisonburg since September, 1910; Commonwealth's Attorney for Rockingham County and the city of Harrisonburg, January 1, 1920, to December 31, 1939; deacon in the Harrisonburg Presbyterian Church; member of the Masonic fraternity, Odd Fellows, Elks, and professional organizations; long-time member of the Republican State Executive Committee of Virginia; chairman of the Republican County Committee.

Mr. Earman's birthplace on Cub Run is on or near the Lawyer Road, the trail thus named a century and a half ago because the famous lawyer, Gabriel Jones, traversed it on his horseback journeys between his home and Harrisonburg. Possibly the traditions of the Lawyer Road may have had an influence in giving bent to young Earman's professional inclinations. He is the eldest of the seven sons of Joseph B. and Mary Burtner Earman, and a grandson of Samuel Earman and his wife, Syvilla May. His mother's father was George P. Burtner; his paternal great-grandfather was Peter Earman. Both the Earmans and the Burtners came to Virginia from Pennsylvania, as did so many of the Shenandoah Valley pioneers.

After early schooling, as already indicated on the opposite page, in Keezletown and Harrisonburg, Wampler Earman entered upon the study of law in Washington and Lee University, where he received his degree in the early summer of 1910. The following September he opened his office in Harrisonburg where he has ever since been actively and successfully engaged in the practice of his profession. During the twenty years that he was commonwealth's attorney for the county and city he established an enviable record as an efficient and fearless officer. It has been said of him, and justly, that during his long period of official service he made safe the bulwarks of life and property and struck terror to the hearts of criminals; yet even those who, because of their wrongdoing, feared him, yet at the same time respected his courage and his stand for justice. Though an active and prominent Republican, his friends are by no means limited to those of his own political party. His personal qualities are such as to make him a congenial associate with all classes of good citizens. He is a member of the state and local bar associations and is affiliated with various fraternal and social organizations. He is a deacon in the Harrisonburg Presbyterian Church, and gives substantial support to civic and benevolent enterprises. In college he was a member of the Alpha Chi Rho fraternity. His immediate forebears were thrifty and prosperous farmers, who at the same time were keenly interested in public affairs. An uncle, George N. Earman, was a member of the state legislature and also a delegate from Rockingham to the state constitutional convention of 1901-02.

On May 27, 1920, Mr. Earman married Miss Frances C. Overlock, born October 12, 1899, daughter of W. H. Overlock of Seattle, Washington. She enjoyed advanced training in Mary Baldwin College, Staunton, and in the University of Washington. Her father was president of the Kent National Bank of Seattle. Mr. and Mrs. Earman have two daughters: Sancie, born in Harrisonburg on March 1, 1921, now the wife of Captain W. L. Bacheler, who is in active service with the U. S. Marine Corps; and Jane, born April 3, 1932, also a native of Harrisonburg and now a student in the city schools.

CHARLES S. ESTEP

FARMER AND COMMISSIONER OF REVENUE

Born October 28, 1886, in Augusta County, Va.; brought to Rockingham at age of six months; grew up on a farm near Dayton; attended local school and Shenandoah College; farmer, traveling salesman, and dealer in livestock; a director of the West Rockingham Mutual Fire Insurance Co.; commissioner of revenue since 1927.

Mr. Estep, though born in Augusta, was brought to Rockingham at such an early age that he is almost entitled to be recognized as a native son. His birthplace was near the historic town of Waynesboro, which is said to have been named for General Anthony Wayne of Revolutionary fame; however, during the Revolution, or at least in the early years of that war, the place was known as Teas's, or the Widow Teas's. Mr. Estep's father, James M. Estep, was born near Forestville in the County of Shenandoah, where the family has been well known for generations. His mother's maiden name was Magdaline Heatwole, of the numerous Rockingham family, and she was born near Dayton. His grandfather Heatwole and two uncles were preachers.

Mr. Estep grew up on a farm and attended school at Stemphleytown, a well-known village about two miles west of Dayton; later he was a student in Shenandoah Collegiate Institute, now Shenandoah College, in Dayton. In the early years of his life he engaged in farming, and has always made his home on a farm. After an experience of some years on the farm, he was employed for a time as a traveling salesman; then for a period of eight years he was engaged as a dealer in livestock. This was conducive to out-door life and comported well with his liking for farms and farming. For two years he engaged in merchandising and then, in 1927, he was elected as commissioner of revenue for Rockingham County on the Republican ticket. In politics Mr. Estep has always been a Republican, and three times since 1927, to wit, in 1931, 1935, and 1939, he has been re-elected to the same office on the same ticket. This is significant, for in Rockingham County the two main parties are nearly evenly matched, and at the same time there are a large number of independent voters. Accordingly, it is quite evident that Mr. Estep has been giving general satisfaction in his office.

Since 1914 Mr. Estep has been a member of the Church of the Brethren. He is also a member of the city-county chamber of commerce, the Kiwanis Club of Harrisonburg, the Ruritan Club of Bridgewater, and the board of directors of the West Rockingham Mutual Fire Insurance Company. His reading preference is for magazines of high standards, and his hobby is handling livestock.

On June 13, 1911, Mr. Estep married Miss Vernie E. Lambert, a native of the Dayton neighborhood. Of this marriage have been born two sons: Dwight L., who was born near Dayton on April 5, 1913; a graduate of Dayton High School and of Bridgewater College; Paul H., born near Dayton on November 21, 1919. He, like his brother, is a graduate of Dayton High School and of Bridgewater College; and is also a graduate of the Textile Institute of Spartanburg, South Carolina.

WELTY BAYARD FAHRNEY, D. D. S.
PROFESSIONAL MAN, POET, AND MUSICIAN

Born November 28, 1878, at Timberville; attended public schools in Timberville; D. D. S., University of Maryland, 1898; councilman and several times mayor of Timberville; member of Stonewall Brigade Band, of Staunton; author of popular verse; member of the Virginia State Dental Society, the American Dental Association, etc.; in active practice at Timberville since 1898.

Dr. Fahrney is a man of versatile talents and varied activities, as will appear from his numerous accomplishments. He is a son of Peter S. Fahrney and his wife, Virginia McInturff. The former was born at Greenmount, March 18, 1854; the latter at Timberville, June 15, 1856. Dr. Fahrney grew up at Timberville and attended the local schools, some of his teachers being Miss Minnie Fishback, D. I. Offman, Thomas Rice, and Elder Daniel Hays. Inclined towards a professional career, he entered the dental department of the University of Maryland, where he graduated in 1898. Since that time he has been actively engaged in the practice of his profession in his native town, where he has proved his interest in civic affairs by serving on the town council, and for several terms he has been mayor. For a number of years he was leader of the Timberville Band. He holds membership in the celebrated Stonewall Band of Staunton, and has been an occasional guest performer with the Hagerstown, Md., Municipal Band. As an amateur musician, he devotes himself to the clarinet and bassoon. He is a member of the Reformed Church of Timberville and has been a teacher in Sunday-school for more than thirty years.

In the field of his profession, Dr. Fahrney has been active and prominent outside the duties of his personal practice. He was one of the founders of the Shenandoah Valley Dental Society, which is now component No. 7 of the Virginia State Society. He is a member of the Northern Virginia Dental Study Club, the Shenandoah Valley Dental Society, the Virginia State Dental Society, and the American Dental Association.

As already indicated, Dr. Fahrney devotes much attention to music as a pastime. In reading, his preference is for poetry, and in recent years he has won a wide reputation as a writer of excellent verse, in which he may be placed in a class with Walt Mason and Edgar Guest. His verses deal generally with subjects of real human interest, and many of them have a clever turn of wit or a touch of contagious humor. Among his numbers that have had a wide acceptance are "His Majesty," "Just to Know," "The House Away from the Road," "My Heaven," "The Touch of a Woman's Hand," and "Homesick." A number of his compositions have been read over the major radio net works.

On December 14, 1904, Dr. Fahrney married Miss Bertie E. Driver, daughter of Cornelius Driver and his wife, Rebecca M. Hoover. Mrs. Fahrney was born at Timberville, January 23, 1879. Her ancestors, both the Drivers and the Hoovers, have been outstanding families of the Timberville community for generations. Her great-grandfather, Samuel Driver, came from Pennsylvania and located on the river near the site of Timberville prior to the Revolution. Her first Hoover ancestor in Virginia was Jacob, who settled on a grant of river land in the edge of "The Plains" in 1773. Most of the early Hoovers were members of the Church of the Brethren. Samuel Driver was a Mennonite.

WILLIAM STUART FALLIS

CIVIL ENGINEER AND HISTORICAL INVESTIGATOR

Born December 17, 1868, in Harrisonburg; early education in Harrisonburg public schools; Acting Engineer and Superintendent of Public Works in Harrisonburg, 1898-1907; director of public works in a number of counties of North Carolina, 1907-15; Acting Highway Commissioner and State Highway Engineer of North Carolina, 1915-21; in related state work in North Carolina, 1921-32; resident in Rockingham since retirement in 1932; member of various engineering societies; author of numerous articles from investigation of historical records.

Mr. Fallis is a native son of Harrisonburg and Rockingham County, who, after extended experience in important engineering positions at home and abroad, has retired to his country home on the historic old Hopkins homestead in the western part of the county, where he devotes himself to rural pursuits and at the same time gives the public the benefit of occasional articles in the local press on persons and topics of historical interest. He is a descendant of Dr. Samuel Gay, a surgeon of the Revolution, who was one of the first residents and business men of Harrisonburg. He is a son of William R. Fallis, whose wife before marriage was Sallie Ossian Gay. His paternal grandparents were Stewart W. and Emmaline Stratton Fallis. His mother's parents were William N. Gay and his wife, Jane Sprinkel. After going through the Harrisonburg public schools he devoted himself to the study and practice of constructive engineering and for nine years, 1898 to 1907, was acting engineer and superintendent of public work in the town of Harrisonburg, which, within that period, was inaugurating many of the progressive improvements that have contributed to its subsequent growth and attractiveness. For a period of 25 years, as already indicated, he held important official positions in North Carolina, first as county engineer (1907-15) of Wilson, Franklin, Iredell, Vance, and other counties, and then for six years (1915-21) he was Acting Highway Commissioner and State Highway Engineer. He organized the State Highway Commission of North Carolina and constructed the first concrete roads in that state and also developed (in the counties named) the first sand-clay-gravel roads that were built on a large scale in the South. From 1921 to 1932 he was associated with the State Highway Commission in general engineering practice. He was a member of the American Society of Civil Engineers and is a past president of the N. C. Section of that society. He is a charter member and past president of the N. C. Society of Engineers, in which society he is a life member as "Fellow"; and he was also affiliated with the Raleigh (N. C.) Engineers Club. At one time he was a member of Co. C, Va. State Guard. Since retiring to his country home in Rockingham he has indulged his penchant for mechanical work of all kinds, with excursions into the old county and city records. He finds diversion in the reading of history and fiction.

In 1906 Mr. Fallis married Miss Mary G. Chrisman, who was born in Rockingham in 1865, a daughter of William J. Chrisman. She died a few years ago. The Chrismans have been one of the prominent families of West Rockingham since colonial and Revolutionary times, with distinguished representatives in other states. The land on which Mr. Fallis resides was one of the tracts which were taken up in the days of early settlement by the Hopkins family, who have been numerous and prominent in the civil and military history of the county.

MARY VIRGINIA KELLEY FARVER

BUSINESS WOMAN, LINGUIST, AND COMMENTATOR

A native of Harrisonburg; graduate of Harrisonburg High School, 1909; student of law and languages; employee of the U. S. Forest Service in connection with the Shenandoah National Forest; a resident of Ohio since her marriage; manager of Community Sales Company, Portsmouth, Ohio; writer of verse and fiction, editorials, and articles on current topics and issues. (See biography of Mrs. Hanora Flynn Kelley, page 224.)

Mrs. Farver, born Mary Virginia Kelley, is a daughter of John E. Kelley, well-known business man of Harrisonburg, and his wife, Frances Vedora Leake. Her father was of Irish parentage, her mother of English descent. Her ancestors on both sides of the family have been outstanding Virginians. Both of her grandfathers, John Kelley and Walter Warfield Leake, fought on the side of the Confederacy in the Civil War, the latter being killed in action. Her paternal grandmother, whose biography appears herein, was Hanora Flynn; her mother's mother was Elizabeth Wade Stevens.

Having gone through the grade school, Mary Virginia Kelley entered in due course the Harrisonburg High School, from which she graduated with the class of 1909. She also graduated from the Harrisonburg Business College, and later from law school. Books and scholastic studies were a passion with her from earliest childhood. She was a hard-working student, and in the field of scholarship achieved a record of high honor, being known for her rare mathematical ability. She also studied and mastered many languages. After graduation, as indicated above, she turned her attention to the field of business, and was employed in the United States Forestry Service during the acquisition period of the Shenandoah National Forest. After her marriage she went to live in Ohio, and has there been identified with various business operations. However, writing continued to be her hobby, and in this field she has achieved notable distinction. She is a writer of both verse and prose, the latter including much fiction, but her editorials and articles on current events and issues of the day are her specialty. She interprets public opinion with uncanny accuracy, and is deeply interested in all civic, educational, political, and religious questions that affect the life of her community. She is always progressive and believes firmly in the great future that lies ahead for the development of our air lanes and its possibilities in the world of commerce, and is a champion of both radio and aviation. Few people really appreciate the delicacy of her feelings, the precision of her insight, the quickness of her sympathy, or realize how sacred sacred things are to her, and what an inviolate treasure to her is the thought of God, or how thoroughly she detests sham and pretense. She has a most kindly feeling for all the youth of the land and its problems. Definite evidence of her dependence on Deity can be found in all her writings, as published in many of the leading newspapers throughout the country.

Along with her constant study of public issues and her continuing literary activity, Mrs. Farver still maintains her place and rank in the world of business as the successful manager of the Community Sales Company of her city, Portsmouth, Ohio. Her hobby, as already indicated, is writing verse, stories, and articles. In reading her preferences are for philosophy, essays, and religious works. She is the mother of one son, Edwin Murray Farver, who is a radio engineer and technician.

ISAAC L. FLORY

BANKER AND BUSINESS MAN

Born September 23, 1872, near Timberville; attended local schools, Bridgewater College, and the Roanoke National Business College; bookkeeper in Roanoke for several years; five years a traveling salesman for the Stoddard Mfg. Co. of Dayton, Ohio; first cashier of the Bank of Elkton, 1904-1912; on the board of directors; since 1912 a manufacturer of soft drinks at Elkton, his specialty Elk Club Ginger Ale; his sons associated in the business in later years; councilman; member of the county school board, a trustee of Rockingham Memorial Hospital, and a steward of the Methodist Church.

Mr. Flory, the youngest of five children of Daniel and Susan Wampler Flory, and a brother of Dr. John S. Flory, president emeritus of Bridgewater College, grew up on the farm of his father near Timberville. After completing his course of study in the National Business College in Roanoke he was bookkeeper a short time for the well-known Bob Angell, then became identified with the Yost-Huff Company, dealers in seeds and farm implements. Later he went to Dayton, Ohio, where for five years he was a traveling salesman for the Stoddard Manufacturing Co., selling their goods over Virginia, West Virginia, and North Carolina. In 1904 he became the first cashier of the Bank of Elkton and continued in that position for eight years, resigning to devote his entire attention to the bottling business previously acquired, which had been established in Elkton by John S. Strole in 1908. He at once erected a commodious block building to give enlarged facilities for the business, and in 1915 constructed another building of two stories, in size 40 by 100 feet, shipping his Elk Club Ginger Ale and other products in car-load lots to a number of different states. In later years his sons, Isaac L., Jr., and D. Randolph, have been associated in the business and the plant has been doubled in capacity. His specialty, Elk Club Ginger Ale, is justly celebrated and is protected under its own registered trade mark.

On October 5, 1905, Mr. Flory married Miss Sarah Clower Saum, daughter of John R. and Julia Clower Saum of Harrisonburg. The Saums and the Clowers are both old and well-known families of Shenandoah County. Mr. and Mrs. Flory have two sons: Isaac L., Jr., born March 27, 1907, and D. Randolph, born February 18, 1910. They are in business with their father, as already indicated.

Mr. Flory since resigning as cashier of the Bank of Elkton has continued his connection with the institution as a member of the board of directors. He took a prominent part in having the town of Elkton incorporated and served as one of the first councilmen under the new charter. He is a steward of the Elkton Methodist Church and was on the building committee that erected the $40,000 house of worship for the congregation. He has also been a member of the county school board and for some time was on the board of trustees for Rockingham Memorial Hospital, representing Stonewall District of the county. In politics he is a Democrat and cast his first vote in a Presidential election for William J. Bryan in 1896. He has been identified with all patriotic movements in his community. During World War I he registered for active service when within 11 days of the age limit. In the present world conflict he is contributing his means and services in various effective ways as opportunities are offered. For years past he has been recognized as one of the outstanding citizens of Elkton and East Rockingham.

WALTER SAMUEL FLORY

TEACHER, RETIRED MAIL CLERK, TRAVELER

Born November 26, 1866, at Good's Mill, Va.; attended public schools, Bridgewater College, and Shenandoah Normal College; A. B., Peabody Normal College, Nashville, now George Peabody College for Teachers; teacher in Rockingham schools 16 years; railway mail clerk 20-odd years; mayor of Bridgewater; on Democratic county committee; traveler in the United States, Canada, Mexico, Europe, and Asia.

Mr. Flory grew up on the farm of his grandfather, Samuel Flory (born December 4, 1801), helping with the farm work in the summer and attending the five-month schools in winter. Samuel Flory and his wife, Elizabeth Young (born in 1805), were both born near Harrisonburg, as was his father, Noah Flory (born December 13, 1836). His mother was Sophia Esther Showalter, born at Dayton, January 16, 1841. Her parents were Adam Showalter, born at Edom, Rockingham County, April 27, 1814, and Sarah E. Beard, also born at Edom, August 10, 1817.

While a student in Shenandoah Normal College, conducted in Harrisonburg by the brothers, George W. and Elmer U. Hoenshel, Mr. Flory decided to become a teacher and accordingly went to Peabody Normal College, where he obtained a scholarship and graduated. He taught eight years in the public schools of Rockingham and then entered the railway mail service in which he continued for over twenty years. After a leisure period of two years he took up teaching again for eight years.

A member of the Church of the Brethren, Mr. Flory has long been interested in Sundayschool work. He superintended the Sundayschool at Mill Creek for several years, and after locating in Bridgewater he served there for many years in the same capacity. He is still a regular attendant at Sundayschool and is now assistant teacher of the men's Bible class. He has always been interested in politics and public affairs; has served on the town council of Bridgewater and was twice elected mayor after serving out the unexpired term of David C. Graham, who resigned as mayor.

On August 17, 1893, in the Mill Creek Church of the Brethren, Mr. Flory was united in marriage with Miss Ella May Reherd by Rev. Henry C. Early. Of the marriage there are three living children: Lillie Katherine, born September 15, 1895, married August 17, 1922, to Carman G. Blough, now of New York City; Annie Virginia, born January 4, 1905, now of Staunton; and Walter S., Jr., born October 5, 1907, now of College Station, Texas.

Mr. Flory says: "My favorite hobby is travel and sight-seeing. I have been in every state in the Union; also have been in Canada and Mexico; have traveled in England, France, Belgium, Holland, Germany, Switzerland, Italy, and Greece; also in Algeria, Egypt, Palestine, Syria, and Turkey. Have seen most of the large cities in Europe and the United States."

Mr. Flory's reading preferences are history and scientific studies. He is also fond of mathematics. With his extended and varied experience as a teacher, a traveling mail clerk for many years, a student of public affairs, a participant in municipal government and a traveler and observer in many parts of the world and a great home lover, he is well qualified to entertain his friends in instructive conversation on many subjects. His son, who is an untiring student, is following in his footsteps and is now doing research work at College Station, Texas.

ODA FRANKLIN FOLEY, D. V. M.
POULTRY AND ANIMAL SPECIALIST

Born March 12, 1890, at Mt. Sidney, Va.; attended public schools in Rockingham and Augusta and Bridgewater College Academy; graduated at McKillip Veterinary College, Chicago, 1915; practiced in Bridgewater 1915-34; office in Harrisonburg since 1934; opened animal hospital in 1940; Bridgewater councilman and mayor; president Va. Veterinary Assn. 1938-39; a director Harrisonburg Chamber of Commerce; member of the United Commercial Travelers; poultry inspector at Va. State Fair five years.

Dr. Foley is a son of David Addison and Louisa Catherine McKee Foley of Augusta County; his paternal grandparents were Samuel Henry and Sarah Sheets Foley; his mother's parents were Simon Peter and Susan Thomas McKee. He started to school at St. Michael's, south of Bridgewater, in Rockingham County, but most of his early schooling was obtained in Augusta at Middlebrook. From 1912 to 1915 he attended McKillip Veterinary College in Chicago and later was a special student at Bridgewater College. During the 19 years that he had his professional office in Bridgewater he served six years on the town council, was town treasurer two years, and four years mayor. He is a member of the Bridgewater Rotary Club and has served as secretary of the chamber of commerce. After early affiliations with the Lutherans and Presbyterians, he joined the Church of the Brethren in Chicago in 1915, and at Bridgewater has served on various committees and boards of the church. In 1938-39 he was president of the Va. Veterinary Medical Association, and has been chairman of the poultry committee of the same organization for several years. For the past three years he has been a director of the Harrisonburg-Rockingham Chamber of Commerce, and as such has been on various committees. He is also vice-president of the Bridgewater Creamery & Ice Corporation.

Having spent his early years on a farm, Dr. Foley has naturally found a congenial field of work in rural communities. He has been a member of farmers' organizations in Rockingham since their beginnings. He has been active in eradicating bovine tuberculosis and Bang's disease in this county and Augusta. After having an office in Harrisonburg for six years, he, in 1940, purchased a site on W. Water Street and opened an animal hospital which he operates in connection with his general practice. He pioneered in poultry practice in the state, and for five years was poultry inspector at the Va. State Fair.

On July 5, 1915, Dr. Foley married Miss Barbara Anna Huffman, born near Staunton, April 19, 1887, daughter of Saml. L. and Mary J. Craun Huffman. She attended Augusta County schools, Madison College, and graduated from Bridgewater College in 1914. For six years before her marriage she taught in the public schools of Virginia and Iowa. Dr. and Mrs. Foley have three children: Alma Winnifred, born Aug. 18, 1916; Ferne Amelia, born June 27, 1922; and Oda Franklin, Jr., born Oct. 22, 1925.

Dr. Foley does not have any special hobby, unless it is attending professional lecturers and meetings of medical associations. In reading he prefers books and articles on veterinary subjects, but is interested in whatever makes for health and progress. Versatile in enterprise, he and his family have operated a tourist home since 1928, and he is chief airplane observer at Bridgewater.

HENRY FORRER
FARMER AND CHURCH OFFICIAL

Born December 23, 1845, at Stuart's Draft, Va.; attended local schools; served the Confederacy at Elizabeth Furnace; came to Rockingham in 1876; an efficient and successful farmer; a tireless reader of history and illustrated travels; a public-spirited citizen; an elder in Cook's Creek Presbyterian Church 44 years; died near Harrisonburg, February 1, 1937.

Mr. Forrer's father, Jacob (1808-1896), was born near Luray; married Susan Whitmore (1817-1880) of Mt. Meridian, Augusta County. His grandparents were Samuel (1773-1799) and Catherine Forrer (1767-1850), who came to Luray in 1826, building a fine brick house still standing, the first floor arranged for meetings of worship. His great-grandfather Christian and his wife came from Switzerland in 1750 and settled near Harrisburg, Pa. Christian was a maker of beautiful tall clocks.

Henry Forrer, one of a family of six boys and five girls, at 16 years of age went to Elizabeth Furnace, in Buffalo Gap, iron-works owned and operated by his uncle, Daniel Forrer of Mossy Creek. Here some of the armor-plate was made for the *Merrimac;* also cannon balls for the Confederate army. He was there in charge of the commissary until the furnace was destroyed just before the close of the war. On May 21, 1874, he married Maria Eversole Showalter (1846-1927), born at Mt. Solon, and two years later moved to the estate of his wife's uncle, John Eversole, near New Erection. He looked upon farming as a real business enterprise and loved it. He had a fine sense of humor, was jovial, fair in dealing and sound in judgement; loved people, and lived by the Golden Rule. His church, his home, and his country were always his chief interests; a Democrat in politics, he sought the best leadership for his community and the country at large. Living to the age of 91, he witnessed horseback riding give place to carry-alls, buggies, and carriages, and finally automobiles and airplanes. The radio was a great pleasure to him, and he never ceased to wonder at the miracle of it.

Mr. Forrer and his wife had four children: Katherine Eversole—Mrs. D. Hinton Rolston of Mt. Clinton; Miss Sue, Harrisonburg; D. Harry, Harrisonburg; and J. J., now of Richmond, maintenance engineer of the Va. Highways Dept.

Mr. Forrer's ancestors and relatives, among them lawyers, doctors, merchants, iron-workers, and ministers of the Gospel, were pioneers in a number of the states. One of them, Samuel Forrer, was among the first engineers to invent and fashion his own surveying instruments. This outfit he used in surveying the canal across the state of Ohio in 1822. This project at that time, with the country sparsely settled, with malaria prevalent and Indians still numerous, was a great undertaking. Thanks to his robust health and staunch courage, he was able to carry on the job longer than any of his associates.

Mr. Forrer in his long lifetime saw great changes take place in the material development of this country. Before the Norfolk & Western Railway was built through Stuart's Draft and other towns of the eastern side of the Valley, droves of cattle and flocks of turkeys were driven to Richmond, 120 miles distant. His four-score years and ten spanned an era when many dreams came true.

JAMES AMBROSE FRY

FARMER AND BUSINESS MAN

Born April 12, 1852, at Centerville, Augusta County; grew up on neighborhood farms; located in Bridgewater in 1876; representative of the Bridgewater Woollen Mills; Sundayschool superintendent; trustee of Bridgewater College, 1889-1919; secretary-treasurer of the Bridgewater Plow Corporation, 1908-1921; died at Bridgewater, May 22, 1921.

On May 8, 1862, James A. Fry, a boy of ten, while helping to plant corn in a field near Centerville, heard cannonading in the mountains to the west. A few days later, his father, William Harvey Fry, mortally wounded in the battle of McDowell, was brought home, where he died on May 13. William Harvey Fry (1830-62) was a son of Simeon Fry who married Mary Smith, daughter of Peter, in Rockingham County, July 26, 1810. He married Martha Myers (1830-91), and James Ambrose was his second son. Martha Myers was a daughter of Jacob and his wife, Polly Eckhard, daughter of Philip, who was a Revolutionary soldier.

James A. Fry was practically a self-made man. He began life without means and with but little schooling, but lived to be well-to-do and one of the most useful men in his community. He owned and lived on a small farm at the northeast edge of Bridgewater, where the latch-string was always out, and where both friends and strangers were welcomed with unstinted hospitality. Much of his time was given to civic, religious, and educational service. He was a member of the Church of the Brethren and superintended the first Sundayschool held in the local church. For thirty years he was a trustee and director of Bridgewater College, and for different periods was also secretary-treasurer of the board of trustees and steward of the institution, to which he gave liberally of his time, money, and energy. From 1908, when the Bridgewater Plow Corporation was organized, he was a director and the secretary-treasurer until the time of his death. In resolutions passed by his colleagues of the company at his death was the declaration: "His wise counsels, conservative advice, and cheery presence will be greatly missed."

In February, 1875, Mr. Fry married Miss Anna Wine, daughter of Jacob and his wife, Elizabeth Garber. They had four children: Ida Elizabeth, born December 1, 1875; Mattie Virginia, born February 13, 1877; William Franklin, born March 20, 1880; and Effie Warren, born March 9, 1888. She died November 14, 1939. On June 8, 1898, Mattie married John W. Wayland and has two sons, Francis Fry, born May 27, 1907, and John Walter, born April 15, 1909; both in Charlottesville. On June 29, 1935, Francis married Olena Abigail Atkins of Lewes, Del., and has a daughter Jane Abigail, born June 10, 1941, and a son David Stanton, born Nov. 15, 1942; both in McPherson, Kans. Walter was married March 1, 1936, and has a daughter Elizabeth Rose, born June 23, 1937, at Takoma Park, Md. On Nov. 23, 1904, Wm. F. Fry married Dora May Ballentine, and had four children: Anna Mary, Geneva Virginia, Raymond Ballentine, and Lois Kathleen. Anna Mary married Richard Lambert (now deceased), has a son Charles, and lives in Bridgewater; Geneva married Harry Staley of Harrisonburg and lives there; Raymond married Lillian Flesher and lives at Fort Defiance; Kathleen married Janssen Tumer, has a son Thomas William, and lives at Spring Creek.

William F. Fry died at Bridgewater on August 18, 1941.

JOHN RANDOLPH GAMBILL, D. D. S.
DENTAL SURGEON AND BUSINESS MAN

Born March 11, 1883, at Dockery, N. C.; attended local schools, an academy in Virginia, and a normal school in W. Va.; D. D. S., University of Maryland, 1909; practiced first in West Va. and North Carolina; located in Harrisonburg in 1911, where he has since practiced; has been a member of local, state, and national dental associations; owner of valuable real estate in Harrisonburg; Rotarian; member of the Baptist Church.

Dr. Gambill, though a native of the Old North State, has been a resident of Harrisonburg for the past 31 years. His native town of Dockery is in Wilkes County, N. C., on the edge of the "Land of the Sky." His father was J. J.Gambill, son of John; his mother's maiden name was Rosa E. Cornett and his paternal grandmother before marriage was Mahilda Smoot. After attending the public school at Dockery, he spent some time as a student in an academy at Comer's Rock, in Virginia, and then took a course in a state normal school at Athens, W. Va. During the session of 1903-04 he taught school at Saddle Creek, Va., and in 1904-05 at his native town of Dockery in North Carolina. Having decided to study dentistry, he entered the dental department of the University of Maryland in Baltimore, where he was graduated with the D. D. S. degree in June, 1909. He began practice in the coal-mining region of West Virginia, and was engaged professionally for some time in North Carolina, where he was licensed to practice by the state examining board in 1909. The same year he was given license to practice by the state board in Virginia. In 1911 he located in Harrisonburg where he has resided ever since and where he has been successfully engaged in the practice of his profession.

In connection with his professional duties Dr. Gambill has given considerable attention to the purchase of real estate and the erection of buildings. His residence is on Mason Street, a short distance south of Paul Street. This is a comparatively new section of the city, in the neighborhood of Madison College and Rockingham Memorial Hospital, and is a popular residential district. Dr. Gambill has made substantial contributions to its development. He has been a member of the Valley Dental Association, the Virginia Dental Association, and the National Dental Association. He is a member of the Baptist Church and the Rotary Club, and is a volunteer in several defense organizations.

Dr. Gambill's wife was Miss Alice Ethel Filler, born June 30, 1890, near Cross Keys, daughter of John Robert Filler, teacher, surveyor, business man, and farmer, and his wife, Florence Virginia Earman, daughter of John William and Ellen Hendron Van Lear Earman. Her grandfather, Rev. Samuel Filler (1811-1861), was a teacher and Lutheran minister; his wife was Rebekah Hook, sister of Col. Wm. Walker Hook, family historian.

Dr. and Mrs. Gambill are the parents of two daughters and six sons: Aurelia Filler, born July 11, 1914; Emerson Cornett, March 16, 1916; John Randolph, Jr., April 21, 1918; Joseph Foch, May 25, 1920; Victor Persons, July 4, 1922; Kenton Filler, November 17, 1924; Florence Virginia, October 22, 1926; and Hamilton Scherer, October 29, 1929. Emerson is a student in dentistry; Randolph is a ministerial student, planning to be a medical missionary; and several of the other boys are in the U. S. armed service.

F. BARTH GARBER

BUSINESS MAN AND PROMINENT MASON

Born April 21, 1886, near Fort Defiance, Augusta County, Va.; taken to Stuart's Draft at age of three years; moved to Waynesboro in 1903; sold shoes for Joseph Ney & Sons in 1904; in 1911 became buyer and manager for the T. P. Yager shoe store; in 1932 began business in Harrisonburg for himself; in January, 1942, moved to his present location, corner of South Main and Newman Avenue; member of the Methodist Church and active in Masonry.

Mr. Garber is one of the best known and most popular of Harrisonburg's young business men. He and his wife come of families that have been prominent in the Shenandoah Valley since the Revolution. He is a son of Charles David Garber and his wife, Mary Virginia Pirkey. The latter is a daughter of Elias Pirkey of Grottoes (formerly called Shendun) and his wife, Susan Baker. Charles D. Garber's father was Isaac; his mother, Rebecca Jane Armentrout. Barth was born at the old homestead of his great-grandfather, near Fort Defiance. When he was about three years old his parents moved to Stuart's Draft, where his father went into business as a general merchant, and as Barth grew up he got his start in business as a salesman over the counters in his father's store. When he was about 17 his father moved to Waynesboro and went into the milling business. The five sons each selected a line of work for himself. Barth chose to be a shoe merchant and says that he has never regretted his choice. About 1904 he became a shoe salesman in the store of Joseph Ney & Sons in Harrisonburg, when they opened a shoe department. In 1907 he left Harrisonburg but returned in 1911 and has been here ever since. From 1911 for a number of years he was a buyer and manager for the shoe store of T. P. Yager. In 1932 he went into business for himself, with an associate. After the death of the latter, Mr. Garber bought out his partner's interest and has since conducted the business under the name of F. Barth Garber, Inc. In January, 1942, he moved his store into quarters newly refitted at the corner of South Main Street and Newman Avenue, where he has a modern and up-to-the-minute shoe store that will compare favorably with the best found in the largest cities.

On June 25, 1919, in the Methodist Church at Parnassus, Augusta County, Mr. Garber married Miss Ellen Elizabeth Mohler, daughter of the late John Newton Mohler and his wife, Alice Armstrong, of Mt. Solon. Prior to her marrriage Mrs. Garber had been a student at Harrisonburg in what is now Madison College. Mr. and Mrs. Garber are members of the Methodist Church in Harrisonburg. Mr. Garber is a member of Rockingham Union Lodge No. 27, A. F. &. A. M., Rockingham Royal Arch Chapter No. 6, the Knights Templars, and the Mystic Shrine. His favorite hobbies are reading and fishing, and he is fond of sports. His four brothers and four sisters are widely distributed: Harry is a clothing merchant in Bluefield; John H. is a Baptist pastor in Hampton; Albert is a druggist in the same city; Charles is a resident of Waynesboro. One of his sisters lives in Portsmouth, Va., another in Florence, Ky., and the other two are residents of Waynesboro. The numerous Garbers in Augusta County are probably all descendants of Abraham Garber who settled on Middle River more than 100 years ago. Abraham was one of the sons of John Garber who purchased land and located at Flat Rock in Shenandoah County in 1775 or 1776.

HARRY J. GARBER

FARMER AND BUSINESS MAN

Born July 14, 1889, in Shenandoah County; at age 9 moved with parents to farm near Timberville; attended Garber's Academy and Valentine School of Telegraphy, Janesville, Wis.; began farming in 1913; from 1926 to 1928 traveling salesman; since 1926 secretary-treasurer Rockingham County Natl. Farm Loan Assn., which he helped to organize in 1917; operator of large peach and apple orchards and stock farms.

John Abram Harry Garber, known familiarly and in business as Harry J. Garber, is a son of Jacob A. and Mary Frances Garber, who were married April 3, 1881, by Elder Samuel Myers. Jacob was born October 14, 1852, son of John and Lydia Getz Garber; died April 15, 1940; Mary Frances was born July 21, 1856, daughter of Abram and Catherine Good Knupp; died January 2, 1940. From the age of nine years Harry J. grew up on his father's farm three miles west of Timberville. After attending a two-room school known as Garber's Academy, working between sessions on the farm, he took a course in telegraphy as already indicated, then returned and became manager of his father's farm, on which he still lives. From 1926 to 1928 he was a traveling salesman for Bowers, Hoover & Co. of Timberville. In 1926 he took over the job of secretary-treasurer of the Rockingham County Natl. Farm Loan Assn., which he had helped organize in 1917, and of which he is a charter member. He still holds this position, and in addition operates peach and apple orchards of 350 acres and stock farms of 700 acres.

On November 16, 1911, in Washington, D. C., Mr. Garber married Miss Fannie Talmar Arehart, who was born near Timberville, August 6, 1892. Mr. and Mrs. Garber have four children, all born near Timberville: Wilda Virginia, December 26, 1912; John Arthur, February 8, 1914; Ernest Arehart, January 25, 1920; and Billy Franklin, October 19, 1922.

At the close of World War I Mr. Garber's two bachelor brothers, who went through the war, came back home, and he, with them, organized a business in the name of H. J. Garber & Bros., which has been carried on in that name ever since. As his sons, John Arthur, Ernest Arehart, and Billy Franklin, finished high school they were taken into the business as partners. Ernest Arehart and Billy Franklin have now been called into the service of their country but still retain their interest in the business.

Mr. Garber is a member of the Elks Club of Harrisonburg, Knights of Pythias of New Market, D. O. K. K. of Roanoke, and Modern Woodmen, Miller's Store, Va. At the age of 20 he became a deacon in the Church of the Brethren. All his life he has been an independent voter in politics, but has always taken an active share in community and county civic work. In the field of hobbies and recreation he enjoys horseback riding and salt-water fishing. These afford him relaxation from the routine duties of a strenuous business life. His offices in Harrisonburg are located at 71 East Market Street. He is typical of the thrifty and enterprising families of Shenandoah and Rockingham that have tilled the farms and carried on successfully the business, social, and religious life of this part of Virginia from colonial and Revolutionary times.

JACOB AARON GARBER

TEACHER, LEGISLATOR, AND BUSINESS MAN

Born January 25, 1879, near Harrisonburg; grew up near Timberville; graduate of Bridgewater College, 1899; of Emerson College, Boston, 1907; teacher in Bridgewater College and Wells Memorial Institute, Boston; secretary of Emerson College; cashier of Timberville Bank; member of Va. House of Delegates; treasurer of Rockingham County; member of the 71st Congress; U. S. internal revenue official; director of the Rockingham Turkey Festival.

Jake Garber, as he is familiarly and widely known, was born in an old house that used to stand five miles southwest of Harrisonburg on the site now occupied by the radio tower of WSVA. He grew up on the river below Timberville on the farm owned by his father, Jacob B. Garber. His mother's maiden name was Rebecca Early. After schooling at Timberville under Professor Daniel Hays and other teachers, he attended Bridgewater College, where he was also a teacher. For one session he was principal of Prince William Academy at Brentsville, Va. A summer session was spent in the Northern Indiana Normal School and Business College, and later he was a student and teacher for several years in the city of Boston, where elocution, oratory, and dramatics were his specialties. In 1905 he was business manager for the history of Bridgewater College, published in that year; and 25 years later he was on the editorial staff that compiled a second volume on the same institution. From 1908 to 1924 he was cashier of the Farmers & Merchants Bank of Timberville, and for the next five years he was treasurer of Rockingham County. This position he resigned to serve a term in Congress. From 1920 to 1922 he had been a member of the Virginia House of Delegates. From 1931 to 1935 he had headquarters in Richmond as an official in the U. S. internal revenue service. Since that time he has lived in Harrisonburg and has been engaged in operating commercial orchards and in handling grain and other farm products. He was the successful director of the first Rockingham Turkey Festival in 1939, and in 1941 he was again put in charge.

For many years Mr. Garber has been active in church and Sundayschool work as a teacher and organizer. For some time he was president of the Rockingham County Sundayschool Association. He is in much demand as a public speaker and has frequently given broadcasts over the radio. For some time he was a member of the city-county Kiwanis Club and for one term was its president. The Alumni Association of Bridgewater College has had no more enthusiastic member than Mr. Garber, and he has served that organization in various official capacities. In politics he is a Republican, but he has a wide acquaintance and many friends in both great parties. His public spirit and active interest in all civic, educational, and philanthropic movements are well known, and it is doubtful whether any man in the city or county has given more of his time and energy, freely, to such enterprises. Though skilled and widely experienced in business, he maintains a keen interest in art and literature, with a preference in his reading for poetry and drama. He is much in demand as a director of amateur theatricals.

On November 24, 1910, Mr. Garber married Miss Lucy Winfield Hite of Lunenburg County, Va. She is a daughter of Eppa and Mary Wilkinson Hite, and is a sister of B. Wilkinson Hite of Timberville.

MINOR W. GARBER
MILLER AND BUSINESS MANAGER

Born March 24, 1891, at Mt. Sidney, Augusta County; grew up on a farm; graduate of Bridgewater College; miller at Knightly and Fort Defiance; promoter of rural electrification; rural engineer at Staunton and Waynesboro; came to Harrisonburg in 1935; division manager, Valley Division, Virginia Public Service Company, since 1936; past president Harrisonburg Rotary Club.

Mr. Garber is a son of Daniel S. Garber, who was born at Mt. Sidney, a son of Elder Levi Garber. His mother, the wife of Daniel S. Garber, was Lizzie M. Click, born at Weyers Cave, the daughter of Samuel Click. The Garbers of Augusta and Rockingham are probably all descended from Elder John Garber and his sons, who began to purchase land and locate at Flat Rock, Shenandoah County, about 1775. John's son Daniel later settled two miles west of Harrisonburg and founded Garber's Church. Abraham established himself on Middle River, in Augusta County, and built up Middle River Church. Samuel organized churches in Tennessee. There were two John Clicks, probably father and son, heads of families in Shenandoah County as early as 1783. They are supposed to have been the progenitors of the Clicks and Glicks now living in the counties southwest of Shenandoah, that is, in Rockingham, Augusta, and adjacent regions.

Mr. Garber grew up and worked on his father's farm, attending local schools. In 1910, after completing his course in Bridgewater College, he entered into the flour-milling business in the Cline Mills at Knightly, his father having a half interest in these mills. Further of his work, he says:

"In 1912 I purchased a one-third interest in this mill. In 1913 our firm purchased another mill, known as the Ft. Defiance Mill. In 1914 I persuaded our firm to enter into the electric light and power business by purchasing the necessary machinery and using the available water power. The necessary franchises were secured to extend lines in the greater portion of Middle River District in Augusta County. This was the beginning of rural electrification in this State. The electrical business developed to the point that by 1927 the milling end was discontinued. In 1929 we sold this business to the Virginia Public Service Company. I was transferred to Staunton as rural engineer, following this sale, and had charge of the rural development in Staunton and Waynesboro in addition to supervising all construction in these areas. In 1935 I was transferred to Harrisonburg in a similar capacity and in June, 1936, was made Division Manager of the Valley Division of the Company, which is my present position."

Mr. Garber is a member and past president of the Harrisonburg Rotary Club, and a director of the chamber of commerce. He, like many of his family have been, is a member of the Church of the Brethren. He gives golf, bowling, and fishing as his favorite recreations.

In 1912 Mr. Garber married Miss Rena B. Western of New Hope. They have one daughter, Catherine Louise, who is a seamstress and lives at home. She is a graduate of Madison College, class of 1934.

PAUL NEFF GARBER
EDUCATOR AND AUTHOR

Born July 27, 1899, near New Market; graduate of Timberville High School, 1915; A. B., Bridgewater College, 1919; student in Crozer Theological Seminary; A. M., University of Pennsylvania, 1921; Ph. D., 1923; assistant instructor in history, Univ. of Pa., 1921-23; instructor in history, Brown University, 1923; assistant professor of history, Trinity College (now Duke University), 1924-26; professor of church history, Divinity School of Duke University, 1926-41; dean of the same since 1941; active in affairs of the Methodist Church; author of "The Gadsden Treaty" (1923), "The Romance of American Methodism" (1931), "The Methodists Are One People" (1939); etc.

Dr. Garber's birthplace, a mile west of New Market, on the south bank of the Shenandoah River, and just southwest of the Fairfax Line, is historic. For many years it was the home of Anderson Moffett, a celebrated Baptist minister, who died here in 1835, aged 90. The fertile bottom lands surrounding have been known as "The Plains" since early white settlement and are thus designated on the Fry-Jefferson map of 1751. When Paul was six years old his parents, Samuel and Ida Alice (Neff) Garber, moved to Timberville where they remained until 1914, when they located in Bridgewater. Samuel Garber, son of Abram, was a farmer and surveyor; his wife was a daughter of Abram and Elizabeth (Cline) Neff. Abram was an honored minister in the Church of the Brethren, a great-grandson of Dr. John Henry Neff, who took up land at Rude's Hill in 1750. Abram Garber was a descendant of Rev. John Garber, first of the name in the Shenandoah Valley, who located near Flat Rock in 1775 or 1776.

As student, teacher, author, and educational leader, Dr. Garber's career has been notable. At Bridgewater College he was salutatorian of his class; while a graduate student in the University of Pennsylvania he was made assistant instructor in history and was awarded the Harrison Fellowship in History; in 1926, when the Divinity School was organized in Duke University, he become professor of Church History, continuing as such until 1941 when he was elected Dean of the Divinity School. From 1928 until 1941 he was also Registrar of the same school. He is a clergyman in the Methodist Church; is affiliated with Delta Sigma Phi, Tau Kappa Alpha, and Theta Phi; holds membership in the Wesley Historical Society; is president of the Association of Methodist Historical Societies; on the Executive Committee of the American Assn. of Theological Schools; and is a trustee of Crozer Theological Seminary. As an influential leader and a member of important Methodist conferences and boards, he has been vitally interested in the union of the several Methodist churches and is justly credited with a large contribution in the unification of American Methodism. Among his books, in addition to those already mentioned, are: "That Fighting Spirit of Methodism" (1928), "John Carlisle Kilgo—President of Trinity College, 1894-1910" (1937), and "The Methodist Meeting House" (1941). His biography appears in "Who's Who in America" and other standard publications.

On August 21, 1927, Dr. Garber married Miss Orina Winifred Kidd of Fall River, Mass. She is a daughter of Dr. and Mrs. F. O. Kidd and a graduate of Brown University. She is specially interested in religious and educational affairs. Dr. Garber, in the midst of his busy life, finds diversion in golf and other outdoor activities. It can hardly be expected or desired that the habits of his early years in the fields and along the streams of Rockingham should be entirely cast off.

J. SILOR GARRISON, D. D.
PASTOR, EDUCATOR, AND HISTORIAN

Born near Middlebrook, Augusta Co.; educated by tutors and in local schools, Mercersburg College, Catawba College, Franklin & Marshall Seminary, and Univ. of Va.; A. B., A. M., D. D.; organized St. Stephen's Reformed Church, Harrisonburg; pastor, 1894-97 and 1908 to the present; first president Massanutten Academy, 1899-1903; professor in Catawba College, 1904-08; head of mathematics dept. Harrisonburg High School, 1908-38; stated clerk Virginia Classis since 1918; author of historical works relating to the Reformed Church.

Dr. Garrison's father, Jacob Silor Garrison, married Rebekah Fix; enlisted in his early 20s and served in the Stonewall Brigade in all actions in which that force was engaged; paroled at Appomattox. Both grandfathers were teachers, one of them, Philip Fix, was author of two volumes on arithmetic.

When licensed to preach in 1894, Dr. Garrison was commissioned to organize the Reformed Church in Harrisonburg. The organization (St. Stephen's) was effected with seven members in a small frame store room still remaining in the northern part of the city. In 1896-97 a small brick church was erected on High Street. In 1897 he accepted the Edinburg charge and in 1898 was appointed to establish a classical academy, which became Massanutten Academy at Woodstock, of which Dr. Garrison was first president, 1899-1903. Resigning because of ill health, he spent the summer recuperating in Harrisonburg. Early in 1904 he was called to head the department of English in Catawba College, N. C. He returned to Harrisonburg in 1908 as pastor again of St. Stephen's and as head of the mathematics department in the high school, in which he taught for 30 years. His pastorate of St. Stephen's is the longest in the history of Harrisonburg. In 1931, under his leadership, the present splendid native gray limestone church building at the corner of South Main and Campbell Street was erected. The design is in the style of the 14th century English parish church, and it is fully equipped for modern church purposes.

Dr. Garrison is an effective and instructive preacher. His diction is chaste and elegant, and his style is direct, logical, and incisive. He is a Knights Templar Mason and a member of the Zeta Chapter of the Chi Phi Fraternity at Franklin and Marshall College. He has beeen a life-long Democrat. His hobby is historical research and he has done yeoman work in the history of his denomination. Several of his works have been published and he has in preparation a history of the Reformed Church in Virginia. Several years ago he was a leader in the celebration at Germanna, where a colony of German Reformed located in 1714 under the patronage of Governor Spotswood. He has come a long way from the log school house on his father's farm at Middlebrook, but no doubt the inspiration he has passed on to his thousands of pupils dates its beginning from early as well as later influences. Catawba College honored him in 1934 with the D. D. degree.

In 1900 Dr. Garrison married Miss Mary Moore Fletcher, daughter of Mr. A. K. and Mrs. Virginia Paul Fletcher of Harrisonburg. Of this marriage were born five children: Mary Fletcher, who died in childhood; Virginia Rebekah, now Mrs. Francis Drake of Lexington; Mary Irene, Mrs. Lambert Molyneaux of A. and M. College, College Station, Texas; Mildred Fletcher, Mrs. Sidney Acker of Harrisonburg; and Jay Silor, Jr., pvt. Medical Dept., Station Hospital, Camp Gordon, Ga.

JOSEPH PAUL GLICK
PRESIDENT OF BLACKSTONE COLLEGE

Born December 23, 1896, near Bridgewater; attended Centerville schools and academy at Bridgewater College; B. A., Bridgewater College, 1921; student in University of Illinois, 1922; M. A., University of Virginia, 1926; graduate student in Harvard, 1928-30; high-school principal and college teacher; president of Blackstone College since 1936.

President Glick was born and reared on a farm five miles from Bridgewater, near the village of Centerville; his father, Joseph M. Glick, was born March 13, 1847; his mother, whose maiden name was Dianna Margaret Miller, was born April 13, 1853; both parents born near Bridgewater. His father's parents were Joel Glick (1821-1880) and Elizabeth "Betsy" Miller (1819-1905). On his mother's side his grandparents were John M. Miller (1821-1888) and Eva Catherine Coffman (1825-1862). He attended school at Centerville through the elementary grades and three years of high school, completing his high-school course in the academy that was then operating in connection with Bridgewater College. His college and university work has already been indicated.

As a teacher and school administrator President Glick has had a wide experience. During the session of 1920-21 he taught in Bridgewater Academy. The following session he was principal of New Hope High School in Augusta County; during 1922-23, of the high school of Lillington, N. C.; from 1923 to 1928, of the Dinwiddie High School, Dinwiddie, Va. At Harvard University, 1928-30, he was Scholar and Assistant in the Graduate School of Education, and worked with the Harvard Growth Study, completing all requirments for the Ed. D. degree except the dissertation. For two sessions, 1930-32, he was associate professor of education in the University of Richmond. After a year as teacher in the Clifton Forge High School, he was principal of the Amherst, Va., High School from 1933 to 1936, when he was elected to the presidency of Blackstone College, Blackstone, Va.

On June 14, 1923, President Glick married Miss Maytie Elizabeth Burns, who was born at Burnsville, Bath County, Va., February 5, 1895. They have one son, Joseph Paul Glick II, born in Richmond, December 17, 1931.

President Glick is a member of the Methodist Church, is District Layleader, and a member of the Virginia Council of Religious Education, the Virginia Academy of Science, and the Virginia Education Association. He holds membership also in Phi Delta Kappa (national honorary educational fraternity), the Masonic Order, and the Rotary Club. He is listed in "Who's Who in America" and "Who's Who in American Education." In politics he is an independent. He is author of a geography of Dinwiddie County, Va., which was used in the schools of the county for a number of years. His studies in "The Functional Differences between Negro and White Intelligence," for his Harvard dissertation, represent extended research, but the work has not yet been published. His special interests are antiquities, history, historical shrines, and genealogical records; his hobby, collecting and refinishing antique furniture. He engages in farming as an avocation, and in this he is following the bent of his ancestors and the best traditions of the Old Dominion. The Glicks have been known for generations in the counties of Shenandoah, Rockingham, and Augusta, Va., and in other parts of the world for their devotion to the soil and their skill in mechanical arts.

MRS. WILLIAM H. GOECKERMAN

REGISTERED NURSE AND HOSPITAL SUPERVISOR

Born in Brooklyn, Iowa; brought to Virginia when a small child; attended Pleasant Hill and Harrisonburg schools and the State Normal and Industrial School for Women, now Madison College; graduated in nursing at Georgetown University Hospital, Washington, D. C., in 1915; supervisor of surgery in City Hospital, Washington, Delaware General Hospital, Wilmington, and Kahler Hospital, Mayo Clinic, Rochester, Minn.; now living in Los Angeles.

Mrs. Goeckerman, born Magdalena Sara Moore, and known to her old friends and schoolmates in and around Harrisonburg as Lena, is a daughter of the late James Martin Moore and his wife, Frances Elizabeth Spitzer. Her parents and grandparents were all Virginians, and Lena, although a Hawkeye by birth, grew up in Rockingham among her kinsfolk. After attending the public schools, as already indicated, she entered the new State Normal and Industrial School for Women at Harrisonburg, where she was a student for one full session and part of another. Her inclinations led her toward hospital service, and in July, 1912, she entered Georgetown University Hospital, Washington, D. C., for nurses' training, and in 1915 she was graduated from that institution. For some time following her graduation she was supervisor of surgery at the Washington City Hospital, now Gallinger Memorial Hospital; for one year she held a like position in the Delaware General Hospital in Wilmington, Delaware; then she entered upon her career at Rochester, Minnesota, where she was supervisor of surgery for thirteen years in Kahler Hospital, in the celebrated Mayo Clinic. On October 18, 1933, she married Dr. William H. Goeckerman of the Mayo Foundation staff. Since her marriage she and her husband have been residents of the city of Los Angeles, California.

Dr. Goeckerman was associate professor of dermatology in the Mayo Foundation until 1932, when he entered upon the private practice of dermatology in Los Angeles. He is the author of many articles relating to his specialty; is a member of the American Dermatological Association; is clinical professor of dermatology at the University of California; and is chief of the dermatological staff of the California Hospital in Los Angeles. He is a member of Sigma Xi.

Mrs. Goeckerman is chairman of the social activities committee in the Woman's Auxiliary to the Los Angeles County Medical Association, a vice-president and associate chairman of the courtesy committee of Town and Gown of the University of Southern California, and a member of University Affiliated of the University of California at Los Angeles. Since the development of the present emergency in connection with the war, she has volunteered as a nurse and is working two days each week for the duration at one of the hospitals of Los Angeles, where her wide experience and devotion to patriotic duty are most valuable.

Mrs. Goeckerman says that her hobbies are needlepoint and interior decorating. She is also an enthusiastic collector of china—teacups and figurines, also bisque statuettes. Her preferences in reading are for biographical and historical novels. Her most recent visit to Harrisonburg was in January, 1929, when she spent a vacation here, in Charlottesville, Baltimore, and Washington City.

CARTER VICTOR GOOD

EDUCATOR AND AUTHOR

Born September 16, 1897, near Dayton; attended Dayton schools and Shenandoah College; A. B., Bridgewater College, 1918; A. M., University of Virginia, 1923; Ph. D., University of Chicago, 1925; principal and superintendent of schools in Virginia and West Virginia; professor of education, Miami University, 1925-30; in the University of Cincinnati since 1930; member of various educational societies; Phi Delta Kappa, Kappa Delta Pi, Kappa Phi Kappa; editor of Dictionary of Education and other works; author of "How to Do Research in Education," "Teaching in College and University," etc.

Dr. Good is a son of Professor Jacob S. H. Good and wife, Anna Victoria Early, of Dayton. His paternal grandparents were Daniel Henry and Lydia Shank Good; his mother's parents were Noah and Sarah Kidd Early. His brother Warren is a professor in the University of Michigan; his sister Virginia is a teacher in Cincinnati. After going through the elementary and high school in Dayton he attended Shenandoah College one year, 1914-15, then spent the next three years in Bridgewater College, graduating in 1918. He was assistant principal of Shenandoah (Va.) High School in 1919-20; the next year principal of New Hope elementary and high schools; in 1921-22 he held a similar position at Marshall, in Fauquier County, and in 1922-23 was superintendent of the Burnsville, W. Va., schools. During the intervening summers he completed his work at the University of Virginia for the A. M. degree. The next two years he spent in the University of Chicago, where he was awarded the Ph.D. degree in 1925. Since then he has been professor of education in Miami University at Oxford, Ohio, and in the University of Cincinnati, as already indicated. At intervals, in summers, he has been professor of education in the University of Chicago, the University of Michigan, and the University of Wisconsin. He holds membership in the American Psychological Association, the National Society of College Teachers of Education, the National Society for the Study of Education, the National Education Association, and the National Council of Education; is a Fellow of the American Association for the Advancement of Science, and in 1940-41 was president of the American Educational Research Association.

As editor and author Dr. Good has done notable work. He has made frequent contributions to educational and professional journals; is editor-in-chief of the Dictionary of Education and is on the editorial staff of the *Journal of Educational Research* and the *Journal of Experimental Education*. He is the author of the following books: "Supplementary Reading Assignment" (1927), "How to Do Research in Education" (1928), and "Teaching in College and University" (1929); and is co-author, with Barr and Scates, of "The Methodology of Educational Research" (1936). In 1918-19 Dr. Good was an ensign in the U. S. Navy. He is a member of the Presbyterian Church; in politics, non-partisan. His hobby is gardening; in reading he naturally prefers works in psychology, sociology, and education.

On September 6, 1920, Dr. Good married Miss Irene Cooper, daughter of Alexander S. and Eugenia Hall Cooper of Nashville, Tenn., and has a daughter, Gene Ann Good, born January 23, 1924, at Chicago, Ill. Dr. and Mrs. Good have their residence at 266 Hillcrest Drive, Wyoming, Ohio. Additional particulars of Dr. Good's life and work may be found in the current volumes of "Who's Who in America" and other biographical publications.

JACOB HENRY HALL

TEACHER, COMPOSER, AUTHOR, AND PUBLISHER

Born January 2, 1855, near Harrisonburg; attended singing schools taught by Timothy Funk and others; student in the Normal Music School at New Market, 1877; studied under B. C. Unseld and P. J. Merges; author of "Hall's Songs of Home" and co-author of "The Star of Bethlehem"; attended Dana's Musical Institute, 1890; under eminent teachers in Philadelphia, 1894; taught in many states and published many music books; author of "Biography of Gospel Song and Hymn Writers," 1914; died in Harrisonburg, December 22, 1941.

Professor Hall as a boy delighted in music and learned to play on various instruments. Inspired by Timothy Funk and H. T. Wartman, he decided to make music his special art. Solicited by the Ruebush-Kieffer Company, he joined with them in bringing out numerous books. Among the early works in which he collaborated, the "Star of Bethlehem" was a great success. In 1891 he invented "Hall's Music Chart," of which Aldine S. Kieffer said, "It is the most comprehensive and complete chart in the world." In the same year he brought out "Practical Voice Culture" and studied under the Roots at Silver Lake, New York State, and H. R. Palmer at Chautauqua, same state. He assisted Mr. Kieffer in editing the *Musical Million*, which had a wide circulation. A complete list of his musical works would be very long, but among them the "Practical Music Reader," "Crowning Day," issued in a series of six numbers, and "Hall's Quartettes for Men" deserve special mention. With him, in some of his publications, were associated such eminent composers as C. C. Case, William J. Kirkpatrick, and the Ruebushes of Dayton.

As a teacher of singing classes and as a conductor of choruses and musical institutes, Professor Hall had a wide and successful experience of 60 years. He taught in 20 different states, returning to the same places year after year, to meet the enthusiastic groups of singers and musicians that eagerly welcomed him. At Raleigh, Miss., in 1897, the National Normal School of Music, at the instance of Judge E. G. McGarr, conferred upon him the degree of Doctor of Music, Judge McGarr himself officiating. In later years Dr. Hall collected many interesting facts concerning men and women who were distinguished as hymn writers, singers and composers, and in 1914 a handsomely illustrated volume of 419 pages was brought out for him by F. H. Revell Co. of New York under the title, "Biography of Gospel Song and Hymn Writers." This is a valuable work for all students of music and an interesting volume for the general reader. Later important works are "The Standard Music Reader" (1926) and "The Standard Manual for Music Teachers" (1928), both published by the Gospel Trumpet Co., Anderson, Ind. At the "Old Folks' Singings," held for years past in Rockingham and adjacent counties, Dr. Hall was a familiar figure.

On January 23, 1883, Dr. Hall married Miss Elizabeth Frances Bowman, daughter of Rev. Joseph and Sarah Flory Bowman. Their son, Charles Ernest Hall, born September 29, 1888, is an auditor in the accounting department of the engineering firm, the Foster Wheeler Corporation, New York City. Dr. Hall's father was George Gordon Hall; his mother was Elizabeth, daughter of John and Susan Miller Thomas. George G. Hall was born in Albemarle County, Va., February 26, 1827, son of Thomas Hall, whose father was from England; his mother was from Scotland. John Thomas came to Virginia from Pennsylvania; his ancestors were from Wales.

CLAUDE W. HANLEY

OIL OPERATOR, LAND DEVELOPER, AND BUSINESS MAN

Born February 16, 1882, at Shamokin, Pa.; attended Shamokin High School and completed correspondence courses; came to Harrisonburg in 1905; engaged here with D. F. Detwiler in wholesale produce business; in railroad service; development agent for Gen. J. E. Roller in Texas and other states; since 1917 with the Gulf Oil Corporation; active in the scientific development of natural resources and the production of crude oil; member of Texas Archaelogical and Paleontological Society, West Texas Historical Society, etc.

Mr. Hanley, by long residence here, by subsequent visits, by entertaining old friends in his home in Fort Worth, and otherwise, has kept in touch with Harrisonburg for more than 37 years. His father, Fiske Hanley, born June 23, 1858, and his grandfather, Albert N. Hanley, born January 29, 1816, were for many years connected with the Philadelphia & Reading R. R. at Shamokin, pioneers in various capacities in opening the coal and iron regions of Pennsylvania. His mother, born October 27, 1863, was Mahala Jane Helt of Reed Station, Pa., and his grandmother, Amelia Vanderslice, was born February 3, 1826, at Pottsville, in the same state. Mr. Hanley supplemented his high-school work by courses with the International Correspondence Schools of Scranton, by study at night, and by the use of Gen. J. E. Roller's library in Harrisonburg, which, with helpful direction, General Roller placed at his disposal. When he left Harrisonburg it was as manager of oil and gas development for General Roller in 20 counties of Texas and in other states. For four years, 1913-17, he handled the legal and geophysical work and research on the Roller properties with marked success.

In 1917 he entered the employ of the Gulf Oil Corporation, then the J. M. Guffy Petroleum Co. of Pittsburgh, in the land department, and today, after more than 25 years, is still with the same corporation, now in charge of 54 counties in the Lone Star State. But his large business interests have not absorbed all his energies. He is active in the Texas Archaeological and Paleontological Society, the West Texas Historical Society, and the Texas Science Society. He is a member of the Presbyterian Church, the Colonial Country Club of Fort Worth, the Wichita Club, of Wichita Falls, the Masons, the Elks, and other organizations. His hobbies are scientific research, geology, and archaeology. He is now active in our common war effort. At the age of 18 he captained companies in the United Boys Brigades of America, predecessors of the Boy Scouts.

Mr. Hanley's wife was Esther O. Flynn, daughter of Elijah H. Flynn, one of the early settlers of Brown County, Texas. She was born in Brown County, March 14, 1897. Her father was born February 11, 1862, at Houston, Miss. Her mother, born Alice Madora House, May 10, 1864, was also a native of Houston, Chickasaw County, Miss. Mr. and Mrs. Hanley have three sons and two daughters: Fiske, born January 14, 1920, who, while completing his senior year in engineering at Texas Tech, enlisted as an aviation cadet in the Aeronautical Engineers; Alice Mahala, born September 16, 1921, graduate of the University of Texas; in war work until her marriage in Minneapolis, Dec. 5, 1942, to Alfred Giles of San Antonio, a pilot officer in the Royal Canadian Air Force; Claude W., born August 24, 1923, who enlisted as an aviation cadet in the U. S. forces while in the second year of his engineering course at Texas A. and M. College; Alvin Weaver, born June 15, 1925, first-year student in mechanical engineering at Texas Tech.; and Edna May, born March 9, 1927, a student in Central High School at Fort Worth.

JAMES ARTHUR HARMAN
MUSICIAN AND TEACHER OF MUSIC

Born at Dry Fork, near Harman, Randolph County, W. Va., January 7, 1882; attended neighborhood schools; student in Dana's Musical Institute 1903-04; ten years concert violinist in the Virginia Theater, Harrisonburg; teacher and director of orchestras in Shenandoah College, Bridgewater College, and the State Teachers (now Madison) College; founder and president of Harman's School of Music.

Professor Harman's father was Noah Harman, son of Moab Harman of Harman's Hills, W. Va.; his mother was Sarah, a daughter of Hugh Nash of Upper Tract. On the Harman side his great-grandfather was Noah, a son of Isaac. Isaac Harman married Christina Henkel of New Market, and was the first of the line to settle in what is now Pendleton County, W. Va. Harman Hills in Pendleton and the town of Harman in Randolph County bear the family name.

James Harman's talent for music appeared in childhood and he received instruction from local teachers. As a student in Dana's Musical Institute in Ohio he won notable distinction. In 1906 he came to Rockingham County, Va., and for the next 17 years headed the violin staff of Shenandoah College at Dayton. In 1920 he founded Harman's School of Music in Harrisonburg, which he still carries on successfully and of which he is president. At intervals he was violin instructor in Bridgewater College and the State Teachers College, Harrisonburg, and conducted orchestras in these institutions. He is a member of the National Academy of Music and the Virginia Federation of Music Clubs; is affiliated with the Federated Teachers' Service Corporation, and is certified by the Virginia State Board of Education. He has been a member of the local chamber of commerce and the Rotary Club, and in the latter had a perfect attendance record for eight years. He and his family are members of the Dayton United Brethren Church. In politics he is a Republican.

On August 25, 1905, at Richwood, W. Va., Professor Harman married Miss Della Margaret Emigh, who was born in Tyrone, Pa., December 25, 1883. They have six children: James Gordon, Emigh Dosler, Priscilla Pauline, Dorotha May (Mrs. Everett Varner), Mary Jane, and Hubert Blaine (now with the U. S. Marines). The whole family is musical, and they have been called on frequently for concerts in churches and at social and musical gatherings. In May, 1929, the eight of them (a full musical scale!) were the Virginia winners in the Home Music Contest, which was nation-wide. The Harman home is in Dayton, but the main studios of the Harman Music School are in Harrisonburg. Professor Harman's main assistants are his daughters Priscilla and Mary Jane. They have studios also in Elkton, Shenandoah, and Luray, and give instruction in schools at intermediate points.

In 1928 was published the Harman-Harmon Genealogy, by John William Harman of Parsons, W. Va. This is an 8vo volume of 472 pages. Opposite page 54 is a picture of the old Harman home in Harman Hills; and facing page 58 is a picture of Professor Harman, his wife, and their six children, with their musical instruments: violins, cello, clarionet, saxophone, etc. This photograph was taken only a year or two before they participated so successfully in the contest mentioned above.

CHARLES GRAVES HARNSBERGER
CIVIL ENGINEER, FARMER, AND BANKER

Born October 23, 1853, at "Maplewood, " his mother's ancestral home, two miles south of Elkton; student in Roanoke College, 1870-72; graduated, civil engineer, at the University of Virginia, 1875; surveyor for new railroads in western Texas; helped survey the railroad through East Rockingham, 1878-80; purchased and lived at "River Bend," his father's ancestral home; moved to Harrisonburg about 1908; president of the Bank of Elkton and the Rockingham National Bank of Harrisonburg; compiler of Harnsberger family history; a member of the Methodist Church; died in Harrisonburg, January 22, 1938.

Mr. Harnsberger was for many years one of the outstanding farmers and business men of Rockingham County and the city of Harrisonburg. His parents were Thomas Kennerly and Anne Virginia Yancey Harnsberger, representing two old and well-known Rockingham families. Having attended Roanoke College for two years, he entered the engineering dpartment of the University of Virginia where he graduated in 1875. Going then to Texas he was there engaged for several years in the work of laying out railroads in the western part of that state, after which he returned to Rockingham and assisted in surveying the right of way for the railway which was opened about 1880 through the eastern part of the Valley, connecting Big Lick, now Roanoke City, with Hagerstown, Md. This is now the Shenandoah Division of the N. & W. Railway. He made his home at River Bend, a short distance southwest of Elkton, in the house built by his grandfather, Jeremiah Harnsberger. A successful farmer and business man, he was soon called on to participate actively in the business life of the county, and for a number of years served as president of the Bank of Elkton and also of the Rockingham National Bank of Harrisonburg. About 1908 he moved to Harrisonburg where he made his home the remainder of his life. He rendered a valuable service in compiling a history of the Harnsberger family.

On May 23, 1888, Mr. Harnsberger married Janet Love Harnsberger (died 1942), a daughter of Henry Baker and Elizabeth M. Hopkins Harnsberger. Henry B. Harnsberger was a member of the Va. House of Delegates for two terms, 1869-70 and 1881-82. Mr. Harnsberger's father, Thomas K., served in the same body in 1889-90. Mr. and Mrs. Harnsberger had four children: Thomas Kennerly (1889-1934), a distinguished geologist, whose biography appears on succeeding pages; Elizabeth Mary, Ann Virginia, and Grace Rolston. Elizabeth is a graduate of Randolph-Macon Woman's College and the General Assembly's (Presbyterian) Training School, Richmond. For seven years she taught in Broadway and Harrisonburg and for six years was director of religious education in Dallas Presbytery, Texas. She has restored the old homestead at River Bend, where she now resides. Virginia graduated at R-M Woman's College and Pratt Institute, N. Y. City. For some time she was a librarian in New York, and for a number of years preceding her death in 1931 was librarian at Madison College. She was active in establishing the Rockingham Public Library and in organizing the A. A. U. W. in Harrisonburg. At one time she was president of the Va. State Library Assn. Grace is also a graduate of R-M Woman's College; is an M. A. of Teachers College, Columbia University; taught mathematics nine years in the high schools of Virginia and other states. In 1934 she married Paul H. Jamison of Roanoke and has a daughter, Janet Love, born in June, 1938.

THOMAS KENNERLY HARNSBERGER

GEOLOGIST

Born April 26, 1889, at "River Bend," a short distance southwest of Elkton; attended Fishburne Military Academy, Waynesboro, and Harrisonburg High School, graduating at the latter, 1908; B. S., University of Virginia, 1911; M. S., 1912; laboratory assistant to Dr. Thos. L. Watson; five years with U. S. Geological Survey in S. W. Va.; three years with petroleum corporation in the Rocky Mountain area; two years (1920-22) in South America; after 1922 chief geologist of the Wolverine Petroleum Corp., Tulsa, Okla., and later divisional chief for the Shell Co. in the mid-continental area; retired in 1931; died at Highland Park, Ill., September 27, 1934.

Mr. Harnsberger was the only son of Charles Graves (1853-1938) and Janet L. Harnsberger (1856-1942) Harnsberger, and was born at "River Bend" in the house built by his great-grandfather, Jeremiah Harnsberger. His paternal grandfather was Thomas Kennerly Harnsberger (1826-1894), member of the Va. House of Delegates, 1889-90, and state senator, 1892-95. His mother's father, Henry B. Harnsberger, a graduate of Dickinson College (1841), member of the Va. House of Delegates, 1869-70 and 1881-82, was the eldest son of Stephen (1787-1870) of "Cherry Grove," near Port Republic. An older Stephen, first Harnsberger to settle in East Rockingham, is said to have been with Spotswood in his expedition across the Blue Ridge in 1716. Thomas's father, Charles G., was a civil engineer, farmer, and banker.

After graduating from the Harrisonburg High School in 1908, Mr. Harnsberger entered the University of Virginia, where, after several years, he was made laboratory assistant to Professor Thomas L. Watson, State Geologist. He was honored in 1911 by election to the Raven Society and Phi Beta Kappa. His first important field work was as assistant to Henry Hinds of the U. S. Geological Survey in mapping an extended coal area in S. W. Virginia. Of this work a University publication says:

"By 1918 the map of Tazewell County, done under the direction of the Virginia Geological Survey with the coöperation of the U. S. Geological Survey, was printed. The text of this region was published in 1919 under the title: *The Geology and Coal Resources of the Coal-Bearing Portion of Tazewell County, Virginia.* This was Mr. Harnsberger's finest contribution to the geology of his native state, and one which will long be used as a reference in the study of coal of southwestern Virginia."

Altogether, Mr. Harnsberger was with the U. S. Geological Survey five years. In July, 1917, he joined the staff of Roxana Petroleum (Shell) Corporation, and for three years was in the Rocky Mountain area, with headquarters at Cheyenne. In December, 1920, he went to South America for the Asiatic Petroleum (Shell) Corporation. Returning in 1922, he was appointed chief geologist of the Wolverine Petroleum Corporation of Tulsa, Okla., and later was divisional chief of land and geological service for the Shell Company in the mid-continental area. He retired in 1931 because of impaired health. He was a member of the American Institute of Mining and Metallurgical Engineers, the American Assn. of Petroleum Geologists, the Geological Society of Washington, and the Pick and Hammer Club, joining the last while studying paleontology at George Washington University. He was also a 32d degree Mason, and helped to establish the Morris Plan Bank in Oklahoma. He was the author of a monograph on the origin of rivers.

On June 1, 1918, Mr. Harnsberger married Miss Norine Jane MacDonald of Glengarry County, Ontario, Canada, daughter of Alexander Hugh and Janet Routhier MacDonald, who is now the wife of Captain Willis S. Bryant, residing at "Blue Water," Kilmarnock, Va.

JOSEPH PHILIP HARPINE

BUSINESS MAN AND MAYOR OF BROADWAY

Born November 5, 1892, at Daphna; grew up on his father's farm; attended Daphna Graded School, Broadway High School, Shenandoah College, and Dunsmore Business College; bookkeeper and credit manager in Huntington, W. Va.; served in World War I in the United States and France, rising to the rank of captain; traveling salesman three years; with Miller & Co., Ford dealers, Broadway, 1922-28; president and manager Broadway Motor Co., Inc., since 1928; president Brock's Gap Oil & Gas Co. since 1936; member and president (1939) of Harrisonburg-Rockingham Chamber of Commerce; mayor of Broadway since 1928.

Mr. Harpine is a son of William M. Harpine, born at Moore's Store, Shenandoah County, November 21, 1857, and his wife, Mary Alice Harpine, born at Forestville, August 12, 1859. They moved to Rockingham in the early 80's and engaged in farming until 1928, when they retired and moved to Broadway. There William died, July 30, 1939; his wife, September 6, 1928. After graduation at Dunsmore Business College in April, 1914, Joseph became bookkeeper with the C. C. Huddleston Lumber & Supply Co., Huntington, W. Va., and after a year was credit manager until he resigned to enlist in the First Officers Training Camp, Fort Benjamin Harrison, Ind. He was assigned to duty as assistant to the Division Quartermaster, 83d Division, Camp Sherman, Chillicothe, Ohio, and was promoted to 1st lieutenant, March 12, 1918. The next month he went overseas and was in service near Chateau Thierry, France, from July 7 to July 27, when he returned to his division and served as property officer. In October, 1918, he was ordered back to the United States as an instructor in quartermaster work. He was assigned special work in the Quartermaster General's Office, Washington, D. C., and on several occasions made talks in the War College on subjects concerning quartermaster activities in France. On October 8, 1918, he was promoted to captain, Q. M. C. After completing special work in Washington he was assigned Assistant Division Quartermaster, 95th Division, Camp Sherman, where he remained until discharged on December 12, 1918.

After leaving the army Mr. Harpine traveled as a salesman three years, then returned to his home at Daphna and took a position with the Ford dealers, Miller & Co., in Broadway, continuing therein till August, 1928, when he was appointed Ford dealer, and the Broadway Motor Co., Inc., was organized to take over the business of Miller & Co. The Broadway Motor Co., with Mr. Harpine as president and general manager, has been most successful. In addition to his business and his duties as mayor, Mr. Harpine is chairman of the Democratic Committee of Broadway Precinct, a member of the Selective Service Board of the county, the Rion-Bowman Post, V. F. W., the Plains District Ruritan Club, the 83d Co., Va. Minute Men, the Police Relief Association of Harrisonburg, the Rockingham Game and Fish Association, and the Broadway Volunteer Fire Department. For seven years he has been a member of the Harrisonburg-Rockingham Chamber of Commerce, of which he was president in 1939, when it promoted the first Turkey Festival. He is a member of the Methodist Church, and is on the Board of Stewards. He also holds membership in the Elks lodge of Harrisonburg and Shenandoah Council No. 205, U. C. T. His hobbies are hunting big game and deep-sea fishing.

On November 4, 1925, in Harrisonburg, Mr. Harpine married Miss Sarah E. Revercomb, daughter of the late James W. Revercomb of Clover Hill, and has one daughter, Alice Elise Harpine, born at Broadway, May 11, 1927.

JOHN HOUSTON HARRISON
MECHANICAL ENGINEER AND HISTORIAN

Born July 8, 1887, at the old Martz-Harrison homestead, between Court Manor and Tenth Legion; grew up on his father's farm; attended Ohio Northern Univ. and Univ. of Va.; graduated, a mechanical engineer, U. Va., 1910; in employ of the Southern Railway since 1911, holding important posts at Charlottesville (residence while traveling), Atlanta, Ga., and Washington, D. C.; residence in Alexandria since 1921; now Mechanical Engineer, handling valuation and other cost and utilization studies, with office in Washington; member American Society of Mechanical Engineers; author of "Settlers by the Long Grey Trail" (1935) and other valuable works.

Mr. Harrison is the son of David Warren (1845-1933) and Anna A. Houston (1856-1921) Harrison, grandson of John and Barbara Katherine Harrison, and through his mother a descendant of Rev. Wm. Houston, early Methodist missionary to the Indians, whose wife was a granddaughter of Thomas Harrison, founder of Harrisonburg. His sister, Rita Catherine, is Mrs. Thomas Moore and lives near Court Manor and the old Harrison homestead. A picture of the latter (birthplace of Houston Harrison and his sister) may be seen on page 197 of Wayland's "Historic Homes." Their father, David W. Harrison, was a successful farmer and stockman, served for a number of years on the county school board, and took a keen interest in public affairs. Houston Harrison, after completing courses in mechanical and electrical engineering at the Univ. of Virginia, specializing in the former, on June 4, 1912, married Berta Steptoe Watson, daughter of A. Sidney Watson and wife, Mary Louise Wheeler, of Albemarle Co., Va. Mr. and Mrs. Harrison are members of the Methodist Church. He is a Mason, a member of the Virginia Historical Society and professional organizations; she is a member of the United Daughters of the Confederacy and the natl. society D. A. R.

Mr. Harrison, as an avocation, spent many years in studying local and family history and in 1935 rendered a signal public service by having published "Settlers by the Long Grey Trail," subtitled "A Contribution to the History and Genealogy of Colonial Families of Rockingham County, Va." This is an 8vo volume of 665 pages, with numerous illustrations, relating to the early history of the region, including genealogies of the Harrison and many other prominent families of northern Virginia. It merits a place in the first rank of similar works in this country. He assisted Wm. Herring Chrisman in editing his father's (Herring Chrisman's) "Memoirs of Lincoln," published in 1930, and is the author of the Introduction and footnotes thereto. An enthusiastic engineer, applied mathematician, and collector of technical and scientific data relating to his profession, he has found restful diversion in historical research. He has assembled much data on the "makers of machines" as affecting scientific thought, and vice versa, besides other related items, more especially regarding the steam and Diesel engine.

Mr. and Mrs. Harrison have three daughters and three sons: Anna Louise, born Aug. 1, 1913; Pearl Elizabeth, Jan. 21, 1917; John Houston, Jr., Sept. 30, 1918; David Warren, Nov. 30, 1920; Daniel Edward, March 27, 1923; and Nancy Byrd, Jan. 26, 1926. Anna Louise on March 8, 1935, married Harry P. Shaffer of Alexandria, now Lieutenant (jg) U. S. Navy, and they have a son Harry P., Jr., born May 21, 1941. Pearl Elizabeth, March 17, 1943, married Lieut. Robt. E. Craddock, U. S. A., of Alexandria, now stationed at San Francisco. All three of the sons are now enlisted in the armed forces of the United States, the first two in active service: John H., in the Coast Guard, and now in Chicago; David W. in the Cavalry, now at Fort Bliss, Texas; and Daniel E., in the Army Reserve Corps, now at V. P. I., Blacksburg, Va.

MICHAEL HOWARD HARRISON
FARMER, SUPERVISOR, AND COUNTY TREASURER

Born September 14, 1868, at Melrose; grew up on a farm and attended public schools; clerked in a store at Front Royal; deputy postmaster at Front Royal; worked at the carpenter trade for many years; a county supervisor of Rockingham; commisioner of revenue for Stonewall District for eight years; deputy commissioner for four years; elected county treasurer in 1931; re-elected in 1935 and 1939; died on June 25, 1941.

Mr. Harrison's chief ambition was to be a successful business man, and he was for many years one of the outstanding men of Rockingham County. He was a son of Reuben W. Harrison (May 27, 1830—August 19, 1913) and his wife, Hannah Sellers (February 29, 1832—July 3, 1900), married November 26, 1850. His grandfather was Nathaniel Harrison (January 22, 1803—February 26, 1839) who, on July 29, 1829, married Mary High (February 9, 1810—December 31, 1898). The Harrison home was on the Valley Pike, north of Melrose.

After his boyhood in Rockingham County and some years in Front Royal, as indicated on the preceding page, Mr. Harrison returned to Rockingham where he spent the remainder of his life. He was a skilled carpenter and worked as such on a number of buildings in the county. He was interested in public affairs and served for many years on the county board of supervisors and as commissioner of revenue, as already indicated. For two full terms he was treasurer of the county, and in 1939 was elected for his third term. He made his home on a valuable farm in the eastern part of the county, and was successful in farming and stock-raising. His reading preferences were in the field of history and related subjects.

On June 20, 1894, Mr. Harrison married Miss Emily W. Wood, born February 16, 1870, at Island Ford, the daughter of Captain John I. Wood and wife of Island Ford. She died October 12, 1941. Mr. and Mrs. Harrison had three children: Hannah Elizabeth, born September 29, 1896; Michael Howard, Jr., born November 22, 1902; and Russell Maggard, born May 25, 1905; all natives of Island Ford. Hannah Elizabeth married W. R. Sipe and has four children: William Howard, born May 6, 1928; John Harrison, born August 15, 1929; Harry Wood, born February 9, 1931; and Mary Emily, born February 9, 1931. Michael Howard Harrison, Jr., married Miss Virginia Yancey and has two children: Elizabeth Ann, born December 20, 1925; and Virginia Yancey, born January 28, 1928. Russell Maggard Harrison married Miss Lucile Richards and has two children: Warren Richards, born September 7, 1925; and Dabney Russell, born March 29, 1931.

Upon the death of Michael H. Harrison, Sr., on June 25, 1941, Judge H. W. Bertram of the circuit court appointed Mr. Harrison's son, Russell M. Harrison, as county treasurer to fill out his father's unexpired term.

Mr. Harrison was interested in things historical, as already indicated, and at his home may be seen an unusual relic of past times. In 1889, at the time of the Johnstown Flood, he found washed out on the river bank a smooth stone, almost globular, about a foot in diameter, supposed to be a glacial stone. This he preserved by mounting it on a stone column which was formerly a lintel in the old county court house which was torn down in 1896.

DANIEL JACOB HARTMAN

AVIATOR AND MASTER OF TRANSPORTATION

Born March 4, 1899, at Dale Enterprise; attended grade schools and Bible terms at Eastern Mennonite School; dairy farmer and dealer in farm machinery; mechanic for the Nicholas & Shepherd and the J. I. Case companies; trucker to the eastern cities; opened the Harrisonburg airport in 1938; director and treasurer city-county chamber of commerce; director Virginia Highway Users Association; expert aviator.

Mr. Hartman's father, Jacob David Hartman, was born at Dale Enterprise, November 23, 1870; his mother, born Eurie Frances Showalter, October 31, 1869, is a native of Broadway. His grandfather was Peter S. Hartman of Harrisonburg, whose wife was Fannie Weaver of Dale Enterprise.

Mr. Hartman says: "My childhood days were spent on the farm, working hard most of the time from early morning till late at night. We were taught strict obedience in the home and attended church and Sundayschool regularly. We were allowed from three to five months of schooling per year. I completed the 7th grade and in my later teens attended two six-week terms of Bible School at E. M. S. The remainder of my education was acquired by costly experience. At the age of 20 I started in business for myself on a dairy farm, retailing milk from house to house in Harrisonburg. At the same time, in addition to my own farm, I was farming my father's farm and that of my grandfather, with the machine business as a side line. This continued for five years; then I was expert mechanic two years for the machine companies. I then started in the produce business, trucking to Washington, Philadelphia, and New York, being the pioneer freight hauler from this section. Because of my competition, railroad and freight rates were greatly reduced, saving our farmers thousands of dollars in their shipments. Working hard, I often went as long as four nights and days without sleep, and as a consequence had pneumonia three winters in succession. But I was determined to win out. In 1938 I rented what was then known as the Burke Field and opened an airport, a project on which I was severely criticized, just as I had been in the pioneer trucking days. In 1940 I purchased the flying field, 44 acres, now known as the Hartman Field. Now I am sure that our freedom as a nation depends on aviation."

Early in his boyhood Mr. Hartman was received into the Mennonite Church by water baptism. His wife, Miss Lena Pearl Good, was born at Dale Enterprise, June 10, 1898. Their children are: Dwight Wilson, born March 25, 1923; Geraldine Ann, born October 1, 1925; Brownie Virginia, born September 24, 1926; Raymond Carroll, born October 27, 1928; Evelyn Blanche, born August 6, 1930; Rhea Joan, born March 5, 1932; and Ewell Daniel, born March 27, 1933. Says Mr. Hartman:

"I am giving these children a high-school education; also a good education in instrumental and vocal music. The oldest son at age of 19 is now mechanic in my truck terminal. He is also a licensed airplane pilot. Two of the other children have finished their high-school courses.

"My favorite hobby is owning and flying airplanes. I make good use of them in my business, saving much time, energy, and money. I have done very little reading, as my time has been taken up by my various activities of work and business."

FRANK HENRY HEATWOLE

SECRETARY-TREASURER AND MANAGER AUGUSTA DAIRIES, INC.

Born Dec. 11, 1902, near Dayton; graduate of Dayton High School, 1922; of Shenandoah College, 1924; student of V. P. I.; supervisor of Dairy Herd Improvement Work, 1925-27; Field Supervisor and Asst. Mgr. Valley of Va. Coöperative Milk Producers Assn., 1928-42; Secretary-Treasurer and Manager Augusta Dairies, Inc., since 1942; former steward Dayton Methodist Church; member and past president of Harrisonburg Lions Club; member of Staunton Rotary Club; member and a director of Staunton-Augusta Chamber of Commerce; Mason; etc.

From Mr. Heatwole's boyhood on his father's farm he has had a growing interest in livestock and all phases of farm life; he was an active member of the Dayton 4H Club and president the year it was the champion club in the state. He was for some years a Boy Scout and served as master of the Dayton troop. For several years after finishing school he managed his father's farm. His parents, David Grove and Rebecca Swartz Heatwole, represent two well-known Rockingham families. His father's parents were Rev. Daniel S. and Elizabeth Grove Heatwole; his maternal grandparents were Abram and Mary Swope Swartz, the latter a descendant of the Swanks. All these families have contributed largely to the thrifty rural life of Rockingham. Bishop L. J. Heatwole, Dr. C. J. Heatwole, and Dr. W. J. Showalter (a Swank descendant) were distinguished in educational, religious, and literary work. Dr. T. O. Heatwole, a brother of L. J. and C. J., was for many years a teacher and offical in the University of Maryland.

At Virginia Polytechnic Institute Mr. Heatwole specialized in the course on dairying. In 1925 he was appointed official dairy herd supervisor for the counties of Rockingham, Shenandoah, and Frederick. For efficiency in this work he, the first year, was awarded first prize among Virginia supervisors, due largely to his genial personality, honesty, and energy. In connection he was for several years a state poultry inspector and tester, but in January, 1928, he resigned this work to become field manager of the Valley of Va. Coöperative Milk Producers Assn., Inc. Promoted to plant superintendent, he displayed such alert and tireless efforts to improve the business that he was made assistant manager. During his more than 14 years with this plant he saw the dairy industry in Rockingham and parts of Augusta and Shenandoah grow into one of the leading sources of income on many farms.

Early in 1942 Mr. Heatwole resigned from his position with the Valley of Va. Milk Producers Assn. to enter private business in Staunton, where he is now secretary-treasurer and manager of Augusta Dairies, Inc., and part owner. He has always been keenly interested in civic clubs and community activities, as already indicated. In Harrisonburg he was a valued member of the Lions Club, and served a term as president. He belongs to Rockingham Union Lodge No. 27, A. F. & A. M. In Dayton he served for some time as a steward of the Methodist Church and now holds membership in the Central Methodist Church in Staunton and in the Staunton Rotary Club. He is a director in the Staunton-Augusta Chamber of Commerce. His favorite recreations are fishing and hunting. He is also an ardent ball fan.

In 1936 Mr. Heatwole married Miss Lucille V. McGlaughlin of Harrisonburg, who is a graduate of Madison College, and was for some years a supervisor in the college training school. Mr. and Mrs. Heatwole have a son, Davis Grove Heatwole, born May 30, 1941.

BAYARD M. HEDRICK
EDUCATOR AND BUSINESS MAN

Born Feb. 22, 1880, at Churchville, Va.; grew up in Rockh. Co., where he attended public schools; student in Bridgewater College, Valparaiso Univ., Temple Univ., Univ. of Chicago; teacher in Rockh. schools and Bwtr. Coll.; Y. M. C. A. Sec'y., Camden N. J.; organizer of Y. M. C. A. war work for N. J., Camp Lee, Va., and the Vannes area, Brittany, France, 1917-18; member N. Y. Southern Society, Rockefeller Luncheon Club, board of directors of Juniata College, Associated Boards of Christian Colleges in China, etc.; pres., Pierce & Hedrick, Inc., 30 Rockefeller Plaza, New York, N. Y.

Mr. Hedrick, following the traditions of his paternal ancestors and his own personal inclinations, has had a notable career in educational and religious service as well as in closely related business fields. His father, Joseph M. Hedrick, was a Lutheran minister; his grandfather, David M. Hedrick, was a newspaper publisher at New Market and served as Director of the Bureau of Patents during the administration of President Pierce. The maiden name of Rev. Joseph M. Hedrick's wife was Mary Katherine Murphy; that of David M. Hedrick's wife was Barbara Rohrback.

Bayard M. Hedrick, orphaned at the age of seven by the death of his mother, and at eleven by the death of his father, was brought up by relatives of his father near Pleasant Valley, in Rockingham County. After attending public schools, he took courses in Bridgewater College and Valparaiso University, graduating from the latter as Bachelor of Accounts in 1900. Already in 1898 he had taught public school, and in 1901-02 he was principal of the Broadway High School. For a number of years, 1902-05 and 1906-11, he taught business courses in Bridgewater College. From 1911 to 1917 he was Y. M. C. A. Secretary at Camden, N. J. In April of 1917 he organized the Y. M. C. A. war work for the National Guard in the state of New Jersey, later being engaged in similar organizing work at Camp Lee, Va., and in the Vannes area in Brittany, France. From 1918 to 1927 he was engaged in business and as a fund-raising counsel. In 1927, with Lyman L. Pierce, he organized the firm of Pierce & Hedrick, Inc., for business of the same character. This firm has handled many of the great national financial campaigns for good causes, such as the China Christian Colleges, the Boy Scouts of America, and the Northern Baptist convention, as well as numerous local appeals. At this writing (October-November, 1942) Mr. Hedrick is directing the $7,000,000 campaign for United China Relief. He was one of the pioneers in developing unique and effective methods of raising funds for philanthropic purposes. He is a member of the Baptist Church and an independent in politics. Besides other affiliations already indicated, he is a member of the International Council of Religious Education. He finds recreation in reading and farming.

On February 7, 1901, Mr. Hedrick married Miss Betty A. Wenger, born January 10, 1882, a daughter of John A. Wenger of Harrisonburg and his wife, Sallie R. Driver of Mt. Clinton. Of this marriage there were born four children: Raymond M., born April 29, 1902; John Randolph, born July 9, 1904; Esther M., born July 16, 1907, who died in 1938; and Bayard M., Jr., born July 29, 1916. Mrs. Hedrick's father, Mr. John A. Wenger, was a well-to-do farmer and business man, and served for a number of years as a trustee and a member of the board of directors of Bridgewater College.

J. MAURICE HENRY

EDUCATOR, AUTHOR, AND LECTURER

Born August 7, 1880, at Roanoke, Va.; attended a "little red school house," Grisso Gate; student in Daleville Academy and Daleville College; B. A., Bridgewater College, 1909; teacher at Daleville, 1909-13, 1914-17; graduate student at the University of Virginia; M. A., George Washington University, 1919; Ph. D., 1924; evangelist in the Middle West; pastor Church of the Brethren, Washington City, 1917-22; president of Blue Ridge College, Md., 1922-27; traveler in Europe, 1927; lecturer, 1928; "Heart of the Crimson Cross" published, 1929; head of history department in Bridgewater College since 1928.

Dr. Henry is a minister, a public speaker, a writer of ability, and an experienced educator. He is a son of John T. and Jane Frances Henry. His father's parents were Samuel J. and Jane Henry; his maternal grandparents were John and Fannie Grisso. Dr. Henry in his early career taught seven years at Daleville and pursued advanced studies at the University of Virginia, as already indicated; and while pastor of the Church of the Brethren in Washington City and president of Blue Ridge College, at New Windsor, Md., he completed his work in George Washington University for his Master's degree in 1919 and that for his Doctorate in 1924. Following an extended tour in Europe in 1927, he spent the next year lecturing on Europe and World War I. In the spring of 1928 he wrote his well-known novel, "The Heart of the Crimson Cross," which was published in Boston the next year in a volume of 394 pages. This is a story of college life and war, prominence being given to the Red Cross, with an effective presentation of Edith Cavell. The hero is a country boy whose naivete is well offset by his sterling qualities. During World War I Dr. Henry served on the peace committee of the Church of the Brethren as secretary. For more than ten years he was chairman of the church's peace and welfare committee, and later for nearly 15 years was a member of the denominational Board of Christian Education.

For his doctor's dissertation at George Washington University, Dr. Henry presented a history of the Church of the Brethren in Maryland, and in 1930, when the semi-centennial history of Bridgewater College was published, he supplied a valuable chapter on the first board of trustees of the institution. He has written numerous articles of a religious and historical character for the periodicals of his denomination, and although a busy man as head of the department of history in Bridgewater College, he finds time to go out to various churches and educational institutions to deliver occasional sermons and lectures, for which he is much in demand. He also devotes considerable time to civic duties in various capacities. At present he is serving his second term as a member of the Bridgewater town council. Biographical sketches of Dr. Henry may be found in "Who's Who in America," vols. 14 and 15, the "Educational Blue Book of the Church of the Brethren," and other standard works.

On August 11, 1909, Dr. Henry married Miss Vergie Wickline, born in 1884 at Amsterdam, Va., daughter of James T. and Kate Wickline. Dr. and Mrs. Henry have two living children: Maurice Kent, born January 27, 1917, a graduate of Bridgewater College and George Peabody College for Teachers, Nashville, Tennessee, who married Miss Helen Kincaid, daughter of Dr. and Mrs. R. L. Kincaid of Lincoln Memorial University. Maurice K. is now principal of Jeter Junior High School, Covington, Va. His sister, Margaret Henry, is also a graduate of Bridgewater College and is now a teacher of home economics in Mt. Clinton High School.

KENNETH MALCOLM HIGGS

FUNERAL DIRECTOR AND BUSINESS MAN

Born August 4, 1890, at Lacey Spring; attended public school at Lacey Spring, Professor Taylor's academy, and a business school in Harrisonburg; served an apprenticeship of three years under William Fultz, Harrisonburg funeral director; graduated from Barnes' School of Embalming in New York City and was employed in the same city for several years; established his business in Harrisonburg in 1913; member of the Presbyterian Church and fraternal organizations; owned and operated the Plecker Greenhouse and the Blue Stone Inn at Lacey Spring; died in Harrisonburg, March 9, 1941.

Mr. Higgs was a native of the historic Lacey Springs community, in which he grew up. His father was Joseph O. Higgs, whose wife before marriage was Amanda Virginia Huddle. His paternal grandparents were Isaac Higgs and his wife, Catherine Hagey. His mother's parents were David and Mary C. Jones Huddle. After attending elementary public school in his early years at Lacey Spring he became a pupil in the private academy which was conducted at the same place for many years by Professor John W. Taylor. Among the latter's pupils were many who were later numbered among the well-known and successful men and women of the county. Having continued his training by taking a business course in Harrisonburg, Mr. Higgs entered into an apprenticeship under the late William Fultz, a well-known funeral director of Harrisonburg, with whom he worked for three years. He then went to New York City where he took a course in the Barnes School of Embalming. Following his graduation therefrom he was employed by a New York firm for several years before coming to Harrisonburg, where he established his own business in July, 1913. This he carried on successfully until his death in 1941, with office, storerooms, etc., in the Dr. James Harris property on Graham Street, which he purchased and fitted up in an attractive manner suitable for his purposes. He also purchased the Plecker Greenhouse, in the northern part of the city, from the late J. E. Plecker, which he operated and developed into the largest establishment of its kind between Washington and Roanoke. He introduced the first private ambulance in this section of Virginia.

In addition to his extensive businesses in Harrisonburg, Mr. Higgs built and operated the Blue Stone Inn at Lacey Spring, with a large and attractive tourist camp in connection therewith. This is one of the conspicuous landmarks along the Valley Pike (U. S. Route No. 11), and has long been a favorite stopping place for travelers and sojourners in this part of the country. He was a member of the Presbyterian Church of Harrisonburg; was a member of the Harrisonburg-Rockingham chamber of commerce, and was affiliated with several fraternal and benevolent organizations—Benevolent and Protective Order of Elks, the Independent Order of Odd Fellows, and the Modern Woodmen of America. Through these organizations and otherwise he was active in charitable work.

On August 18, 1915, Mr. Higgs married Miss Margaret Rebecca Tyerman, daughter of Ambrose S. Tyerman and his wife, who was before marriage Miss Elsie D. Clinger. Mr. and Mrs. Higgs had no children. Since the death of the former, Mrs. Higgs has carried on as a memorial to him the businesses established by her deceased husband, with headquarters at the well-known site on Graham Street, in Harrisonburg.

HERMAN LAMAR HOLLAR
ORCHARDIST AND SHIPPER OF PRODUCE

Born September 16, 1903, at Timberville; attended Timberville graded and high schools; employed in Pennsylvania; farming in Rockingham; trucking for produce dealers; in the produce business for himself; planting orchards and raising poultry; now a large shipper of fruit, meat, and poultry; a pioneer Ruritan; an enthusiastic traveler.

Mr. Hollar, in his life and achievements, provides an example of what young men of thrift, energy, and resourcefulness can accomplish in their home communities. He is typical of those substantial citizens who, for generations in the Shenandoah Valley and other rural sections of our country, have developed the resources and possibilities that lie at hand, and have thus made valuable contributions to the general welfare of the nation at large, as well as to their own counties and states. For them it has not been necessary to seek distant fields of opportunity or the noise and rush of great cities.

He is a son of Davis M. Hollar, who was born at Timberville on February 3, 1884, whose parents were Crist Hollar and Anna Wampler Hollar, the former born at Singers' Glen, the latter a native of Timberville. His mother, the wife of Davis M. Hollar, was Elizabeth Branner, born at Forestville on December 5, 1886. She was the daughter of Silas Branner of Forestville and his wife, Mary Kipps, a native of New Market. From the old Branner homestead at Forestville, where Casper Branner and John Branner were heads of families as early as 1783, their descendants have scattered widely. The late John Casper Branner, distinguished in California and South America, published extended studies in the history of the family.

Herman Hollar, after going through the grades and the first three years of the Timberville High School, went to York, Pennsylvania, where he spent a short time working for the York Safe and Lock Company. Returning home, he started farming for himself. In or about 1925 he began hauling with his own trucks for produce dealers, and in 1932 he started in the produce business for himself, and in a short time had built up a trade of about half a million dollars a year. In 1935 he cut down his business as a dealer and expanded it as a producer in raising turkeys and chickens. At the same time he planted out a peach orchard of about 180 acres. Since then he has increased his poultry-raising to about 25,000 birds a year and has bought additional orchards. His 1942 crop aggregated some 85 carloads of fruit and about 12 carloads of meat, including turkeys and chickens.

Mr. Hollar has been a member of the Harrisonburg Elks Club for the past fifteen years, and has been connected with the local Ruritan Club since it was organized in 1939. He is an independent in politics, voting for the man he regards as the best candidate. In sports, he is very fond of seashore fishing. For reading he prefers the *Time* magazine to any other. He finds much pleasure in traveling, and for the past two years has spent part of the winter in Florida.

On March 28, 1932, Mr. Hollar married Miss Louise Andes in Washington City. She was born at New Market, August 14, 1914. They are the parents of a daughter, Nancy Lee Hollar, who was born August 16, 1933.

DAVID HENRY HOOVER

SOCIOLOGIST AND ECONOMIST

Born April 26,1878, on Mossy Creek, near the line of Rockingham and Augusta; grew up on a farm near Bridgewater; attended local school and Bridgewater College; taught in Rockingham County schools; B. A., Bridgewater College, 1913; M.A., 1914; M.S., Vanderbilt University, 1916; B.D., University of Chicago, 1918; Th.D., Baptist Theological Seminary, Louisville, 1919; professor of sociology in McPherson College, 1920-22; graduate student, University of Illinois, 1922-23; on teaching staff, University of Illinois, since 1923; author of various social and economic studies.

Dr. Hoover says, "I was born in Isaac Glick's tenant house on Mossy Creek; lived on a fifteen-acre farm near Cook's Creek; went to school at Harmony, a one-room school." He does not say that his father, Abram Hoover, was one of the best farmers in the community and made a good living on his farm of 15 acres, which is also true. His mother's maiden name was Susana F. Garber; his paternal grandparents were Henry and Matilda Hoover. Having completed a business course in Bridgewater College in 1903, he taught in different public schools and was principal for one year each at Pleasant Hill, near Harrisonburg, and at Singers' Glen. In the meantime, at intervals, he continued his studies in Bridgewater College, where he received the degrees of B.A. and M.A., as already indicated. Then, after two years of advanced study in Vanderbilt University, two years in the divinity school of the University of Chicago, a year in the Southern Baptist Theological Seminary, and a summer in George Peabody College for Teachers in Nashville, he was professor of sociology for two years, 1920-22, in McPherson College, Kansas. Not yet being satisfied with his scholastic training, he entered the University of Illinois for further study. There, before the end of the session (1922-23), he was offered a teaching position, in which, with appropriate advancements, he has continued until the present.

It is doubtful whether any man or woman of Rockingham County has had more comprehensive or extended college and university training than Dr. Hoover. Besides the usual courses for college graduates, he has specialized in theology, sociology, and economics, and has made important social surveys in different cities and rural communities. For a number of years past he has been teaching in the field of economics. Among the special studies he has prepared are the following: "The Health of the Teacher," "The Development of the Papal Hierarchy in the Middle Ages," "Juvenile Probation in Cook County, Ill.," and "The Effectiveness of Juvenile Probations." He did city survey work in Louisville, Ky., and Nashville, Tenn., and after World War I he was county organizer, under the general direction of Herbert Hoover, in the state of Kentucky in the extensive organization to feed the starving peoples of Europe.

On December 24, 1920, Dr. Hoover married (1) Miss Arta Lee Demy, born March 16, 1886, daughter of Jesse L. and Dove Geiman Demy. After her death he married (2) Mrs. Elva Miller Craik of Lawrence, Kansas, widow of the late Dr. E. L. Craik. Although Dr. Hoover has had no children of his own, he and his wives have been foster parents to six different children, one at present.

Dr. Hoover confesses to no particular hobby, but he has a kit of tools which he enjoys using. He is fond of reading, and among current periodicals he devotes a good deal of time to the *Reader's Digest*.

JOHN HENRY HOOVER
FARMER AND BUSINESS MAN
AND MRS. HOOVER

Born December 4, 1863, near Timberville; educated in local schools and Bridgewater College; farmer, grazer, and dealer in livestock; merchant in Timberville; an organizer and the first president of the Timberville bank; a director of the First National Bank of Harrisonburg; director of the Rockingham Memorial Hospital; a promoter of the water and lighting systems of Timberville; a trustee of Bridgewater College.

Throughout a long life Mr. Hoover has been active in various lines of business and in numerous civic, religious, financial, and philanthropic enterprises. He is a son of Emanuel Hoover, grandson of Samuel Hoover, and a great-grandson of Jacob Hoover. Jacob was the first of the family in this part of the Shenandoah Valley, settling on a tract of river land a short distance east of the site of Timberville, granted to him in 1773 by King George III. This land has ever since been held by the family. While a student in 1882-83 at Bridgewater College, then in its beginnings, Mr. Hoover saw furrows plowed through the field on the southeast side of the town to indicate where College Street was to be.

On November 5, 1885, at Timberville, Mr. Hoover married Miss Annie R. Flory, daughter of Daniel and a sister to Dr. John S. Flory of Bridgewater, president emeritus of Bridgewater College. In 1887 he took charge of a portion of the home farm and began his long experience in agriculture and stock-raising. In 1902 he built his present residence adjoining the Timberville town site. Ten years later he turned over the management of part of his large land-holdings to his oldest son, Ernest Hoover, who continued in that capacity until his death by accidental drowning in 1921. After 1912 Mr. Hoover devoted more time to the agricultural and livestock business of C. Driver & Company, in which he had a financial interest, and to various other activities. In Timberville he engaged in merchandising with his sons and others; he was an organizer and the first president of the Farmers and Merchants Bank of Timberville, and was one of the leaders in providing the town with a good water supply and joined with his sons, Ernest M. and Stanley F., and Frank H. Driver in building an electric light plant. He was one of the original board of trustees for the Rockingham Memorial Hospital, and is now the only surviving original member on that board.

A member of the Church of the Brethren, Mr. Hoover was chairman of the building committee in erecting the new church of the denomination at Timberville in 1928. He was for 20 years a trustee of the Old Folks Home at Timberville, and he has participated in various other church enterprises. A Democrat in politics, he has not held public office, but has always been keenly alive to the public welfare. For a number of years he was a member of the Kiwanis Club of Harrisonburg and Rockingham County. He is a careful reader of the newspapers; does not claim to have any hobby.

Mr. and Mrs Hoover have had eight sons and one daughter: Ernest Miller, deceased; Flora, now Mrs. Bowman, wife of President Paul H. Bowman of Bridgewater College; Stanley Franklin of Timberville; Lester Daniel, a well-known business man of the county and city of Harrisonburg; Charles E., who died August 14, 1920, from the effects, as it is believed, of poisoning by factory gas in war service; Merville John, living near New Market; Saylor C., of Timberville; Raymond Isaac, and Lawrence Harold. The daughter and most of the sons are graduates of Bridgewater College; two of Blue Ridge College, Md. Charles attended Cornell University. Lawrence is now commonwealth's attorney of Rockingham County.

LESTER DANIEL HOOVER
FARMER AND BUSINESS MAN

Born November 19, 1892, at Timberville; attended Timberville Graded and High School, Bridgewater College, and Virginia Polytechnic Institute; agent for life insurance companies; insurance adjuster for teachers in Harrisonburg, Rockingham, and other counties; farmer and raiser of livestock and poultry; operator of service stations and other business enterprises; active in Red Cross work; trustee Church of the Brethren; a promoter of the Spotswood Country Club, Virginia Craftsmen, and the Harrisonburg Loan & Thrift Corporation.

Mr. Hoover is typical of the progressive young business men who have played such an important part in his home town of Timberville, Rockingham County, and the city of Harrisonburg during the past quarter of a century. He is a son of John Henry Hoover and his wife, Ann Rebecca Flory, who represent two of the families that have long been prominent in the Timberville area. His brother Lawrence is now the efficient commonwealth's attorney of Rockingham County. Other brothers are successful farmers and business men. His paternal grandfather was Emanuel Hoover (born April 4, 1827), whose wife was Anna Cline (born July 6, 1831), daughter of John; his mother's parents were Daniel Flory (born Aug. 16, 1833) and his wife, Susannah Wampler (born Jan. 6, 1832).

After his boyhood on his father's farm near Timberville, and early education in the Timberville schools, Mr. Hoover attended Bridgewater College; later took a course in Virginia Polytechnic Institute in horticulture. This has been of great practical value to him in operating his farm of 375 acres, on which livestock and poultry, as well as fruit and farm crops, are produced. In these operations one of his brothers was associated with him for several years. While a student in Bridgewater College he began selling life insurance, in which he is still a licensed agent, and in which he has made an enviable record. For many years he has been a member of the $250,000 Field Club, personal production, of the Mutual Life Insurance Co. of New York, in which a handsome medal and extended tours are given each year. He has also been the recipient of recognition from fire insurance companies, through the W. L. Dechert Insurance Corporation of Harrisonburg, for 25 years of continuous service. In addition to his insurance and agricultural interests, he operates oil and gasoline service stations in Timberville and Harrisonburg and a bowling alley in Timberville. He opened the first private parking lot in Harrisonburg, primarily for business and professional men. At Timberville he owns and operates the only public scales for weighing livestock and farm products on the Southern Railway right-of-way. For years he was vice-president of the Rockingham Red Cross and was formerly chairman of the nursing service committee. He is a member and trustee of the Timberville Church of the Brethren. He belongs to the Masonic lodge, the Shrine, and B. P. O. E. He was formerly a member of the Harrisonburg Kiwanis Club and the Ruritan Club of Plains District. In politics he is nominally a Democrat, but is independent in local elections. He was interested in the beginnings of the Spotswood Country Club, the Virginia Craftsmen, and the Harrisonburg Loan and Thrift Corporation. He finds recreation in fishing. In reading he prefers *Time*, the *Reader's Digest*, and works of biography.

On November 11, 1922, Mr. Hoover married Miss Ethel Vaughan of Timberville, their place of residence.

LAWRENCE HAROLD HOOVER
COMMONWEALTH'S ATTORNEY

Born March 27, 1906, at Timberville; grew up on his father's farm; graduated from Timberville High School, 1923; B. A., Bridgewater College, 1927; LL. B., University of Virginia, 1930; claims adjuster and attorney for Employers' Liability Assurance Corp., Ltd., four years; began practice in Harrisonburg, 1934; Commonwealth's Attorney for Rockingham County and City of Harrisonburg since 1940; member Church of the Brethren, Kiwanis Club, Masonic lodge, Elks, and professional organizations; active in Red Cross work and other civic and benevolent enterprises.

Mr. Hoover is a son of John H. and Annie R. Flory Hoover of Timberville. For more particulars concerning ancestors and family connections the reader is referred to the biographies of his father and his brother Lester, on preceding pages. After going through the Timberville schools and graduating from high school in 1923, Lawrence entered Bridgewater College, where his father had been a student in the early years of the institution, and completed the work of the freshman and sophomore years, serving as president of his class; then after a year in Emory and Henry College he returned to Bridgewater for his senior year, graduating in June, 1927. At Bridgewater he was president also of the Virginia Lee Literary Society, manager of the football team, and business manager of the college annual. In the fall of 1927 he entered the law department of the University of Virginia, where he received his degree in 1930. For the next four years or thereabouts he was claims adjuster and attorney for the U. S. branch of the Employers' Liability Assurance Corporation, Ltd., at first with his office in Roanoke, then in Harrisonburg. This is an English corporation, the pioneer in its field, which provided the first liability policies ever written.

In June, 1934, Mr. Hoover took up the private practice of law in Harrisonburg. In 1935, following his first year of practice, he was candidate for Commonwealth's Attorney on the Democratic ticket. In 1939 he ran again for the same office and was elected for the four-year term beginning January 1, 1940. Since that date he has been discharging the duties of his office with fidelity and efficiency.

From boyhood and throughout his career in college and university, Mr. Hoover took a special interest in debating and oratory. While still in high school he participated in numerous debates with representatives of other high schools, and won through to the finals in Charlottesville. At Bridgewater College he was a charter member of the chapter of Tau Kappa Alpha, national forensic fraternity, and engaged in debating contests with colleges and universities over a wide area. In his senior year at Bridgewater he won in the Virginia state intercollegiate oratorical contest, nine colleges participating. At the University in his first year he was elected captain of the debating squad and debated in contests with outstanding institutions, including the universities of North Carolina, West Virginia, Pittsburgh, and Princeton. In his first year at the University he was given the best debater's award. In his whole long series of debates he was on the losing side only once.

On June 18, 1927, Mr. Hoover married Miss Ola May of Timberville, daughter of the late Lee May (1874-1942) and Ida F. Hinegardner May, who now makes her home with Mr. and Mrs. Hoover. Of the marriage there are two children: Ann (Rebecca Anne), born May 5, 1928, and Lawrence H., Jr., born May 3, 1934. Ann is now a freshman in Harrisonburg High School; Lawrence is a pupil in the grades.

SAMUEL BEERY HOOVER

BUSINESS MAN AND CERTIFIED PUBLIC ACCOUNTANT

Born June 18, 1898, in Winchester; attended private school in Winchester; came with his parents to Harrisonburg in 1908; graduated from Harrisonburg High School in 1916; attended V. P. I., University of Virginia, and Pace Institute of Accounting, New York City; passed Virginia Certified Public Accountant examination in 1927; engaged in business in North Carolina and Virginia; farmer and apple-grower; head of the S. B. Hoover and Company, Certified Public Accountants, Harrisonburg.

Mr. Hoover spent the first ten years of his life in Winchester, where his father, Samuel Lewis Hoover, pioneered and organized the Winchester Telephone Co., which was later purchased by the Bell System. He also organized the Northern Virginia Power Co., which later was acquired by the Potomac Edison interests. Mr. S. L. Hoover was born near Timberville, September 28, 1857, son of David and Mary Zigler Hoover. He married Miss Minnie D. Beery, born December 22, 1864, near Edom, daughter of Noah W. and Kate Neff Beery. Mrs. Beery was a daughter of Daniel Neff of Shenandoah County.

Beery Hoover graduated from the Harrisonburg High School in 1916, the youngest member of his class. After leaving the University of Virginia he was assistant manager of a lumber manufacturing concern in North Carolina, and later managed a farmers' cooperative organization at Timberville, and at the same time engaged in farming and apple-growing. In 1924, following his bent for mathematics, in which he made a record in high school and at the University, he took up accounting, and in 1927 was certified by the Virginia state board. He was the first resident C. P. A. in the Valley. His firm, with offices and staff in the National Bank Building in Harrisonburg, enjoys a wide reputation. He was a cadet at V. P. I. and at present is an aircraft observer in the U. S. Army Aircraft Warning Service. He is a member of the Presbyterian Church. In the Harrisonburg Rotary Club he has a perfect attendance record since joining, September 1929. He was president of the club in 1941-42. He is also a member of the American Institute of Accountants and the Virginia Society of Public Accountants, and in the latter has served as a director. His hobbies are farm work, baseball, and other games. In 1941 he bought the famous "Fort Egypt" farm in Page County, adjoining his wife's old home. This farm and the old house on it are described in Harry M. Strickler's book, "Forerunners." The "Egypt" log house of 8 rooms, built about 1735 and believed to be the oldest in Page County, has both an inner and outer fort cellar built for defense against the Indians, and various Indian relics are preserved around the place. These historic features comport with Mr. Hoover's reading preferences in history and biography. He is fond, also, of detective stories and general news, as well as works relating to public accounting and taxation. He is secretary and a director of the Wetsel Seed Company, Inc., of Harrisonburg.

On January 26, 1923, Mr. Hoover married Miss Mary Strickler of near Luray, daughter of Elder Reuben T. and Talitha Cornwell Strickler. They have a daughter and a son: Janice Marylyn, born near Luray on February 22, 1925, and now a senior in Harrisonburg High School; and James Beery, born at Harrisonburg on October 16, 1934, and now a student in the schools of Harrisonburg.

ABNER KILPATRICK HOPKINS

DIRECTOR OF INDUSTRIAL ARTS, HARRISONBURG HIGH SCHOOL

Born August 19, 1880, near Mt. Clinton; grew up on his father's farm; attended a one-room school and West Central Academy; advanced training in Washington and Lee University (1904-8), Madison College and the University of Virginia (summer session); teacher at Dale Enterprise, principal of Mt. Clinton High School, S. Main Street Graded School, Harrisonburg, 1909-20, and coach of high-school athletics; director of industrial arts in Harrisonburg High School since 1920; elder in Presbyterian Church since 1932; member of N. E. A. and other professional organizations, Sons of Confederate Veterans, etc.

Professor Hopkins is the 9th child of Lewis Chrisman Hopkins (b. Sept. 4, 1843) and wife Cornelia Whitmore (b. Aug. 1838). He is a great-great-grandson of Archibald Hopkins, who, with his brothers John and William, came from New York State to what is now Rockingham County, Va., about the middle of the 18th century. Archibald and his brothers acquired large tracts of land here, including the homestead and farm now owned and occupied by William S. Fallis and neighboring areas. In a census of Rockingham County taken in 1784, and published as part of the first Federal census (1790), Captain John Hopkins is listed as head of a family of 10 and Archibald Hopkins, Sr., as head of a family of five, besides himself. Archibald, a son of Archibald, Sr., had a son Archibald who married Sarah Ann Hopkins, whose 7th child was Lewis Chrisman Hopkins, father of Abner K., the subject of this sketch. Lewis Chrisman Hopkins was a V. M. I. cadet in 1861-62, and for the remainder of the Civil War served in the Virginia cavalry, C. S. A.

After schooling in West Central Academy under Principal I. S. Wampler and his able associates, Professor Hopkins taught a year at Pine Grove (Dale Enterprise). For the next four years he was a student at Washington and Lee. During the session of 1908-09 he was principal of the Mt. Clinton High School. Since 1909 he has been connected in various capacities with the schools of Harrisonburg, where his efficient service of 30-odd years has won for him an enviable place in the affection of his pupils and in the history of the city. In 1914-15 he was president of the Rockingham Teachers Association. For some years he was a member of the local Kiwanis Club. From 1918 to 1932 he was a deacon in the Harrisonburg Presbyterian Church, and since 1932 has been an elder. He is a lover of music and all kinds of athletic sports and contests. In his reading he gives preference to current history and works on industrial art. The construction of novelties and projects in handwork, first a hobby, then an avocation, has become a regular employment, in which he directs the students under his charge. The work of his classes in manual arts has won merited recognition.

On August 22, 1912, Professor Hopkins married Miss Anna Price Firebaugh, born March 22, 1878, near Rockbridge Baths, daughter of Robert Dunlap Firebaugh (b. May 13, 1842) and his wife, Sarah Jane Clemmer (b. Oct. 20, 1845). Mrs. Hopkins died March 18, 1934, leaving two daughters: Evelyn Price and Janet Cornelia; a son, Robert Lewis, died in infancy. Evelyn Price, born October 20, 1914, educated in the Harrisonburg and Rockingham public schools, is now her father's housekeeper. Janet Cornelia, born December 13, 1915, is a graduate of Harrisonburg High School and Madison College. After teaching a year (1937-38) in Beltsville, Md., she entered upon her present work as a teacher in the Pleasant Hill School, near Harrisonburg.

CHARLES HERBERT HUFFMAN
EDUCATOR AND AUTHOR

Born February 27, 1887, near Bridgewater; attended public schools in Rockingham and Augusta; B. A., Bridgewater College, 1914; M. A., Clark University, 1915; Ph. D., University of Virginia, 1920; teacher in public schools of Augusta; assistant professor of English, U. Va.; professor, Austin College, Texas, Roanoke College, and Madison College (since 1924); Raven, Pi Gamma Mu, Tau Kappa Alpha; past master Rockingham Union Lodge No. 27, A. F. & A. M.; Lt. Gov. 5th Div., Capital District, Kiwanis International.

Dr. Huffman's father was Brown M. (1849-1915), his mother, Mary M. Landis (1850-1906); his sisters and brothers: Cora V., Mrs. Arey, born 1875; Sarah R., Mrs. Alexander, 1877; Clinton C., 1879; Walter B., 1882; Hattie E., 1884-1887; Jesse Wade, 1890. His grandparents were Benjamin (1803-1877) and Rebecca Thuma Huffman (1809-1896), and William and Sarah Reeves Landis. Benjamin's father, Solomon Hoffmann (the spelling prior to 1825), was born in Berks Co., Pa., February 17, 1774; in 1780 came with his father, Valentine (c. 1720-1803), to Rockingham; in 1796 married Elizabeth Dinkle (born in Frederick Co., Md.), daughter of Daniel and Susanna Dinkle. Solomon had brothers and sisters: George, Christian, Abraham, Elizabeth Messerly, Catherine Black, Mary Venices, and Ester Butt.

In recent years Dr. Huffman has devoted a good deal of attention to the history of his forebears; and such items as are given above will in time to come be one of the most valuable features of this book. Always of a studious and inquiring disposition, he has been distinguished as a painstaking student, and as a teacher his procedure is methodical and scholarly. At the University of Virginia the high class of his work was attested by his election to the Raven Society and by his appointment as a teacher in the English department. After further experience in the teaching of his specialty at Austin College, Sherman, Texas, and in Roanoke College at Salem, Va., he was called to Madison College in 1924, where his work has been outstanding. He is a member of the National Council of English Teachers, the American Association of University Professors, and the Virginia Education Association. His work has not been limited to teaching. He is the author of various notable publications including "The Eighteenth Century Novel in Theory and Practice," "The Types of Literature," and numerous articles and book reviews.

Dr. Huffman grew up in sight of St. Michael's Reformed Church, south of Bridgewater; he is now a member of St. Stephen's Reformed Church in Harrisonburg, and one of the Consistory. In 1935 he served as master of the Harrisonburg Masonic lodge, and he holds membership in Rockingham Royal Arch Chapter No. 6. An active Kiwanian, he was president of the Harrisonburg club in 1939, and has recently been elected lieutenant-governor of the Fifth Division, Capital District, of Kiwanis International.

In 1917 Dr. Huffman married Miss Roxie R. Riddle, daughter of the late James A. and Rebecca Obaugh Riddle of Bridgewater. Dr. and Mrs. Huffman have two children: Vesta Gwendolyn, who, in June, 1941, married Lieut. Claude V. Smith, Jr., of Harrisonburg, and Herbert Garland, who is now a student in the University of Virginia and volunteer in the U. S. Naval Reserve.

ZIMMERMAN DAVIS JACKSON

AUDITOR AND BANKER

Born August 8, 1903, in Summerville, S. C.; attended schools in Blacksburg, Warrenton, and Alexandria, Va.; graduated from Alexandria High School in 1920; student in George Washington Univ. two years; while employed in an Alexandria bank, completed night classes in accounting and business administration in Benjamin Franklin Univ., receiving the Bachelor of Commercial Science degree in 1929; special agent F. B. I., 1929-32; senior examiner, Maryland State Banking Department, 1932-37; executive vice-president First National Bank of Harrisonburg since 1937; a director of the Harrisonburg-Rockingham Chamber of Commerce; etc.

Mr. Jackson is the eldest of four sons of Rev. Eugene B. Jackson, D. D., well known Baptist minister of Harrisonburg, now retired, son of John Richard Jackson (1820-1879), prominent lawyer and state's attorney of Warren Co., Va., during the Civil War, and Cornelia Maria Kerfoot (1834-1900). His mother, Nela McIver (Davis) Jackson (1870-1932), was a daughter of Col. Zimmerman Davis (1834-1910), influential military and civil leader, and Cornelia Jeannette McIver (1838-1912), of Charleston, S. C. His ancestors in both Virginia and South Carolina have always been active in civil life and have served their country in its wars, including the Revolution. By reason of his father's residence as pastor in different cities, he enjoyed opportunities for wide acquaintance and schooling. In Alexandria High School he played football, basket-ball, and baseball. After two years in George Washington University he, at age 18, entered business as an employee of the Alexandria Natl. Bank, but continued his study of commercial science in Benjamin Franklin University night classes. During his senior year he was chief auditor of Science Service, Inc., newspaper syndicate of Washington. In the spring of 1929 he became a special agent (accountant) of the F. B. I., Dept. of Justice, and for three years traveled throughout the South and East investigating criminal violations of Federal statutes, principally in national banks. In 1932, by competitive examination, he won appointment as senior examiner with the Md. State Banking Dept., and as such participated in and planned reorganization of Maryland banks in the famous banking holiday of 1933. In 1937 he accepted his present position as executive vice-president of the First Natl. Bank of Harrisonburg. His coming to Harrisonburg, he says, was in accordance with his desire to quit traveling, to live in the Shenandoah Valley, and to raise his children in a cultural atmosphere removed from the hubbub of big cities.

In 1930 Mr. Jackson married Miss Harriet Nourse Myers of Baltimore, upon her leaving Goucher College in that city. She is the daughter of Dr. and Mrs. J. Sidwell Myers of Baltimore, and was born in Westminister, Md., June 4, 1910. Her uncle founded the famous Sidwell Friends' School in Washington and operated it until his death in 1934. She is also descended from James Nourse, prominent in Revolutionary affairs under appointment of George Washington. Mr. and Mrs. Jackson have two children: Edith Nourse, born in Charlotte, N. C., January 26, 1932, and Zimmerman Davis, Jr., born in Baltimore, July 25, 1935.

Mr. Jackson is a member of the Baptist Church; a Democrat, though not active in politics; and is identified with various civic and patriotic enterprises. Besides those already mentioned, he is a member of the War Bond Committee of the Va. Bankers Assn., Va. Reserve Militia (Minute Men), an air raid warden, and actively participated in and led in the sale of war bonds in Harrisonburg and Rockingham County. He has no special hobbies, but enjoys outdoor activities.

JAMES CHAPMAN JOHNSTON
EDUCATOR, SCIENTIST, AND AUTHOR

Born April 29, 1875, in Harrisonburg; attended Mercersburg Academy and Columbian Univ.; graduate student at Harvard, Johns Hopkins, and Georgetown Univ.; principal of Harrisonburg High School; professor in State Teachers (Madison) College, 1910-27, and eight years secretary of the faculty; editor of the *Daily News* and the *Virginia Teacher;* active and prominent in Masonry; a charter member and one year president of the Harrisonburg Kiwanis Club; a promoter of the Rockingham Public Library; a vestryman of Emmanuel Episcopal Church; author of "Biography, the Literature of Personality" and other works; died in Harrisonburg, June 18, 1927.

Professor Johnston was a son of Judge Robert and Laura Criss Johnston. Robert was a native of Rockbridge, and after law study in Lexington was State Auditor of Virginia for several years; he served in the Confederate Congress and later practiced law in Harrisonburg where he was judge of th county court from January 1, 1880, until his death in 1885. Of him Judge James Kenney said: "I knew Judge Johnston well, and admired him for his ability and sterling integrity. As a lawyer he had but few equals at the bar of this State; as a Judge, his ermine was pure and unspotted; as a man, his integrity was never questioned." Judge Johnston's mother was Jane Montgomery, daughter of Humphrey, a Revolutionary soldier, who died in 1799.

Thus descending from distinguished families of the Old Dominion, Professor Johnston inherited the best traditions and well maintained them in his own career. As a finished scholar, a skilful teacher, a trenchant writer, and a man of delightful personal qualities, he won the esteem of his thousands of pupils and other friends. A graduate of Harrisonburg High School, he later served as its principal for a number of years, and under his guidance the institution took first rank and won general recognition from the best accrediting agencies. Within the period of 17 years that he was a member of the faculty of the State Teachers (now Madison) College he founded the *Virginia Teacher*, a high-class educational magazine, and served as its editor. Following his untimely death, one of the college buildings was named in his honor, as a tribute to the love and esteem in which he was held. Shortly after his death the Century Company of New York City brought out his notable book, "Biography, the Literature of Personality," a volume that was highly rated by competent critics. The book is typical of the author, whose discriminating taste, companionable disposition, and gentleness among family and friends won him admiration and affection.

On April 15, 1911, Professor Johnston married Miss Althea Loose of Harrisonburg and Manassas, daughter of Rev. Elmer Palm Loose, Presbyterian minister, and his wife, Althea Maitland Bennett, a native of London, Ontario. Of this marriage were born five children: Jaqueline Palm, B. S. of Madison College, who married William Thomas Rice, now a captain in the U. S. Army, and has a son, John Thomas; James, Jr., B. S. and A. M. of V. P. I., now a captain in the U. S. Army; Robert Maitland, now in the armed forces of the United States in the Pacific area; Aaron Montgomery, A. B. and A. M. of Columbia University, now a member of the U. S. Air Force; and Althea Margaret, now a senior in Westhampton College, Richmond.

The Harrisonburg Kiwanis Club endowed the Rockingham Public Library with a fund of $1000 in memory of Professor Johnston, and his portrait was recently placed in Madison Library by one of the senior classes. Mrs. Johnston, one of the first teachers in the college, has been on the faculty again since 1927.

ELMER ANDREW JORDAN
FARMER, STOCK-RAISER, AND SUPERVISOR

Born June 10, 1897, 7 miles west of Bridgewater; educated in public schools and Bridgewater Academy; with his brother and others, owner of farms in Rockingham and Loudoun; director of Rockingham Farm Bureau, Planters Bank of Bridgewater, Southern States Marketing Cooperative, Shenandoah Valley Electric Cooperative, Rockingham Turkey Festival; member of Rockingham Board of Supervisors; president Farmers Mutual Telephone Co.; a deacon in Beaver Creek Church of the Brethren.

Mr. Jordan's father, George Samuel Jordan, died when Elmer was 18, and his mother, born Almira Jane Hess, became an unfailing and wise guide. His father was born November 27, 1869, near Bridgewater, son of Andrew J. Jordan (born August 20, 1842) and his wife, Catherine Wine (born July 6, 1841). His mother, born at Sangersville, April 26, 1865, was a daughter of Andrew Hess (born January 17, 1829) and his wife, Annie Miller (born May 24, 1832).

In 1920 Mr. Jordan and his brother, Oliver W., rented the home place and began a partnership as Jordan Brothers, which is still continued. In 1921 they started a small hatchery, which in 1932 was enlarged in capacity from 7200 eggs to 31,000. In 1938 they installed new and complete electric equipment, increasing the capacity to 56,000 eggs. In recent years they have raised about 100,000 broilers annually. In 1923 they bought the home place and in 1936 the P. S. Miller farm. The next year they purchased the Charlie Painter farm near Mt. Crawford, and in 1939, with J. Abe and Nelson Craun, they acquired a livestock farm in Loudoun County on which they have about 900 hogs, sheep, and cattle. In 1941 they bought the Paul Myers farm at Mt. Crawford.

Although still a young man, Mr. Jordan has had an unusual career as a successful business man and as an active participant in commercial, civic, and religious enterprises, as already indicated. Besides the connections mentioned on the preceding page, he has been vice-president since 1939 of the Rockingham Poultry Cooperative, and since 1941 has served on the executive committee as well as the board of directors of the Southern States Marketing Cooperative, with headquarters in Richmond. He took office as a member of the Rockingham County Board of Supervisors in 1940. He is a member of the Bridgewater Rotary Club and of the Defense Savings Committee of Rockingham County. As a member and deacon of the Beaver Creek Church of the Brethren, he serves on the ministerial committee. His favorite hobby is traveling. He states that on account of a nervous breakdown when he was eight years old, and the death of his father ten years later, he was not able to get much schooling, but he has evidently profited from the school of experience. He gives much credit to his mother.

On February 18, 1920, Mr. Jordan married Miss Fay Anna Huffman of Luray, who died July 8, 1933, leaving two children: Ruth Almira, born May 2, 1921, and Dwight Huffman Jordan, born April 24, 1923. On July 18, 1934, at Bridgewater, Mr. Jordan married for his second wife Miss Nannie V. Miller, a native of Pendleton County, West Virginia. Of the second marriage there is one child, Evelyn Catherine Jordan, born October 14, 1941.

WILLIAM M. JOSEPH

FARMER, LIVESTOCK DEALER, AND BUSINESS MAN

Born October 19, 1879, near Rawley Springs; grew up on his father's farm and became an expert teamster; on an engineering corps about one year, surveying railroads in West Virginia; at the age of 21 began dealing in livestock; moved to Harrisonburg in 1911; engaged extensively in farming, buying and selling farms, and handling livestock; served several terms on the city council; a director of the Rockingham National Bank; appraiser for the Federal Land Bank of Baltimore; an organizer, a director, and president of the Shenandoah Valley Livestock Sales; died at Harrisonburg on January 13, 1941.

Mr. Joseph was a son of John C. and Sally Ann Hoover Joseph. His father served under Captain E. A. Shands in Co. I, 7th Va. Cavalry, C. S. A. John C. bought a farm about three miles from Rawley Springs where William was born and reared. The latter bought the farm and part of it is still held by his estate. William attended the local public school and helped his father haul bark and lumber to market in Harrisonburg, taking two days to make a round trip with the four-horse team. On these trips William always took along his bird dog and gun, with which he killed rabbits, turkeys, and pheasants. By this means he earned enough to buy his first horse and buggy. After about one year with a corps of railroad engineers in West Virginia he, at the age of 21, began purchasing small lots of livestock in Highland County, making the four-day drive to Harrisonburg where they were shipped to eastern markets. This business he developed to large proportions, continuing it after he moved to Harrisonburg in 1911, where he built his splendid residence at the northeastern edge of the city. He was a strong believer in farms for investment and at one time owned as many as seven in different parts of the Valley. He would sell one and buy another which promised better to suit his needs.

At the same time that Mr. Joseph was handling farm lands and dealing extensively in livestock he participated in various civic and financial activities. He was a director of the Rockingham National Bank and of the Federal Land Bank, and served for some time on the Harrisonburg city council. He was an organizer and the first president of the Shenandoah Valley Livestock Sales, with headquarters in Harrisonburg, in which capacity he was succeeded by his son Albert. He was a lover of good horses, having always on hand a large number of the best. He was recognized as an expert judge of horses and other livestock. He was a member of the Methodist Church, and was a Republican in politics. With a sincere interest in his fellow men, he had a host of friends, with whom he always was ready to converse in a discussion of their interests and problems. A friend said of him: "Mr. Joseph was one man big enough and human enough to be willing to help all who came to him for assistance of any kind, sympathy, cash, or endorsements. His greatest weakness was in being unable to say No to any who came to him for help." He took a keen interest in public affairs. For recreation, he was fond of fishing and hunting.

On Dec. 23, 1904, Mr. Joseph married Miss Sadie Lynn Arey, born June 25, 1882, daughter of John W. and Katherine Roberson Arey. Of the marriage were born four children. Evangeline Arey, June 23, 1906, who married David H. Liskey, Feb. 9, 1929; Albert John, May 14, 1908, who married Miss Louise Yancey, Dec. 10, 1941; Virginia, June 23, 1914, now Mrs. George Joseph Kagey, married Nov. 29, 1936; and Gladys Roselie, Sept. 21, 1919, who married Raleigh William Shifflett on August 10, 1941.

JAMES M. KAVANAUGH

HOTEL PROPRIETOR

Born December 25, 1869, on a farm two miles north of Harrisonburg; educated in Harrisonburg schools; as a young man, was active in athletics and in the fire companies; owner and driver of winning horses for 45 years; Democratic committee-man for 50 years; amateur horticulturist; owner and operator of the Kavanaugh Hotel since 1905.

Mr. Kavanaugh's parents, James Kavanaugh, a native of Ireland, and Mary Hicky, born in Hardy County, W. Va., moved to Rockingham County about 1857 to a farm on Crotzer Road, where the subject of this sketch was born. About 1859 the elder Kavanaugh bought and operated the Virginia Hotel. About 1875 Mr. Kavanaugh senior sold his farm and moved his family to town and they made their home in the hotel.

James M., who was fond of baseball and other sports, was also on the lookout for profitable employment. He says: "When I was a boy of 14 or 15 I would work for 75 cents a day. My first money was earned in the harvest field at 75 cents a day; later I received $1.00 a day." As a young man he was considered the best athlete in the city and county. In 1923 the Valley League baseball team, which he managed, won the league pennant.

Some years after his father's death, Mr. Kavanaugh and his brother Joseph built the Kavanaugh Hotel, with 53 rooms, on the site of the old Virginia Hotel. The new hotel was opened May 1, 1905. Joseph died in 1911 from the effects of an automobile accident. About 1913 James M. built an annex to the hotel of 32 rooms, and in or about 1923, due to the growth of business, he added another annex of 32 rooms. In this well-known and popular hotel he takes a just pride. It is enrolled in the American Hotel Association, the Virginia Hotel Association, and the Southern Hotel Association.

Mr. Kavanaugh has always been fond of horses. For some 45 years he drove his own horses in races. In 1910 or thereabouts he had the best horse in the Grand Circuit and defeated Pop Geers, the greatest driver of his time.

On November 18, 1891, Mr. Kavanaugh married Miss Addie I. Conrad, who was born September 30, 1870, near Charles Town, W. Va. In 1941 they celebrated their golden anniversary at a dinner in the Kavanaugh Hotel, with more than 100 friends. They have no children. On top of a little mountain at Rawley Springs Mr. and Mrs. Kavanaugh have a summer home with all modern appointments. There they spend much time, and Mr. Kavanaugh takes great pleasure in growing flowers. Every year he grows 350 or 400 beautiful dahlias, which he tends himself. The house is supplied with water from the Harrisonburg city system, and river water is forced to the top of the mountain for the lawn and flower garden. The grounds comprise about 18 acres. Here Mr. and Mrs. Kavanaugh live every year from June 1 to October 1.

As already indicated, Mr. Kavanaugh has always been active in politics, and he is a careful reader of the newspapers. Born a Catholic, he is a member of the Holy Name Society of the Church. His charities are well known—he has never turned a deaf ear to any one in need, and has often assisted others when he could ill afford it. He was a charter member of the Harrisonburg Elks and a long time member of the Kiwanis Club, but resigned from both some years ago.

QUINCY G. KAYLOR

FARMER AND BUSINESS MAN

Born February 8, 1859, at Kaylor's Mill, now Harriston, Augusta County; attended local schools in Augusta and Rockingham; a farmer, merchant, and shipper of apples and vegetables; a charter member and a director of the Rockingham Farm Bureau; judge of elections at Pleasant Valley precinct; owner of Kaylor's Park; active in advancing genealogy and local history.

Mr. Kaylor's father was Lewis Washington Kaylor, born at Crimora, Augusta County, Va., November 12, 1823, a son of Peter Kaylor, who was born February 14, 1795, near McGaheysville, one of 10 children, all of whom except Peter went with their mother to Bellefontaine, Ohio, between 1828 and 1832. Their father, George Kaylor, son of Michael, came from Pennsylvania soon after 1760 to East Rockingham, then a part of Augusta County. Lewis Kaylor's wife was Elizabeth D. Cline, daughter of Peter Cline of near Friedens Church; his mother, Quincy's grandmother, was Sarah Kyger, daughter of Jacob Kyger.

Q. G. Kaylor's earliest memory goes back to a day when he was two and a half years old and got lost in the Blue Ridge Mountain, having wandered away from his home. With more than 100 people hunting for him, he was out from eight o'clock one morning until nine the next, when George Peters, Henry Weast, and Billy Bunch found him near Black Rock Springs.

He attended six different country schools, three in Augusta County, three in Rockingham. The first was a pay school in a log house about 12 by 15 feet, between Grottoes and Hariston; the next, the Gillie Hamner school, a free school, between Hariston and the Rockfish Gap road; then one, in another small log house, at Port Republic, taught by Clay Lewis; another was called the Battle Glen School; it was in a log cabin at Mt. Meridian and the teacher was Dr. Harnsberger; the last one was Mt. Carmel, between Dayton and Kaylor's Park; there, he says, he graduated.

Most of his life Mr. Kaylor has been a farmer. He also engaged, in partnership with his brother William, in milling, then in merchandising at Rushville and Mt. Crawford Depot. Around 1890, as a member of the firm of Kaylor & Irvine, he engaged in the business of buying and barreling apples from farm orchards and selling them in carload lots in the South and West. When there was a shortage of apples in Rockingham they bought Baldwin apples in New York State, also potatoes and cabbage, and sold them to local merchants and others at the Coffman warehouse in Harrisonburg. For some years Mr. Kaylor was engaged in selling and building wire fence for the farmers.

On October 12, 1897, Mr. Kaylor married Miss Annie Lee Bowman, daughter of John S. and Mary Elizabeth Bowman. From this union were born five children: Robert Dewey, who died in infancy; Harry Roy, born April 11, 1901, who married Lula Firebaugh, October 10, 1929; Irene Virginia, born February 4, 1903, who married Tracy Claytor, June 6, 1930; John Lewis, born November 18, 1906; and Elmore Baxter, born July 16, 1911, who married Nureta Airey, October 23, 1937.

Mr. Kaylor's home is near Kaylor's Park. He is owner, also, of the General Samuel Lewis farm on Port Republic battlefield, where he is accustomed to assemble several hundred of his friends each summer for a watermelon feast. He and his family are members of the Reformed Church at Mt. Crawford.

WILLIAM JACKSON KAYLOR
FARMER AND BUSINESS MAN

Born October 23, 1862, at Harriston, Augusta County; grew up in Augusta and Rockingham; attended schools at Port Republic, Mt. Meridian, and Mt. Carmel; merchant at Mt. Crawford Station, Rushville, and again at Mt. Crawford Station; miller at Pleasant Valley; B. & O. station agent at Mt. Crawford, 1905-37; a director of The National Bank of Harrisonburg; member of the Methodist Church; Jr. O. U. A. M.; farmer and raiser of livestock.

Mr. Kaylor is a son of Lewis W. (born November 12, 1823) and Elizabeth Dorcas Cline Kaylor (born June 15, 1832), and a grandson of Peter (born February 14, 1795) and Sarah Kyger Kaylor (born February 27, 1804). He is a direct descendant of the Revolutionary soldier, Michael Kaylor (Kohler), who came from Germany to Philadelphia on the ship *Britannia,* October 26, 1767. He spent the first six years of his life at Harriston, then three years at Port Republic, where the family lived during that time. He saw the bridge over North River at Port wash away in the great flood of October, 1870. The family then moved to Mt. Meridian, from there to Leroy, and then to Kaylor's Park, near Harrisonburg, where his parents died. In 1882 he and his brother, P. C. Kaylor, opened a mercantile store at Mt. Crawford Station. Next he clerked for four years in Emanuel Roller's store near Friedens Church. He then bought out the Roller stock and, with T. J. Johnson, resumed merchandising at Mt. Crawford Station. Selling his half interest in this business to W. H. Wine, he bought a half interest in the Pleasant Valley flour mill. Later he traded his mill property to E. W. Carpenter for store property at Rushville, where he was in business for seven years. Selling at Rushville to Jasper Smith, he, in 1904, bought the farm and store property which he now owns at Mt. Crawford Station from W. H. Wine, thus returning to the place where he had been in business twice before. Since then he has been farming and merchandising, and is probably the oldest country merchant in the county. For 32 years he was B. & O. station agent at Mt. Crawford, until November 30, 1937, when he was retired with a pension. He is a member of the Methodist Church and the Junior Order United American Mechanics, and has been a director of The National Bank of Harrisonburg since its beginning. In politics he is a Democrat. His hobby is fine horses and other livestock. His favorite reading is in the *Reader's Digest* and current literature.

On September 10, 1889, Mr. Kaylor married Miss Minnie Margaret Showalter, born March 11, 1868, daughter of John H. Showalter and his wife, Hettie Whitesell. Mr. and Mrs. Kaylor are the parents of five daughters: Lillye (Mrs. Ralph S. Monger), born July 8, 1892; Rose (Mrs. Elmer O. Rodes), born October 5, 1896; Violet Grace, born June 16, 1901; Ivy (Mrs. John S. Peters), born September 6, 1903; and Pansye (Mrs. Ralph P. Phillips), born July 19, 1905.

Mr. Kaylor and his brothers, Quincy G. and the late Peter Cline Kaylor, have taken a commendable interest in genealogy and local history. Due to their efforts in this field many records of old families and churches have been preserved and made available to the public. The house in which Mr. Kaylor lives at Mt. Crawford Station is an excellent example of the brick dwellings that were erected in many parts of the Valley between 1810 and 1850. Several mantels in this house are fine specimens of the old-time woodcarver's art.

NATHANIEL HARRISON KEEZELL
CIVIL ENGINEER, FARMER, AND MERCHANT

Born June 25, 1898, at Keezletown; attended graded and high school at Keezletown and (1913-15) Harrisonburg High School; student in civil engineering at Virginia Military Institute, receiving the B. S. degree in 1919; high school principal for two sessions; engineer for Atlantic Coast Realty Co. in North Carolina and South Carolina; manager of his father's farm, 1923-31; owner and operator of the farm until May, 1942; since then in business in Harrisonburg; member of the Presbyterian Church, Elks lodge, Ruritan Club, etc.

Mr. Keezell is the youngest son of George Bernard Keezell (1854-1931), a successful farmer and business man and distinguished legislator, and his wife, Mary Kathryn Hannah (1858-1902). His grandfather, George Keezell (1795-1862), was a soldier in the War of 1812. The latter's wife was Amanda Fitzallen Peale (1815-1890). His great-grandfather, George Keezell, in 1781, laid out 100 acres of his plantation for a town in which a number of his neighbors at once purchased lots. Among these purchasers were John Harrison, Cornelius Cain, Abraham and Thomas Lincoln, John Armentrout, and David Laird. This town (Keezletown) was established by Act of Assembly, December 7, 1791. It is located on the old Indian Road which in early times was the main highway through the Valley, and it has long been familiar as the Keezletown Road. The Keezell homestead is located on this highway, a short distance northeast of the village. Keezletown was a rival of Harrisonburg for the location of the county-seat, and interesting traditions have come down concerning the competitive efforts of George Keezell and Thomas Harrison on behalf of their respective establishments.

After his graduation from Harrisonburg High School in 1915, Nat H. Keezell spent four years as a student in Virginia Military Institute at Lexington, graduating in 1919. The next two years he engaged in teaching as principal of the high schools at Keezletown and Chatham Hill, Smyth County, Va., and then for the next year worked as an engineer for the Atlantic Coast Realty Company in the Carolinas. Returning to Keezletown in 1923, he managed his father's farm until the death of the latter, June 22, 1931. He inherited part of the farm and operated it until May, 1942, when he sold out and bought an interest in the shoe store in Harrisonburg, which is now carried on under the firm name of Williams & Keezell, Inc.

For some time preceding the close of World War I, Mr. Keezell was in officers training at Camp Lee, Va. His brother, Captain Rembrandt P. Keezell, who died some years ago, had a distinguished record in war service overseas. Nat H. has always taken an active interest in civic and political affairs. In 1939 he was a candidate for Rockingham County Treasurer, but was defeated by Mr. Michael H. Harrison. He is a member of the Presbyterian Church, the Benevolent and Protective Order of Elks, and the Keezletown Ruritan Club. Of the last named he was president in 1941. He finds recreation in fishing and hunting, and in his reading prefers informative works. He also keeps abreast of current affairs by means of newspapers and magazines.

On July 24, 1931, Mr. Keezell married Miss Helen Anne Carper, who was born on June 14, 1900, at Blacksburg, Va., daughter of Mr. and Mrs. J. B. Carper. Mr. and Mrs. Keezell have a son, Nathaniel Harrison Keezell, Jr., born January 18,1938. Since leaving the farm they have established their residence in Harrisonburg.

WILLIAM HAMPTON KEISTER

SUPERINTENDENT OF HARRISONBURG SCHOOLS

Born August 18, 1865, in Highland County, Va.; attended Doe Hill schools and McDowell Academy; student four years at Washington and Lee University; summer student at the University of Virginia and the University of the South; teacher in McDowell Academy; came to Harrisonburg in 1894; principal of the High School; superintendent of the city schools since 1916; elder in the Presbyterian Church.

Mr. Keister's parents were William Renick and Martha McCoy Keister. He was named for his father, a C. S. A. veteran, and General Wade Hampton. His father transmitted to him wit and good fellowship; his mother, by strict discipline, taught him respect for law and authority; the family doctor, Harrison Jones, by a chance expression of confidence, gave him his first great inspiration. Early in life he learned to endure hardships, face dangers, and follow rugged paths, day or night.

In 1894 he began his career in Harrisonburg as principal of the public school, which then was by no means so popular as now. For the first three years he taught all the high-school branches, working every period of the day. In a few years he was made supervising principal of both white and colored schools, and in 1916 was appointed superintendent of the city division, but continued doing some teaching until 1927. He has seen six permanent school buildings added to those of 1894, and the white enrolment grow from 165 to 1584, while the colored enrolment has reached 200. He is held in affection by the 1,135 graduates of the high school, each of whom he remembers personally. Since 1909 the city schools, under his guidance, have cooperated successfully with the State Teachers College, now Madison College, in teacher-training. He has been justly honored by the teachers of Virginia in their various organizations. In 1911 he was elected president of the State Association in Richmond. He is a life member of the National Education Association, in which he has been Virginia Director. His high school has received highest ranking by all accrediting agencies.

On May 24, 1934, when he rounded out forty years of service in Harrisonburg, Superintendent Keister was the guest of honor at a notable meeting in Wilson Hall, at the State Teachers College, when the city school board presented his portrait and distinguished graduates of his high school and leading educators of the State participated in an elaborate program.

On September 4, 1900, Mr. Keister married Miss Virginia Fletcher of Harrisonburg, daughter of Abner K. Fletcher. The city has been his home and in a real sense is his town. In it he has stood by his job through thick and thin, always an asset, long an institution. His fellow teachers have given him loyal support, and with him many have become distinguished. The school board, the city council, and other officials have upheld him in merited confidence; the patrons of the schools trust him as a friend, the children love him as a father. Even his enemies recognize his honesty and generosity. In his church and in the Masonic fraternity he has been placed in offices of honor and trust. As a member of the Rotary Club, in the local chamber of commerce, and in other associations and activities he has demonstrated his comradeship and public spirit. The schools of Harrisonburg are his hobby; the welfare of the children in the schools and the men and women who have gone out from them is his chief life interest. He can look to the past with justifiable pride, while he faces the future with unshaken courage.

GEORGE WARDER KELLER

PHARMACIST AND BUSINESS MAN

Born September 8, 1880, at Massanetta Springs; grew up in Bridgewater where he attended schools; employed in G. R. Berlin's printery; registered pharmacist while in Ott's drug store, Harrisonburg; student in W. & L. University, 1903-04; manager drug store, Lewisburg, W. Va., 1904-08; located in Huntington, W. Va., 1908; druggist and promoter of natural gas wells; secretary-treasurer and general manager of Huntington-Oklahoma Oil Co. and Midway Gas Co.; vestryman in Trinity Episcopal Church, Huntington.

Mr. Keller's father, who died September 1, 1880, was George W., born at Tom's Brook, Shenandoah County, Va., a son of Samuel Keller and his wife, Frances Baxter, a native of Spotsylvania County. His mother was born Elizabeth Rebecca McLeod, near Dayton, Rockingham County. She died in Bridgewater, September, 1913. Her daughters: Clara, Mrs. E. R. Harrison (died in September, 1921); Margaret, Mrs. J. A. Raum; Stella, unmarried. The Kellers have been a prominent family of Shenandoah County since colonial times. George Keller, born in Bavaria in 1712, came to Bucks County, Pa., where he married Barbara Ann Hottel about 1734. He located in Shenandoah County, Va., where he, his son John, and other members of the family took part in the Revolution. An extended genealogy of the Keller-Hottel-Fravel families has been published.

George W. Keller, the subject of this sketch, early gave evidence of the business ability that has since distinguished him. While in Ott's drug store, Harrisonburg, he was offered a place in the firm. When he located in Huntington, in the fall of 1908, he purchased a half interest in the Frederick Pharmacy, one of the largest drug stores in West Virginia at that time. Later he sold a part interest to Roy Bird Cook of Charleston, the well-known pharmacist and historian, and the firm did business under the name of the Keller-Cook Drug Company. After some years Mr. Keller disposed of his drug business to devote his whole time to the development of gas in the natural gas fields of West Virginia. He organized the Sovereign Gas Company, with several of the leading business men of Huntington. They drilled 72 gas wells on their property. Later he organized the Huntington-Oklahoma Oil Company and the Midway City Gas Company. At present he is secretary-treasurer and general manager of these two companies, with offices in the First Huntington National Bank building.

On June 3, 1908, Mr. Keller married Miss Mary Simms of Huntington. Their children: Katherine Elizabeth, born April 2, 1910, died September 6, 1912; George Simms, born June 26, 1921, attended Washington and Lee University three years. He is now (1942) in the Naval Air Corps under training for the air service. He is a member of the Phi Kappa Sigma Fraternity, as is his father.

Mr. Keller and his family are Episcopalians, members of the Trinity Episcopal Church, in which he is a vestryman. He says that he enjoys reading biographical sketches, history, current literature, etc. He claims no hobbies— "Not much for clubs or sports; never had time." He is a 32d degree Mason.

Further in regard to his family, Mr. Keller states that his father was for a time in Captain Sites's company, C. S. A. Due to ill health, he was transferred to the commissary department. His grandfather, John Henry McLeod, was born in Nova Scotia. He married Elizabeth Fishburn of near Fort Defiance, Augusta County, Va.

MRS. HANORA FLYNN KELLEY

HARRISONBURG RELIGIOUS LEADER AND BENEFACTRESS

A native of Limerick County, Ireland; married John Kelley in Rockingham County, Va.; long a resident of Harrisonburg, where she was known for hospitality and good works; a leader in providing a place of worship for the Catholics; an astute business woman, active in buying and handling real estate; died in Harrisonburg, March 17, 1885.

(This sketch was written by Mrs. Kelley's granddaughter, Mary Virginia Kelley Farver, q. v., page 130.)

At an early age Hanora Flynn came to America, settling in Rockingham County, where later she met and married John Kelley, also from Ireland. He was employed in building the railroad, which was so vital to the Valley's growth and development. To this union were born five children: the late Martin J. Kelley of Chicago; John E. Kelley, the oldest living active merchant and property-owner of Harrisonburg; Mary, who died early in life; the late Bridget A. Wallace, proprietress of the old Revere House on S. Main Street; and Edward, who died in infancy.

Mrs. Kelley was very active in the religious and community life of the county and city, and for this she is most remembered and loved. During the Civil War, when the Valley was battle-scarred, she successfully concealed in a secret attic at her home, still standing, flour and meat, that her neighbors might not go hungry. In fact, her home became in reality a Civil War canteen center. No one left her home without food. Her greatest feat and daring came when the Confederacy was about to fall, when she, a lone woman afoot, set out through enemy lines and multiple dangers, over the Blue Ridge Mountains and on down to Richmond, to exchange the worthless Confederate money for gold. Secretly and prayerfully she made that journey, not to enrich herself, but that her community might have a church in which to worship. Her first act, on returning, was the purchase of the lot on which the new postoffice building now stands. Her intention was to build the church on this lot, but inasmuch as there was no money among those of her faith, she forthwith traded off this lot and purchased the old Methodist Church on W. Market Street, which had served as a hospital during the war, repaired and rebuilt it, thus accomplishing a life's dream of a church for her people. Thus the first Catholic church for Harrisonburg became a reality, and today a new church stands right next door to where she originally planned it, a lasting and imposing monument to her and those of like deep and abiding faith.

Mrs. Kelley was a woman of rare and keen business judgment, and was known far and near for her hospitality and helpfulness to her fellow-countrymen. It was a common thing for anyone who was in any difficult straits to be advised to go and tell Mrs. Kelley, knowing full well that she would find a way out for those in distress. Her business acumen and activity became notable along with her philanthropic qualities and habits. She entered extensively into buying, trading, and investing in property, and at her death on March 17, 1885, she was the owner of much valuable real estate and other property. One of the streets of Harrisonburg still bears her name. It is adjacent to the site of her residence and near the place where John E. Kelley, the latest survivor of her children, lived and carried on his business. He died February 19, 1943, aged 86.

E. L. KLINGSTEIN

BUSINESS MAN AND WORLD TRAVELER

Born February 4, 1894, in Harrisonburg; educated in Harrisonburg schools and those of Pueblo and Denver, Colo.; early business experience in western states, Mexico, Hawaii, and Alaska; Captain Battery B, 337th Field Artillery, World War I; owns and operates Friddle's Restaurant, Klingstein Realty Co., Harrison Hotel, Revita Products Co., etc.; president Rocco Feeds, Inc., Empire Construction Co.; vice-president Loewner Granite & Marble Works; chairman of trustees Hebrew Friendship Congregation; Past Commander American Legion and Veterans of Foreign Wars, Dept. of Va.; Chief Precinct Air Raid Warden, City of Harrisonburg.

E. L. Klingstein early aspired to be a business man, an ambition that has certainly been realized. His record in business, civic, and patriotic activities is unusual. In the First World War he was instructor and radio expert at the University of Colorado and Camp Dodge, Iowa; served 17 months overseas; was wounded in action and decorated for bravery by the American, French, and Russian governments. Returning to his native city in 1922, he has built up successful enterprises in numerous fields. At the same time he has rendered notable service in veterans organizations and benevolent orders, Moose, Elks, and others. He has given liberally of his time, energy, and means to individuals and charitable institutions. He has traveled in every continent and has a wide acquaintance among public figures in many departments of life.

His father, Samuel Klingstein (1857-1912), was a native of Bavaria; his mother, Anna B. Loewner (1854-1922), was born in Bohemia. Her father, Samuel Loewner (1818-1894), and her mother, Augusta Loewner (1830-1893), were both natives of Bohemia. Klingstein is named for his uncle, Emanuel Loewner (1831-1894), a native of Bohemia, who was a soldier in the Confederate Army from Harrisonburg.

Mr. Klingstein, in addition to connections already mentioned, is serving his eleventh term on the Executive Committee of the Shenandoah Valley, Inc. He is a member of the local chamber of commerce and has been a director in the State Chamber of Commerce. He is a director of the Rockingham Turkey Festival and the Virginia State Restaurant Association, and has served in a like capacity in the National Restaurant Association. He has held important offices in the American Legion and the Veterans of Foreign Wars, and in 1937 was Cheminot Nationale, Dept. of Virginia, 40 et 8. He has been active in the local fire companies, and is a member of the Rockingham Game and Fish Association, the National Aeronautic Association, and the American Tourist Association.

On March 4, 1928, Mr. Klingstein married Miss Beulah A. Loewner, born January 26, 1893, in Harrisonburg, daughter of A. M. and Theresa Loewner. One child, Maxine Birch Oakes, born in Harrisonburg on December 26, 1917, and is grandfather of Richard Oakes, aged 3, and Sherry Oakes, aged one year. His brother, Albert Klingstein, and his sister, Ruth Shwayder, live in Denver, Colo. His sister, Mrs. Eva A. Friddle, lives in Harrisonburg. All three were born in Harrisonburg.

Mr. Klingstein's favorite hobbies are fishing, hunting, baseball, and other athletic sports which, as an officer and director in the Harrisonburg Athletic Club, he has done much to promote, notably baseball and athletics. Years ago he was captain and left half-back on the Harrisonburg football team and captain of the city baseball team. His reading preferences are for current magazines and newspapers.

WILLIAM CLYDE KOONTZ
FARMER AND COUNTY SUPERVISOR

Born in 1892 near Elkton; attended Coffman School one year, then the graded and high school in Shenandoah, Page County; student in Shenandoah College, Dayton, 1909-10, and in Virginia Polytechnic Institute, 1910-11; dairy, grain, and stock farmer; member board of supervisors of Rockingham, second term; president League of Virginia Counties; past president Harrisonburg-Rockingham Chamber of Commerce; on Virginia Advisory Legislative Council; Mason; member of Elks and Rotary Club and of St. Peter's Lutheran Church.

Mr. Koontz represents one of the old and well-known families of East Rockingham and the Page Valley. He is a son of Charles E. Koontz and his wife, who before her marriage was Lula A. Kite. His paternal grandparents were Isaac Koontz, Sr., and Rebecca Koontz. After attending the graded and high schools of Shenandoah City he spent a year in Shenandoah College at Dayton, and then took a year's course in Virginia Polytechnic Institute at Blacksburg, specializing in agriculture. At the same time he received military training as a member of the cadet corps. Since then he has been successfully engaged in farming, stockraising, and dairying. From his dairy farm he carries on a retail milk business in the neighboring towns of Shenandoah and Elkton. He takes a keen interest in public affairs, and is now serving his second term on the Rockingham County Board of Supervisors. Of this board he has twice been chairman. He is a member of the city-county chamber of commerce and was president of that body for one term. Upon invitation, he became a member of the Virginia Advisory Legislative Council, and is president of the League of Virginia Counties.

Near Mr. Koontz's home is the historic St. Peter's Lutheran Church, of which he is a member. He belongs to Ashler Lodge No. 125, A. F. & A. M., and to the Shenandoah Royal Arch Chapter, No. 16, both in Shenandoah City. He is also a member of the Shenandoah Rotary Club and the Elks Lodge, No. 450, of Harrisonburg. In politics he is a Democrat. He says that his hobby is horseback riding; and in his reading he prefers history and good detective stories. He is handy with carpenter tools and takes pleasure in woodwork. Nothing delights him more than to perform obliging favors for his neighbors and friends. Like other normal persons, he has his troubles, but is not disposed to burden others with them.

Mr. Koontz has natural ability as a public speaker, and is frequently called on to exercise his talents in that line. In October, 1940, he made the address of welcome to the queen of the second Rockingham Turkey Festival at Harrisonburg, and on June 13, 1942, when the portrait of Governor O'-Ferrall was placed in the circuit court room in Harrisonburg, he made the presentation speech on behalf of the board of supervisors. His optimistic outlook on life and his jovial disposition make him an agreeable companion.

In 1930 Mr. Koontz married Miss Frances Huffman, a native of Page County, born in 1906, the daughter of J. F. Huffman, deceased, and his wife, Mrs. Alice Huffman. The latter before marriage was Miss Alice Strole. She now makes her home with her daughter, Mrs. Koontz. The Huffmans have been represented in the counties of Madison, Page, and Rockingham since colonial times. Mr. and Mrs. Koontz have two daughters: Frances Ann, born in 1931, and Betty Jo, born in 1934.

WILLIAM HERMAN KYGER
ELECTRICIAN AND UNDERTAKER

Born August 9, 1880, in Rockingham County; attended Pineville School and Oak Hill Academy; a natural electrician; installing and operating telephones an avocation for 35 years; graduate Champion College of Embalming, Baltimore, 1899; a charter member of the local Ruritan Club, member of the board for three years, and acting president at this time (1942).

Mr. Kyger was the only child of Daniel S. Kyger and his wife, Laura Virginia McAllister. Daniel was a son of Benjamin F. and Sallie Miller Kyger. Laura V. was a daughter of William C. and Margaret C. McAllister.

In the one-room school at Pineville W. H. Kyger had P. B. F. Good as teacher; at Oak Hill Academy, in McGaheysville, he was under Miss Lula Yates and Professor Hamrick. His home for 59 years and his present place of business is Kyger's Shop, named for his father who there, for a number of years, had a cabinet and carpenter shop and conducted an undertaking establishment. Mr. Kyger, who is a natural electrician and is known as the "Telephone Spirit" of East Rockingham, installed the first exchanges (1900) at McGaheysville, Elkton, and Stanardsville, and was electrician for the McGaheysville Company until 1932, when the Harrisonburg Telephone Company took over the McGaheysville exchange. On January 6, 1942, when dial service was inaugrated at McGaheysville, Mr. Kyger was honored by being appointed to receive the first call.

Evidently, however, telephone service for Mr. Kyger has been in the nature of an avocation, for he has carried on the undertaking business since 1899. He owned and operated the second motor hearse in the county. The area which he serves has a population of approximately 50,000. He has conducted the funerals of Rev. Henry C. Early, Michael H. Harrison, Senator George B. Keezell, and other well-known citizens of the county. The funeral of Senator Keezell, June 25, 1931, was one of the most largely attended of those ever held in this part of the country. In 42 years Mr. Kyger has missed only one funeral to which he was called—a remarkable health record. Interrogated as to difficulties encountered because of bad weather and other untoward conditions, he says:

"I have experienced a number of difficulties in the way of high waters and storms in connection with the undertaking business. One occasion well remembered from the horse-drawn hearse days was the funeral of John Huffman of Penn Laird, in February 1899—snow four to six feet deep. The pallbearers rode ahead of the hearse in a four-horse road wagon, with shovels, breaking through drifts to Woodbine Cemetery, in Harrisonburg."

He recalls other trying experiences in the floods of 1924 and 1936.

His hobby, he says, is playing with electricity and telephones. He still looks after the Good's Mill telephone exchange for the amusement and pleasure that he gets out of it. As the "Telephone Spirit," he has been serving the people of this community for 35 years. An association so cordial and so long continued must give pleasure to Mr. Kyger's friends no less than to himself.

Mr. Kyger's wife, born March 15, 1879, was Miss Annie P. Gooden of McGaheysville, daughter of John P. and Elizabeth Gooden. They have no children.

DANIEL SHEFFEY LEWIS

LAWYER, PUBLIC OFFICIAL, AND PUBLISHER

(Photograph made at age 40)

Born October 16, 1843, at Lynnwood, southeast Rockingham; attended schools in Rockingham, Augusta, and Albemarle; graduated in law at the University of Virginia in 1866; practiced in Harrisonburg; owner and publisher of the *Spirit of the Valley* and the *Daily Times;* Federal Court official; delegate to national conventions; mayor of Harrisonburg one term and treasurer from 1889 to 1908; died October 3, 1912, at Clifton Forge.

Mr. Lewis was descended from two sons of John and Margaret Lynn Lewis, pioneers of Augusta. His grandfather, Gen. Samuel Hance Lewis, was a grandson of Thomas, John's eldest son, and his grandmother, Nancy (Lewis) Lewis, was a granddaughter of Charles, John's third son. His father, John Francis Lewis (1818-1895), was lieutenant-governor of Virginia, 1869-70, U. S. Senator, 1870-75, and again lieutenant-governor, 1882-86. His mother was Serena Helen Sheffey, daughter of Daniel (1770-1830), a distinguished lawyer and member of Congress, who was a native of Frederick, Maryland, and who, after a number of years in southwest Virginia, lived in Staunton.

Mr. Lewis, as a boy, attended private schools in his native county of Rockingham, and others in the adjoining counties of Augusta and Albemarle. Later he took a course in law at the University of Virginia, graduating in 1866, in a class which contained many men who were later prominent in state and national affairs. He located in Harrisonburg, where he engaged in the practice of his profession. In 1886 he purchased the *Spirit of the Valley,* a weekly newspaper that had been established in 1878 by Daniel Dechert & Son; to this in 1905 he added the *Daily Times,* which he edited and published for a number of years, and which was published later by Rickard & Voorhees, with D. S. Lewis, Jr., as editor.

Mr. Lewis was a Republican and always took a very active and deep interest in politics. For some time he was Assistant District Attorney, an later was District Attorney, for the Federal Courts in the Western District of Virginia. He was delegate to several national conventions and was the recipient of a medal that was given to the 306 delegates who favored the nomination of General Grant for a third term as President. He served one term as mayor of Harrisonburg, and was treasurer of the town from 1889 to 1908. He was a great reader of history and fiction, as well as current events. Unusually well informed on genealogy and local history, Mr. Lewis was frequently called upon for information in these fields, and was generous and obliging in his responses. He did not belong to any clubs or secret organizations, and was not a church member, but he was an attendant of the Episcopal Church all his life.

On July 3, 1868, in Washington, D. C., Mr. Lewis married Isabella McLain Botts, daughter of Hon. John Minor Botts and his wife, Mary Whiting Blair. Mrs. Lewis was born in Richmond on February 3, 1841. She was the mother of eight children: two daughters, who died in infancy; the sons now living are Minor Botts Lewis of Clifton Forge, John Francis Lewis of Brooklyn, Daniel Sheffey Lewis of Harrisonburg, and Archibald Aiken Lewis of Atlanta, Ga. The two other sons were Beverley Blair Lewis, who died on June 2, 1914, at Sag Harbor, N. Y., and Dr. Lunsford Hoxsey Lewis, whose death took place on March 7, 1941, at Elkton, Va.

ERNEST REID LINEWEAVER

BUSINESS MAN, FARM MANAGER, AND CIVIC LEADER

Born October 23, 1883, near Harrisonburg; attended Weaver's Church and Harrisonburg schools and Shenanodah Collegiate Institute; graduate of Eastman Business College; bookkeeper in New York City, 1902-04; bank bookkeeper and teller in Roanoke and Harrisonburg, 1904-19; member of Lineweaver Motor Co., Inc., 1915-24; owner and manager, 1924-39; on city school board 25 years, ten years clerk, fifteen years chairman; charter member Kiwanis Club, president 1925; a director chamber of commerce, president 1932, 1933.

Mr. Lineweaver was born on the farm now owned by W. S. Shover, just east of Harrisonburg. His father was Abram N., his mother Harriet I. Lineweaver. His father's parents were John and Margueret Beard Lineweaver; his maternal grandparents, Harvey and Margueret Liskey; all successful in the agricultural development of the county. Following his graduation in accounting at Eastmen Business College, Poughkeepsie, N. Y., in 1902, he spent two years in the accounting department of the American Tobacco Co. in New York City; then entered the First Natl. Bank, Harrisonburg, as clerk, going after two years to the Natl. Exchange Bank, Roanoke, as bookkeeper. In 1907 he returned to Harrisonburg where he was general bookkeeper and teller in the Rockingham Natl. Bank for 13 years. In 1915, while still in the bank, he became a stockholder in the Lineweaver Motor Co., Inc., and in 1919 resigned from the bank to take active management of the motor company. In 1924 he acquired full control of the company and became president and manager. In 1929, due to the expansion of the business, larger facilities were necessary and he purchased the large garage at the corner of S. Mason and Water Street. Here he operated successfully until 1939, when he sold the business, but still owns the building.

In 1925 Mr. Lineweaver served as president of the Kiwanis Club, of which he was a charter member. He was a director of the chamber of commerce for a number of years and was president of 1932 and 1933. Under his leadership in 1932 the chamber sponsored the splendid historical pageant in which many incidents in the life of the city and county were portrayed. His long service on the county and city school boards was notable. Supt. Keister declares: "Because of his interest in the progress of the city as a whole, and the schools in particular, for a quarter of a century he gave unstintingly of his time and talents to the promotion of the schools, particularly the purchase of ample grounds for playgrounds and physical development, the erection of buildings, and providing furnishings and equipment for them. It was through the interest of himself and others that the Kiwanis Club donated the splendid playground equipment at Main Street School, which was erected under the supervision of himself and other members of the club." He, as chairman of the board, led in providing the present modern high school building. He is a member of the Presbyterian Church, and, as he says, an "inactive" Democrat. He reads current events; and, if he has a hobby, it is his present job as manager of Dogwood Hill Farm, producing pure-bred and grade Hereford cattle and Hampshire sheep.

On November 28, 1906, Mr. Lineweaver married Miss Susan Bennett Yancey, daughter of John G. and Frances Bennett Yancey. Of the marriage there are two sons: John Yancey, born February 12, 1908, now a major in R. O. T. C. Engineers, stationed in Washington, D. C.; and Ernest Reid, Jr., born May 15, 1912, now a sergeant in the Marine Corps, stationed at Parris Island, S. C.

ETHEL IRWIN LINEWEAVER

ATTORNEY, MUSICIAN, AND COURT OFFICIAL

Born July 13, 1907, in Woodstock; moved with her family to Harrisonburg in 1914; attended Harrisonburg elementary school and the commercial department of the High School; stenographer for Ward Swank, who directed her study of law; passed State Bar examination June 29, 1929; since then practicing in Harrisonburg; music an avocation; from 1935 to 1943 deputy clerk in Harrisonburg of the U. S. District Court of the Western District of Virginia.

Mrs. Lineweaver (in business still Ethel Irwin) is the first woman practicing attorney in the Shenandoah Valley. She is the daughter of Clarence Patterson Irwin (now deceased), who was born in Woodstock, March 22, 1874, and his wife, Stella Mae Shaffer, also a native of Woodstock, born November 19, 1878, a daughter of Francis Marion and Ella Lonas Shaffer. Both the Shaffers and the Lonases have long been prominent in Shenandoah County. Clarence P. Irwin was a son of Dr. Joseph Swift Irwin and his wife, Catherine Smoot. Practically all of the Irwin men for generations have been doctors and druggists.

In 1922 Mrs. Lineweaver (Ethel Irwin) accepted a position as stenographer in the office of Hon. Ward Swank, and began the study of law under his direction. Having passed the State Bar examination in 1929, she at once opened an office in Harrisonburg. She has practiced in the courts of Rockingham, Augusta, Page, Shenandoah, and Frederick; has argued cases before the Supreme Court of Virginia, and has been admitted to practice before the U. S. Supreme Court. She is a member of the Virginia State Bar Association, a charter member of the Harrisonburg Bar Association, of which she was vice-president in 1933; is a charter member of the local Business and Professional Women's Club, of which she was president in 1936-37. She is chairman of the Harrisonburg and Rockingham County Women's Division of the Democratic Party and a member of the Harrisonburg Community Council. Besides her activity in civic affairs, she has also given much time to the work of the Harrisonburg Muhlenberg Lutheran Church, of which she is a member, and has frequently been called upon to make addresses before various groups and organizations. For many years music has been a special hobby. At the age of seven she began violin study under Professor James A. Harman, and she has since played on practically all instruments of band and orchestra. She has played in the University of Virginia, Shenandoah College, Massanutten Military Academy, Madison College, Manch School of Music, Shenandoah Valley, and other concert orchestras; in the Harrisonburg, Bridgewater, Luray, Shenandoah Valley, and other concert bands; in the Shenandoah Valley Stringed Quartet, and in practically all the churches of Harrisonburg and Rockingham County. For two years she was orchestra chairman of the Virginia Federation of Music Clubs.

On April 17, 1933, Miss Irwin married James Reherd Lineweaver, whose biography appears herein. Since the birth of her son, Joseph Reherd Lineweaver, June 28, 1938, she has naturally developed new interests. According to her own statement, her hobbies are now chiefly limited to those that she and her son can enjoy together, and at present take on largely the character of nature study, art and poetry. Her reading preferences are for the classics, law periodicals, and related fields of research.

JAMES REHERD LINEWEAVER

EDITOR AND JOURNALIST

Born March 3, 1902, in Harrisonburg; attended private and public schools; graduate of Harrisonburg High School, 1919; student two years in Georgetown University; reporter for *Daily News-Record* during World War I, while still a student in high school; except two years in college, on staff of this paper ever since; appointed managing-editor in 1940 upon the death of John R. Crown, under whom he worked 1923-40; correspondent Associated Press since 1922; member of Harrisonburg City Council, 1936-40.

Mr. Lineweaver is the son of C. C. and Louisa May Lineweaver. The former, who was a well-known Harrisonburg merchant, died in 1939; the latter, November 7, 1942. C. C. Lineweaver's father was James M., a popular public school teacher in West Rockingham. Mrs. Lineweaver was a daughter of the late Dewitt Clinton and Mary Ward Reherd, born and reared at her father's home place on the old Furnace Road, on the southeast edge of Harrisonburg.

During World War I, while still a student in Harrisonburg High School, Mr. Lineweaver entered the employ of the *Daily News-Record* as reporter, and, with the exception of the two years he spent in Georgetown University, at Washington, he has ever since been on the staff of this newspaper. In 1923 the late John Randolph Crown became editor, and Mr. Lineweaver profited greatly from his training under that able and experienced journalist. He has covered all types of news events, from Presidential visits to Rockingham and the Valley to the slightest incidents. For two decades he has attended and reported most of the important court trials, state and federal, and has recorded the growth of the poultry industry and farm cooperative marketing since its early days, along with many sports events and other incidents of general or special interest. He has served as Harrisonburg correspondent of the Associated Press since 1922. Following the death of Mr. Crown, November 14, 1940, Mr. Lineweaver was appointed managing-editor of the *Daily News-Record,* and continues in that position.

Mr. Lineweaver is a member of the Catholic Church, the local Kiwanis Club, and the city Democratic Committee. He was on the Harrisonburg City Council from 1936 to 1940, retiring after four years and two months. Within this period there were five mayors, owing to retirement, death, two appointments, and election. He was a member of Mayor Ward Swank's special committee which reorganized the city government in 1938-39. He is a director of the Rockingham Turkey Festival, Shenandoah Valley, Inc., and is now serving his second term as a director of the Harrisonburg-Rockingham Chamber of Commerce. He reads extensively in newspapers and current news magazines. He takes a keen interest in local history, particularly as it relates to the early government and growth of Harrisonburg and Rockingham County, and does much to encourage investigation in the available records of the city and county by according generous space to communications on such matters in the columns of his newspaper. Files of the paper are valuable sources for local historians and genealogists.

On April 17, 1933, Mr. Lineweaver married Miss Ethel Irwin of Harrisonburg, and has one son, Joseph Reherd Lineweaver, born June 28, 1938. Mrs. Lineweaver, whose biography appears herein, is prominent in the civic and professional life of the city and county.

GOODRICH WILSON LINEWEAVER

NEWSPAPER MAN, EDITOR, AND GOVERNMENT OFFICIAL

Born Jan. 4, 1887, at Harrisonburg; attended Harrisonburg High School; newspaper man and editor in Harrisonburg, West Virginia, and Norfolk; secretary Hampton Roads Port Commission; secretary Federal Power Commission; secretary Reclamation Repayment Commission; chief of Research Section, Bureau of Reclamation; Chief of Information, Bureau of Reclamation, U. S. Dept. of the Interior, Washington, D. C.; Presbyterian; Democrat; member Rockingham Union Lodge No. 27, A. F. & A. M., Harrisonburg; Bethesda-Chevy Chase Post, American Legion, Bethsada, Md.; specialist and consultant on power, irrigation, and conservation, especially water resources in arid and semi-arid areas of the western United States.

Mr. Lineweaver's parents were James M. and Sallie C. Ralston Lineweaver of Rockingham County. His father, commissioner of revenue of Central District and deputy county clerk, was a son of John and Margueret Beard Lineweaver. His mother's parents were Benjamin and Salome Neff Ralston. He is a brother of Rev. Jesse L. Lineweaver of Beckley, W. Va., Mrs. L. P. Little of Williamsburg, Va., Mrs. W. Ward Beam of Philadelphia, and of the late Dr. Walter T. Lineweaver, W. Price Lineweaver, and Clifford C. Lineweaver of Harrisonburg. His career as a newspaper man began on the Harrisonburg *Daily News*, which he served as a reporter from 1903 to 1907. For the next five years he was editor of newspapers in Hinton, Pineville, and Elkins, W. Va., and printing clerk of the W. Va. House of Delegates in 1911. Returning to Harrisonburg in 1912, he was connected with the *Daily Times*, the *Daily Record*, and was managing editor of the *Daily News-Record* from 1913 to 1917.

In 1907 he was quartermaster-sergeant, Co. C, 2d Va. Inf., under Captain (now Judge) John Paul. At the beginning of the World War he attended the First Officers' Training Camp at Fort Myer, was commissioned a 2d lieutenant, U. S. Army, and later a 1st lieutenant. Until 1918 he was transport quartermaster, making four round trips to France. He was assistant troop-movement officer, port of debarkation, Newport News-Norfolk, 1918-19, and superintendent of army inspectors, Norfolk, 1919-20.

From 1920 to 1934 Mr. Lineweaver was city editor and associate editor of the Norfolk *Ledger-Dispatch*. Within the same period he was secretary of the Hampton Roads Port Commission (1921-26) and secretary of Governor Byrd's Seafood Conservation Commission (1927-28). From 1934 to 1936 he was secretary of the Federal Power Commission; the next three years consultant of Brookings Institution, Washington, the Pennsylvania Anthracite Coal Commission, the National Reclamation Association, and secretary of the Reclamation Repayment Commission, Department of the Interior; from 1939 to 1942 chief of Research Section, Bureau of Reclamation. In 1942 he became chief of information of the Bureau. He is a member of the Interdepartmental Committee, Civilian Defense; secretary of the Guiding Committee, Central Valley (California) Project Studies; and assistant to the chairman of the advisory committee on the Central Valley Project.

In 1921 Mr. Lineweaver married Miss Evelyn M. Koogler of Harrisonburg, daughter of the late DeWitt Clinton and Elton Helphenstine Koogler. Clinton Koogler was a son of John R. Koogler, sheriff of Rockingham County, 1857-60 and 1865-66. Sheriff Koogler's wife was Sarah Jane Harnsberger. Mrs. Lineweaver's maternal grandparents were Perry and Margaret Martin Helphenstine.

Mr. and Mrs. Lineweaver reside at 3511 Davenport Street, N. W., Washington, D. C.

CONRAD TRAVIS LOGAN
TEACHER, EDITOR, AND AUTHOR

Born July 15, 1890, in Harrisonburg; graduate Harrisonburg High School, 1907; A. B., Randolph-Macon College, 1910; A. M., Columbia University, 1915; graduate student, Univ. of Cincinnati and Teachers College, Columbia Univ.; teacher in Danville (Va.) School for Boys, Hughes High School, Cincinnati, and Horace Mann School for Boys, New York City; professor of English and head of dept. Madison College since 1919; summer school instructor George Peabody College for Teachers, 1922, 1923; visiting professor Teachers College, Columbia Univ., summers 1927-32, and instructor, Extension Dept., Univ. of Va., since 1929; editor and author.

Mr. Logan is a man of versatile talents and interests and has had a wide experience in literary and educational work. He is a son of John Lester Logan (Aug. 13, 1863—Aug. 29, 1895) and Margaret Elizabeth Conrad (b. July 16, 1864). His paternal grandparents were Joseph Travis Logan (1834-1885) and Margaret Adelaide H. Haas (1836-1923); his mother's parents, George Oliver Conrad (1823-1907) and Diana Smith Yancey (1831-1895). He is a descendant of John Lewis, founder of Staunton, Isaac Gore, one of the founders of New Market, John Smith, of Smithland, Adam Miller, first settler of the upper Shenandoah Valley, and William Strother, high sheriff of King George County, Va., in 1694.

In his senior year (1910) at Randolph-Macon College he was editor of the *Randolph-Macon Monthly;* had later experience as a newspaper reporter and correspondent, and from 1923 to 1939 was editor of the *Virginia Teacher*. He has served on the editorial board of the *English Journal,* the *Elementary English Review,* the *Madison Quarterly,* and is now editor of the *Madison Quarterly*. He helped to revise the Va. state course of study in English in 1924, and was consultant in English for the core curriculum of Va. secondary schools in 1935. In 1932 he was alumni speaker at Randolph-Macon College and has frequently lectured before clubs and organizations. As a member of the board of trustees of Rockingham Library Assn. since its establishment in 1928 and president of the board since 1937, he has done effective and notable work in assembling an unusual collection of books and manuscripts. He is a vestryman of Emmanuel Episcopal Church, Harrisonburg; a Mason since 1912; and was president of the local Kiwanis Club in 1930. He is a member of Phi Beta Kappa, Phi Kappa Sigma, and other college fraternities; Modern Language Assn., Amer. Assn. of University Professors, College English Assn., and Natl. Council of Teachers of English. In the last he has held official positions.

Professor Logan is author (with Elizabeth P. Cleveland and Margaret V. Hoffman) of "Practice Leaves in English Fundamentals," four forms of which were published between 1926 and 1937 by D. C. Heath & Co.; "A Test in Children's Literature" (with Miss Hoffman), Rand McNally, 1927; "Practice Leaves in Junior English" (with Katherine M. Anthony), Heath, 1928; and "Literary Background Tests" (with Carrie Belle Parks), Heath, 1930. He has contributed numerous articles to *American Speech,* the *English Journal,* the *Virginia Journal of Education,* the *Virginia Teacher,* and other magazines.

On December 23, 1913, Mr. Logan married Miss Mary Harnsberger Jarman, daughter of Miletus Miller and Elizabeth A. (Taliaferro) Jarman of Elkton. Mr. and Mrs. Logan have three children: Conrad Jarman, born 1916, graduate of Randolph-Macon College, now an ensign in the U. S. Naval Reserve; Jane Taliaferro, born 1918, graduate of Madison College, now wife of Lieut. Peter James Long, 309th Inf., 78th Div., U. S. Army; and Joseph Talfourd, born 1920, who, after three years at Randolph-Macon, enlisted and is now a sergeant in the 81st Btn. of the Chemical Warfare Division, U. S. Army.

LUTHER E. LONG

ENTREPRENEUR AND COMMUNITY-BUILDER

Born September 5, 1881, in Rockingham County; attended Timber Ridge School, Bridgewater College, and National Business College; clerk and stenographer for Hon. Wm. E. Humphrey, M. C., 1903-04; stenographer in R. O. Armstrong's brokerage office, Harrisonburg, 1904-05; bookkeeper for Harrisonburg Milling Co., 1905-09; operator of mills at Pleasant Valley and Weyer's Cave, 1909-38; manager Shenandoah River Power Co., 1925-30; manager Elkton electrical department, 1932-38; organized Valley R. E. A., 1935; manager Shenandoah Valley Electric Cooperative; president Shenandoah Valley Defense Cooperative.

Mr. Long grew up on the farm of his parents, Isaac and Sarah Catherine Craun Long, at Meyerhoeffer's Store. Professor M. A. Good headed him towards Bridgewater College and a business career. In Washington the patient guidance of Congressman Humphrey gave him a lasting inspiration toward achievement, and this was sustained by the friendship of Mr. and Mrs. Humphrey as long as they lived. This inspiration Mr. Long has been able to pass on to other men whom he has employed, some of whom he raised from a "down and out" condition to a high plane of efficiency, failing in only one or two cases. As a mill operator he proved his ability by transforming a bankrupt business into a paying enterprise, and as a pioneer in rural electrification he has accomplished wonders in the face of doubt and discouragement. In 1911 rural electrification was practically unknown—the power companies said that it could not be done. Starting with 20 customers and an income of $20 a month, he has built up a system through the Shenandoah River Power Co., the Virginia Public Service Co., and the Shenandoah Valley Electric Cooperative whose income exceeds $35,000 a month, with more than 8000 customers and over 2000 miles of line in the three counties of Augusta, Rockingham, and Shenandoah. He has continued as general manager of the Shenandoah Valley Cooperative from its beginning to the present. The Diesel Power Plant at Dayton has been built at an outlay of a quarter of a million dollars. He has mainly engineered and assisted in raising funds for constructions costing over $4,000,000 in generating plants, transmission, distribution lines, substations, etc. Many of the lines have been built under his personal direction. The influence of his work has extended far beyond the Shenandoah Valley. He was appointed a member of the executive committee of the Virginia Public Utilities Association. He was on the ground floor when the State Corporation Commission took over direction of the utilities, and has been in close touch with the Commission ever since. He has never been cited by the Commission on any charge. His success in the recent lining up of local shops in defense work has been remarkable.

Mr. Long's wife was Miss Sadie Washington Wagner of Port Republic, born February 22, 1884. Their children are: Isaac Clinton, born August 7, 1906; Faye Wagner, born July 29, 1909 (deceased); Harry Paxton, born September 19, 1916; Luther Winston, born September 15, 1917; and Maxine Maye (Mrs. Tillette), born May 14, 1919. Practically all are now engaged in defense work. Maxine has a daughter Virginia Ann, and Clinton a daughter Glory Ann.

Mr. Long is a Mason and U. C. T. He is an elder in the Evangelical and Reformed Church; is active in Sundayschool and the Parent-Teachers Association. He says that he is 90% Democrat. His hobbies are bowling and major-league baseball. He loves livestock. "It is restful," he says, "to be about them."

CALVERT RANDOLPH McGAHEY

ENGINEER, INVENTOR, MUSICIAN, WRITER

Born June 4, 1871, near McGaheysville; attended neighborhood schools and studied at home; at 16 built a generator and made the first electric light he ever saw; superintendent of machine shops and steel mills; organizer and chief musician 4th Ga. Regimental Band; writer for technical journals and other publications; collector of antiques, student of local history, and commentator on current events.

William McGaughey, first of the name in Virginia, was born in Glasgow, Scotland, October 26, 1741. In 1761 William came to Dover, Del., where he married Ann Kincade in 1764. Their son, Tobias Rheudolph McGaughey, born in Dover, March 24, 1765, came in 1783 to Rockingham County, Va., where he married Mary Eva Conrad in 1801. In 1802 he established the postoffice at McGaheysville, using the Gaelic spelling of the name. Mary Eva Conrad McGahey died in 1819, and in 1821 Tobias married Elizabeth Anderson of Woodstock, Va. Their son, Warren Tobias McGahey, was born in Harrisonburg, March 27, 1825. In 1827 T. R. McGahey moved to Bonny Brook, his farm home near McGaheysville, where he died, 1843.

Calvert R. McGahey, born at Bonny Brook, was the seventh child of Warren T. McGahey and his wife, Frances Mauzy Winsborough, who was born at Ruckersville, Va., July 16, 1829. As a youngster, Calvert did not care for games—was more interested in making something. He learned the alphabet at his mother's knee, and the first word he spelled was "gold." At eight he was playing a cornet. His first school was in a log cabin with slab benches, the teacher an old cobbler whose only text was a blue-backed spelling book. His next school was in the village, where in 27 months he went from the second reader to algebra, physics, and chemistry. At 16 he, from reading a "Scientific American Supplement," built a generator and made the first electric light he ever saw. Already he had organized a boys band, and later he graduated from the McLane School of Metallurgy. For years he worked as a mechanical and electrical engineer in various states and Canada and was manager of large machine and power plants, supervising all classes of construction from steel hull steamers to intricate equipment. He was granted a number of patents on inventions. The 4th Ga. Regimental Band, which Mr. McGahey organized, participated in the Dewey parade in N. Y. City and later was selected to lead the Brumberry parade in Atlanta. It was the first organization to play "Hot Time in the Old Town Tonight" and Sousa's march, "Stars and Stripes Forever."

In December, 1893, Mr. McGahey married Miss Emma Virginia Lambert, who was born in Harrisonburg, December 23, 1870. Their children are: Mary Virginia, born November 27, 1899, now Mrs. Stephen P. Lee of Miami; Lillian Frances, born August 23, 1901, now Mrs. James Gordon Bennett of Richmond; Randolph Winsborough, born March 24, 1904; married Miss Wanda King; Lelia Katherine, born March 4, 1907, now Mrs. Basil G. Watkins of Lynchburg; and Dorothy Louise, born September 20, 1908, now Mrs. Charles B. Marvin. Major Marvin is at an army flying field in Australia. The daughters are graduates of Randolph-Macon Woman's College. Randolph is a graduate of the University of Virginia. He is chemical engineer for the B. F. Goodrich Co., Akron, Ohio, and has secured a patent for this company on synthetic rubber. Mr. McGahey disclaims hobbies. In reading he prefers history and scientific works. He says that he has never read novels, but in his younger days found the *Youth's Companion* of interest.

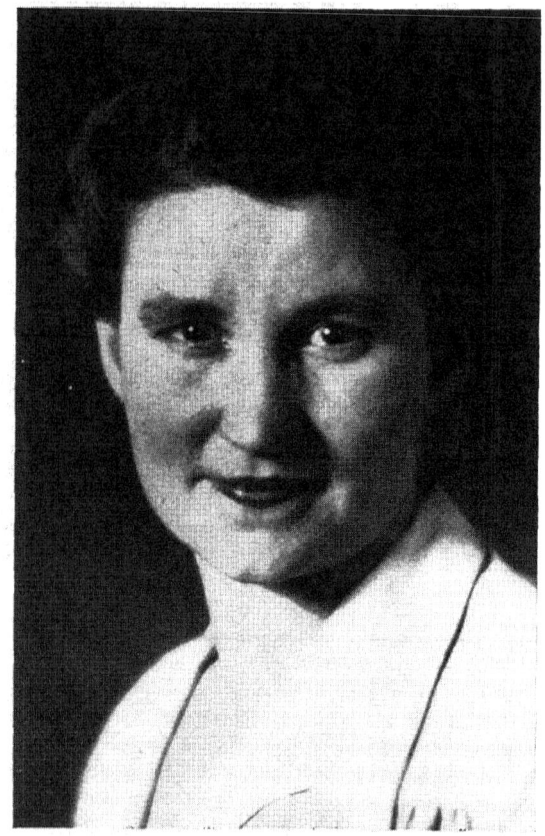

MRS. WILLIAM HOLMES McGUFFIN

EDUCATOR AND CIVIC LEADER

Born February 19, 1907, near Timberville; graduated from Timberville High School in 1923; an active 4H Club member for a number of years and winner of outstanding honors in state and national competitions; student in Bridgewater College, Madison College, the University of Virginia, and the College of William and Mary; principal Montezuma Graded School, Rockingham County, and teacher in Monterey High School, Highland County, since 1927; elected president of Department of Classroom Teachers, Virginia Education Association, 1942; Chief of Civilian Mobilization for Highland County.

Mrs. McGuffin, born Reefa Belle Hoover, is typical of the Rockingham girls who have won distinction in the wholesome activities of rural life, in the field of education, and as leaders in civic and religious service. Her father was Rev. William C. Hoover (1870-1924), a well-known minister in the Church of the Brethren and a successful farmer, who was also an active participant in public affairs, serving for a term in the Virginia House of Delegates at Richmond. He was a son of Emanuel Hoover (1827-1898) and his wife, Anna Cline (1831-1898), and a brother of John H. Hoover, whose biography appears in this work. Her mother, Mrs. Maggie Miller Hoover, born in 1872, is a daughter of the late George and Sallie Whitmere Miller, of the Mill Creek neighborhood of southeast Rockingham. These several families have long been substantial and estimable members of their respective communities.

While still a student in the Timberville schools, Reefa Belle Hoover entered with characteristic energy and efficiency into the various organizations that offered opportunities for improvement and useful achievement to the young people of her community. For ten years she was affiliated with the local 4H Club, and in 1923 she won a trip to the World's Dairy Congress in Syracuse, N. Y. In 1924 she was awarded the 4H All Star membership. She was also a winner in the Virginia State Contest in Dairy Calves. Following her graduation from Timberville High School in 1923, she took advanced courses of training in Bridgewater College, the State Teachers (now Madison) College, the University of Virginia, and the College of William and Mary, partly in recent years at intervals while teaching in the public schools. In 1927 she was principal of the graded school of Montezuma, and for the past 16 years she has been a member of the high-school faculty in Monterey. In the summer of 1941 she was a member of the Curriculum Conference at William and Mary. From 1940 to 1942 she was a representative of the Department of Classroom Teachers of District G in the state organization, and in November, 1942, at Richmond, she was elected president of the same department of the Virginia Education Association. She is a member of the Monterey Garden Club; is teacher of the young peoples class in the Monterey Presbyterian Church; and is chief of civilian mobilization for the county of Highland. Her hobbies are needlework and the collecting of china. In her reading she gives preference to works of fiction that are based on history. She still keeps in close touch with her native county of Rockingham, and is a frequent visitor at Madison College, where her sister, Miss Ferne Hoover, is a member of the library staff.

On June 1, 1928, Miss Hoover married William Holmes McGuffin, who was born July 30, 1903, in Bath County, the only child of William B. and Hamie Revercomb McGuffin. His paternal grandfather was Colonel James McGuffin of Warm Springs, Va.

WILLIAM McATEE MENEFEE

FARMER AND BUSINESS MAN

Born August 6, 1866, near Mt. Crawford; grew up on farms and attended schools at Mt. Crawford and Pleasant Valley; farmer and dealer in livestock; moved to Harrisonburg in 1909; dealer in feed, grain, hay, and coal; president of the Rockingham County Fair Association; director of Valley Fertilizer Co.; a charter director Harrisonburg Loan and Thrift Corp.; on city council 3 terms, 1924-36; a member at the time of his death; director of chamber of commerce; vice-president of Rockingham National Bank at time of death; elder in the Reformed Church; died April 5, 1936.

Mr. Menefee's paternal ancestors were from Rappahannock County, Va., where the family has been prominent for generations. His grandfather, Jonas Menefee, married a Miss Britton and had sons Garland, Thomas, Britton, Samuel M., James (killed while a Confederate soldier), and Hanson; daughters, Jane (Mrs. John Shank), Lucy (Mrs. Laula), and Bettie (Mrs. Jack Pounds). Jonas Menefee died in Page County. Samuel M. Menefee, father of William M., was a native of Rappahannock County, but grew up in Page. He served in the Confederate army, part of the time under Stonewall Jackson. At the end of the war he came home without a dollar, to take a fresh start in life. He married Miss Virginia Tutwiler of Rockingham, a daughter of Jonathan, and rented Rev. Mr. Hensel's farm. Later he bought land near Mt. Crawford, the birthplace of his children: Mary L. (Mrs. Daniel Stoner), William Mc-Atee, Thomas J., who died in Galesburg, Ill., the late Edgar Warren, who resided at Deal's Ford, Rockingham County, and Robert Tilden, now a resident of Harrisonburg.

When William M. Menefee was fifteen years old his parents moved to Pleasant Valley, a neighboring village in Rockingham County, where a farm of 200 acres was acquired. There Virginia Tutwiler Menefee died in 1891, at the age of 49; her husband, Samuel M., survived until 1907. Their son, William M., devoted his labors mainly to the home farm until he was twenty-five. On March 25, 1892, he was united in marriage with Miss Alice Roberta Roller in the Pleasant Valley Reformed Church, Rev. S. N. Callender officiating. Mrs. Menefee was born in September, 1866, a daughter of George W. Roller and his wife, Louise Ann Sherman. She was the youngest of eight children among whom were Mrs. Margaret A. Carpenter and W. M. Roller of Harrisonburg. Mr. and Mrs. Menefee were the parents of one son, Wade Whitfield Menefee, who is a well-known business man of Harrisonburg.

After his marriage in 1892 Mr. Menefee began his independent career as a farmer on the paternal estate. He was a successful grower of grain, but gave special attention to the raising of livestock. As a buyer and shipper of horses, cattle, hogs, and hay he became well known in his part of the county. In 1909 he sold his farm and moved to Harrisonburg. Here he continued to deal in livestock for some time, but after several years he devoted himself to carrying on a large business as a dealer in feed, grain, hay, and coal, suceeding the firm of Swank & Hoover in this field.

Mr. Menefee was never active in politics, but was always keenly interested in good government and practical affairs, as shown by his participation in local enterprises of civic, financial, and religious character. His father was a Methodist, but Mr. Menefee connected himself with the Reformed Church, in which he was an honored and influential member. In 1923 he was chosen to represent his church in Harrisonburg at the synod, which was held that year at Hickory, N. C.

WADE WHITFIELD MENEFEE

BANKER AND BUSINESS MAN

Born February 4, 1895, near Mt. Crawford; grew up on a farm; attended neighborhood schools, Harrisonburg High School, and Bridgewater College; located in Harrisonburg in 1910; employee of the Harrisonburg Telephone Co. 1912-28, and manager at the time of resignation; entered business with his father in 1928; merchant and operator of mill; member of city council; director of Rockingham National Bank; treasurer of St. Stephen's Reformed Church; past president Chamber of Commerce; past master of Masonic lodge.

Mr. Menefee's forebears, on his father's side, were the Menefees and Brittons of Rappahannock County and the Tutwilers of Rockingham; on his mother's side, the Rollers, Shermans, and others of Rockingham. One of his grandfathers was Samuel M. Menefee, who followed Stonewall Jackson; the other was George W. Roller, a representative of a family that has long been prominent in Rockingham in affairs both civil and military. For more particulars in regard to family connections the reader is referred to the biography of his father, William McAtee Menefee, whose wife was Alice Roberta Roller.

Like numerous other men of Rockingham whose careers have been notable in character and achievement, Mr. Menefee was reared on a farm, and profited by a close contact with nature and the training afforded by early rising, a variety of chores, and the handling of implements of agriculture and livestock. At an early age he enjoyed also an association with men of reputation and influence in the chief city of the Commonwealth when he served as a page during the legislative sessions of 1908 and 1910 in Richmond. The acquaintances he formed in the personal contacts he enjoyed in that service have proved of great educational and social value. Entering upon employment with the Harrisonburg Telephone Company at the age of seventeen, and continuing in that work for a period of sixteen years, he gave evidence of administrative ability as well as mechanical skill by rising to the position of manager of the company.

For eight years, 1928-36, he was associated with his father, William M. Menefee, in business operations in Harrisonburg, and since that time he has carried on the same business with important expansions. At present he operates a large business in coal and feed and in manufacturing flour, feed, and corn meal in the Mutual Mills, and also operates a farm on the edge of the city.

In addition to his own business concerns, Mr. Menefee has devoted much time to various activities in municipal, philanthropic, and religious service. He has been president of the city-county chamber of commerce and was a member of the city council from 1938 to 1942. He is treasurer of the William M. Bucher Memorial Fund for the relief of distressed Masons, their widows and orphans; is a member of the consistory and treasurer of St. Stephen's Reformed Church; a member of the Benevolent and Protective Order of Elks. He serves also as a director of the Harrisonburg Loan & Thrift Corporation and the Rockingham National Bank. His hobby is farming.

In 1922 Mr. Menefee married Miss Pearl Mauck, who was born in the county November 19, 1895. They have two children: Wade Whitfield, Jr., born February 28, 1924, a graduate of the Harrisonburg High School and now a cadet at V. P. I., and Mary Jane, born December 4, 1927, a student in the city high school.

ERNEST BRUBAKER MILLER, M.D.

PHYSICIAN AND SURGEON

Born May 12, 1891, at Elkton; graduate Elkton High School, 1909; student in Randolph-Macon Academy, Front Royal, 1909-10; pre-med course in R-M College, Ashland, 1910-11; student in medical dept., University of Virginia, 1911-15; M. D., 1915; interned at Mercer, Trenton, N. J., 1915-16; in U. S. Army from Jan. 13, 1918, to March 16, 1919—6 months in U. S. and 8 months overseas as surgeon; since 1919 in practice at Elkton; surgeon for N. & W. Ry.; consulting physician for Merck & Co., Inc.; medical examiner for Harrisonburg Selective Service Board; charter member American Legion, Rockingham Post No. 27; Mason; member Rockingham Mem. Hospital staff, etc.

Dr. Miller in his immediate forebears and other lines of ancestry represents several old families of East Rockingham and the Page Valley. The Millers, Bears, Kites, and Brubakers have all been well known in this region since early colonial times. His father was Charles E. Miller; his mother, before her marriage, was Sallie E. Brubaker. His grandfather was S. P. H. Miller, M.D., whose wife was Sallie C. Bear; his maternal grandparents were F. John Brubaker and Elizabeth Kite. The pioneer, Adam Miller, was the first settler in this part of the Shenandoah Valley, and his son-in-law, Jacob Bear, purchased land in 1764 at the great spring, since familiar as the Bear Lithia Spring.

Having completed the course in the Elkton High School in 1909, Dr. Miller attended Randolph-Macon Academy at Front Royal for a year, and then took a year's course in preparation for the study of medicine in Randolph-Macon College at Ashland. Entering the medical department of the University of Virginia in 1911, he continued therein until 1915, when he was awarded his M.D. degree. After his interneship in Mercer Hospital, Trenton, N. J., he spent the next 14 months in the U. S. Army, serving the greater part of that time as a surgeon overseas. Returning to Elkton in the spring of 1919, he opened an office and has since then been successfully engaged in the practice of his profession at this place. He is a member of the county, state, and national medical societies and is on the staff of Rockingham Memorial Hospital in Harrisonburg, with other professional connections as already indicated. He is a charter member of the American Legion, and is an active Mason, holding membership in the blue lodge No. 72, Elkton, the Milnes Royal Arch Chapter No. 16, at Shenandoah, the Harrisonburg Commandery, No. 10, K. T., at Harrisonburg; and is a Shriner, of Acca Temple, Richmond. He operates a farm on which he raises cattle and high-grade race horses, and as a hobby he carries on the breeding and training of bird dogs. In addition to his reading in medical journals, he devotes much time to the study of psychology, by the perusal of books and periodicals in that field. He no doubt appreciates the intimate relation of mental conditions with nervous affections and diseases of the human body.

On November 4, 1942, Dr. Miller married Miss Arlene Vertis Davis, born September 10, 1913, daughter of Charles and Irine Davis of Elkton. By a former marriage with Miss Mary Regan of Morrisville, Pa , Dr. Miller has two children: Mary Elizabeth, born November 21, 1920, who received her B.S. degree at Madison College in 1942 and is now a graduate student in chemistry in the University of North Carolina at Chapel Hill; and Charles Samuel, born October 20, 1923, who is now a student in pre-medical courses at the University of Virginia. The medical profession is evidently well established by tradition in the Miller family, and bids fair to be carried on with succeeding generations.

JOHN DAVID MILLER, M. D.
EDUCATOR AND PHYSICIAN

Born May 7, 1870, near Spring Creek; grew up on his father's farm and attended Beaver Creek School and summer normals; graduated at Peabody Normal College, Nashville; taught in Rockingham schools; B. A., Bridgewater College, 1901; M. D., Medical College of Virginia, 1906; member county board of health, town council of Bridgewater, board cf trustees, Bridgewater College; college physician and president of the alumni association; former member of the College Street Church of the Brethren finance board and now again on the pastoral board.

Dr. Miller is a son of Rev. Martin P. Miller and wife, Rebecca Heatwole, of the Beaver Creek and Spring Creek community; his paternal grandparents were Martin and Anna Sanger Miller. One of his brothers is Dr. E. R. Miller of Harrisonburg, whose biography appears herein. He grew up in a preacher's home and enjoyed the varied experiences of farm life on the banks of Beaver Creek. The old school house he first attended was located on the grounds of Beaver Creek Church; his summer sports were chiefly fishing and swimming. Working in the home garden gave him skills which he still exercises with pleasure, and at the same time he found time for reading, which he now continues in fiction and current events, as well as in professional literature. Having attended summer normals at Lacey Spring and Mt. Clinton, he began teaching, but feeling the need of better preparation, he secured a Peabody scholarship by competitive examination and after two years graduated at Peabody Normal College. Having taught again in Rockingham elementary and high schools, he entered upon a college course at Bridgewater, graduating in 1901. After teaching two years in his alma mater, he took up the study of medicine, winning his M.D. degree at the Medical College of Virginia in 1906. Since then he has been engaged at Bridgewater in general practice and as college physician. He ranks high in his profession as a diagnostician.

In 1889 Dr. Miller was baptized into the Church of the Brethren by Elder Jacob Thomas, and has ever since been active in church work. He served on the building committee for the College Street Church of the Brethren and in other official capacities. For six years he was a member of the Bridgewater town council. He takes a keen interest in all welfare agencies; in politics is an independent voter.

On December 25, 1902, Dr. Miller married Miss Bertha Cline, born November 28, 1879, at Stuart's Draft, daughter of Elder John A. and Mary Wine Cline. Dr. and Mrs. Miller have two children: DeWitt L., born October 12, 1908, and Dorothy, born October 6, 1911; both natives of Bridgewater. DeWitt graduated from Bridgewater College in 1928, from Bethany Biblical Seminary in Chicago in 1931. He has served pastorates: Huntington, Ind., three years, and Cleveland, Ohio, three years, and is now pastor at Meyersdale, Pa. On May 30, 1931, he married Miss Mary Hartsaugh, and has a son, David LeRoy, born February 25, 1936. Dorothy graduated from Bridgewater High School in 1928, from Bridgewater College in 1932, B. A., with certificate in piano. She also holds a certificate in piano from Cincinnati Conservatory of Music and spent two years in Peabody Conservatory, Baltimore. From the University of Pennsylvania she obtained the M. S. degree by attendance upon summer sessions. She is a member of the Mu-Phi-Epsilon Sorority, Peabody Conservatory Chapter. She taught two years in Rockingham, five in the William Byrd High School, Vinton, Va., and is now supervisor of music in the schools of Summit Township, Pa.

EPHRAIM RUFUS MILLER, M. D.
EYE, EAR, NOSE, AND THROAT SPECIALIST

Born November 28, 1872, near Spring Creek, Va.; grew up on his father's farm; attended public schools, Spring Creek Academy, and Bridgewater College; M. D., Medical College of Virginia, 1898; post-graduate student in the Presbyterian Eye and Ear Hospital, Baltimore, New York Eye and Ear Hospital, and St. Bartholomew's Nose and Throat Clinic, New York City; practitioner in Harrisonburg.

Dr. Miller is the youngest son of Rev. Martin P. Miller and his wife, Rebecca Heatwole, who lived on a farm between Spring Creek and Beaver Creek Church. His father was born near Spring Creek, October 8, 1833, son of Rev. Martin Miller of the same locality, who was born July 15, 1800, and died September 19, 1872. The latter's first wife was born Anna Sanger, January 1, 1796, probably in Augusta County; she died June 23, 1849; his second wife, Mary Schaeffer (1803-1894), was a native of Bremen, Germany. Dr. Miller's mother, born Rebecca Heatwole, May 6, 1832, in Rockingham, died May 19, 1921. His father, Martin P. Miller, like his grandfather, was a devoted minister of the Church of the Brethren. Unlike most of his associates in the denomination at that time, he was an advocate of higher education and gave much encouragement to his nephew, Daniel C. Flory, in founding the school at Spring Creek that later developed into Bridgewater College. Martin P. Miller was one of the original trustees of the college.

Dr. Miller grew up on his father's farm, attended local schools, and did some clerking in a store at Spring Creek. When he attended Bridgewater College, 1892-94, he made the trip each day in a buggy. After graduating from the Medical College of Virginia in 1898, he first practiced in Bridgewater, later locating in Harrisonburg as a specialist. For a short time he lived in Hagerstown, then for a longer period in Frederick, Md., where he carried on his practice. In 1917 he returned to Harrisonburg, where he has since been located. He has always taken much interest in church and school work and is an expert in Sundayschool teaching and administration. For one term he was president of the State S. S. Assn. and for a number of years headed the Rockingham County S. S. Assn. He is an interested reader of the magazines and daily papers. He is a member of the Baptist Church and an independent in politics.

On February 16, 1899, Dr. Miller married Miss Susan Virginia Snell, daughter of George W. Snell (1837-1906) and his wife, Malinda Stinespring (1842-1920), of near Dayton. Dr. and Mrs. Miller have two children: Francis Stinespring, born August 2, 1902, and Wellington, born June 19, 1906; both natives of Bridgewater. Francis is now a practicing attorney of Harrisonburg and justice of police court. On February 3, 1926, he married Miss Virginia Bailey Heneberger of Winchester, Massachusetts, and has two daughters: Nancy Bailey, born February 9, 1931, in Kansas City, and Carol Ellis, born March 21, 1935, in Harrisonburg. Wellington, on February 12, 1927, married Harry Sanborn Corey, Jr., of Richmond; she has a son, Harry Sanborn III, and lives in Asheville, N. C., where Mr. Corey is in business.

For a number of years Dr. and Mrs. Miller lived in the house which they built on Campbell Street, Harrisonburg; at present they occupy an apartment in Wellington Hall, of which Dr. Miller is the owner, on South Main Street, opposite Madison College.

MINOR CLINE MILLER
EDUCATOR AND RELIGIOUS LEADER

Born January 16, 1889, at Mt. Sidney, Va.; attended Augusta County schools and the academy connected with Bridgewater College; completed the Bible course in Bridgewater College, 1912, and graduated A. B. in 1914; graduate student Harvard University, 1920-21; master's degree in Religious Education, Boston University, 1921; teacher in Augusta County schools and professor of Religious Education in Bridgewater College; General Secretary of Va. Council of Religious Education since 1924; member of executive committee, International Council of Religious Education; etc.

Mr. Miller is a son of Rev. Samuel D. Miller and his wife, Minnie Cline, of Mt. Sidney. His father's parents were Rev. John Miller of Mt. Sidney and his wife, Fannie Brower of Hermitage; his mother's parents were Rev. Joseph M. Cline of Fort Defiance and his wife, Lydia Neff of Quicksburg, Shenandoah County. On both sides of the family his ancestors have been active members and leaders in the Church of the Brethren for generations in Augusta, Rockingham, and adjacent sections of the Shenandoah Valley. Minor C. has kept up the traditions of his forebears and extended his work in wider fields. As a teacher in the schools of Augusta County for four years, as professor of religious education in Bridgewater College, as a contributor to periodicals and as the author of books, as well as in organizing and directing religious work in the schools of Virginia, he has exercised a far-reaching and potent influence.

In January, 1924, he became general secretary of the Virginia Council of Religious Education. He is a member of the commission on the educational program of the International Council of Religious Education, and is on the executive committee of that organization. He is chairman of the Southeastern Regional Council of Boards, Church of the Brethren. As a traveler he has gone over many parts of America and in 1936 he visited most of the countries of Europe, including the Soviet Union. He is the author of three books: "Heroic Lives," "Conquests for God," and "The Lost Bible," and is general editor of "Adventures in Christian Living," a curriculum guide for use in Virginia week-day church schools. In the midst of a busy life he finds time to make frequent contributions to the *International Journal of Religious Education* and similar publications, and is much in demand as a speaker before many religious and educational meetings. With headquarters in Bridgewater, he carries on a wide correspondence and at the same time gives his personal attendance upon conferences in various parts of the country.

On June 7, 1916, Mr. Miller married Miss Mary Agnes Shipman, daughter of James R. and Mollie Young Shipman of Bridgewater, and is the father of eight children, five girls and three boys. Vera is teaching in the Bridgewater High School; Alice teaches home economics in the schools of Arlington County; Lawrance is a student in the medical school of the University of Virginia; others are in school in Bridgewater.

Mr. Miller takes an active part in the affairs of his own community. He is a charter member of the Bridgewater Rotary Club and is an influential member of the Bridgewater Church of the Brethren. In his reading he prefers, in addition to books and periodicals in the religious field, works in history and biography.

MARTIN OLIVER MILLER

BANKER AND BUSINESS MAN

Born November 4, 1886, on his father's farm near Bridgewater; attended Bridgewater College and completed the B. E. course; clerk in general offices of the N. & W. Railway at Roanoke 1907-08; traveling salesman in West Virginia 1908-09; with a Philadelphia firm 1909-10; farmer at Broadway 1910-14; in 1914 became bookkeeper in the First National Bank of Broadway; now vice-president and cashier of the same; member of Rockingham County School Board.

Mr. Miller's father, John W. Miller, who lived a mile south of Bridgewater, was a substantial farmer and public-spirited citizen, born May 21, 1855, son of John M. Miller, who was born July 6, 1821. His mother, Fannie Pifer Miller, was born near Mt. Crawford, March 18, 1857. The wife of John M. Miller was Catherine Coffman, born January 13, 1825. Mrs. John W. Miller was a daughter of Adam Pifer.

Mr. Miller grew up on his father's farm; attended a local school; then entered Bridgewater College, of which his father was a trustee, and completed the course leading to the B. E. degree. Following his work in the railway offices in Roanoke, he accepted a position as caretaker, then as salesman, at Moundsville, W. Va., with a man who bought and sold registered horses. This work, mainly out of doors, he found more healthful than office work. After traveling a year for a book and novelty company of Philadelphia, he married Miss Bess B. Helbert of Broadway, October 4, 1910. She was born July 12, 1888, a daughter of B. F. Helbert. For several years following his marriage Mr. Miller farmed for his father-in-law; then, on December 1, 1914, he entered the First National Bank of Broadway as a bookkeeper, with which institution he has remained to the present. For some time past he has been vice-president and cashier. He also represents the W. L. Dechert Corporation, the well-known insurance agency of Harrisonburg.

Mr. Miller has been active in fraternal, civic, and religious organizations, being a past master of the Rockingham Union Lodge No. 27, A. F. & A. M., of which he is a member. He has been high priest of Rockingham Royal Arch Chapter No. 6. He is past councilor of Broadway Council No. 46, Jr. O. U. A. M. He is vice-president of the Plains District Ruritan Club. He is a steward, trustee, and the treasurer of the Broadway Methodist Church, superintendent of the Sundayschool, and teacher of the adult Bible class; also lay leader of the New Market charge of the Methodist Church. He is treasurer of the local school board at Broadway and a member of the Board of Public Welfare of Rockingham County.

Mr. and Mrs. Miller have had three children: Frances A., born January 20, 1912, now Mrs. Daniel F. Yancey of Broadway; Genevieve I., born September 21, 1914, now Mrs. Sam C. Heltzel, Jr., of Bridgewater; and Morris Eugene, born December 19, 1923, who died March 3, 1928.

Mr. Miller's hobby is poultry, especially fancy or purebred strains. His reading preferences are found in current events as presented in the newspapers and magazines. He does not claim to have any outstanding achievements to his credit, but is interested in any and every project that makes for the betterment of his community or that of the country at large.

OMEGA LEVI MILLER, D. O.
PRACTITIONER AND CIVIC LEADER

Born July 19, 1891, at Sangerville, Augusta County; grew to manhood on a farm at Nokesville, Prince William County; attended school at Sangerville and Nokesville; student in Hebron Seminary and Bridgewater College; B. A., Bridgewater, 1919; student in Andrew T. Still College of Osteopathy and Surgery, Kirksville, Mo., 1921-25; received the degree of Doctor of Osteopathy, 1925; licensed by Va. Medical Board, 1925; has since practiced in Harrisonburg; active with Boy Scouts of America since 1933; teacher of Red Cross first aid courses; member of professional organizations.

Dr. Miller is a son of Levi Miller (Aug. 2, 1853—Feb. 10. 1891) and his wife, Catharine S. Glick (Oct. 27, 1851; living). His paternal grandparents were Daniel Miller (1815-1888) and wife, Hannah Huff. His mother's parents were Joel Glick (1820-1880) and wife, Elizabeth Miller (1819-1905). The son of a cabinet-maker and builder of buggies, he learned early in life to use tools and made most of his own toys. He did much farm work and fished in near-by streams for diversion, attending the Sangerville school during the terms they were in session. When he was ten years old the family moved to Nokesville, where he worked on a dairy farm, which meant early rising and a long day's work. Accordingly, when the evening chores were done he was ready for the sleep of the weary and just. Owing to his home duties, his time in school was now limited to three or four months a year, but he did manage to get two years of high-school work completed in Hebron Seminary. After the farm was sold to allow him, a brother and a sister, to attend school, he finished his high-school work in Bridgewater College Academy, and then took up the college course which he completed in 1919, receiving his B. A. degree. During his junior year he had charge of the college wood-working shop, thus paying all of his expenses for that year. Most of the other years he supplemented his finances by working in the college library. During all of his vacations he sold books or aluminum ware or did carpentering. After serving as superintendent of the Mutual Cold Storage, Inc., at Broadway from 1919 to 1921, he took up his course at Still College, graduating after four years, as already indicated.

In Harrisonburg, in addition to his extensive professional work, Dr. Miller has been active in church and various social services. For the past ten years or more he has been a steward in the Methodist Church, and was for two years chairman of the board. Since 1927 he has been a member of the Kiwanis Club—was president in 1935. He is a member of the local chamber of commerce. The latter in 1940 awarded him a plague for distinguished community service with the boy scouts, and he holds the Silver Beaver Award from the Stonewall Jackson Council. In politics he is an independent voter. His hobbies are gardening, wood-working, and furnishing leadership for boy scouts. His reading is mainly along professional lines, with newspapers, magazines, and an occasional novel.

On June 8, 1920, Dr. Miller married Miss Eunice Estelle Early of near Harrisonburg, daughter of the late Daniel and Ida Kiser Early. She received her B. A. degree from Bridgewater College on May 30, 1919. For three years she taught in Rockingham County schools. Dr. and Mrs. Miller have three sons: Orland Lloyd, born March 5, 1922; Waldo Glenn, born January 16, 1925; and Dwight Earl, born November 5, 1929.

RALPH SHOWALTER MONGER
MECHANIC, FARMER, AND BUSINESS MAN

Born February 4, 1888, at North River, Rockingham County; attended public school, Mt. Crawford Military Academy, and Bridgewater College; operated a cannery at Mt. Crawford Depot; rural mail carrier, 1909-20; started lumber business in Harrisonburg, 1920; in 1937, with his sons, expanded his business as R. S. Monger & Sons, Inc., dealing in lumber, coal, and building supplies; steward in the Methodist Church; member of the Elks Club of Harrisonburg; farmer and producer of livestock.

Mr. Monger is a son of John H. (1859-1913) and Amanda S. Showalter (born 1867) Monger; his paternal grandparents were William H. Monger (born 1832) and Margaret Vaughter (born 1833); his mother's parents were Isaac Showalter (born 1825) and Isabelle Huffman (born 1833). During the war,1861-65, his grandfather Showalter was captured by Federal troops and sent to his brother's farm in Indiana. Ralph attended public school near North River and later Rockingham Military Academy, which was conducted for some years at Mt. Crawford by Captain Frank Byerly. In 1905 he entered Bridgewater College and in 1907 received his diploma in the commercial department. While he grew up he had access to tools and machinery in connection with a water-power sawmill, buggy and wagon factory which his grandfather Monger had built about 1870, and in which were many of the tools that had been used by his father, his grandfather, and his great-grandfather. A grain and hominy mill was operated in connection with the sawmill. The old mill pond was a favorite place for him and neighbor boys for swimming in summer and skating in winter. His grandfather had made grain cradles for which he, as a young mechanic, made repairs. After operating a cannery at Mt. Crawford Depot for a time, and serving as carrier on a rural mail route for 11 years, he became a dealer in lumber and building supplies in Harrisonburg, moving to town in 1922 and adding coal to his business. As his coal and lumber business expanded he took his sons into partnership and in 1937 they organized as R. S. Monger & Sons, Inc., with R. S. Monger president and treasurer, W. K. Monger vice-president, and J. H. Monger secretary. This business is being successfully carried on at the well-known location between S. High Street and the C. W. Railway.

Mr. Monger serves the Methodist Church of Harrisonburg as a steward and is a member of the Brotherhood Bible Class. He also belongs to the Benevolent and Protective Order of Elks. He tries to live by the Democratic ideals of our American government. In childhood his favorite hobby was fishing; now he finds recreation in farming and looking after livestock. In reading he prefers historical works, and he enjoys the radio, especially news broadcasts.

On May 31, 1916, Mr. Monger married Miss Lillye Fern Kaylor, born July 8, 1892, the marriage taking place at Greenbank, farm home of her parents, Mr. and Mrs. William J. Kaylor. Mr. and Mrs. Monger have five children: William Kaylor, born Feb. 28, 1917; John Henry, Aug. 18, 1918; Unity Fern, Jan. 2, 1922; Anita Chloe, July 31, 1923; and Margaret Susan (Peggy Sue), May 16, 1929. The sons are graduates of Harrisonburg High School and Virginia Polytechnic Institute and are now serving in the U. S. Army, John H. as captain. Unity graduated from high school and Madison College and is now a student in the Medial College of Virginia at Richmond. Anita is a graduate of high school and is now a junior in Madison College. Peggy Sue is attending the city high school.

KARL CECIL MOORE

LAWYER AND JUDGE OF JUVENILE COURT

Born Sept. 16, 1898, in Augusta County, near Mt. Sidney; grew up on his father's farm; attended West View Graded School and Weyers Cave High School, graduating from the latter in 1917; in 1918 entered the academic department, Univ. of Va., in 1919 the law department, from which he was graduated LL.B. in June, 1922; has practiced in Harrisonburg since 1922; Juvenile Judge, 1933; a director of and since 1937 attorney for the First National Bank; City Attorney since June, 1942; Trial Justice and Juvenile Judge for the city and county since November, 1942; Kiwanian; Episcopal vestryman; chairman city Democratic Committee.

Mr. Moore is a native of that fertile and prosperous section of Augusta County lying east of the village of Mt. Sidney, between the Valley Pike and Middle River, in which the Moores, Landises, Garbers, Wamplers, Clines, and other well-known families have been numerous and well-to-do for generations. His father is Robert Letcher Moore; his mother's maiden name was Josephine Landis, a daughter of John Landis. His paternal grandfather was Hamilton Moore, whose farm lay on one of the ox-bow curves of Middle River, two miles southeast of Mt. Sidney. Having obtained his elementary education in West View Graded School, which is located two miles northeast of Mt. Sidney, he attended Weyers Cave High School where he completed the prescribed course and was graduated as a member of the class of 1917. In the autumn of 1918 he entered academic and in 1919 matriculated in the law department of the University of Virginia, of which William M. Lile was then dean, pursued the regular course from year to year and was graduated with the degree of LL.B. in June of 1922.

Coming to Harrisonburg in November, 1922, Mr. Moore entered upon the practice of his profession in which he has been successfully engaged here since that date. In 1933 he served the city as Juvenile Judge; for two years, 1933-34, he was district counsel for the Home Owner's Loan Corporation. For the past eight years he has been a director of the First National Bank of Harrisonburg and since 1937 has been attorney for that institution. Since April, 1942, he has been city attorney for Harrisonburg, and since November of the same year he has been Trial Justice and Juvenile Judge for Harrisonburg and Rockingham County.

In 1918 Mr. Moore was enrolled under S. A. T. C. from October to December. He is a member of the city-county Kiwanis Club, a vestryman of Emmanuel Episcopal Church, chairman of the Harrisonburg Democratic Committee, and is affiliated with a number of professional organizations. In his reading he gives preference to current events, fiction, and biographies. He does not list any hobbies, but enjoys most sports and diversions with which the normal American becomes acquainted during his growing-up period of outdoor life on a farm. City life quickens rather than cures the capacities for such pleasures.

On October 20, 1927, Mr. Moore married Miss Ellen Kagey, born July 17, 1902, a daughter of Noah I. and Aphelia Crickenberger Kagey of Weyers Cave. Mrs. Moore is a graduate of Madison College, class of 1923. Her father, Noah I. Kagey, a native of the Bridgewater community, is the ninth son and next to the youngest child of David Neff and Mary Miller Kagey. Her mother is the daughter of Samuel and Elizabeth Crickenberger. Mr. and Mrs. Moore are the parents of two children: Mary Ellen, born January 3, 1934, and Robert Letcher II, born February 25, 1939, both natives of Harrisonburg.

W. O. MOWBRAY
TEACHER AND WRITER

Born November 14, 1870, at Mt. Clinton; attended Rockingham public schools, West Central Academy, and Madison College; teacher in Rockingham and Shenandoah schools 33 years; retired in 1930; engaged in newspaper work since retirement; census enumerator in 1930; Sundayschool superintendent, 1896-1931; antiquarian—devoted to local history and neighborhood traditions, on which he makes frequent contributions to periodicals.

Mr. Mowbray is a son of Benjamin W. and Kate Thacker Mowbray; his paternal grandparents were Zachary Lewis Mowbray and wife, Polly Clayton. The first school he attended was Liberty Hall, with Miss Hattie Driver as teacher, at Myers's Mill, later known as Rodeffer's, on Muddy Creek. Later teachers at other places were Boyd H. Funk, Dee Witt Rodeffer, Benj. F. Kirkpatrick, Jacob A. Miller, and S. P. Beery. Mr. Funk and Mr. Miller later became ministers in the Church of the Brethren. When West Central Academy was opened at Mt. Clinton in 1890, by Dr. B. T. Hodge, he was one of the charter pupils, and from 1892 to 1896 he was in the same school, with Prof. Isaac S. Wampler as principal. Entering the teaching profession himself, he taught one term each at Melrose, Dayton, and Linville, two terms at Mt. Clinton, and 27 at Singers' Glen. For one year he was principal of the school at Quicksburg in Shenandoah County. Within the period of his service as a teacher he took a summer course at the State Teachers (now Madison) College in Harrisonburg. In 1930, upon his retirement from teaching, he was enumerator in Rockingham for the 15th Federal Census, and from the same time to the present he has been engaged in newspaper work, chiefly in connection with the Harrisonburg city papers. In his reading he prefers historical works and declares his hobby to be digging into the "archives of antiquity." He has contributed numerous articles to the press on old schools, roads, local geographical names, and incidents of personal and historical interest. He is a member of the United Brethren Church and served the Donovan Memorial Church of Singers' Glen for a number of years as Sundayschool superintendent. In politics he classifies himself as a "hard-boiled, stand-pat Republican of the Mark Hanna School."

In 1913 Mr. Mowbray married Miss Lena Myers, daughter of Mr. and Mrs. W. Frank Myers of Mt. Clinton. Of the marriage there are two daughters: Virginia Glen, born December 5, 1915, and Minnie Myers, born June 12, 1918. On February 25, 1939, Virginia Glen, who is a registered nurse, married Virgil Lane Mathias and has a daughter, Marilyn Myers Mathias, now three years old. Mr. Mathias is postmaster at Mathias, Hardy County, W. Va., where his family has been well known for generations. On June 29, 1941, Minnie Myers Mowbray married Sebastian Richard Rio, who is an architect and for the past five years has held a position with the Federal Public Housing Authority in Washington, D. C. Both daughters are graduates of the Mt. Clinton High School. Virginia Glen completed her course in nursing at Rockingham Memorial Hospital in 1938. Minnie Myers, after her graduation at Mt. Clinton, took a special course in stenography and typewriting at the Harrisonburg High School and for four years prior to her marriage held a position with the Potomac Telephone Company in Washington City.

CHARLES SAMUEL MUNDY

FARMER, BUSINESS MAN, AND BUILDER

Born April 30, 1884, at Scott's Ford, Rockingham County; educated in public schools of southeast Rockingham; began his business career as a farmer and producer of pure-bred shorthorn cattle; successful milk distributor in Harrisonburg; operator of the Mundy Stone Company; contractor and builder of stone houses; member of the Church of the Brethren.

Mr. Mundy, a son of Archibald and Lucy Mundy of the Scott's Ford community near Good's Mill and Port Republic, is the second child in a family of eight brothers and sisters. His early education was received mainly in one-room schools in the southeastern part of Rockingham, the section in which he grew up. His subsequent career as a farmer, producer of livestock, milk distributor, operator of large stone quarries, and as a builder of modern dwelling houses, has supplemented his schooling with the valuable lessons of extensive experience. He began his business career as a farmer and in raising pure-bred shorthorn cattle, and later, to have convenient facilities for the education of his children, he purchased a farm a short distance north of Harrisonburg, where he engaged extensively in dairying and retailing milk to customers in the city and adjacent suburbs. In this he was eminently successful and won merited recognition as a leader in improving the service and the quality of the commodity. In connection with dairying he developed a large business in producing and distributing crushed stone for use in the improvement of roads and in the construction of buildings and bridges. In this business he and his sons operated quarries at Harrisonburg, Port Republic, Elkton, Broadway, and Cootes's Store. Having sold his farm, in order to give his full time to the stone business, Mr. Mundy began to indulge a hobby for construction work, and in recent years he has completed seven stone dwelling houses. These domiciles are unique in design and ultra-modern in every respect.

Mr. Mundy's wife was Miss Letitia Josephine Wampler, daughter of Rev. David B. and Elizabeth Cline Wampler, born December 19, 1887. The marriage took place April 24, 1906, at her home a short distance east of Penn Laird. Of this marriage were born four children: Theodore Wampler, born at Pleasant Valley; a graduate of Bridgewater College and a student of the University of Virginia; now owner and operator of the Elkton Stone Co.; Nellie Elizabeth, born at Penn Laird; also a graduate of Bridgewater College; now Mrs. Mark Wampler, and a teacher in the public schools; D. Clement, born at Cross Keys; he attended Bridgewater College and is now owner and operator of the Mundy Stone Co., Harrisonburg; and Avis Rosalind, born at Cross Keys; a graduate of Bridgewater College; now Mrs. G. W. Swartz, and a teacher in the public schools.

Mr. Mundy's hobbies, in addition to building houses, are hunting and fishing, and, to go back to his start in life, farming. In reading he prefers the leading magazines and newspapers, and gives preference in them to scientific articles relating to his business. He is a member of the Church of the Brethren; in politics he is a Republican. Mrs. Mundy has always been much interested in educational and religious work. Her father was a teacher as well as a minister of the Gospel.

FRED P. MYERS

LAWYER, AUTHOR, AND EDUCATOR

Born at Greenmount; attended local schools; B. A., Bridgewater College; M. A., University of Virginia; LL. B. and LL. M., D. C. universities; graduate student at Johns Hopkins; charter member and treasurer Society of Virginia in Washington; Historian-General for United Confederate Veterans; member American Legion; author of poems and historical and legal works; principal and treasurer of Emerson Institute; member of law firm of Abbott, Puller, & Myers, Washington, D. C.

Fred Myers, Pete to his intimate friends, is versatile in his talents and cosmopolitan in his interests. At intervals in his busy life, he has been a teacher for 31 years without losing a day on account of illness. He writes poetry, practices law, organizes clubs, and is a lay reader in church. He grew up on the North Mountain "Vineyard Farm" and has never lost his love for Rockingham. As a boy he was never bad, but was notorious for mischief. He was fond of playing Indian, soldier, and "preaching" to other boys in an old shop on Sunday afternoons. He liked wild west stories and history, especially of the War between the States. In the latter his interest is unabated, and his hobby is collecting old histories and documents on the war and related subjects. His father was Peter Harvey Myers of Greenmount; his mother, Elizabeth Burkholder of Dale Enterprise. His paternal grandmother was Elizabeth Hagerdon Myers, born in 1822 in Darmstadt, Hesse-Cassel, Germany. His father was a cannoneer in Chew's Battery, attached to Ashby's cavalry.

After four years in the preparatory department of Bridgewater College, Fred taught school at Tenth Legion and Edom. Then he took four more years at Bridgewater, graduating as class poet and valedictorian, after serving as magazine editor, president of two literary societies and the athletic association, and manager of the glee club. He was high-school principal at LaCrosse, Mecklenburg County, Shenandoah City, and McGaheysville, and, while attending the University, a teacher in the Charlottesville High School. At the Natl. Univ. Law School in Washington he graduated LL. B., and LL. M. at the American University, at the latter on a fellowship. Elected a Hopkins Scholar, he commuted to Johns Hopkins three years, finishing for the Ph. D. degree, except the dissertation. As a lawyer in Washington for the past 20 years, he has had a wide experience. One year he tried more murder cases than any other member of the District bar during the same term of court. In civil practice, to which he now devotes himself, he has exposed several gigantic fraudulent institutions and sucessfully prosecuted them through the courts. For the past 21 years he has been a teacher in Emerson Institute, and for nine years in National University on law, economics, and government. He has made a special study of the Constitutional opinions of Chief-Justice Taft and is the author of "The Challenge of the Market-place," "Wars and Rumors of Wars," "England's Attitude toward the Monroe Doctrine," "The Latin-American Policy of the Wilson Administration," and related works.

At Harrisonburg Mr. Myers was a member of the home guards, and the first of that body discharged to join the U. S. Army in 1918. He served in the Va. Natl. Guard and the 121st Engineers, D. C. Natl. Guard. On April 19, 1930, he married Mrs. Myra McCathran Marks. His stepson, Harold M. Marks, is an officer in the Naval Air Service. Mrs Myers is a singing teacher, church soloist, and radio and concert artist.

JOHN CLARENCE MYERS
SUPERINTENDENT OF ROCKINGHAM PUBLIC SCHOOLS

Born January 18, 1876, near Mt. Crawford; grew up on his father's farm near Broadway; attended a one-room country school and Broadway High School; B. A., Bridgewater College, 1900; graduate student at University of Virginia 1901-03; teacher in Bridgewater College 1900-01, 1903-1908, and 1910-1912; located on home farm near Broadway in 1912; principal of Broadway High School 1913-17; division superintendent of Rockingham schools since 1917.

Superintendent Myers is a son of Benjamin Allen (December 6, 1841—September 28, 1931) and Sallie Garber Myers (December 20, 1846—May 7, 1912), both born near Timberville. The Myerses and the Garbers have been well known in the Shenandoah Valley since Revolutionary times. B. A. Myers was a successful farmer, an efficient business man, and an active worker in the Church of the Brethren. He and his wife had 10 children: James O., Vancouver, B. C.; Mrs. Edna Bowman, Washington, D. C., who died Jan. 16, 1943; Bessie, who died years ago; Robert E., Olney, Texas; John C.; Walter A., Bridgewater; Weldon T., Spartanburg, S. C.; Mamie K., Broadway; Mrs. Nellie Wampler, Broadway; and Harold B., Rosetown, Sask.

John C. Myers taught one session before entering Bridgewater College in 1896. After graduation there and graduate work in the University of Virginia he taught in Bridgewater College as already indicated, eight years in all, and for part of the time was business manager of the college. On the faculty he was associated with Walter B. Yount, John S. Flory, Justus H. Cline, R. H. Latham, and other well-known educators. From his ancestors he inherited a love for the land and livestock and country life, and in 1912 he located on the home farm, which he now owns, on Linville Creek. After heading the Broadway High School four years he, in 1917, was made division superintendent of Rockingham public schools, and has six times been reappointed. Under his direction and capable leadership the schools of the county have made remarkable progress. At the same time he participates actively in civic and religious work. He is a member of the Plains Ruritan Club; is elder of the Linville Creek Church of the Brethren, and is president of the board of trustees of Bridgewater College.

On August 10, 1904, Mr. Myers married Miss Ottie F. Showalter, who was born August 20, 1877, near Port Republic, daughter of P. H. Showalter and wife, Magdalene Heatwole. She, too, has been a teacher and is active in civic affairs and the women's work in the Church of the Brethren.

Mr. and Mrs. Myers have had five children: Rachel Edna, born July 20, 1905, now with her husband, Earl M. Zigler, married in 1937, a missionary in India; Allen Showalter, born July 18, 1907, who died at age of two years; Rebecca Virginia, born May 26, 1910, B. A. of Bridgewater College and M. S. of Richmond Professional Institute of William and Mary, now a social worker in St. Elizabeth's Hospital, Washington, with the American Red Cross; Dorothy Katherine, born March 28, 1913, a graduate of Madison College, married in 1938 to Thomas Hugh Stafford and living in Henderson, N. C., where Mr. Stafford is rate clerk in the Southern Railway freight office; one son, Thomas Stafford, Jr.; and Anna Margaret, born February 24, 1915, B. A. of Bridgewater College, married to Snyder S. Harman in 1935; sons John, Dannie, and Richard. Mr. Harman is a teacher at Harman, W. Va.

JOHN HENRY NEFF, M. D.
SURGEON AND SPECIALIST IN UROLOGY

Born September 12, 1887, in Harrisonburg; graduate of Harrisonburg High School, 1903; A. B., University of Virginia, 1907; M. D., 1910; interne and house surgeon, U. Va. Hospital, 1910-16; acting associate professor of surgery, 1917-19; adjunct professor of urology, 1916, later associate professor, and from 1928 until his death professor of urology; fellow American College of Surgeons; member American Urological Association, Southern Surgical Association, American Association of Genito-Urinary Surgeons; Phi Beta Kappa, Sigma Xi, Pi Kappa Alpha, Phi Rho Sigma, Alpha Omega Alpha. Died November 8, 1938.

Dr. Neff came of a long line of professional ancestors, family tradition having it, "There was always a Doctor Neff." His father, John Henry Neff (1842-1912), was for many years a leading physician of Harrisonburg. His first ancestor in Virginia was Dr. John Henry Neff, who received grants of land at Rude's Hill, Shenandoah County, Va., in 1750 and 1756. Jacob, one of the pioneer's five sons, was a doctor. Another son, Francis, had a son John (1776-1852), and among this John's several sons was Daniel (1810-76), grandfather of the subject of this sketch. Daniel's wife was Elizabeth Garber, married in 1837; his son John Henry's wife was Brownie Morrison, married November 1, 1883. Dr. John Henry (1887-1938) had a sister, Brownie, older, and three brothers, Mitchell, Harold, and Douglas, and a sister, Mary, younger than himself.

During his student days at the University of Virginia Dr. Neff was distinguished in football, one of the outstanding backs of the South, and later he was an efficient football coach. He was fond of outdoor sports and an ardent fisherman, familiar with many Virginia streams and some in Canada. Tennis, card-playing, music, and reading were also among his diversions and cultural activities. He was a member of St. Paul's Episcopal Church in Charlottesville, and although professional duties often kept him from attending, he kept in touch with the work of the church and contributed generously to its support. On the night preceding his death he was elected a member of the vestry. He was outstanding in the community and among his colleagues for his kindliness, cheerfulness, good judgment, and courage.

During the seven years of his house training in surgery Dr. Neff enjoyed notable advantages in his association with Dr. Stephen H. Watts, these associations being continued in succeeding years as he advanced steadily in rank and professional standing. It is said of him that his professional life was unusual in two respects: (1) "He had perhaps the soundest background of general surgery upon which any urologist of his age has based his specialty;" and (2) his remarkable qualities of mind and character appeared in the fact that he was entirely a self-taught urologist. "He evidenced on every occasion almost faultless surgical judgment, based upon a wide knowledge of pathology. As an operator, he was methodical, careful and thorough, respecting tissue profoundly, bold where boldness was justified."

On June 1, 1916, Dr. Neff married Miss Harriet Louise Fitzgerald of Houston, Texas, born October 16, 1887. Of the marriage were born three children: Mary Elizabeth, June 13, 1919; John Henry, May 11, 1921; and George Fitzgerald, August 10, 1923. Biographical sketches of Dr. Neff appeared regularly in "Who's Who in America" for the ten years preceding his death.

BARUCH NEY
MERCHANT, PHILANTHROPIST, AND ARTIST

Born February 16, 1846, at Niederstetten, Wurttemberg, Germany; came to New York in the fall of 1865; soon after, to Harrisonburg; worked for Leopold Wise; operated a confectionery store under the name of Ney & Wise; in 1874 began business on the site of the present store of B. Ney & Sons; in 1895 took his sons Isaac and Henry into partnership; at age of 21 began a course of self-education; at age of 50 took up oil portraiture; died on March 10, 1915.

Baruch Ney, always known as B. Ney, came to America in the fall of 1865, at the age of 19. He was inclined to come earlier, but on his father's advice waited until the war here was over. With the limited education acquired in the home schools and $50 over and above his traveling fare, given him by his father, he started peddling in New York State, but soon lost his small capital. Then, by selling pictures of Abraham Lincoln in front of Trinity Church, New York City, he earned enough to go to Baltimore. From there Leopold Wise of Harrisonburg brought him here, where he drove Mr. Wise's cow and worked around the house for one dollar a week, his board, washing, and patching. One of his main objects in coming here was to learn the English language. Captain C. A. Sprinkel set him up in business and rented him the quarters now occupied by the McCrory Store, then owned by Captain Sprinkel. He opened a confectionery store under the firm name of Ney & Wise. In 1874 he dissolved partnership with Mr. Wise and purchased the site on the north corner of Elizabeth Street and North Main, where the store of B. Ney & Sons is still located, and began merchandising, specializing in men's clothing. In 1895 he took his sons Isaac and Henry into partnership, and later his sons Albert H. and Carl. Accordingly, the Neys have been in business at this familiar stand for 68 years, and the firm has for a long time been well known over a large area of Virginia and adjacent states. One of B. Ney's grandsons is now a member of the firm. About 1898 the store added ladies' wear and became a general department store.

In 1870 Mr. Ney married Miss Kattie Wise, a sister to Leo J. (not the Leopold mentioned above), and of the marriage were born seven children: Isaac, Henry, Albert H., Carl, Hulda (Mrs. I. Iseman), Olga (Mrs. Clarence Wise), and Dr. Grover Cleveland Ney, of Baltimore, who married Selma Straus. Mrs. Ney died in 1887, and in 1889 Mr. Ney married (2) Miss Bertha Rosenfeld, who, a year earlier, had come to Harrisonburg from Atlanta, Ga. Of the second marriage were born four children: Carrie (Mrs. Morris Scheurer of Front Royal), Manhattan R., now of Chattanooga, Ferdinand, now of Washington City, and Miriam (Mrs. Leon Scheurer of Baltimore).

Mr. Ney was a member of the Hebrew Friendship Congregation of Harrisonburg and instrumental in building the synagogue. By correspondence with rabbis and others in all parts of the country he raised money for the purpose. This, added to local contributions, made the building possible. At the age of 21 Mr. Ney began a course of self-instruction by extensive reading, especially in history, and at the age of 50 he took up oil painting and, without ever having a lesson, carried the art to a high degree of excellence. At his death in 1915 his collection of paintings was divided among his children. His final work, and in his judgment his masterpiece, is a portrait of General R. E. Lee.

Mrs. B. Ney died March 5, 1943, aged 87, widely known and well loved for her benevolent and patriotic activities.

HENRY NEY

PRESIDENT OF B. NEY AND SONS COMPANY

Born September 28, 1874, in Harrisonburg; attended the city schools and Bryant & Stratton Business College; a charter member of the Harrisonburg Rotary Club and the Elks Lodge; member of the chamber of commerce; past secretary of the Hebrew Friendship Congregation; president of the firm of B. Ney & Sons, merchants; member of the Rockingham Memorial Hospital board, successor to Joshua Wilton, who died Nov. 17, 1928.

Henry Ney is the second son of Baruch Ney (1846-1915) and his first wife, whose maiden name was Kattie Wise. Of this marriage there were six other children: Isaac, who was Henry's senior, and Albert H., Carl, Hulda, Olga, and Grover Cleveland, who are younger. Baruch Ney's parents were Alfred Hirsch Ney and his wife Miriam, whose family name is unknown.

Henry Ney as a boy attended the schools of Harrisonburg and then continued his education in the Bryant & Stratton Business College of Baltimore. He then entered business in Harrisonburg with his father and older brother as a member of the firm of B. Ney & Sons, and since the death of his brother Isaac, November 26, 1941, he has been president of the company.

Mr. Ney was one of the 18 men who established the Elks Lodge in Harrisonburg, and he is now the only one of the number living. He was also a charter member of the Harrisonburg Rotary Club, in which he was active for some years. He is now an honorary member of that club. For a number of years he was secretary of the Harrisonburg Hebrew Friendship Congregation, of which he is a member. His interest in civic welfare and all progressive movements is well known. He was one of the prime movers in the launching and organizing of Shenandoah Valley, Inc., in 1924 or thereabouts. Encouraged by Frank L. Sublett, he wrote to three or four outstanding men in each of 13 counties, who came together in an enthusiastic meeting in Harrisonburg and effected an organization which has been functioning efficiently ever since. This organization has done much to develop and make known the natural resources and beautiful scenery of this part of Virginia, and has been instrumental in increasing largely the number of tourists who, every year, come as sightseers and sojourners. Mr. Ney's quiet manner and wholesome companionship have earned him thousands of friends, not only in business connections but also in the various civic and fraternal activities in which he has taken part.

On January 10, 1898, Mr. Ney married Miss Julia Salomon of Baltimore. Of this marriage have been born five children: Kattie, named for her grandmother; she is single and lives in Chicago; Alvin H., who is now a member of the firm of B. Ney & Sons; he married Miss Margaret Putzel of Baltimore; Helen, who married Dr. E. S. Edlow of Baltimore and lives in that city; Blanche Clinton, who married E. P. Berney of Baltimore and lives there; and Dr. Charles Ney, single, who is a surgeon in the Morrisania City Hospital of New York.

Reading is Mr. Ney's recreation, and so habitually and eagerly does he devote himself to it that it may be termed his hobby. He does not take up much time with books, but goes through all of the newspapers available, finding his chief interest in current topics. This is no doubt in keeping with his business activities and his concern for civic, social, and political welfare and progress.

ALBERT HIRSCH NEY

MERCHANT AND BUSINESS MAN

Born July 8, 1878, in Harrisonburg; attended the public schools of Harrisonburg; student in the Bryant & Stratton Business College; a member of the mercantile firm of B. Ney & Sons of Harrisonburg; in 1923 retired from the firm and located in Washington City; now engaged in business, handling building materials.

Mr. Ney is the third son of Baruch Ney and his first wife, Kattie Wise. His grandparents on his father's side were Alfred Hirsch Ney and Miriam Ney. His father, Baruch Ney, came to Harrisonburg in or about 1866, where he first worked for Leopold Wise, but soon went into business for himself. In 1874 he purchased the house and lot on the north corner of Elizabeth and North Main Street, where he first specialized in handling men's clothing; later, with his sons, he expanded the business into a large department store which is still being operated under the firm of B. Ney & Sons Company.

Albert H. Ney, after attending the Harrisonburg public school, naturally turned toward the business world, in which his father and older brothers were active and prominent, and to qualify himself for the work he anticipated he took a course of training in the Bryant & Stratton Business College in the city of Baltimore. At the age of nineteen he entered business with his father and his brothers Isaac and Henry, and continued in that relationship for about twenty-five years, giving evidence of excellent judgment and executive ability. Persons who know him well are unreserved in attributing to him business qualities of a high order.

Retiring from the mercantile firm in Harrisonburg in 1923, Mr. Ney went to Washington City, where he sought an occupation that would release him from indoor confinement and give him the advantages of an outdoor life. Accordingly, he engaged with others in the purchase and distribution of materials and supplies that are needed in building operations, in which he has since carried on a successful business. At present he is connected with the Hechinger Company, which is operating in the field just indicated.

On June 20, 1904, Mr. Ney married Miss Berdie Frank, a daughter of Mr. and Mrs. Lewis Frank of the city of Baltimore. She died at Woodley Park Towers, in the city of Washington, on September 25, 1942, following an illness of about two months. Besides her husband, she is survived by a daughter, Miss Audrey Jean Ney, of Washington, and two sisters, Mrs. Sylvia Hechinger and Mrs. Rena Wolsheimer, both of Washington, and one brother, Nathan Frank, also of Washington City. During her long residence in Harrisonburg, Mrs. Ney made many friends who regret her untimely death.

Mr. Ney is a member of the Masonic fraternity and is also affiliated with the Benevolent and Protective Order of Elks; and he is a member of the Washington Hebrew Congregation. He maintains intimate connections with Harrisonburg, his boyhood home and the scene of his business activities over a period of many years.

JOHN JACOB NICHOLAS

FARMER, CHURCHMAN, AND BUSINESS MAN

Born June 11, 1889, at Port Republic; grew up on his father's farm and attended Port Republic schools, completing high school; took a commercial course under Professor Mitchell; began farming for himself in 1917; purchased the Madison Hall farm after the death of his parents; continued farming and raising of livestock; official in the Methodist Church and superintendent of Sundayschool; treasurer of the Port Republic Ruritan Club; county member of the A. A. A.; member of the board of the county Farm Bureau; one of the five elected supervisors of the Shen. Valley Soil Conservation District (Augusta and Rockingham).

Mr. Nicholas is a member of one of the families that have been well known in East Rockingham and the region of historic Port Republic for many years. His father was William S. Nicholas, who was born at Port Republic on December 16, 1861. He was a successful farmer and business man, whose death occurred on September 26, 1932. He was a son of Jacob Bright Nicholas, whose wife's maiden name was Elizabeth Koiner. The name of William S. Nicholas's wife before marriage was Bettie R. Harper. She was born at Port Republic on April 5, 1864, the daughter of John and Sara Trout Harper. She died on March 14, 1934.

Having gone through the graded school at Port Republic, John Jacob Nicholas entered the high school, which was then under the principalship of Professor B. B. Mitchell. After finishing the regular high school course he continued his studies in more special fields and completed a business or commercial course under Professor Mitchell. In the year 1917 he rented a farm from his father and operated it for nine years; then due to the failing health of his parents and the fact that his sisters, Miss Bessie H. Nicholas and Mrs. Jennie S.Groah, were away at that time, he located near the home place to be near his parents. They lived at an old homestead which is historically known as Madison Hall, from residence there in early times of John Madison, the first clerk of Augusta County. This place Mr. Nicholas purchased after the death of his parents, and there he now resides. He is a member of the Methodist Church at Port Republic (has been from boyhood), and has been superintendent of the Sundayschool since 1935. He is secretary and treasurer of the board of stewards, having been chosen to that office in 1910; and since the same year has been recording steward of the Port Republic Circuit. He is a member and the treasurer of the Port Republic Ruritan Club, a county member of the A. A. A., and has been on the board of the Rockingham Farm Bureau for years. In politics he is a Democrat. His hobbies are farming and livestock, and he takes much pride in the thrifty upkeep of his farm, the buildings, and the general equipment. His dwelling house was built by his father in 1916 on the site of old Madison Hall. The latter, which was torn down, was a large house, the main (front) part built of logs, the rear extension frame. A picture from a photograph of the old house made in 1911 may be seen in Wayland's "Historic Homes," page 226, and in "Stonewall Jackson's Way," page 150. General Jackson had his headquarters in June, 1862, at Madison Hall, which was then occupied by Dr. George W. Kemper, Sr. Tradition has it that a fort was located here in Indian times. Mr. Nicholas, in recent excavations, found remains of an old foundation.

On March 16, 1915, Mr. Nicholas married Miss Stella Lupton, daughter of Silas and Catherine Lupton of near Martinsburg, W. Va. The Luptons have lived in that region since early colonial days.

MRS. CHARLES E. PALMER

EDUCATOR, TRAVELER, AND CIVIC LEADER

Born in Harrisonburg in 1879; graduate of Harrisonburg High School in 1895; of Peabody College, Nashville, in 1897; teacher in Virginia, Washington, Oregon, and California, 1897-1906; married in 1906; traveler with her children in America and Europe; collector of Virginiana; executive director of the City Planning and Zoning Commission, Sioux City, Iowa; president of the Iowa Housing League.

Mrs. Palmer, born Mary Vance Clary, is a daughter of J. O. A. Clary and his wife, Mary Vance Hern. The latter's mother was Martha Vance of Mountain Grove, Bath County, Va., a direct descendant of John Vance, who died in 1782, and his son, Colonel Samuel Vance of the Revolutionary War. The family built the colonial Fort Vance at Mountain Grove. During the Civil War Mary Vance Hern lived in Harrisonburg with her aunt, Margaret Vance Wartman, and her uncle, Harvey Wartman. The Wartmans were the famous Harrisonburg printers and publishers, Lawrence Wartman (1774-1840) having founded the *Rockingham Register* in 1822. Her paternal grandfather was Dr. Jonathan Clary, who practiced in Harrisonburg and Rockingham; his wife was Frances Newman, daughter of James Newman of Orange County and Rockingham.

When Mrs. Palmer (Mary Vance Clary) graduated from Harrisonburg High School she won a scholarship, in competitive examination, to Peabody College. After graduating at Peabody, she taught as assistant principal, then principal, at Port Republic, 1897-1900, making a name for herself as one of the most progressive and popular teachers of the county. From 1900 to 1903 she taught Latin and science in Brunot Hall, an Episcopal young ladies seminary in Spokane, Washington. She then headed departments of science and philosophy in St. Helen's Hall, Portland, Oregon, and St. Margaret's Hall, San Mateo, California, until her marriage in 1906 to Charles E. Palmer, a prominent business man of Sioux City, Iowa. In succeeding years, though busy with her family, Mrs. Palmer found time for many social and civic duties and for frequent travels with her husband and children in Europe and the Orient, as well as in America. After Mr. Palmer's death in 1924 she continued directing the education of her children and in many business duties as trustee of the estate. She has one son and three daughters: (and five grandchildren): Charles Vance, B. S. of the University of Virginia and M. A. of Harvard; his wife, Miss Catherine Dunford of Charlottesville; Mrs. Virginia Dare Palmer Klingler of Sioux City; Mrs. Mary Vance Palmer Whiting of Whiting, Iowa; and Mrs. Penn Palmer Sturdivant of Hollywood, California.

Mrs. Palmer, during the past five years, has devoted much time to state and local civic work, as indicated on the preceding page. She does much writing and lecturing, and is a prominent social and civic leader in her city. She is a member of the Episcopal Church, various clubs, the Woodbury County Historical Assn., the American Assn. of University Women, the Turner Ashby Chapter, Daughters of the Confederacy, of Harrisonburg, and is chairman in her city of the Va. Div. of the Society of Southerners. One cherished corner of her large library is devoted to Virginiana. There may be found pictures of Washington, Lee, and Jackson; an old Confederate flag; a *Rockingham Register* of 1841; a large volume on the Harrison family (to which she is related); one of Mrs. Emma Lyon Bryan's books; and hundreds of others. In a prominent place is an old picture of the "Big Spring" in Harrisonburg. She has attended many reunions of Harrisonburg High School alumni, and never fails to pay a tribute to her old principal, W. H. Keister.

CHARLES GRATTAN PRICE

INSUROR AND BANKER

Born Sept. 6, 1883, near Harrisonburg; attended private and public elementary schools, Dayton High School, and Shenandoah College; stenographer for Sipe & Harris; clerk, bookkeeper, and assistant cashier, Rockingham Natl. Bank; deputy treasurer of Rockingham County; in 1912 organized general insurance agency of Burke & Price; trustee Massanetta Springs Conference and president board of trustees of Lexington Presbytery, Inc.; trustee from Virginia of Southern Presbyterian Church; sec'y-treas. Harrisonburg Realty Corp.; member board of visitors Mount Vernon Assn.; past master Rockingham Union Lodge No. 27, A. F. & A. M.; president Rockingham National Bank.

Mr. Price since early manhood has been actively engaged in various business enterprises and has held important official positions in many of the civic, educational, benevolent, and religious organizations of Harrisonburg and Rockingham County, as well as others beyond our local borders. He is a son of James Robert and Mary Marshall Price. His paternal grandparents were Addison H. and Mary Cox Price; his mother's parents, Mansfield Marshall and wife, Mary Parsons. After completing a business course in Shenandoah Collegiate Institute, now Shenandoah College, at Dayton, he was employed for a year in the law office of Sipe & Harris in Harrisonburg; for the next 10 years he worked in the Rockingham National Bank, advancing to the position of assistant cashier. In 1911 he was deputy treasurer of the county, and the next year was Va. Secretary of the Natl. Citizens' League for Banking & Currency Reform. In 1912 he organized the general insurance agency of Burke & Price, of which he is now sole owner. This is one of the larger agencies in Virginia, representing 18 fire companies, and is general agent for two casualty companies. For some years he has been president of the Rockingham Natl. Bank of Harrisonburg. He holds official positions in the Presbyterian Church and has been prominently identified with the Democratic party in politics; has served for many years as secretary-treasurer of the Rockingham Memorial Hospital of which he is a trustee; is also a trustee of the Richmond Hospital Service Assn., and is president of the Woodbine Cemetery Company. Besides the business connections already mentioned, he is secretary-treasurer of the Harrisonburg Realty Corp. and president of Shenandoah Apartments, Inc. In World War I he participated officially in selective service registration and Liberty Loan drives; and at present he is in the selective service registration and is a member of the Shenandoah Valley Defense Council.

In social and fraternal bodies Mr. Price has been active for many years. He is a member of the Commonwealth Club, Richmond; a charter member and past president of the Harrisonburg Rotary Club, and has held various important offices in Masonry as master of the local lodge, high priest of the Royal Arch Chapter, eminent commander of the Harrisonburg Commandery, and district deputy grand master of the Grand Lodge of Virginia. He is a member of the Scottish Rite Consistory, Alexandria, and Acca Temple (A. A. O. Nobles of the Mystic Shrine), Richmond. He finds recreation in golf; in reading he gives preference to current events.

On June 12, 1917, Mr. Price married Miss Julia Page Pleasants, born Aug. 9, 1893, daughter of Mr. and Mrs. Howard Peterkin Pleasants of Fort Worth, Texas, and Richmond, Va. Mrs. Price is active in social and civic affairs. Mr. and Mrs. Price have two sons: Lieut. Chas. Grattan Price, Jr., born May 31, 1919, now at Camp Holabird, Baltimore, and Page Pleasants Price, of Harrisonburg, born Feb. 15, 1924, student of U. Va., now at Camp Lee.

SAMUEL JAMES PRICHARD
CASHIER OF THE NATIONAL BANK

Born January 6, 1891, in Petersburg, Va.; attended Petersburg public schools; started work in a bank at the age of 16; in the U. S. Armed Forces, 1917-19; sold life insurance in Harrisonburg and Rockingham County, 1919-20; entered employ of the Peoples (now The National) Bank of Harrisonburg in 1920; cashier of this bank since 1930; vestryman Emmanuel P. E. Church; past president Kiwanis Club and past commander American Legion, Post No. 27, Harrisonburg; served on the Harrisonburg school board and now a member of the city council.

Mr. Prichard, who has been a resident of Harrisonburg for the past 24 years, is a native of Petersburg, Va., the "Cockade City," so termed by President Madison because of the valor of Petersburg volunteers at Fort Meigs, in the War of 1812, and the fact that the said volunteers wore a cockade as part of their uniform. His father was Robert White Prichard, whose wife before marriage was Martha Cuthbert Bragg. Her father, Thomas Bragg (1810-1872), a native of Warrenton, N. C., was governor of that state from 1855 to 1859, having served previously in the legislature for a number of years. He was re-elected for a second term as governor, then entered the U. S. Senate, from which he withdrew in 1861. For about two years, 1862-63, he was attorney-general in the Confederate Cabinet. His wife was Isabella Margaret Cuthbert. Mr. Prichard's paternal grandfather was William Irwin Prichard of Greenville County, Va., who married Mary Margaret Hammett.

After going through the Petersburg public schools Mr. Prichard, at the age of 16, began work in the National Bank of Petersburg where he was employed from 1908 to 1917. He then entered the armed service of the United States, which was then engaged in the First World War. He enlisted at Petersburg and for some time was stationed at Camp Lee. Later he served at Fort Myer, where he was honorably discharged in 1919. He then located in Harrisonburg, and was engaged in selling life insurance in the city and county for about a year, when he accepted a position with the Peoples Bank, now The National Bank, of Harrisonburg, with which institution he has since been connected. He has been cashier of this bank for the past 13 years.

Along with his work as a banker, Mr. Prichard has been actively connected with various religious, civic, educational, and business organizations. For 20 years he has been a vestryman of Emmanuel Episcopal Church. He is part owner and manager of the Rosehill Orchard Co., Inc. He has served as president of the local Kiwanis Club and commander of the American Legion of this post. For some time he was on the city school board, resigning to accept a place on the city council. For recreation he plays golf; he and Mrs. Prichard enjoy walking. He is an intereested spectator at games of baseball, football, and basket-ball. In reading he gives preference to current events and works of biography and history.

On January 22, 1918, Mr. Prichard married Miss Bessie Wilson Arthur, who was born October 13, 1891, in Union, S. C., daughter of Benjamin Franklin Arthur and his wife, Josephine Hooker Farrar. Mr. and Mrs. Prichard have three sons: Samuel James, Jr., born February 17, 1920; Benjamin Wilson, born February 6, 1924; and Thomas Bragg, born April 3, 1927. Samuel J., Jr., graduated (B. S.) from Hampden-Sydney College in 1941; Benjamin W. is a freshman (1942-43) in Bridgewater College; and Thomas B. is a student in the Harrisonburg High School, having entered the freshman class last autumn (1942).

JAMES ANDREW RIDDEL

BUSINESS MAN, POSTMASTER, AND MAYOR

Born July 22, 1861, near Mt. Solon, Augusta County, Va.; attended the common schools; worked on sawmills and learned shoemaking; merchant at Moscow eight years; bought a drug store in Bridgewater in 1898; operated sawmills and lumber mills; engaged in contracting and building; member of the Bridgewater town council; postmaster from 1910 to 1914; mayor of Bridgewater, 1920-24; died at his home in the same town on January 9, 1929.

Mr. Riddel had the same name as his father and his grandfather. The latter and his wife, Bettie Gilmer, were natives of McGaheysville. After the Civil War they moved to the vicinity of Muncie, Indiana. James Andrew Riddel, father of the subject of this sketch, was a Confederate soldier and lost his life in the war. His wife was Mary E. Furr, daughter of Harrison Furr and his wife, Elizabeth Johnson. She was an active member of the United Brethren Church, and died in 1875. She and her husband were the parents of four children: Jennie, who married Samuel H. Ellinger; Annie, who married Harvey Ellinger, a brother of Samuel H., and lived near Basic City; Maggie, who married D. L. Perry and lived at Stokesville, Augusta County, Va.; and James Andrew, born July 22, 1861.

Bereft of his father when but an infant, James A. Riddel was under the care of his mother until the age of fourteen, when she died. His parents left no estate, and he and his sisters, without a home, had to make their own way in life. With but little schooling, he worked on sawmills and at various other kinds of hard labor. At the age of 21 he learned the shoemaking trade, but followed that work only a few years. After eight years in business in the village of Moscow as a merchant, he located in Bridgewater where he bought out a drug store. To this, however, he did not give his main attention, but devoted himself chiefly to the buying and selling of tanbark and the manufacture of lumber into building supplies. Soon he built up a large business in operating sawmills, planing mills, dealing in lumber and builders' supplies, and in erection of dwelling houses and other buildings. He served on the town council of Bridgewater; was postmaster in that town for four years, under the Taft administration; and in 1920 was elected mayor. Two years later he declined re-election, but continued in the office for another term at the urgent request of the citizens and the other officials. While he was on the council the town installed a modern water supply system, and the corporate limits were extended.

In October, 1885, Mr. Riddel married Miss Sarah Rebecca Orebaugh of Augusta County, daughter of George A. Orebaugh and his wife, Bettie A. Stoutermyer. Mrs. Riddel was a member of the Lutheran Church. She and her husband were the parents of four children: Pearly V.; Clifford Thurston, whose sketch appears in this work; Roxie R., who is the wife of Dr. Charles Herbert Huffman of Madison College; and Dewey R. Clifford and Dewey were associated with their father in his business for some years prior to the latter's death.

Mr. Riddel's life and achievements afford an inspiring example of what may be accomplished by energy, perseverance, and diligent attention to business and civic responsibilities.

CLIFFORD THURSTON RIDDEL, SR.
BUILDING CONTRACTOR, CHURCH OFFICIAL, AND MAYOR

Born December 28, 1889, at Moscow, Augusta County, Va.; student in Bridgewater College; began business as operator of a restaurant in Bridgewater; became manager of the J. A. Riddel lumber business in 1911; in 1929 purchased the business and added construction work; Bridgewater councilman 12 years; precinct chairman in the county Republican organization since 1929; elder in the Presbyterian Church; elected mayor of Bridgewater, 1942.

Mr. Riddel is the older son of James Andrew Riddel, whose biography appears herein, and his wife, Sarah Rebecca Orebaugh. More particulars concerning his forebears will be found in the preceding pages that relate to his father, James Andrew Riddel.

Clifford Riddel grew up in and around Moscow, his birthplace. In 1898 the family moved to Bridgewater, where James A. Riddel had acquired business interests. There Clifford continued his education in public school, graduating in 1907. From 1908 to 1910 he was a student in Bridgewater College, where he took much interest in the athletic games and excelled as a baseball player. Leaving college at the age of 21, he started business for himself by opening a restaurant in Bridgewater. This he operated for about a year and then entered the wholesale and retail lumber business, as manager, with his father. Upon the death of the latter in 1929 he purchased the business and expanded it by undertaking construction work upon contract. This phase of his operations he has developed to large proportions in recent years. Some of his contracts have provided for the construction of school buildings at Fairfax, Va., Warwick, Alexandria, and Falls Church; another for the building of a court house in Lawrenceville. At present he is engaged in erecting barracks and other government buildings in and near Norfolk. Like his father, Mr. Riddel has been an active participant in the affairs of his home town. For 12 years he served as councilman; from 1930 to 1934 he was postmaster; and recently he has been elected mayor. He is a charter member of the Bridgewater Rotary Club, and in 1940 was elected president. At the age of nine he joined St. Paul Lutheran Church; in 1930 he transferred his membership to the Presbyterian Church of Bridgewater. In this he was for nine years a deacon; he is now an elder.

On October 10, 1911, Mr. Riddel married Miss Grace Dell Andes, daughter of J. M. and Elizabeth Stickley Andes of Fort Defiance. Of this marriage were born three children: Clifford T., Jr., born May 30, 1913; James Andrew IV, born December 22, 1915, who died September 30, 1921; and Janet Arlene, born October 23, 1922. Clifford Riddel, Jr., is a B. A. of Bridgewater College (1933) and an M. A. of Columbia University (1942). He is a talented singer, and has been a high-school principal for the past five years. On December 19, 1932, he married Miss Wilma Moyers, daughter of Dr. and Mrs. B. F. Moyers of Mathias, W. Va. Janet Arlene graduated from Bridgewater High School in 1937 and is now a senior in Bridgewater College.

Mr. Riddel, in his early career, faced great difficulties on slender resources, but by confidence and perseverance has built up a large and successful business. He lives by the Golden Rule, and may take just pride in his achievements. For recreation, he enjoys hunting and fishing; is fond of all sports; and for many years was active in baseball as player, umpire, and manager.

JOHN EDWIN ROLLER

SOLDIER, LAWYER, AND LEGISLATOR

Born October 5, 1844, at "The Dale," near Mt. Crawford, Virginia; tutored by the eminent Dr. White; under fire at First Manassas; honor graduate of V. M. I., 1863; lieut. of scouts and engineers; teacher at V. M. I.; in active service again, 1863-65; lawyer in Harrisonburg, 1867-1918; member of Va. Senate, 1869-73; appointed major-gen. of Va. militia, 1872; LL. D. of Heidelberg University, 1905; large landowner and real estate operator; collector of books and documents; died in Harrisonburg, August 10, 1918.

General Roller was a man of varied interests and accomplishments. From boyhood he was stirred by ambition. In 1861, when, at the age of 16, he was about to enter the University of Virginia, he heard the sound of war, he hurried to the nearest camp to enlist. Refused because of his youth, he soon found a place in Co. I, 1st Va. Cavalry. He was called the "infant of the regiment," but proved at First Manassas that he could stand fire like a veteran. In 1862 he was appointed a cadet at V. M. I., and graduated the next year second in his class. Elected lieutenant of Blacksford's scouts, he served in that capacity till the death of Captain Blackford, when he became lieutenant of engineers in the regular army. Ordered to the Institute, he taught Latin and mathematics to the cadets later distinguished at New Market. In 1863 he was ordered to Charleston, where he was under General Beauregard during part of the siege of that city. He then accompanied Beauregard to Virginia. Assigned to Hoke's Division as engineer officer, he was promoted two grades in 1864 and in the defense of Petersburg. In the winter of 1864-65 he organized Cos. G and H, 2d Regt. Engineers, commanding them until relieved by Major Harrod. Continuing in service, he was in the last line at Appomattox, where he was paroled.

John Edwin was the oldest of eight children of Peter S. Roller and Frances Sidney Allebaugh, grandson of John and Elizabeth Whitmore Roller. The first Roller of this family in America was John Peter, a Huguenot, who came from France to Philadelphia in 1752. Early members of the family were leaders in the French and German Reformed Church. General Roller was a devoted member of St. Stephens in Harrisonburg. He was untiring in advancing the traditions and history of his church.

On June 27, 1878, General Roller married Margaret Rector Shacklett of Harrisonburg, descendant of Samuel Henry, John Rector, and Micajah Glasscock. She was born September 11, 1856, and died May 12, 1888, leaving two daughters: Frances Lewis, Mrs. George G. Grattan, Jr., and Margaret Stuart, who married (1) Dr. John Egerton Cannaday and (2) Dr. Hanson S. Ogilvie. In March, 1896, he married Lucy Brown Cabell, daughter of P. H. Cabell of Nelson Co., Va. Of this marriage are three daughters: Miss Lucy Cabell Roller; Elizabeth Henry, Mrs. Wm. G. Bottimore; and Anne Woolston, Mrs. Wilfrid Pyle; all of Richmond.

General Roller lived on S. Main Street, Harrisonburg, corner of Bruce, in the brick house built in 1826 by Col. James Hall. His law office was adjacent, in the old stone house of Thomas Harrison, founder of the town. In this he had much of his valuable library, including many manuscripts. His practice covered a wide field. A distinguished U. S. judge said of him, "He has no superior as a land lawyer." He was one of the first trustees of Hood College, Md., and was often called upon to lecture before historical societies, religious bodies, and educational institutions.

ARTHUR RUSSELL ROSENBERGER
BANKER AND BUSINESS MAN

Born at Rosendale, Rockingham County, October 3, 1857; educated in a home school at Rosendale and in the New Market Polytechnic Institute; began business in a mercantile store in New Market; engaged in banking, building telephone lines, handling real estate, and operating hotels; located in Harrisonburg in 1897; the prime mover in building the community mausoleum in Woodbine Cemetery.

Mr. Rosenberger is a great-grandson of the Rev. John Kagey who, a hundred years ago, went up and down the Shenandoah Valley preaching the Gospel without money or price, and carrying something with him nearly every time for the poor. He was widely known as "Kagey, the Good Man." His wife was Elizabeth Breneman. Their son Abraham married Frances Yount, and his daughter Barbara Kagey was the wife of George W. Rosenberger of Rosendale and the mother of Russell Rosenberger. The latter's great-grandfather, George Rosenberger, of Zurich, Switzerland, was a Revolutionary soldier, who settled in what is now Page County, Va. His son George married a Zirkle and located at Rosendale where he built the older part of the house now occupied by Major E. M. Brown. In this house Russell Rosenberger and his father were born. George W. Rosenberger was a prosperous farmer and was one of the first to introduce improved livestock in Rockingham County.

Russell Rosenberger has certainly lived a progressive and constructive life. He has owned and jointly owned property in eight or ten different states and has built houses in four or five. He has had some of the nicest and best buildings erected in Harrisonburg, one of special note and character being the community mausoleum in Woodbine Cemetery, which will be a beautiful monument to him for ever. He has lived in Harrisonburg since 1897. He has had a very wide and varied experience in business—has employed and paid fees to about 50 different lawyers from the Gulf of Mexico to Canada, east of the Mississippi River, and never lost but one case, and that one involving less than one hundred dollars.

Whilst Mr. Rosenberger has not belonged to any particular church, he has been mostly affiliated with the Lutherans and the Presbyterians. Many years ago he helped considerably, materially and otherwise, to build a Lutheran church in New Market; also the Presbyterian church in Harrisonburg, and many others elsewhere, to some extent. He has always been an earnest believer in churches and the Christian principle, and has demonstrated the fact by living the good life.

On April 26, 1883, Mr. Rosenberger married Miss Eva Kirk Long, daughter of William Long of Point Pleasant, W. Va. She died in December, 1921, leaving a daughter Lucile, now Mrs. John G. Yancey of Harrisonburg. Her daughter Dorothy is Mrs. John Roller Grattan.

Holding Democratic principles, Mr. Rosenberger is an independent voter. He has never been a candidate for office and has held no public commission except that of notary public. He is a member of the Sons of the American Revolution through his great-grandfather, George Rosenberger. His preferences in reading are for history, law, poetry, and architecture. His hobby is making canes, watch charms, and other trinkets which he distributes with much pleasure as keepsakes among his friends.

EPHRAIM RUEBUSH

TEACHER OF MUSIC, PRINTER, AND PUBLISHER

Born September 26, 1833, near Stover's Shop, Augusta Co.; student under the Funks at Mountain Valley (now Singers' Glen); teacher of music in Virginia and West Virginia; publisher at Singers' Glen, with John W. Howe, Cornelius Hammack, and Aldine S. Kieffer, of patent note music books; founder, with Aldine S. Kieffer, of the Ruebush-Kieffer Co. in 1868; moved to Dayton in 1878; associate publisher of the *Musical Million*, established in 1869; died at Dayton, November 18, 1924.

Mr. Ruebush was a son of John (1782-1874), a grandson of John (who died in 1784), and a great-grandson of Henry, who came to America in 1732, settling in York County, Pa., where he died in 1784. His mother was Mary Huffman (1792-1884), a daughter of George (1762-1855), and a granddaughter of Valentine, who died in 1803. On March 28, 1861, he married Lucilla Virginia Kieffer (1843-1919), a daughter of John (1814-1847), who was a son of George (1786-1856), a grandson of Abraham (1758-1855), a great-grandson of Dewald (who died in 1830), and a great-great-grandson of Abraham, who came to America in 1748. Abraham Kieffer (1758-1855) was a Revolutionary soldier. Lucilla's mother was Mary Funk (1815-1888), a daughter of Joseph (1777-1862), a granddaughter of Henry, and a great-granddaughter of Bishop Henry Funk, who came to America in 1719 and died in 1760.

In boyhood Mr. Ruebush studied music, printing, and bookbinding at Mountain Valley, now Singers' Glen, under Joseph Funk, "Father of Song in Northern Virginia," and his sons. Later he taught music in Rockingham, Shenandoah, and other counties of Virginia, as well as in adjacent sections of West Virginia, and engaged in the publishing of music books and periodicals at Singers' Glen. His outstanding work was done at Dayton, to which place he and his brother-in-law, the talented Aldine S. Kieffer, in 1878, moved their printing and publishing house, under the name of the Ruebush-Kieffer Company. As senior member of the firm, Mr. Ruebush lived at Dayton and was actively engaged in the publishing business until a short time before his death at the advanced age of 91. The Ruebush-Kieffer Company produced a large number of books and other musical publications which were deservedly popular and were widely used over many parts of the United States and Canada. The monthly magazine, the *Musical Million,* which was continued until about 1915, had a wide circulation.

Mr. and Mrs. Ruebush had six children: Linneus Edgar, James Hott, William Howe, Joseph Kieffer, Mary John (Mrs. W. L. Andrews), and Anna K. (Mrs. Isaac M. Andrews). Edgar lives at Dayton and is a printer and bookbinder. James H., musican, educator, and publisher, for many years was a leader in the operation of Shenandoah Collegiate Institute, now Shenandoah College, at Dayton. He has done much to promote the study of music in the public schools. Will H., who also lives at Dayton, is a musican, teacher, a talented composer, and a distinguished director of bands and orchestras. He and his military band won signal honors in France in World War I. His compositions have been published in the best musical journals in the country. Joseph K. lives in Harrisonburg and is a publisher and bookseller, specializing in Virginiana and other historical and genealogical works. His collection of books and manuscripts is recognized as one of the best in Virginia, and he has a large number of regular customers in all parts of the United States. His catalogues are welcomed by dealers and private collectors.

JOSEPH KIEFFER RUEBUSH
BOOKSELLER AND PUBLISHER

Born October 26, 1878, in Dayton; educated in local schools, Shenandoah Collegiate Institute, and Ohio State University; business manager of the Ruebush-Kieffer Co., music publishers of Dayton, 1902-1923; Rockingham County chairman of the War History Commission of Virginia, 1920-24; publisher of numerous works on local history and genealogy; extensive collector of books and manuscripts; dealer in books and other publications, especially Americana and Virginiana; moved from Dayton to Harrisonburg in 1936; traveler in America and Europe.

Mr. Ruebush is the youngest son of Ephraim Ruebush, whose biography appears on preceding pages, and his wife, Lucilla Kieffer. Though widely traveled and acquainted with the life of great cities, he has not lost his love for rural scenes and outdoor life. Brought up among printers and publishers, with traditions of corresponding activities handed down to him from many generations, he naturally has found a congenial career among books and literary occupations. In 1744 his great-great-great-grandfather, Heinrich Funck, had "Ein Spiegel Der Tauffe mit Geist mit Wasser and mit Blut," a volume of 94 pages, published by Christoph Saur in Germantown, Pa. Four years later this same Henry Funk was the leading member of a committee that saw through the publication at Ephrata of T. J. Van Braght's Book of Martyrs, which Samuel W. Pennypacker declared to be the noblest specimen of American colonial bibliography. Henry Funk was responsible for other notable publications. His grandson, Joseph Funk of Singers' Glen, Mr. Ruebush's great-grandfather, was perhaps the most outstanding literary figure in this remarkable family. Mr. Ruebush, accordingly, enjoys a literary inheritance of almost 200 years from his ancestors and other relatives. For some time he was literary editor of the *Musical Million,* the well-known monthly magazine which his father and Aldine Kieffer founded in 1869. For several years he edited the *Rockingham Outlook,* a weekly newspaper published at Dayton. In 1912 he and P. H. Elkins brought out Wayland's History of Rockingham County, an 8vo volume of 475 pages. In 1923 he published the first edition of the "Scenic and Historical Guide to the Shenandoah Valley," which was the first work of its kind in this part of Virginia.

Among other notable volumes that Mr. Ruebush has published are Morton's History of Pendleton County, a History of Alleghany County, by the same author, Strickler's Rockingham Marriages, Harrison's "Settlers by the Long Grey Trail," Prichard's Abstracts of Culpeper County Records, Coffman's "The Conrad Clan," and White's "King's Mountain Men." Dr. George P. Jackson of Nashville, in the preface to his splendid volume, "White Spirituals of the Southern Uplands," acknowledges the "immense value" of materials furnished him by Mr. Ruebush, who was also the main promoter of the History of the United Brethren Church, by Funkhouser and Morton, published in 1921. He is a recognized authority on the valuation of old and rare books, his catalogs, of which he has issued over 70, being used as a guide to such values in many libraries.

On December 29, 1908, Mr. Ruebush married Miss Nancy Byrd Rhodes, daughter of J. B. D. and Emma Sipe Rhodes, the latter the oldest daughter of Col. Emanuel Sipe. Mr. and Mrs. Ruebush have traveled widely over the United States, Mexico, and Europe. Mrs. Ruebush, who is a graduate of Elon College, an M. A. of the University of Virginia, and was some time a student at Oxford, is assistant professor of English in Madison College.

GLENN WHITMORE RUEBUSH
LAWYER, FARMER, AND REFEREE IN BANKRUPTCY

Born October 30, 1891, near Hinton, Rockingham Co.; attended Hinton school, Shenandoah College, and University of Virginia; school principal in Henrico Co., Va.; in World War I served at Ft. Myer, Camp Sevier, and in France; student in Cambridge University; major in Judge Advocate General's Office; B. S., U. Va., 1920; LL. B, Yale, 1921; lawyer in New York, 1921-30; in Harrisonburg, since 1930; referee in bankruptcy; trustee of Shenandoah College; past commander American Legion and V. F. W.; active in fraternal orders.

Mr. Ruebush, only child of James Addison Ruebush and wife Esther Whitmore, was born at the brick homestead of his grandfather, Peter Whitmore, on Muddy Creek, near Hinton. His grandfather Ruebush was George. The Ruebushes came to Rockingham from York County, Pa., the Whitmores from Lancaster, prior to 1800. Both were of German extraction. See "George Ruebush" and "Peter Whitmore" in Part II.

In the one-room school at Hinton classes from primer to 7th reader were taught from 8 a. m. to 4 p. m., five months in a year. To attend Shenandoah College, Glenn walked the four miles twice daily except on infrequent occasions when he rode the old bay mare Maud, doing farm chores morning and night. He also worked on the farm in summer and in pinches during school sessions. After he entered the University of Virginia he had to bolster his finances by teaching. From the principalship of Glendale High School in Henrico Co. he returned to the University in 1916, taking law. In April, 1917, he enlisted and was stationed at Ft. Myer. There, August 9, 1917, he was commissioned 2d lt. and sent to Camp Sevier, where he helped to convert cotton fields and pine thickets into a military camp, serving there with the 30th Division and as Summary Court-Martial Officer. He was sent overseas with the 81st (Wildcat) Division. In October, for gallantry in action, he was made 1st lt. by order of General Pershing. On the morning of November 11 he was with the 322d Inf. at the front in action in the Meuse-Argonne Drive. Transferred to the Third Army, 3d Div., he marched with it to the Rhine; was stationed at Mayen where, for a while, 1918-19, he commanded Co. A, 30th Inf. In March, 1919, he was ordered to England where he enrolled as a student in Caius College, Cambridge, studying English literature and attending lectures of Sir Arthur Quiller-Couch and others until June. On June 29, at Brest, he received his certificate that he was "free from lice," and sailed for New York. For some years after discharge at Camp Lee, July 30, 1919, he held a reserve commission in the Judge Advocate General's office, rising to the rank of major. Returning to U. Va., he graduated B. S. in 1920. At Yale in 1921 he graduated LL. B. and was admitted to the New York Bar, soon becoming junior member of the Civil and Admiralty firm of Loomis & Ruebush, 52 Broadway. In 1926 he was admitted to the U. S. Supreme Court Bar. In 1930 he returned to his old home and opened an office in Harrisonburg where he has a large practice and is recognized as a lawyer of marked ability. He is also a successful farmer. For some years he was U. S. Commissioner; was the first commissioner for Shen. Natl. Park; and now is Referee in Bankruptcy for Rockingham and six other counties. He belongs to the Va. and American Bar Assns.; is a member of the United Brethren Church; is active in veteran organizations; Past Exalted Ruler of Elks; a Mason, Moose, Kiwanian, member Chamber of Commerce; Air Raid Warden for Harrisonburg. He is an ardent reader of detective and other short stories, and is author of the Handbook of the Republican State Committee of Virginia.

WILLIAM THOMAS SANGER

PRESIDENT OF THE MEDICAL COLLEGE OF VIRGINIA

Born September 16, 1885, at Bridgewater; early boyhood at Bridgewater, later in Indiana; graduate South Bend (Ind.) High School, 1906; B. A., Bridgewater College, 1909; M. A., Indiana University, 1910; Ph. D., Clark University, 1915; LL. D., Hampden-Sydney, 1926; L. H. D., Bridgewater, 1939; LL. D., University of Richmond, 1939; fellow in psychology, Clark University; professor and dean, Harrisonburg State Teachers (now Madison) College and Bridgewater College; executive sec'y and editor, Va. Educa. Assn., 1921-22; sec'y Va. State Board of Educa., 1922-25; president of the Medical College of Virginia since 1925.

President Sanger's father, Rev. Samuel F. Sanger, born Feb. 4, 1849, son of John, born Nov. 28, 1801, was an outstanding minister of the Church of the Brethren. Leaving Bridgewater in middle life, he moved to Indiana, whence, after some years, he went to California. His mother was Susan Thomas, born Feb. 8, 1850, daughter of Rev. Daniel, born July 7, 1821. If eloquence is not hereditary, the powers thereto may be. At any rate, Dr. Sanger has the logical and incisive qualities of speech, as well as the administrative ability, that distinguished his father and his maternal grandfather. An outstanding student, he was a debater and the editor of the college magazine at Bridgewater, where later (1910-12, 1913-16) he was a teacher, and from 1919 to 1921 professor and dean. At Clark University (1912-13) he was a fellow in psychology, where in 1915 he received his doctor's degree. While teaching at Bridgewater he spent a summer in Columbia University. During the session of 1916-17 he was registrar and instructor in education in the State Teachers (now Madison) College at Harrisonburg, and from 1917 to 1919 dean and head of the education department in the same institution. After serving a year (1921-22) as executive secretary of the Virginia Education Association and editor of the *Virginia Journal of Education*, he was for three years (1922-25) secretary of the Virginia State Board of Education. In 1925 he was made president of the Medical College of Virginia, in which position he has enhanced his distinguished record. Under his direction this honored institution has had a remarkable expansion along all progressive lines.

Among the civic, educational, benevolent, and professional organizations in which Dr. Sanger holds membership may be mentioned the Richmond Kiwanis Club, Torch Club, the National Education Association, American Association for the Advancement of Science, the Virginia Academy of Science, the Medical Society of Virginia, Richmond Academy of Medicine, Phi Delta Kappa, Alpha Omega Alpha, and Phi Beta Kappa. He holds or has held official positions in the Westhampton Citizens Association, the Cooperative Education Association, the Association of Virginia Colleges, the Virginia Hospital Association, the Richmond Chapter of the Virginia Cancer Foundation, and others. He is a member of the Church of the Brethren, a Democrat in politics, and a loyal alumnus of his several *alma maters*. His hobbies are flowers, particularly lilacs and peonies; wild flowers; colonial architecture and furniture, and music. Other items of interest concerning him may be found in "Men of Mark of Virginia," "Who's Who in America," and other well-known biographical publications.

On August 20, 1913, Dr. Sanger married Miss Sylvia Gray Burns of Burnsville, Va., whose literary and aesthetic tastes comport well with his own. His son, Julian Douglass Sanger, born March 23, 1918, is a graduate of the University of Richmond.

JAMES THOMAS SCRUGGS
MERCHANT AND ELKTON COUNCILMAN

Born October 11, 1912, at Concord, Campbell County, Va.; attended Concord school; in 1926 came to Elkton, where his father continued in business; graduated from Elkton High School, 1931; auto salesman and bookkeeper; in 1936 entered business with his father; in charge of Scruggs & Co., Inc., after April 28, 1940; member of Elkton town council since 1938; chairman of Civic Improvement Committee, Elkton Lions Club; promoter of East Side Highway and active in efforts to bring the Merck Plant to Elkton.

Mr. Scruggs is typical of Virginia's young business men, with a keen interest and active participation in civic and industrial enterprises. His father was James Preston Scruggs, who was born in Appomattox County, June 16, 1877, and died in Elkton on April 28, 1940. His mother, Nannie D. Scruggs, born March 27, 1881, is also a native of Appomattox.

At his boyhood home in Concord, Mr. Scruggs completed the 7th grade in school. At Elkton, to which place the family moved on September 1, 1926, and where the father continued in the mercantile business, the boy entered high school, finishing in June, 1931. Then, at the age of 19, he went to work for an auto dealer as salesman and bookkeeper. In June, 1936, he entered his father's store as clerk. In a year or two he purchased stock in the business and was put on the board of directors; was made president in 1938 and held the office about nine months. Because of the death of two members of the corporation and the ill health of his father, Mr. Scruggs then had to take full charge. With lack of experience in management his task was a difficult one, and, together with the death of his father on April 28, 1940, it subjected him to a severe strain. Sometimes he saw little chance of keeping things going, but by constant effort and with advice and encouragement from friends he got through the first year. Since then, with continuing hard work and discerning foresight, he has made a notable success.

In June, 1938, Mr. Scruggs was elected to the Elkton town council, second from the lead. In 1940 he was re-elected with the largest number of votes; and in 1942 he was chosen for a third term. For four years he has served on the street committee, of which he is now chairman. Among the important matters to which he, with his colleagues, has given much time and hard work, were the securing of a right of way through town for the East Side Highway and bringing the Merck Company plant to the vicinity. In 1940 he was chosen a director of the great county Turkey Festival. In this capacity and in his office as councilman in Elkton Mr. Scruggs has been instrumental in promoting a closer cooperation and more fruitful friendship between the eastern and western parts of the county and the towns of Elkton and Harrisonburg. He is a member of the Elkton Methodist Church, is chairman of the board of stewards, and active in the Sundayschool. He also belongs to the Lions Club and is chairman of the Civic Improvement Committee. His hobbies are horseback riding and outdoor sports. In reading he prefers the *Reader'sDigest* and works on civic affairs.

On June 16, 1934, Mr. Scruggs married Miss Margaret Anne Duff, the ceremony taking place in the home of Miss Duff's aunt, Mrs. Lillian Gooden, at McGaheysville. Mrs. Scruggs was born March 15, 1914, in Orange County, Va. Mr. and Mrs. Scruggs have one son, James Thomas II, born June 5, 1935.

LEMUEL RAY SHADWELL

PHARMACIST

Born May 4, 1896, at Forestville; came to Harrisonburg at the age of 12; graduated from Harrisonburg High School in 1914; from the Medical College of Virginia in 1917; in U. S. Army 1917-18; president Virginia Pharmaceutical Association 1925; president Richmond Retail Druggist Association about 1935; commander Legion of Honor of Acca Temple Shrine, 1939; proprietor of large drug store at corner of Boulevard & Broad streets, Richmond.

Dr. Shadwell's birthplace is the historic town of Forestville, located near the line of Shenandoah and Rockingham. This line was surveyed for Lord Fairfax in 1746 by Thomas Lewis, Peter Jefferson, and other men well known in Virginia history. The families in and around Forestville have been known for energy and thrift ever since the days of early settlement.

Dr. Shadwell lived on a farm until the age of 12, when his father, Lemuel Lee Shadwell, died. His mother, Mrs. Lydia Carrie Shadwell, then moved to Harrisonburg with her family, where Lemuel attended both grade school and high school, working in Fletcher Brothers' drug store while a high-school student. He writes: "I looked to Mr. W. H. Keister for counsel and advice in those days, and shall always feel grateful to him for helping me to find a way to get through high school. With a loan from Dr. B. F. Wilson and Mr. George E. Sipe, I was able to attend and graduate from the Medical College of Virginia, in pharmacy, in 1917."

On December 10, 1917, Dr. Shadwell enlisted in the U. S. Army at the Medical Supply Depot, Camp Lee, Va. He was discharged a sergeant at Camp Meigs, Washington, D. C., December 24, 1918. For one year he was assistant manager of one of the Peoples Drug Stores in Washington; then for three years he was manager of a chain store in Charlottesville. On July 1, 1923, he purchased in Richmond the store which is located at the corner of Boulevard and Broad streets. He is still carrying on business at this location, open 24 hours a day, and doing four times as much business as the store was doing when he purchased it.

Notwithstanding his close attention to business, Dr. Shadwell has found time for recreational and cultural diversions in different fields. In Charlottesville he was a charter member of the municipal band. His activity in Masonry and in various professional organizations has already been indicated. His hobby is hunting and fishing, and for convenience and recreation in his favorite sports he maintains a cabin on the James River. In selecting his reading he shows a preference for the *National Geographic Magazine,* the *Reader's Digest, Time Magazine,* and *Kiplinger's Letter.*

In September, 1920, in Washington, D. C., Dr. Shadwell married Miss Blanche Delaney, a native of Richmond, who died on April 24, 1925. His present wife, married in Washington in June, 1926, was Miss F. Genevieve Andrews, a native of Blacksburg, Va. His children are: Lemuel R., Jr., born March 20, 1922, a student in the junior class in the Medical College of Virginia, department of pharmacy; Elizabeth Minor, born June 18, 1923, now a sophomore at Madison College, taking the pre-nursing course; and Jeanne Andrews, born May 10, 1927, who is a junior in Westhampton High School.

Dr. Shadwell and his family are all members of the Grace Covenant Presbyterian Church in Richmond.

DAVID EDGAR SHANK
BANKER AND BUSINESS MAN

Born on August 21, 1889, at Broadway, Rockingham County, Va.; attended schools in his native town; at age of 20 went to the West, where he spent six years; returned to Rockingham and engaged in dairy business; member and director of the Harrisonburg-Rockingham Chamber of Commerce; vice-president Rockingham National Bank; member of the Rotary Club; secretary-treasurer and general manager Valley of Virginia Cooperative Milk Producers Association, Inc., Harrisonburg.

Mr. Shank is a native of the progressive town of Broadway, grew up there and in the vicinity, and attended the graded and high school of the town. His parents are John F. and Elizabeth Zigler Shank; his grandparents, on his father's side, were Samuel and Katherine Rhodes Shank; those on his mother's side were Michael and Mary Knupp Zigler; all of Broadway and the surrounding community. All these families have been represented in this part of Rockingham County for generations and are typical of the thrifty and industrious folk that have peopled the Linville Creek Valley since colonial times. Just who the first settler in this region was cannot be determined at this time, but certainly one who was on the ground very early was William Linville, or Linwell, from whom the stream and the valley took their name. He evidently was there prior to 1739, for in that year, when a grant for 7009 acres of land was made to Hite, Duff, McKay, and Green, the stream was already known as Linville Creek.

After a practical training on the farm and a fair education in the Broadway schools, Mr. Shank, at the age of twenty, went to Chicago where, for three years, he was employed in the Drug Sales Department and general offices of Armour & Company. Leaving Chicago, he went to the Twin Cities, and for the next three years held a position in the Sales Department of Swift & Company, in South St. Paul, Minnesota. Returning to the East, he engaged in the dairy business and related industries. This was eminently appropiate in view of the remarkable development of poultry-raising, stock-raising, and dairying that has taken place in recent years in the communities surrounding his native town of Broadway. He is at this time president of Augusta Dairies, with headquarters in Staunton; a member of the board of directors of the Rockingham Poultry Association; the board of directors of the Lynchburg Dairy, Lynchburg, Va.; secretary-treasurer and general manager of the Valley Cooperative Milk Producers Association, Inc., Harrisonburg; and vice-president of the Rockingham National Bank. He is a member of the Rotary Club of Harrisonburg, past president and member of the board of directors of the Chamber of Commerce, past president and member of the board of directors of the Virginia Dairy Products Association, and treasurer of the Agricultural Conference Board of Virginia. His hobbies are dairy farming and fishing. In reading, he prefers newspapers and magazines.

On September 20, 1916, in Chicago, Mr. Shank married Miss Bertha B. Bare of Broadway. Of this marriage were born three children: Maxine Mardelle, born May 31, 1919, in Broadway; Donald Eugene, born September 12, 1926, in Harrisonburg; and Charles Lewis, born April 26, 1931, in Harrisonburg.

JACOB ANDREW SHENK
BUSINESS MAN AND CHURCH WORKER

Born February 17, 1900, at Denbigh, Va.; went as far as the 7th grade in local schools; assisted his father in clearing timber lands and in farming; self-supporting student at Eastern Mennonite School, Harrisonburg; graduated in June, 1927; carpenter and student of architecture; proprietor of electric hatchery; Mennonite deacon; member of important building committees of his church.

Mr. Shenk's father, Abram P. Shenk, is a native of Ohio; his mother, Fannie Coffman Shenk, is a daughter of Bishop Samuel Coffman, of the Mennonite Church, born and reared in the Dry River section of Rockingham County, Va. In 1898 his parents located in Warwick County, Va., where he was born and grew up, assisting in converting a native forest into productive farm land. At age 20 he entered the Eastern Mennonite School at Harrisonburg, paying his way by working at odd jobs and at a local hatchery in season during school terms and as a carpenter in summers. Because of working his way, his time in school was extended a year or two longer than the usual period for graduation. As a carpenter he became interested in architecture and architectural drawing and entered upon a correspondence course in these subjects with the International Correspondence School, completing his course after several years. In the meantime he continued work at the local hatchery and became more interested in this business, and about 1932 he decided to undertake this work on his own account. His success in this enterprise may be indicated in his own words:

"The hatchery formerly known as the Garber Hatchery came on the market and I decided to purchase that. This hatchery had a capacity of about 30,000 eggs. In the ten years that I have owned this plant it has grown from the original capacity of 30,000 to the present capacity of 600,000 eggs. The first year's production was about 80,000 chicks, while the production for the current year will be approximately 4,000,000 chicks. This hatchery at this time is the largest in Virginia."

Since the age of twelve Mr. Shenk has been a member of the Mennonite Church, and since 1940 he has been a deacon. Within the last few years he has served on several building committees, namely, that of Zion Mennonite Church, near Broadway, recently completed; that of the north wing of the main building of the Eastern Mennonite School at Harrisonburg, completed about January 1, 1942; and that of the new college auditorium now under construction. For the last he made the working plans and blue prints. He is also on a committee for supervising the enlargement of the church-owned Nurses' Training School, Hospital and Sanitarium at LaJunta, Colorado.

On December 8, 1926, Mr. Shenk married Miss Lucy Blanche Wenger, born November 4, 1902, daughter of the late Jacob and Virginia Suter Wenger of near Edom. Mr. and Mrs. Shenk have four children: Jacob Paul, born January 7, 1931; James Allen, born March 3, 1934; Virginia Ann, born October 17, 1938; and Ellen Joyce, born November 22, 1941.

Mr. Shenk says that the nearest thing to a hobby he has is salt-water fishing. His reading preferences are in national and international current events and books of a religious and devotional nature. He attributes his success to an aim to produce the best in his line, generous dealing, and the providential leading and direction of God.

DAVID ROLLIN SHOWALTER
MERCHANT AND BUSINESS DIRECTOR

Born May 31, 1872, in Rockingham County; grew up on his father's farm and attended the neighborhood school; general merchant at Hollar and Lacey Spring; salesman in Harrisonburg for B. Ney & Sons and the Valley Hardware Company; factory representative for the Round Oak Stove Company, 1907-42; president of the Valley Hardware Company since 1922; chairman of the official board of the Harrisonburg Methodist Church.

According to the late Dr. W. J. Showalter of this county, the Showalters came to America from Switzerland and settled first in Northampton County, Pa. The family has been represented in this part of Virginia for a century and a half, perhaps longer. Among a large number of substantial farmers and business men, they have been distinguished by several singers and musicians, as well as by an outstanding journalist.

David Rollin Showalter's birthplace was about midway between Singers' Glen and Cherry Grove, on the farm of his father, Benjamin Anthony Showalter. His mother was Mary Catherine Hollar, a daughter of Philip and Rebecca Thomas Hollar. In boyhood he attended school in a log school house near his home, in which the teachers were Laban McMullen, Michael Hollar, Ida Funk (later Mrs. Harvey Foltz), and Maggie Grandle.

On September 4, 1895, at Broadway, Mr. Showalter married Miss Maggie Reeves Grandle, who was born at Lacey Spring on August 2, 1863, a daughter of William Cutler Grandle and his wife, Adaline Margarette Cave. Her paternal grandfather was Elijah Grandle; her mother, a native of Albemarle County, Va., was a daughter of Reuben Cave and his wife, Elizabeth Yager.

From 1893 to 1899 Mr. Showalter was a general merchant at Hollar. After his store burned he moved to Harrisonburg for a few years and then operated a store at Lacey Spring for several years. Returning to Harrisonburg, he clerked for B. Ney & Sons and later for the Valley Hardware Company. In 1907 he began work with the Round Oak Stove Company of Dowagiac, Mich., continuing in that capacity until February 1942, when the factory was taken over for national defense work. His work as factory representative for the Round Oak Company was notably successful. For a number of years he led their large sales force in percentages of increase and was awarded a valuable diamond ring by the company as a token of their appreciation. For the past twenty years he has been president of the Valley Hardware Company.

Mr. and Mrs. Showalter have two daughters: Aera Olivia, born March 15, 1898, who is a teacher in the city schools of Greensboro, N. C., and Grace Elizabeth, born April 26, 1901, who, on August 20, 1934, married Ward B. Adams and lives in Kent, Ohio, Mr. Adams' native state.

Mr. Showalter's reading preference is for current events; his hobby is playing pool; in politics he is an independent. He and Mrs. Showalter are members of the Methodist Church, in which he is chairman of the official board. He is an active and honored Mason, having taken all the degrees. For three years he was Grand Trustee in the State of Virginia for the Eastern Star, and is now the Illustrious Potentate's grand representative in this territory. Much of his time recently has been devoted to the rationing of gasoline, for which he is chairman of the local board.

J. HENRY SHOWALTER
TEACHER, COMPOSER, AND PUBLISHER

Born November 2, 1864, at Cherry Grove, Rockingham Co.; educated in public and private schools of Virginia, Ohio, and Chicago; took voice training under F. W. Root and other eminent teachers; teacher of normal music schools and composer of many pieces of music, mostly for church use; author of 40 or more musical publications of various kinds, notable among them "Psalms, Hymns, and Spiritual Songs," a series, the first of which appeared in 1892; associate author the "Brethren Hymnal," 1901; a successful publisher of musical works at West Milton, Ohio, for many years.

Mr. Showalter, third son and 5th child of John A. and Susannah Miller Showalter, comes of a distinguished musical family and is himself entitled to eminent rank among the teachers, authors, and publishers of musical works in this country. His father, a teacher of "pay schools" and a pioneer in advancing church music and higher training for music teachers, was a fine singer and for more than 50 years was an outstanding song leader and teacher of singing classes in Virginia and other states. In 1873, while teaching in Maryland and Pennsylvania, he, with Aldine Kieffer, secured B. C. Unseld and others to hold the New Market Normal Music School which continued in summers till 1882 and was attended by young men who later became distinguished as teachers, composers, and publishers. Among these was Anthony J. Showalter, J. Henry's older brother, who also won first rank among teachers and composers and was for many years head of the leading firm of music publishers in the South. Two other brothers, B. F. and J. M. Showalter, were also well-known teachers and composers of sacred music.

J. Henry Showalter was endowed with a voice of large compass and high quality. One of his teachers, Frederic W. Root of Chicago, termed his voice one of the best. He is a skilled teacher of classes and one of the best leaders of large singing assemblies. His compositions are to be found in many collections for church and Sundayschool, including hymnals of the Church of the Brethren, of which he is a member, and many other standard works. For many years he has been established at West Milton, Ohio, as composer and publisher. The 40-odd books of which he is author, many of which have been issued by him as publisher, include works on the rudiments of music, theory and practice of teaching, voice culture, harmony, and musical composition, as well as many Gospel song books and hymnals. One of his most notable and successful publications is entitled "Psalms, Hymns, and Spiritual Songs," a book that first appeared in 1892, and was continued in a series of four additional numbers in later years. This work changed the singing in the Church of the Brethren from the old "lining out" procedure to the more modern method of rendering hymns in religious services. In 1901, when a new edition of the church hymnal was published, Mr. Showalter was one of the associate editors. He was frequently called upon to lead the singing at the annual meetings of the church, in assemblies made up of thousands from all parts of the United States.

On June 27, 1886, Mr. Showalter married Miss Emma Brumbaugh of Ohio, member of a family long eminent in the history of the Church of the Brethren. He terms himself a "farmer, teacher, composer, editor, and publisher." His address is 646 South Miami Street, West Milton, Ohio. After a long and distinguished career in active service, he is taking life more easily on his farm, bringing out an occasional composition and doing some editing, publishing, and teaching by correspondence.

WILLIAM HENRY SIPE

MERCHANT AND BANKER

Born Nov. 12, 1858, near Sparta (now Mauzy), Rockingham; acquired business training in his father's mercantile stores; with J. B. D. Rhodes, opened a store at Lilly in 1882; soon purchased his partner's interest and expanded the establishment; moved to Bridgewater in 1899, where he operated a store with William Arey; after a few years became sole owner; later took his sons into partnership as the W. H. Sipe Co.; county supervisor, 1901-05; an organizer and director of the Bridgewater Creamery & Ice Corp.; a director of the Merchants Grocery & Hardware Co. of Harrisonburg; a trustee of Bridgewater College; president of the Planters Bank of Bridgewater.

Mr. Sipe in his later years was justly termed one of Rockingham's "grand old men." His genial manner, honest dealing, public spirit, and active benevolence won enduring esteem and affection. He was a son of Emanuel and Penelope Jennings Sipe. His father, as lieut. colonel, commanded the 7th Va. Cavalry in the Confederate service and for many years later was a successful merchant, a pioneer chain-store operator, owning at one time as many as eight places of business, with headquarters in the village of Linville. In 1882 William, in partnership with his brother-in-law, Jacob B. D. Rhodes, opened a store at Lilly, of which he was later sole owner and which he expanded into one of the largest department stores in the county. It was a favorite marketing center not only for the surrounding rural communities of Rockingham, it also drew a large trade from the neighboring counties in West Virginia.

After Mr. Sipe moved to Bridgewater in 1899, where he at first was in partnership with William Arey, he continued operating the store at Lilly until it was taken over by his son Herbert. In later years the Lilly store was leased to others and Mr. Sipe's sons joined with him in the Bridgewater store under the firm name of the W. H. Sipe Co. Since his death, on January 9, 1939, one of the surviving sons, Herbert B. Sipe, purchased the stock of merchandise from the estate and carries on the business under the name, W. H. Sipe Co.

Not long after Mr. Sipe located at Bridgewater he became a member of the Church of the Brethren and entered actively into the work of the denomination as a trustee of Bridgewater College and otherwise. For four years he served the county on the board of supervisors and also was connected with various business enterprises in Bridgewater and Harrisonburg. For 20 years preceding his death he was president of the Planters Bank of Bridgewater. His career as a successful merchant, extending over a period of 58 years, is probably without a parallel in the mercantile history of the county.

On December 21, 1882, Mr. Sipe married Miss Maggie Elizabeth Beery (1861-1933), eldest daughter of Noah W. and Kate Neff Beery of Edom. Noah Beery was a prosperous farmer of the Edom vicinity; his wife was a daughter of Daniel Neff of Shenandoah County. Mr. and Mrs. Sipe had seven children: Penelope (Nelle), wife of Col. Paul M. Thrasher of Porter Military Academy, Charleston, S. C.; one child, Paul, now a senior in Lehigh University; Herbert B., who married Grace Orndorff; W. Edgar, deputy clerk of circuit court since Jan. 1, 1932, who married Edith Rothgeb; sons William H. and James R.; Irene, wife of C. W. Waters, Long Beach, Calif., lieutenant U. S. Navy; Jennings, who died Feb. 3, 1937; Ethel, single, acting dean of women, Bridgewater College; and Minnie, wife of Rev. R. J. Kirby, Baptist minister, Portsmouth, Va.; one son, Robert.

HARRY BRUCE SLAVEN

BUSINESS MANAGER, DAILY NEWS-RECORD

Born September 21, 1889, in Monterey, Va.; attended Monterey High School; served printing apprenticeship in the offices of the *Highland Recorder*, at Monterey; came to Harrisonburg in 1910 where he was employed on the *Daily News*, the *Daily Independent*, and since 1917 has been with the *Daily News-Record;* business manager of the *Daily News-Record* since 1932; member of the Harrisonburg Methodist Church and active in various official capacities in denominational work; member of the local Rotary Club and president during the year 1939-40.

Mr. Slaven is a native of the town of Monterey, county-seat of Highland County, Va., widely celebrated for its beautiful location and environs between parallel ranges of the Alleghanies, in a fertile and populous valley. He is a son of Harry F. Slaven, whose wife before marriage was Maude V. Siple. His paternal grandparents were Thomas H. and Margaret C. Fleisher Slaven. After completing his course in the Monterey High School he entered upon an apprenticeship in the printing offices of the Monterey newspaper, the *Highland Recorder*, which had been established in 1878 by Witts & Jordan, and was being published when he entered its offices by the late W. H. Matheny. Leaving Monterey in 1910, he came to Harrisonburg where he accepted a position with the *Daily News* which was then being edited by Professor James C. Johnston. In 1913 the *Daily News* and the *Rockingham Record* were merged and came out as the *Daily News-Record*, Mr. Slaven continuing in connection. From 1916 he worked with the Harrisonburg *Daily Independent*, edited by R. B. Smythe and others, until it was discontinued in 1920, when he returned to the *Daily News-Record* as advertising manager. In 1932 he was promoted to the office of business manager, in which position he continues at present.

On June 4, 1913, the date of the first issue of the *Daily News-Record*, Mr. Slaven married Miss Lottie Mae Nisewander, born June 24, 1894, daughter of the late C. T. and Mary Jane Nisewander of near Harrisonburg. Of the marriage were born a son and three daughters: Harry B. Slaven, Jr., March 9, 1914; Dorothy Mae, May 21, 1916; Mary Rebecca, January 18, 1920; and Charlotte Jean, November 12, 1923. Harry, who married Clara E. Hopkins and has a son, Lynn Fleisher, is employed on the *Daily News-Record*. Dorothy, Mrs. L. L. Tourgee, Jr., of Harrisonburg, has a daughter, Ann Slaven. Mary, Mrs. Chas. E. Quatse of Greensburg, Pa., has three children: Terry, Ann, and Barbara. Charlotte married Pvt. N. Jack Wood, who is now stationed at Camp Grant, Ill.

Mr. Slaven says that he enjoys fishing. This is no doubt a natural experience for one who must have had an early acquaintance with the trout streams of the Alleghanies. He has been a member of the Harrisonburg Rotary Club since 1935 and during the year 1939-40 served as its president. As a member of the Methodist Church he has been active in the work of the local congregation as superintendent of the church school and in other capacities, and has extended his services through various organizations to wider fields. He is lay leader of the Board of Lay Activities of Winchester District, having held a similar position for a number of years in the old Rockingham District; secretary of the Va. Conference Board of Lay Activities; chairman, Advisory Board of the local Salvation Army branch, and president pro-tem. of the Harrisonburg Council of Churches.

CLAUDE VIRGIL SMITH

FARMER, BANKER, AND BUSINESS MAN

Born August 22, 1885, at Marksville, Page County, Va.; attended Page Valley Academy, Luray High School, and Eastern College; merchant and farmer; treasurer and a director of the Virginia Farm Bureau Federation; a director of The National Bank, Harrisonburg, Frozen Foods, Inc., United Wool Growers Association, Rockingham Petroleum Cooperative, and the Richmond Hospital Service Association; a trustee of Rockingham Memorial Hospital; secretary-treasurer and manager Rockingham Cooperative Farm Bureau, Inc.

Mr. Smith's father, Jesse Walter Smith, was born at New Windsor, Md., January 14, 1854; his mother, born Elizabeth Biedler, August 8, 1861, was a native of Marksville, Va. His grandfathers were John J. Smith and Martin Biedler; his grandmothers, Sarah Quigley Smith and Mary Brumback Biedler. His childhood was spent at the Biedler homestead near Marksville, and he attended schools as already shown. He clerked in stores in Luray and Roanoke and operated a grocery store in the latter city. He had further experience as a member of the firm of T. P. Yager, Inc., at Cross Keys and Penn Laird, and also engaged in farming. For a number of years past Mr. Smith has resided in Harrisonburg and has been identified with a number of important business, civic, and philanthropic organizations, as indicated on the preceding page. His position as secretary-treasurer and manager of the Rockingham Cooperative Farm Bureau has given him a wide influence. He is a Mason and an elder in the Presbyterian Church. In politics he is a Republican.

Mr. Smith married Miss Kathryn Keezell, born at Keezletown, August 2, 1890, a daughter of Senator George B. Keezell. There are four children, all born at Cross Keys:

George Bernard, born November 10, 1912, who attended Timber Ridge School, Harrisonburg High School, and Virginia Polytechnic Institute, B. S. in chemical engineering, V. P. I., 1935, and at graduation commisioned 2d lieutenant in the U. S. Army Reserves. He was commissioned 1st lieutenant in 1938; called to active service May 6, 1941; now serving in Co. F, 55th Coast Artillery, Hawaiian Dept. He was serving at Pearl Harbor when it was attacked on December 7, 1941.

Martha, born August 22, 1915; educated at Timber Ridge, in Harrisonburg High School, William & Mary College, and Madison College, graduating at Madison in 1938. On August 24, 1939, she married William L. Coleman; has a son, William L. Coleman, Jr., born at Charlottesville, June 3, 1940.

Claude Virgil, Jr., born April 24, 1917; educated at Timber Ridge, in Harrisonburg Graded and High School, and Virginia Polytechnic Institute; B. S. in agricultural economics at V. P.I., 1941; commissioned 2d lieutenant at graduation in the U. S. Army Reserves; called to active service July 1, 1941; commissioned 1st lieutenant in June, 1942. On June 28, 1941, he married Miss Gwendolyn Huffman of Harrisonburg. He is now stationed at Fort Eustis, Va., battalion headquarters, executive officer of the 14th Battalion.

Edward Lee, born June 2, 1919; educated in the Harrisonburg schools and Virginia Polytechnic Institute; B. S. in chemical engineering at V. P. I., 1941; commissioned 2d lieutenant at graduation in the U. S. Army Reserves. In his senior year he was major of the 3d Battalion, V. P. I. Cadet Corps. He was called to active service July 1, 1941; commissioned 1st lieutenant in April 1942. He was for some time stationed at Fort Eustis, post headquarters, Assistant Post Adjutant. He is now a captain.

HERBERT P. SNAPP

BUSINESS MAN, CIVIC LEADER, MAYOR OF GROTTOES

Born in 1879 at Parnassus, Augusta County; employee of N. & W. Railway; state manager for Wood Harmon & Co.; circulation manager of the Waynesboro *News-Virginian;* promoter of the Shenandoah National Park; active leader in securing the Eastside Highway; president Grottoes Chamber of Commerce; councilman and mayor of Grottoes since 1927; active in successful movements for improving travel and transportation facilities in Rockingham and Augusta.

Mr. Snapp is a son of Rev. Silas R. and Sarah V. Snapp, and a grandson of John; a large landowner of Hampshire County, W. Va., and his wife Elizabeth. In childhood and youth he lived at Port Republic, Gainesboro, Hedgesville (W. Va.), White Post, and Grottoes, where his father, a Methodist minister, was located, and attended school at the three places last named. In his sixteenth year he began working for the N. & W. Railway as warehouse man under the direction of his brother, Robert J. Snapp of Elkton. Within a year he became train messenger and baggage master for the Southern Express Co., resigning after eight years to be manager of the paint department of the Pittsburg Plate Glass Co. in Cleveland, Ohio. Shortly afterward he became a real estate agent in New York for Wood Harmon & Co. and was soon appointed district manager in Virginia for this firm, handling at the same time his own properties near Port Republic and Grottoes. About 1920 he became interested in building a first-class highway through the east side of the Valley, and in 1924 he was appointed chairman of a committee to forward this enterprise. As the movement gained headway he was again put on the executive committee for Rockingham County and was made secretary of the Eastside Highway Association, continuing thus until the work was completed. The wide and effective publicity given the project was due to his earnest efforts. In 1926 he became president of the Grottoes Chamber of Commerce, and thus continues. About 1927 he was elected to the town council and soon thereafter was appointed mayor, and as such has served ever since, with the exception of a brief interval. During his tenure of office Grottoes has secured a modern school building, a large industry, macadamized streets, and the completed Eastside Highway. With others he secured the building of the Scotts Ford bridge and the improvement of highways in Rockingham and Augusta, as well as connections with Albemarle. He was one of the first promoters and organizers in the successful movement for the great Shenandoah National Park. For a number of years he has been engaged in newspaper work, first with the late Geo. G. Jordan, owner of the Waynesboro *Valley Virginian,* which paper was later bought out by the Waynesboro *News* and is now known as the Waynesboro *News-Virginian,* with Mr. Louis Spilman general manager and editor. Of this paper Mr. Snapp is the efficient circulation manager. His hobby is gardening, and his reading is mainly in the Bible, science, and psychology.

In August, 1900, Mr. Snapp married Miss Adeline L. Blackburn, born at Grottoes, April 5, 1881, daughter of John W. Blackburn and wife, Frances Harnsberger. Her brother, J. Frank Blackburn, was clerk of Rockingham County. Their grandfather was Capt. Henry B. Harnsberger, and they are direct descendants of the pioneer Adam Miller. Mr. and Mrs. Snapp have living children: Gladys V. (Mrs. Foster), born Sept. 22, 1903; Letitia B. (Mrs. Martinez), born Feb. 19, 1908; Adelaide C. (Mrs. Pattie), born Sept. 11, 1910; and Herbert P. Snapp, Jr., born May 5, 1914.

JAMES O. STICKLEY
BANKER, BUSINESS MAN, AND CIVIC LEADER

Born September 2, 1869, at Cross Keys, Rockingham County; attended schools at Cross Keys and Port Republic; traveling salesman; came to Harrisonburg in 1905; several years in Florida; J. O. Stickley & Son successors to W. H. Cunningham & Co., dealers in farm implements; Harrisonburg city councilman 22 years; president of The National Bank of Harrisonburg; president of the Rockingham & Cross Keys Mutual Fire Insurance Company since 1899.

Mr. Stickley's father, Phineas Stickley, and his grandfather, Tobias Stickley, were representatives of the Shenandoah family of Stickleys who have been prominent in and around Strasburg for generations. Coming to Rockingham, after serving four years in the Civil War, Phineas married Mary Bowman, daughter of Daniel Bowman of Silver Lake, near Dayton, and located near Cross Keys. James went to school first near home, then went to Port Republic, where his teacher was Prof. J. J. Lincoln. Circumstances did not admit of his going to college; instead, he went to work; but he has kept alive his interest in books, having a partiality for poetry and history, especially the history of the English people and that of our own Southland; and he has taken pleasure in assisting at least six other persons to obtain a college education. During his teen age he clerked in a country store; later went to Baltimore and traveled as a salesman for about seven years. Some years after he located in Harrisonburg he purchased an interest in the large farm implement business of W. H. Cunningham & Co. After the death of Mr. Cunningham, Mr. Stickley and his son purchased the Cunningham interest and have since operated as J. O. Stickley & Son, Inc.

Mr. Stickley's wife was Mrs. Roberta G. Tyler, formerly Miss Turner, daughter of Dr. J. H. Turner and his wife, Annette Tyler, of Front Royal. Mrs. Stickley was a teacher and the author of magazine stories and poetry. Dan C. Stickley, son of James O. Stickley and wife, graduated from the Harrisonburg High School and the Virginia Military Institute at Lexington. Since then he has been in business with his father and is now president of the firm of J. O. Stickley & Son, Inc. In 1930 he married Katherine, daughter of W. W. Sproul of Augusta County. They have two sons, Dan C., Jr., and William S. Both are now in grade school.

Mr. Stickley is a member of the Presbyterian Church; in politics he is a Democrat. His hobbies are farms and livestock. During the 22 consecutive years that he was on the city council he was present at every regular meeting but one, and served on some of the most responsible committees. When the Peoples Bank, now The National Bank, of Harrisonburg was chartered in 1907, Mr. Stickley became a stockholder and one of the original board of directors. In a few years he was elected vice-president; and upon the death of James E. Reherd in 1940 he was chosen president and has been re-elected at each annual meeting since. He is now serving his 43rd year as president of the Rockingham & Cross Keys Mutual Fire Insurance Company, one of the well-established and successful financial institutions of the county. The present building of J. O. Stickley & Son, Inc., in Harrisonburg, erected in 1940, is pronounced by officials of the International Harvester Co. to embody more features of advantage than any other of its kind in the country.

ROBERT EDWARD LEE STRICKLER, D. D. S.

PROFESSIONAL AND BUSINESS MAN

Born June 7, 1877, on a farm near Timberville; attended schools near Timberville and New Market, Tenth Legion High School, and West Central Academy; Bridgewater College, 1897-1900; D. D. S., University of Maryland, 1903; began practice in Bridgewater and North Fork, W. Va.; has lived and practiced at Bridgewater since 1907; on town council for a number of years; owner of stocks and real estate; active in church and professional organizations.

Dr. Strickler's father, Benjamin Franklin (October 21, 1836—January 4, 1887), was known as Frank Strickler; his mother's maiden name was Susan Cline. She was born March 6, 1838, and died May 3, 1893. His father's parents were Benjamin Strickler (1799-1856) and his wife, Margaret (Peggy) Zirkle. Dr. Strickler had three brothers older than himself and three younger. After attending the Bluff School near Timberville, the Roller School near New Market, Tenth Legion High School, and West Central Academy at Mt. Clinton, he, in 1897, entered Bridgewater College where he remained three years. The next three years were spent in the dental department of the University of Maryland, where he received his degree in 1903, with honorable mention for special plate work. Already, in the summer of 1902, he had done some professional work in Bridgewater, and there he practiced for a year or more after his graduation, then located at North Fork, W. Va., where, after three years, he broke down from overwork. Soon recovering, he located in Bridgewater, where he has practiced successfully ever since. Though not a strict tither, he has proceeded on the tithing principle, and has given to the church and to charity more than $10,000, his practice having aggregated over $100,000. He aided his younger brothers in securing their education and loaned considerable sums to his older brothers at various times. He is a member of the Church of the Brethren and has taken an active part in temperance and church work for 40 years. He and Mrs. Strickler are both life members of the Women's Christian Temperance Union. For 20 years he was treasurer of the Bridgewater congregation. He is a general reader, with no special preferences. He is interested in politics and public affairs, but is an independent voter. He finds recreation in walking and climbing mountains, and has been on top of most of the highest peaks east of the Rockies.

As may be perceived from the foregoing, Dr. Strickler has been successful in business. He owns a house in Bridgewater, another in Luray, and has profitable investments in various enterprises. He considers bank stock preferable for investment, and owns stock in a number of different banks.

In October, 1905, Dr. Strickler married Miss Nora R. Andes, born July 12, 1878, daughter of John W. and Bettie Roller Andes of Pleasant Valley. Of this marriage were born three sons: Frank A., born July 12, 1908, now a physician, specializing in nervous diseases, with offices in the cities of Roanoke and Radford; Stanley S., born October 18, 1910, who is a funeral director in Pulaski; and Robert Lee, born December 21, 1915, who is a minister, now pastor of the historic Peter's Creek Church near Roanoke City.

Dr. Strickler's youngest brother, S. Vernon Strickler, is a dentist in Charlottesville; another brother, Harry M., is a lawyer, formerly commonwealth's attorney of Rockingham County, and the author of several well-known books on genealogy and local history.

HARRY M. STRICKLER
LAWYER, AUTHOR, AND PUBLIC OFFICIAL

Born November 5, 1881, at Timberville; attended public schools and West Central Academy; B. A., Bridgewater College, 1906; LL. B., University of Virginia, 1907; lawyer in Arlington County, Va.; located in Harrisonburg in 1910; commonwealth's attorney of Rockingham County, 1915-20; deputy clerk of U. S. District Court, 1920-21; located in Luray, 1929; mayor of Luray, 1931-35; author of valuable works on local history and genealogy.

Mr. Strickler is one of the seven sons of Benjamin Franklin and Susan Virginia Cline Strickler, one of whom, Dr. R. E. L. Strickler, is the well-known dentist of Bridgewater. His paternal grandparents were Benjamin and Margaret Zirkle Strickler. While he was still a boy his parents moved from Timberville to a farm on Smith Creek, near the historic village of Tenth Legion. New Market, five miles to the northeast, was their trading place. After a year in West Central Academy at Mt. Clinton, he matriculated at Bridgewater College, where he spent several years, continuing his work at the University of Virginia in the law department. In 1906 he was awarded the B. A. degree at Bridgewater, and the next year he graduated in law at the University.

Shortly after receiving his law degree Mr. Strickler opened an office in Arlington County, Va., but after a year or two came to Harrisonburg, beginning practice here in 1910. For four years, 1915-20, he was commonwealth's attorney of Rockingham County; then, during the year 1920 and part of 1921, he was deputy clerk of the U. S. Court for the Western District of Virginia. In 1929 he located in Luray, where he continued his practice and where he served as mayor of Luray from 1931 to 1935.

In both Rockingham and Page County Mr. Strickler has found congenial surroundings among the homes of his ancestors, Stricklers, Zirkles, and others, some of whom were among the earliest settlers of these localities. Abram Strickler, with Adam Miller, Mathias Selzer, John Roads, and others, settled in the Massanutten Country, on the Shenandoah River, in what is now Page County, in 1727 or 1728. These pioneers and others have been interesting subjects of study to Mr. Strickler, who has devoted much time to tracing out their history and locating the several tracts of land on which they settled. As a result of his investigations he has published several valuable works relating to many well-known families of Page and Rockingham, among which are the following: "Massanutten," relating to that section of Page County that was first settled by the white people; "Forerunners," a large volume on the Stricklers and kindred families; "Old Tenth Legion Marriages," a marriage register of Rockingham County from 1778 to 1816; and "Tenth Legion Tithables," an interesting work giving much information from old militia records and other sources.

Mr. Strickler is a member of the Presbyterian Church; a Mason, a Rotarian; and in politics a Democrat. At present he is a member of the Selective Service Board of Page County. He is a genial companion and an all-round good fellow. His wife was Miss Virginia Garber Cole, who was born in Shenandoah County, December 30, 1887. She is much interested in educational and related activities. Mr. and Mrs. Strickler make their home at Rosemary Mont, near Luray; they also maintain an apartment at Bridgewater, where Mrs. Strickler has been an outstanding benefactress of Bridgewater College.

FRANK L. SUBLETT

BUSINESS MAN AND CIVIC LEADER

Born March 3, 1869, in Staunton; educated in the public schools, Kable's School in Staunton, Shenandoah Valley Academy at Winchester, and the Kenmore University School at Amherst; began business as an office boy for his father in Staunton; set up for himself as a dealer in coal; then became a wholesale dealer in hay at Staunton, moving in 1900 to Harrisonburg where he carried on extensively for many years; owner and operator of real estate; Harrisonburg postmaster under President Wilson; bank and railway director; first president of Shen. Valley Inc. and promoter of the Shen. National Park; active in all progressive enterprises.

Mr. Sublett is a son of Philip Branch and Ida Caroline Scott Sublett. The latter was a daughter of Col. Thomas Scott of Prince Edward County, Va. His paternal grandfather was Thomas Smith Sublett, of Powhatan County, whose wife was a Dupuy. Both the Subletts and the Dupuys were of the Huguenot colony that settled in and around Manakin Town, Goochland County, in 1700. John Dupuy contributed an interesting account of this settlement to the *Southern Literary Messenger* of April, 1841.

Ten days after his marriage in Brooklyn, January 10, 1900, to Mrs. Nannie Smith, daughter of Washington Patterson and widow of Benjamin Smith, Mr. and Mrs. Sublett located in Harrisonburg. Here Mr. Sublett continued as a wholesale dealer in hay, developing the business to large proportions and making Rockingham hay known over the eastern States. For eight years, under the administrations of President Wilson, he served as Harrisonburg postmaster. At the same time he invested largely in real estate and was a prominent figure in other lines of business. Under his advice, D. F. Detwiler came here from Philadelphia and developed a large business in the shipping of poultry. He was an active member of the chamber of commerce and a director of the Southern Railway and the First National Bank. He was a charter member of the local Rotary Club and was affiliated also with the Elks and U. C. T. During World War I he was a member of the Harrisonburg Home Guards. He was instrumental in organizing the Shenandoah Valley Inc. and served as the first president. About 1920 he began collecting and selling antiques, building up a business in this line that became nationally known. His business as a dealer in hay and grain was continued until about 1928, that in antiques until May, 1931, when he suffered from a severe stroke of paralysis.

It is not too much to say that during his 31 years of active life here Mr. Sublett was a general benefactor. Every movement and enterprise that gave promise of promoting legitimate business and the general welfare received his encouragement and substantial support. His favorable reports of the Shenandoah Valley Inc. to Dr. John P. McConnell of Radford led to a similar organization in Southwest Virginia. He rendered effective service in developing the Virginia Craftsmen and in bringing the shirt factory, the silk mill, and other industries to Harrisonburg. As president of the Shenandoah Valley Inc. and otherwise he took a leading and effective part in the movement which resulted in the opening and development of the Shenandoah National Park.

Mr. and Mrs. Sublett were the parents of three daughters: Eleanor (Mrs. J. E. Catlin), who lives in a suburb of New York City, on the New Jersey side; Frances (Mrs. James M. Warren), of Harrisonburg; and Nancy (Mrs. Charles A. Nelson), who also resides in Harrisonburg. Mr. Sublett is a member of the Episcopal Church; in politics, a Democrat. Though much disabled physically (since 1931), he is still a genial companion and finds diversion in reading detective and adventure stories.

WARD SWANK

LAWYER, LEGISLATOR, AND MAYOR

Born November 10, 1885, at Edom; attended public schools at Edom; graduated from the Harrisonburg High School in 1908; B. A., University of Virginia, 1911; B. L., U. Va., 1913; admitted to the bar in Harrisonburg, 1913; clerk of Harrisonburg City Council, 1915-32; member of Virginia State Senate, 1923-31; mayor of Harrisonburg since 1932, excepting a brief interval; local counsel for the Federal Land Bank of Baltimore, the B.& O. Railroad Co., the Southern Railway Co., the N. & W. Railway Co., Virginia State Highway Department, Merck & Company, Inc., and The National Bank of Harrisonburg.

Mr. Swank for years has been a leading attorney of Harrisonburg, a loyal alumnus of the University of Virginia, and an active participant in local and state government. He is a son of the late John Perry Swank, a successful farmer and stockman of Edom, and his wife, Mary Elizabeth Horn. His paternal grandparents were John and Mary Acker Swank; his mother's parents were Jackson and Mary Moyers Horn. After early schooling at Edom, he entered Harrisonburg High School, where he graduated in 1908. He then matriculated at the University of Virginia, where he, with Tom Harnsberger, Raymond Dingledine, and others kept up their record in mathematics and other subjects that they had begun with Professor Keister in Harrisonburg. Having received his degree in law at the University in 1913 he returned to Harrisonburg where he entered upon professional practice, in which he has been eminently successful. In World War I he took training in the Officers' School at Fort Meyer and served as a member of the draft board for Harrisonburg and Rockingham County. He is a member of the American Legion, the Masonic fraternity, and the Presbyterian Church. At the University of Virginia he was affiliated with the Phi Kappa Psi Fraternity and the Imp Society; professionally, he belongs to the local bar association, the Virginia State Bar Association, and the American Bar Association.

From 1923 to 1931 Mayor Swank was a member of the Virginia State Senate, where his work was effective and always along progressive lines. In local politics and civic affairs he has been active and efficient, devoting much time and energy to constructive service. For 17 years (1915-32) he was clerk of the Harrisonburg City Council, and since 1932 he has been mayor of the city, excepting several months in 1937 when the office was held by John W. Morrison and Raymond Dingledine. In 1938 he appointed a special committee of the council to study the city government, and the next year, in accordance with the recommendations of this commitee, a city manager was appointed and other progressive changes were made. Within recent years the corporate limits of the city have been extended and many material and governmental improvements have been carried out. He has always shown a commendable and helpful interest in all benevolent, educational, and cultural enterprises.

On June 19, 1918, Mayor Swank married Miss Elsie Rebecca Miller, who was born at Stephens City, Va., daughter of Samuel H. and Lura Peery Miller of Frederick County. Mrs. Swank, before her marriage, was a student in the State Teachers (now Madison) College at Harrisonburg, where she graduated in 1917. Mr. and Mrs. Swank are the parents of two daughters: Carolyn Miller, born November 29, 1925, now a student in Harrisonburg High School, and Janice Newton, born October 25, 1930, a student in the Junior High School of the city.

WILLIAM PERRY SWARTZ, JR.
BUSINESS MAN AND REAL ESTATE OPERATOR

Born Sept. 21, 1911, at Seven-Mile Ford, Smyth Co., Va.; brought to Dayton at age of six months; finished Dayton grammar school; graduated from Harrisonburg High School, 1929; B. S., Va. Polytechnic Institute, 1933; sales representative and sales engineer, 1933-42; vice-chairman board of Raleigh Court Methodist Church, Roanoke; commissioned 2d lieut., Officers' Reserve Corps, Coast Artillery, June 1933; 1st lieut., August 1937; honorably discharged, August 20, 1942; operates Wm. P. Swartz, Jr., Co., furnishing building supplies and equipment.

Mr. Swartz's father, Wm. Perry Swartz, Sr., born at Dale Enterprise, Feb. 12, 1865, is one of the few living charter members of the famous Dale Enterprise Literary Society. His mother, Elva Worrell (July 2, 1880—Nov. 5, 1942), was a daughter of Maj. C. C. Worrell, C. S. A., educator, and civic leader of Hillsville, Va., and wife, America Watson. She taught in Va. and Tenn. schools until she married Mr. Swartz in 1907. During his second year in high school, Wm. Perry, Jr., worked mornings, evenings, and Saturdays in B. Ney & Sons' "Bargain Basement"; the last two years he was circulation mgr. in Harrisonburg for the Richmond *Times Dispatch* and in addition carried a paper route himself. While at V. P. I. he had a photo and camera agency, represented a company for military equipment, and was agent for the old Eastern Bus Lines and the Old Dominion Stages, the latter now the Atlantic Greyhound Lines. The last three years he worked in the mess hall; during his senior year he had a filling station, operated for him, military regulations and other work barring him from doing so. He was Sr. Lt. of Hdqrs. Battery. Making honors in his Jr. and Sr. years, he graduated in Electr. Engineering, with extra credit in Bus. Administration. In addition, he was vice-pres., and pres. of the V. P. I. Shen. Valley Club; in his senior year was asst. business manager of the V. P. I. *Skipper* (magazine); was a member of the dramatic club, and during his Jr. and Sr. years was its manager; during the same years he was a member of the Amer. Society of Electr. Engineers and of the Y. M. C. A. cabinet. At his graduation he was given a gold key for outstanding work in the Y. M. C. A.

Since graduation Mr. Swartz has been active as an officer in the V. P. I. Alumni Assn. at Greensboro, N. C., and is now Sec'y of the Roanoke Chapter. He is a member of the Roanoke Symphony Assn. and the Roanoke Civic Theater. He is a 32d degree Scottish Rite Mason, and a York Rite Mason, and is a member of Pleasants Lodge No. 63, A. F. & A. M., Elmwood Chapter No. 33, R. A. M., Bayard Commandery No. 15, K. T., Roanoke Consistory, A. & A. S. R. F., and Kazim Temple, A. A. O. N. M. S.

Mr. Swartz has had a varied business experience, with unvarying success. He is now head of the Wm. P. Swartz, Jr., Co., a sales organization for industrial, institutional, and building supplies, and owns and operates much real estate. On March 29, 1935, in Macon, Ga., he married Miss Suelle McKellar, born Nov. 11, 1911, at Homerville, Ga., daughter of Mr. and Mrs. I. E. McKellar of Macon. Her father is head of the dept. of ancient languages in Wesleyan College. Mr. and Mrs. Swartz have two children: Wm. Perry III, born Dec. 11, 1937, and Elva Anne, born April 26, 1942.

As to hobbies and recreation, Mr. Swartz says: "I find that church, Alumni, and civic activities consume a good part of my spare time. I play some golf and read the *Saturday Evening Post* and the *Reader's Digest*."

WALTER C. SWITZER

BUSINESS MAN AND CHURCH LEADER

Born June 9, 1870, at Mt. Crawford; located in Harrisonburg in 1895; founded the Harrisonburg Telephone Co. in 1902; organizer and manager of the city's first ice plant; first superintendent of the city-owned electric plant; chairman of the Democratic committee of Harrisonburg more than 20 years; member of the Democratic state committee; delegate to the Democratic national convention in Baltimore, 1912; senior elder of St. Stephen's Reformed Church; died November 29, 1924.

Mr. Switzer was the son of John A. Switzer and his wife, Caroline Roller. The Harrisonburg Telephone Company, which he organized in 1902, and of which he was president and general manager until his death, has had a remarkable development and has earned a high rating in efficiency. Carried on by his sons, the company on January 1, 1942, operated 3972 stations, with 2461 service-line stations, making a total of 6433. Its investment in plant and equipment amounted to $511,164.00.

The efforts of Mr. Switzer were at all times far-reaching and effective, and his labors constituted an important element in the advancement of his community and the commonwealth. He was one of the original supporters of Senator Harry F. Byrd and remained one of his loyal champions and ardent admirers. On June 8, 1898, he married Miss Sarah Sherman, daughter of John Wise and Nancy Henkel Sherman. Of this marriage were born four children: Frank C., Margaret (Mrs. Hayes A. Richardson of Kansas City, Mo.), G. Fred, and Homer (deceased). Mrs. Switzer survives and continues to make her home in Harrisonburg.

Frank C. Switzer attended Harrisonburg High School, Mercersburg Academy, and graduated from Washington and Lee University. He married Miss Mamie Omohundro and has two children: Anne Omohundro and Sue Cunningham Switzer. He is a deacon in St. Stephen's Reformed Church and has been active in Masonry, the local chamber of commerce, and the Rotary Club. He is now a major overseas in the U. S. Army, 116th Inf., 29th Division. For some years he was general manager of the telephone company which his father established.

G. Fred Switzer is also a graduate of Harrisonburg High School and attended Washington and Lee University. He is a deacon in St. Stephen's Reformed Church, a director of the First National Bank, a member of the Kiwanis Club, and has been on the Harrisonburg Democratic Committee for many years. He was a delegate to the Democratic national convention at Chicago in 1932 and has been postmaster at Harrisonburg since 1936. He, like his father, is a Democrat of the Harry Byrd type and has been associated with Senator Byrd in politics for the past 20 years. He is president of the Harrisonburg Telephone Company, but considers his chief contribution to Harrisonburg as made through the new Federal Building in the city and St. Stephen's Reformed Church. His efforts to secure the new Federal Building were untiring and eminently successful. This splendid structure was dedicated with appropriate exercises on March 23, 1940.

On June 21, 1930, G. Fred Switzer married Miss Elizabeth Kemper, daughter of Dr. and Mrs. Albert S. Kemper of Lynnwood, Rockingham County. Of this marriage there are two daughters: Elizabeth Blackburn, born January 15, 1933, and Nancy Kemper, born November 23, 1935.

JOHN ROBERT SWITZER
CLERK OF ROCKINGHAM AND HARRISONBURG CIRCUIT COURT

Born December 25, 1883, at Mt. Crawford; attended public schools of Mt. Crawford and Harrisonburg and Randolph-Macon Academy at Front Royal; LL. B., Washington and Lee University, 1906; in law practice in Harrisonburg until appointed deputy clerk of the circuit court in 1920; elected clerk in 1927 and re-elected in 1935; for some years a lieutenant in the National Guard; chairman of the county draft board in World War I; for some time was president of the Harrisonburg Mutual Telephone Co. and of the First National Bank of Harrisonburg.

Mr. Switzer is a younger brother of Walter C. Switzer, whose biography precedes. Their father was John A. Switzer (1837-1909); their mother, Carrie Roller Switzer. John A. was a native of Hardy County, now West Virginia, a son of Valentine and Margaret Moore Switzer. He was a cavalryman under Col. John S. Mosby. After the war he was a farmer and stockman at Mt. Crawford. In 1895 he was elected sheriff of Rockingham County, the only Democrat chosen to a major office in that contest. He held the office of sheriff 12 years, then refused to be a candidate again. John Robert, having completed his training in law at Washington and Lee, began the practice of law in Harrisonburg, continuing until 1920, when he was appointed deputy clerk of the circuit court. In 1927 he was elected clerk without opposition and in 1935 he was re-elected by a majority of over 2000 votes. In 1928 he retired from the presidency of the Harrisonburg Mutual Telephone Company and in 1936 as president of the First National Bank, to be able to devote all his time to his duties as clerk of the court. At the same time he has always been active in civic, fraternal, and religious organizations. He is an elder in St. Stephens Reformed Church, a prominent Mason in the different branches of the fraternity, a member of the Elks lodge, in which he has been secretary for 30 years, and is also affiliated with the Independent Order of Odd Fellows, the Knights of Pythias, and the Junior Order of United American Mechanics. For many years he was a member of the Kiwanis Club, and he is past commander of the D. H. Lee Martz Camp of Sons of Confederate Veterans. For some time he was an officer in the National Guard, and in World War I served as chairman of the local draft board. He has always taken an active interest in politics and civic affairs and since 1916 has held official positions in the local and state Democratic organizations. He is a regular attendant upon the party conventions. For relaxation he occasionally seeks out a mountain stream for trout-fishing.

On December 12, 1911, Mr. Switzer married Miss Virginia Armentrout of Strasburg, daughter of G. W. and Cora Virginia (Willey) Armentrout. Mr. and Mrs. Switzer have a son and a daughter: John Robert, Jr., who was born August 17, 1913, and Virginia Anne, born March 13, 1919. John Robert is a graduate of the Harrisonburg High School, class of 1931, and took his degree in dental surgery at the University of Maryland, in 1935, later taking a post-graduate course at Harvard University. On June 16, 1942, he married Virginia Ramsey of Bassett. Dr. Switzer is now a captain in the Medical Detachment of the 116th Infantry in the U. S. Army and on duty in England. Virginia Anne is also a graduate of Harrisonburg High School, class of 1937, and attended Hollins College. On September 7, 1940, she married L. O. Funkhouser, who is an ensign in the U. S. Navy and now on duty in Norfolk, Virginia.

PETER SWOPE THOMAS
BUSINESS MAN AND CHURCHMAN

Born April 12, 1857, near Spring Creek; attended Beaver Creek School and Spring Creek Academy (later Bridgewater College); teacher at Beaver Creek; came to Harrisonburg in 1881; dealer in farm implements; contractor with W. H. Rickard in construction work; contractor in plumbing and heating; secretary Harrisonburg Board of Trade; active in church work; captain of Fire Company No. 3; founder and first elder of the Harrisonburg Church of the Brethren.

Mr. Thomas for many years was a faithful minister in the Church of the Brethren and a prominent leader in church enterprises; at the same time he engaged in various lines of business and participated actively in civic and philanthropic organizations of Harrisonburg and Rockingham County. He was a son of Elder Jacob Thomas of Beaver Creek and his wife, Elizabeth Swope. His father was one of the early supporters of higher education in the Church of the Brethren, and Mr. Thomas himself was for many years a trustee of Bridgewater College. For 25 years he was secretary of the Brethren orphans home board at Timberville; also for some years general secretary of the child rescue organization of the Church of the Brethren, as well as an active worker for temperance and welfare agencies.

In 1881, in partnership with his father, Mr. Thomas began business in Harrisonburg as a dealer in farm implements and so continued until about 1896, when his building was burned. For several years he and W. H. Rickard engaged in construction work, one of their contracts consisting in grading a part of the roadway for the C. -W. Railway. In 1907 he went into the plumbing business, with his shop on the north side of East Market Street, just east of Federal Alley. About this time he took a correspondence course in heating and plumbing with the International Correspondence Schools. Shortly afterwards he took the contract for laying the first main sewer line in Harrisonburg. He was instrumental in developing the city water system, and was an active member of one of the fire companies, being captain for some time of the old Fire Company No. 3. For 25 years he was secretary of the Harrisonburg Board of Trade, the forerunner of the present chamber of commerce. About 1901 he and several others established the Church of the Brethren in Harrisonburg, and a few years later he was instrumental in building the brick church of the denomination on the hill, on the site formerly occupied by the first Methodist Church. Until a short time before his death he served the congregation as pastor and elder.

On October 11, 1881, Mr. Thomas married Miss Lizzie E. McLaughlin, daughter of John and Hannah J. McLaughlin, and at the time of his death, February 21, 1930, he was survived by Mrs. Thomas and seven children: Nina, Mrs. John D. Garber; Lottie, Mrs. Claude Bowman; Margaret, Mrs. E. V. Crist; Pauline, Mrs. Glenn Cline; Edna, Mrs. Earl Wetsel; Anna, Mrs. Russell Lee; and a son, Charles H. Thomas. He was survived also by a brother, Rev. Abram S. Thomas, and a sister, Miss Susan Thomas, both of the Spring Creek neighborhood. Interment was made in the cemetery of Beaver Creek Church, which is located near the old Thomas homestead. The popularity of Mr. Thomas was indicated by the large congregation in attendance, made up of ministers and members of the various denominations represented in the city and county.

FRANCES CALVERT THOMPSON

CONCERT ARTIST
PIANIST, TEACHER, ACCOMPANIST

Honor graduate of Hollins College; Bac. Mus., University Conservatory, Chicago; student under James Bliss of Minneapolis; in Damrosch School of Music, New York; teacher in Marion College, Va., University of North Dakota, and Sioux Falls Conservatory; Minneapolis and Chicago; teacher in Harrisonburg and organizer of music clubs in the Shenandoah Valley since 1926.

Mrs. Thompson's native talent was encouraged by the literary and musical traditions of her native town, New Market, and the accomplishments of her forebears. She was one of the five children of Judge George R. Calvert and his wife, Anna Clinedinst. Her paternal grandfather was Major John S. Calvert (1806-1870), who was twice elected state treasurer of Virginia. Having given evidence of her serious interest in music at Hollins, she later studied four years with Emil Liebling in Chicago. Her real success she credits to James Bliss of Minneapolis, with whom she worked for protracted periods. She coached with Victor Heinze, the great Leschetizky exponent, and in the Damrosch School of Music in New York she was associated with Arthur Hochmann, John Thompson, Bristow Hardin, and Hans Barth, modern pedagogues. She has concertized extensively in the South and Middle West, and has appeared in Minneapolis, Chicago, Spokane, and San Diego; and has won approval as an accompanist with Madam Bessesen, grand opera star, Sigurd Gran Rishovd, violinist of the Minneapolis Symphony Orchestra, and Minne Hambitzer, coloratura soprano of Milwaukee.

She has served as musical critic for the *Musical Courier* of New York and the *Concert-Goer* of Chicago. Among her students she has brought out many with talent, one having appeared with success before the Thursday Music Club of Minneapolis, and another, of only eight years of age, having won notice over the radio. Mrs. Thompson has played frequently for broadcasting stations in Minneapolis and in Virginia. She has a wide acquaintance among distinguished musicians, composers, lecturers, and teachers. She converses in one or two languages besides her native tongue. Her experience in musical organization is wide and notable. She is one of the charter members of the music club at Grand Forks, North Dakota, and she is enrolled in the Thursday Music Club of Minneapolis, an organization of one thousand members; also in the Twin City Music and Dramatic Club of the same city. She has been recognized by notices in national and international gazetteers of musical celebrities. She holds membership in Federated Virginia music clubs, including Virginia as well as National Music Teachers' Association and the Federation of Music Clubs. Her activity in organizing music clubs in the Shenandoah Valley has been notable. She has frequently acted as a judge in various Federation contests, has served as State Chairman of National Music Week, and has held office in the National Music Club organization. No small part of her success in her chosen field is attributable to her personal qualities of vivacity, humor, and wit, sweetened with sympathy and human kindness. In playing she subordinates her splendid technique to the spirit and meaning of the composition.

In her native town of New Market, Frances Calvert was married to William Bernard Thompson, a talented singer and musician, who died some years ago. There were no children of the marriage. The old home in New Market is still in the hands of the Calvert family.

MERCYE CHILDRESS TUCKER
PIANO TEACHER, SUPERVISOR OF MUSIC, AND SCHOOL PRINCIPAL

Born February 9, 1898, at Berkeley Springs, W. Va.; attended schools in Iowa; graduate of Jennings, La., High School; student of music and art; attended Silliman College and Madison College; teacher in Louisiana, Maryland, and Virginia; member of the executive committee of the Rockingham Teachers Association; supervisor of music in Rockingham schools; now principal of the Singers' Glen School.

Mrs. Tucker, born Mercye Childress, is the daughter of Dr. W. Lomax Childress and his wife, Ada Burtner. Her paternal grandparents were Dr. Abram and Elizabeth Grosvenor Childress of Roanoke. She married George Reginal Tucker, born July 25, 1886, in Hamburg, Arkansas, son of Henry St. George Tucker and his wife, Mattie Cammack. Her husband was directly related to Henry St. George Tucker of Lexington. She has a son, George Reginal Tucker, Jr., born June 25, 1923.

In Cumberland, Md., where Mrs. Tucker taught in the city schools, she was a member of the Cumberland Music and Art Club. In Rockingham County, Va., where she has resided for a number of years, she has been active in various educational services. For three years or more she taught in the Broadway High School, and for eight years she was a member of the faculty of the high school at Singers' Glen. For three years past she was supervisor of music in the schools of Rockingham County, and since the opening of the present school session she has been principal of the Singers' Glen School. For a number of years she has been a member of the executive committee of the Rockingham Teachers Association.

At Singers' Glen, which was the home of Joseph Funk, "Father of Song in Northern Virginia," and his sons, Mrs. Tucker has found inspiring traditions in congenial surroundings. For three years she was president of the Joseph Funk Music Club and was sponsor of the Singers' Glen Choral Club. She sponsored and organized the Rockingham County Teachers Chorus, and was chairman of the music committee for the Rockingham County Turkey Festival of 1941. She has been a choral director of various organizations for the past fifteen years; for an equal period she has been a piano instructor; and she is now in her twentieth year of teaching in the public schools. For two years she was chairman of the music committee of the Rockingham County schools. She is a member of the United Brethren Church. In politics she is a Democrat. Her hobbies, as might be surmised, are music, art, flowers, and reading.

While a student in Silliman College, Mrs. Tucker was president of her class, of the glee club, and of the student body. At Madison College, where she will graduate in 1943, she was elected a member of Kappa Delta Pi. For many years she has been active as church accompanist, choir director, and in organizing and directing music festivals in which large numbers of children and young people have participated. With her father, grandfather, five uncles, and a cousin all ministers, she could hardly avoid being active and enthusiastic in religious and social work. Her father, a talented preacher, was the author of five volumes of poetry, many stories, and numerous articles on various subjects. He received the title of "Poet Laureate of the United Brethren Church." He was a humorist and chautauqua lecturer, and his biography was requested for White's Cyclopedia of American Biography.

FRED CLINE WAMPLER

BUSINESS MAN, FRUIT GROWER, AND TRAVELER

Born September 6, 1873, on his father's farm near Dayton; attended Paul's Summit School, Shenandoah College, and Bridgewater College; in early life traveled and lived in a number of northern and western states; spent one year in eastern Cuba, where he purchased land; has been engaged in business in Harrisonburg since 1911, excepting two years spent in the Rio Grande Valley of Texas, where he built a home and planted an orange grove which he still owns; now a member of the firm of the Wampler Feed & Seed Co.; extensively engaged in poultry-raising in Rockingham.

Mr. Wampler, after traveling widely and sojourning for varying periods in different parts of the United States and neighboring countries, still finds his native county of Rockingham a desirable place for residence and business. In 1931 he purchased lands on the road between Dayton and Dale Enterprise and thereon erected his attractive and commodious stone house, from which he has a fine view of Dayton and Silver Lake. To him the site of his residence has a special interest because of the fact that here stood the old school house, Paul's Summit, where he went to school as a boy. Among his teachers here were Paul Funkhouser, Bishop John Coffman, Elder John Brunk, and Dr. Will Payne. The land was part of the farm of Abram Paul, a great-uncle of the present Judge John Paul, and was given to the school board by Mr. Paul for a place to build a school house. Mr. Wampler's hobby is pitching horseshoes. He has his grounds electrically lighted for night games.

Mr. Wampler's father was John Wampler, a substantial farmer and consistent member of the Church of the Brethren, a son of John Wampler, who was born May 10, 1795. The wife of John Wampler, Sr., was Mary Cline, born May 13, 1802. The maiden name of Fred Wampler's mother was Catherine Miller. After attending Paul's Summit School, as already indicated, Fred attended Shenandoah Collegiate Institute, now Shenandoah College, at Dayton one term; another term was spent at Bridgewater College; he then traveled and lived for some time in a number of northern and western states, and lived for one year in eastern Cuba, where he purchased lands. In 1911 he, with a brother-in-law, went into the grocery business in Harrisonburg, soon expanding the business by adding feeds and seeds, also shoes and dry goods. In 1926 he sold his interest to J. D. Wampler & Sons, who still operate the store. During the next year or two he and his family resided in the Rio Grande Valley of southern Texas, where they purchased lands, built a home, and planted an orange grove. In this balmy region they still spend most of their winters.

In the fall of 1927 Mr. Wampler, with his two brothers, Charles W. and Joseph D., established the now well-known business of the Wampler Feed & Seed Company, of which firm he is still a partner. In connection, the firm carries on an extensive business in the raising and marketing of poultry, in which members of the family have won national distinction.

On April 20, 1912, Mr. Wampler married Miss Laura E. Miller, daughter of G. Edward Miller of Bridgewater. Of this marriage there are two daughters: Janet, born July 8, 1918, and Rosaline, born July 5, 1920. Janet attended Manchester College, Indiana, and completed the B. A. course at the University of New Mexico, majoring in music. She is now teaching at Roswell, N. M. Rosaline attended college in Tennessee and will get her B. S. degree in Home Economics in June, 1943.

HERSHEY HARTMAN WEAVER

BUSINESS ORGANIZER AND EXECUTIVE

Born July 30, 1877, in South River District, Augusta County; grew up on his father's farm; attended the Hall School, near Stuart's Draft, through the 7th grade; at age 21 started work in Philadelphia in poultry and egg business; came to Harrisonburg in 1908 and with the Blosser Brothers organized the City Produce Exchange; president Harrisonburg Grocery Co., Inc., and the Rockingham Milling Co.; elder in the Presbyterian Church; Mason; charter member of the Rotary Club and U. C. T.

Mr. Weaver, like a number of others among our leading business men, who have not enjoyed extended training in the schools, exemplifies the success that may be achieved by industry, integrity, and thrift in fields of work that provide for real human needs. His birthplace, the home of his parents, Samuel H. and Elizabeth Weaver, was on a farm five miles south of Waynesboro, where he remained until he was 21 years of age. His paternal grandparents were David B. and Margaret Weaver. On coming of age he went to the city of Philadelphia where he worked for an uncle in a commission firm that handled country produce, especially poultry and eggs, and continued in this employ for a period of eight years, widening his acquaintance with life by observations in a great city and learning by direction and experience many of the lessons that have proved of value to him in subsequent years. He was also enabled to make contacts and form acquaintances among business men in Philadelphia and other cities.

In 1908 Mr. Weaver came to Harrisonburg and here, with Emanuel and Gabriel Blosser, organized the City Produce Exchange, which they are still operating and which has grown to be one of the largest enterprises of its kind in the United States. It has been one of the chief factors in making Harrisonburg a great center for the purchase and shipping of eggs and dressed poultry, and in advancing the production of chickens and turkeys in an extensive area surrounding the city. In 1919 Mr. Weaver was one of the organizers of the Rockingham Milling Company, which began operations in 1920. He is president of this company and also of the Harrisonburg Grocery, Inc., which carries on a large wholesale business. His connection with the latter enterprise dates from about 1925. He is a member and elder of the Harrisonburg Presbyterian Church and a charter member of the city-county Rotary Club. He is also affiliated with the United Commercial Travelers and the Masonic fraternity. In the latter he is a Master Mason, a member of the Royal Arch Chapter, the Commandery, and the Shrine. He states that he has not had much time to indulge in hobbies and recreational diversions, but he keeps up his reading of poultry journals and other publications that relate to his various lines of business.

In May, 1902, Mr. Weaver married Miss Lillia Brunk, born October 20. 1877, a daughter of Christian H. and Mary Brunk of the Weaver's Church neighborhood. Mr. and Mrs. Weaver have two children: a daughter, Mary Elizabeth, and a son, Charles Oliver. Mary, born October 25, 1906, a graduate of Hollins College, is now Mrs. Paull Shields of Hagerstown, Md. She has a son, Paull Shields, Jr. A daughter died in infancy. Charles, born March 21, 1911, graduated from Randolph-Macon College at Ashland and then took a business course in Richmond. He is engaged with his father in the City Produce Exchange. He married Miss Martha Way and has a son, Charles Stewart Weaver.

MARION ROLSTON WEAVER

BUSINESS MAN AND AIRPLANE PILOT

Born October 1, 1900, near Dayton; grew up on a farm and attended public schools; completed various correspondence courses, including one in business administration under auspices of Northwestern University; manager for some years of the Valley Creamery at Penn Laird; founder in 1934 and operator until 1937 of the Spotswood Transfer Co.; operator since 1937 of the Rockingham Construction Co., Inc.; Kiwanian; member of the Harrisonburg-Rockingham Chamber of Commerce, etc.; licensed airplane pilot.

Mr. Weaver is another Rockingham boy who has made an important contribution to his home county and city through various successful business enterprises. He is a son of Raleigh Jacob Weaver and wife, Sallie Ada Heatwole (1881-1942), and thus represents two old and well-known Rockingham families. His father, born in 1877 at Dale Enterprise, is a son of Abram D. Weaver and wife, Rebecca Shank; his mother was a daughter of Gabriel D. and Lydia Frank Heatwole. He spent his entire childhood on a farm, completed the work offered in the local public schools, and then supplemented and extended his education by taking various correspondence courses, one in business administration from the La Salle School which is operated under the auspices of Northwestern University. In 1921 he left the farm to accept a position with the Valley Creamery, Inc., at Penn Laird, and in 1928 was made manager of the plant, which at that time was producing approximately 200,000 pounds of butter a year. In 1934 the company bought out the Farmers & Merchants Dairy in Harrisonburg, and at present is making over a half-million pounds of butter annually, with considerable quanities of ice cream.

In 1934 Mr. Weaver, in addition to his work with the creamery, started a truck line known as the Spotswood Transfer Company, which at first operated between Staunton and Baltimore. The scope of its operations was later extended to New York City, and when sold in 1937 the system had grown to ten units. In 1937 he became interested in construction and accordingly launched the Rockingham Construction Company, Inc., in Harrisonburg, specializing at first in building transmission and power lines. Later he took contracts for power plants and complete generating equipment. This business has had a remarkable growth until at the present it amounts to over one million dollars a year, work being performed in West Virginia, Delaware, Maryland, and North Carolina, as well as in Virginia.

In 1920 Mr. Weaver married Miss Annie Ruth Shank, a native of the Dayton community, daughter of Jacob L. and Fannie (Susanna Frances) Good. Her father is a son of Michael Shank (son of Jacob); her mother is a daughter of Daniel Good of Dale Enterprise. Mr. and Mrs. Weaver have one son, Winston O. Weaver, born in 1921. He has one semester of his senior year to be completed at Bridgewater College. On July 18, 1942, he married Miss Phyllis Livengood of Cumberland, Maryland.

Mr. Weaver, with his wife, is a member of the Mennonite Church. He is a Kiwanian, a member of the Harrisonburg-Rockingham Chamber of Commerce, and supports various other worthy organizations. For recreation he plays golf, and for some time has been much interested in aeronautics. He began flying in 1940 and now holds a pilot's license. He has traveled by air to Mexico City and other places in the same country. He reads periodicals pertaining to business management, engineering, labor, dairying, manufacturing, and the marketing of dairy products.

RUSSELL MAUZY WEAVER

FARMER, LAWYER, AND LEGISLATOR

Born February 25, 1901, in Rockingham; graduate of McGaheysville High School; student at the University of Virginia 1918-26—four years in the college, then in law; LL. B., 1926; practiced law in Winston-Salem, N. C., 1926-34; in N. R. A. work in Washington City, 1934-36; lawyer in Harrisonburg since 1936; member General Assembly of Va., 1939-40, 1942-43; former trial justice for the city and county and member of Harrisonburg School Board; on Board of Managers, U. Va. Alumni Assn., 1939-42; president of Harrisonburg-Rockingham U. Va. Alumni Assn.; member of the Lions Club and the Elks.

Mr. Weaver, a true Virginian, of Scotch-English and Huguenot descent, is the son of Fannie Mauzy and the late W. P. R. Weaver of Island Ford. He was born at Midford, an old brick house built by his grandfather, James Madison Weaver, adjoining his own place Lethe, near Three Springs. James M. with his wife, born Sarah Carpenter, and brother Robert Weaver, who later married Lucy Teal, came from Madison County. On his maternal side he is a descendant of Daniel Smith, famous jurist of Revolutionary time, Adam Miller, first white settler in the Valley, and Capt. John Lewis of Staunton, pioneer of Scotch Valley settlers. His parents, while he was a young boy, moved to a farm which they purchased near Island Ford. He attended McGaheysville school and learned farming under his father, a leading and progressive farmer of the community. Having finished high school, he entered the academic department of the University of Virginia and, after four years in that department, took up law, receiving his LL. B. degree in 1926. While a student, he entered into all phases of college life, gaining his monogram in football and becoming a member of the Alpha Tau Omega Fraternity and the Eli Banana, Imp, Skull and Keys, P. K., and German Clubs.

After graduating, Mr. Weaver took up the practice of law in Winston-Salem, N. C., where he maintained his office for eight years and was married to Miss Lucia Gordon Wilkinson, whose ancestors in the Swanson, Gordon, and Wilkinson lines were Virginians. They have one son, Russell Mauzy Weaver, Jr.

After a year spent in Washington, in a legal capacity in the code unit of the N. R. A., Mr. Weaver came to Harrisonburg where he has practiced his profession over seven years, with intermissions while serving in the General Assembly at Richmond, as a representative of Rockingham County and Harrisonburg. His interests are wide and varied. In his home town he is a steward in the Methodist Church and a former member of the school board. He has served as assistant to the trial justice, in which office he was especially interested in the questions regarding domestic relations and juvenile troubles. At present he is president of the Alumni Association in Harrisonburg of the University of Virginia, having just finished a four-year term as a member of the Board of Managers of that University. In the legislature he has served on the appropriations, asylums and prisons, schools and colleges, and library committees. He is a member of the Lions and Elks Clubs. He has always kept up his interest in farming. Together with his brother, James Madison Weaver, who is also a resident of Harrisonburg, he operates their farm near Island Ford. Thus he keeps up the traditions of his thrifty rural ancestors and is typical of many generations of Virginians who have been leaders in agriculture, industry, and government.

CLEMENT DAVID WENGER
ORCHARDIST AND SUPPLY MERCHANT

Born November 23, 1874, near Dayton; educated in public schools and Shenandoah Collegiate Institute, now Shenandoah College; farmer, nurseryman, and fruit-grower; shipper of apples and manufacturer of shippers' supplies; life member of the Virginia Horticultural Society; active in civic, religious, and political life; has had his business headquarters in Harrisonburg for many years.

Mr. Wenger's family for generations have been thrifty farmers and successful fruit-growers and nurserymen in the section of Rockingham County between Harrisonburg and Dayton. His father was Abraham Blosser Wenger, farmer, nurseryman, and Mennonite minister, who died in July, 1898. Abraham's wife, who died in 1900, was a daughter of David and Elizabeth Burkholder Hartman. Their children were: Rebecca, who married John H. Barnhart; Isaac B., who married Ella Haldeman; Elizabeth; Rachel, who married Charles Kilburn; Clement D., and Sarah Frances. Benjamin Wenger, father of Abraham B., was a man of large stature and active life as a farmer; devotedly religious, he served as a deacon of the Pike Mennonite Church, which is located about two miles east of the Wenger homestead. On this farm, not far from the family dwelling, on a rainy day in early October, 1864, three Confederate scouts met three Federals, and in the fight that ensued one of the Federals, Lieut. John Rodgers Meigs, of Sheridan's staff, was killed. Because General Sheridan at first supposed that Meigs had been "bushwhacked," he ordered a general burning of houses and barns in the neighborhood, an order that was carried out until the facts were ascertained. The Wengers suffered with a number of their neighbors.

Clement D. Wenger, after being in business with his father as a farmer and nurseryman for 15 years, went into business for himself, planting an apple orchard and engaging as a dealer in buying and shipping apples and as a manufacturer of barrels for the use of himself and other shippers. This business he has expanded successfully and still carries on, with headquarters in Harrisonburg. One of the first members of the Va. Horticultural Society when it was organized, he has done much to promote and improve fruit-growing in the county and state. Like his forebears, he has been an active member of the Mennonite Church. He has been intimately identified with the temperance movement, in which he has demonstrated fine qualities of leadership. As president of the Anti-Saloon League of Rockingham County, he was instrumental in bringing to the county and city such outstanding temperance advocates as Governor Hanley of Indiana and Governor Glenn of North Carolina. After repeated urgings on the part of his friends, he some years ago ran for a seat in the Va. House of Delegates, and although he had incurred the enmity of the liquor interests, strong in the county at that time, he was defeated by less than 50 votes. Genial and companionable, he is a man of strong convictions and strict integrity.

On June 18, 1919, In Washington, D. C., Mr. Wenger married Miss Bessie G. Reiter, daughter of John L. and Jessie Guyer Reiter of Harrisonburg, born November 22, 1895. Their children are: Margaret Elizabeth, born June 21, 1920; Mark Reiter, born August 15, 1921; Lois Virginia, born September 4, 1923; Charlotte Evangeline, born April 20, 1928; and Paul Clement, born August 4, 1932.

DANIEL M. WETSEL, SR.
AGRICULTURIST, HORTICULTURIST, SEEDSMAN, CHURCHMAN

Born January 23, 1861, near Gettysburg, Pa.; attended schools in Adams County; came to Rockingham in 1882; blacksmith, fruit grower, farmer, seed corn breeder; co-founder in 1912 of D. M. Wetsel & Son, Seedsmen, Harrisonburg; widely known as an authority on agriculture, horticulture, the Bible, and prospective weather conditions; member Church of the Brethren; ardent Republican; died in Harrisonburg, February 28, 1933.

Mr. Wetsel's parents, Daniel and Adaline Wetsel, had three sons and three daughters. At age 21 Daniel M. came to Good's Mill, Rockingham County, worked as farm hand, learned blacksmithing, and soon established a shop of his own. In 1896, while a blacksmith at Port Republic, he purchased a small farm and on part of it set out a variety of fruit trees; on the remainder he experimented with seed corn to determine the best strains for this climate. In 1905 he acquired a large farm on the river, and by test selected types of corn best adapted to low land, upland, wet and dry seasons. Thus he became widely known as a breeder of and authority on seed corn. He exhibited at county and state fairs over an area of several hundred miles, and each season won numerous top honors. Each spring he attended courts, public sales, and other places where farmers assembled, displaying samples of corn and taking orders. From year to year he added other farm and garden crops, making his Green Island Seed Farm well known. He and his oldest son operated a seed wagon, painted green, and specially designed to display corn and other seeds. In 1911, in Harrisonburg, the general seed store of D. M. Wetsel & Son was established, the first real seed store in the Shenandoah Valley.

Mr. Wetsel read a large variety of publications, including books on agriculture, horticulture, and plant foods; also the Bible. Thus he became well versed in history, current topics, and the Bible. One of his chief interests was a study of the weather conditions, and he became widely known for his accurate weather forecasts. He was a pioneer in advocating soil improvement through legume crops, commercial inoculation, and proper chemical fertilizers. His advice was much sought after by farmers, and thus, unofficially, he was the first county farm agent in the Valley. He developed a new strain of tomato, the "French-American," non-acid and almost seedless, and received extended publicity through bulletins of the State Department of Agriculture. All his life, from early manhood, he was a member of the Church of the Brethren. An ardent Republican, he took much interest in politics, and, although his official positions were limited to minor roles, his close attention to religious and political activities enabled him frequently to discern important trends well in advance of their actual development.

On February 3, 1888, Mr. Wetsel married Miss Lydia Virginia Wampler, daughter of Samuel and Mary Wampler of Penn Laird. To them were born 14 children: Arnold W., 1888; Lula Viola, 1890; Grace Ellen, 1891; Anna Belle, 1893; Lillian Dare, 1895; Earl H., 1897; Lilly Louise, 1899; Ruth Virginia, 1901; Luella Margaret, 1903; Daniel M. Jr., 1905; Rosalie Elizabeth , 1907; Alma Mae, 1909; Wampler Harrison, 1912; and Beidler Joshua, 1914.

ARNOLD (ARNIE) W. WETSEL
SEEDSMAN, ACCOUNTANT, FINANCIAL ADVISER AND EDITOR

Born November 25, 1888, at Penn Laird, Rockingham County; attended Port Republic schools and commercial classes in Harrisonburg; student by correspondence of Alexander Hamilton Institute; co-founder, 1912, of D. M. Wetsel & Son, seedsmen; first president and managing head to 1927; with Alexander Hamilton Institute and Brookmire Economic Service, New York; president A. W. Wetsel Advisory Service, investment advisers, New York City.

Mr. Wetsel, as a business man in Harrisonburg and as a financial adviser in New York City, has had an outstanding career. His ancestry is outlined in the biography of his father, D. M. Wetsel, which appears on preceding pages. Except for brief periods with the N. & W. and W. M. railroads, repairing and operating locomotives, his boyhood was spent on a farm near Port Republic, with his father. From the age of five he was determined to be a merchant. This led him to the founding of the D. M. Wetsel & Son seed store in Harrisonburg in 1912, incorporated in 1915. While his father's primary interest was in growing and testing seeds, Arnie's chief effort was aimed at commercial distribution. As his father pioneered in growing, he pioneered in the commercial field. Thus he managed and developed to large proportions the first genuine seed business in the Shenandoah Valley. Despite trying times and against great odds in respect to capital, and in the face of adverse advice from all quarters, he persisted and carried the enterprise to success. He devised and installed in the Wetsel Seed Co. in 1923 an accounting system which received national publicity in 1924 and again in 1932.

In 1927 Mr. Wetsel joined the staff of Alexander Hamilton Institute in New York and was soon made president of a subsidiary corporation. Later he was president of the Wetsel Market Bureau, subsidiary of Brookmire Economic Service. He established his own organization, the A. W. Wetsel Advisory Service, Economic and Investment Counselors, in 1931. This organization became one of the most prominent of ten similar companies in the United States, having clients in every state and numerous foreign countries. Thus he became a prominent figure in Wall Street. He has been active in church and civic affairs. In Harrisonburg he was a member of the chamber of commerce and held official positions in the Country Club, the Rotary Club, and the county fair association. In New York he was a member of the Bankers Club, the Advertising Club, and the National Republican Club, and in the last was on the committee of national affairs. He is a member of Riverside Church, New York, widely known for its pastor, Dr. Harry Emerson Fosdick, and its sponsor, John D. Rockfeller, Jr. In his church he has served in official capacities, including the vice-chairmanship of the board of ushers. He served in the army in World War I, and was assigned to special duty as business manager of the Camp Lee newspaper. His hobbies are politics, government, sports, and biographies of scientists, philosophers, economists, financiers, and industrial leaders.

Mr. Wetsel married Miss Ninga G. Brewington of Salisbury, Md. They have a daughter, Charlotte Virginia, born April 18, 1919. She, on October 15, 1938, married Eugene A. Myers of New York, and has a daughter, Barbara Anne, born July 17, 1939.

BENJAMIN F. WILSON, D. D.

PASTOR AND EDUCATOR

Born in Sumter District, S. C., March, 1863; A. B. and A. M. of Davidson College; graduate of Princeton Seminary, 1887; traveler and student in Europe; pastor of the First Presbyterian Church of Spartanburg, S. C., three years; one of the founders and the first president (1890-1902) of Converse College; D. D. of Wofford College, 1902; in graduate work at Harvard and Johns Hopkins, 1902-05; Phi Beta Kappa; pastor of the Harrisonburg Presbyterian Church, 1905-31; pastor emeritus, 1931-32; member of the faculty of Madison College.

Dr. Wilson's father, Benj. F. Wilson, Sr., was an officer in the famous Hampton Legion, C. S. A.; his mother, Rebecca Elizabeth Wilson, was a daughter of Wm. T. Wilson, a South Carolina planter and a member of the state legislature. His great-uncle, Rev. John Leighton Wilson, went out as the first missionary to Liberia. Two sisters, a brother-in-law, and three nephews are distinguished missionaries in China.

The 26 years that Dr. Wilson was pastor of the Harrisonburg Presbyterian Church was a period rich in achievement and the building of friendships. He is remembered with enduring affection by our people of all races and creeds. He inspired the building of the splendid church in which the congregation worships, but his more fitting monument is in the hearts of men. It was but natural that he should lead many to righteousness, and during his pastorate the membership of his church was greatly increased. At the same time its activities in Christian service were widely extended by support of its own representatives in foreign fields. As one of his nephews wrote from Nanking in 1932, "he never stopped growing—he never grew old." In World War I he was furloughed by his church and was thus enabled to render notable service among the soldiers and their families along the Atlantic Coast from Fort Monroe to Camp Morrison. He inaugrated and carried on the home service program of the Red Cross in this region.

Dr. Wilson was an outstanding Mason and was for years chaplain of the Harrisonburg lodge. He was also chaplain of the S. B. Gibbons Camp of Confederate Veterans, and in 1931 was elected chaplain of the Virginia Division. He was a member of the local chamber of commerce and a charter member of the Harrisonburg Rotary Club. As an influential supporter of the church's educational and religious work, he aided greatly in establishing and promoting the Massanetta conferences. For several years he was professor of Bible in Madison College. His wide acquaintance with life in America and Europe, his keen and sympathetic interest in people of all classes, and his extensive reading of the best literature, added to his deep piety and natural talents, made him a genial companion, an entertaining conversationalist and lecturer, and a preacher of power.

At Spartanburg in July, 1889, Dr. Wilson married Mrs. Sallie G. (Farrar) Foster, daughter of J. Clough and Josephine Hooker Farrar. Her mother was a sister of Colonel Hooker, M. C. from Mississippi. The Farrars were an old family of Albemarle County, Va. J. Clough Farrar moved to South Carolina prior to 1861 and became a merchant in Charleston. Dr. and Mrs. Wilson had no children, but from the age of five Mrs. Wilson's niece, Bessie Wilson Arthur, now Mrs. S. J. Prichard of Harrisonburg, lived with them as their own daughter. Dr. Wilson died on May 24, 1932, having been pastor emeritus of his church from the preceding December. Mrs. Wilson died on December 4, 1932. Her grave is beside that of her husband in Woodbine Cemetery, Harrisonburg. (See tribute in Part II.)

JOHN EUGENE WINE, M. D.

PHYSICIAN AND SURGEON

Born July 31, 1889, near Forestville, Shenandoah County; attended Flat Rock School and Timberville High School; B. E., Bridgewater College, 1911; M. D., Medical College of Virginia, 1917; interne, James Walker Memorial Hospital, Wilmington, N. C.; post-graduate work in Rockefeller Institute and Columbia University, New York City; 1st lieutenant, Medical Reserve Corps, January 5, 1918; promoted to captain, February 17, 1919; served on staff of Base Hospital No. 65, A. E. F., August, 1918, to July, 1919; discharged from U. S. Army, August 8, 1919; physician in Harrisonburg since September, 1919.

Dr. Wine, following his foreign service in World War I, opened an office in Harrisonburg, where he has had an extensive and successful practice during the past 24 years. He is one of the sons of Rev. Daniel P. Wine, a well-known minister of the Church of the Brethren, and his wife, Rebecca Good, both now deceased. His paternal grandparents were Elder Jacob Wine (Feb. 24, 1811—Feb. 21, 1880) and Catherine Neff (Dec. 12, 1816—Sept. 28, 1882), daughter of John Neff (1776-1852). His mother's parents were Samuel F. and Sallie Wampler Good. Since 1750, when Dr. John Henry Neff, first of the name in the Shenandoah Valley, took up land at Rude's Hill, there has always been a Dr. Neff; and one of Rebecca Good Wine's brothers, Dr. Eugene Good, was a prominent physician of New Market.

In August, 1918, Dr. Wine went overseas with Base Hospital No. 65, landing at Brest, and continued with his unit until after the armistice. From February to June, 1919, he was stationed at Le Mans, and while there was commissioned captain. In July, 1919, he returned to America on the U. S. *Iowan*, landing at New York, whence he was ordered to Camp Dix. On August 8, following, he was honorably discharged at Camp Lee. He belongs to the American Legion and the Veterans of Foreign Wars; is a member of the Harrisonburg Presbyterian Church, and serves on the board of deacons. When the local Kiwanis Club was organized in 1922 he became one of the charter members. He has also been affiliated with various professional organizations, and for some time was secretary and treasurer of the Rockingham County Medical Society. In politics he is a Democrat. His busy professional life does not permit him much time for diversions, though he does take off a day or two now and then for fishing and hunting. He enjoys general reading, in addition to such research as pertains to his medical practice, and is active in community enterprises that make for health and general welfare. His boyhood and early manhood on his father's farm between Flat Rock and Forestville gave him an intimate acquaintance with wholesome outdoor life and agricultural activities. This, supplemented by extensive travel and wide familiarity with urban centers, enables him to enter into sympathetic association with all classes of people.

On May 11, 1918, Dr. Wine married Miss Nell S. Fennell, born July 11, 1898, daughter of David Carey and Minnie Newkirk Fennell, of Kerr, near Wilmington, N. C. The marriage took place in Greenville, South Carolina. Dr. and Mrs. Wine have one son, Jean Fennell Wine, born July 24, 1920. He graduated from Davidson College, North Carolina, in 1941, and in September of the same year entered the Medical College of Virginia, in Richmond, where he is now pursuing his studies. He is a talented musician, distinguished especially as a pianist, having taken high rank as such in boyhood.

WILLIAM EDWARD WINE

INVENTOR, MANUFACTURER, AND FARMER

Born September 20, 1881, on a farm near Bridgewater; B. S., Virginia Polytechnic Institute, 1904; Mech. Engr., 1905; designer and draftsman for railroads, 1905-13; an organizer, 1912, the Wine Railway Appliance Co. of Toledo, Ohio; 1922, the Industrial Steel Castings Co.; 1934, the Unitcast Co.; president until July 1, 1937, and since then chairman of the board of directors Unitcast Corp. and subsidiaries; past president and a director V. P. I. Alumni Assn.; owner and operator of Winewood Farms in Spotsylvania Co., Va.

Mr. Wine's father was John H., son of Solomon and Susan Harshbarger Wine of Mossy Creek, on the line of Rockingham and Augusta; his mother was Jennie Berry, daughter of William. His second school was at Mossy Creek, on the site of the famous academy started by Jed Hotchkiss in 1847. After attending Bridgewater High School he entered V. P. I., where he graduated B. S. in 1904 and Mechanical Engineer in 1905. For the next eight years he was employed by the Seaboard Air Line, the Atlantic Coast Line, and other corporations, as designer, draftsman, inspector, and chief draftsman. In September, 1913, he began business in Toledo, Ohio, as president of the Wine Railway Appliance Co., an Ohio corporation organized in June, 1912, to manufacture railway car and locomotive devices under his own patents. He is still chief executive of this company and has taken out over 500 patents on railway cars, locomotives, and farm equipment. During the First World War his company made much equipment for the U. S. Railroad Administration. In November, 1936, he represented the Railway Division as guest inventor at the centennial celebration of the American Patent System, held at the Mayflower Hotel in Washington.

In 1922 Mr. Wine and his associates organized the Industrial Steel Castings Co., also an Ohio corporation, and in 1934 they launched the Unitcast Co., a sales and engineering organization. On July 1, 1937, these two and the Wine Railway Appliance Co. were consolidated. E award in 1943.

Some years ago Mr. Wine acquired three adjoining farms, comprising about 2100 acres, in Spotsylvania County, Va., 15 miles west of Fredericksburg, near Chancellorsville, old Catherine Furnace, and the birthplace of Matthew Fontaine Maury. Over part of this tract Stonewall Jackson led his famous flank march on May 2, 1863. On these farms Mr. Wine specializes in raising wild turkeys, brought up in 1933 from the Santee swamps of South Carolina. His plan is to provide each year a sufficient number of turkeys to supply a few state game departments until all the states that wish to avail themselves of this service have a complete foundation stock. With the assistance of the State Experiment Station at Blacksburg, the U. S. Biological Survey, and officials of the Virginia Department of Conservation, much progress has been made in propagation and distribution.

Mr. Wine's wife, Ellanor Worts, was born at Oswego, N. Y., January 30, 1883, daughter of Mannister C. and Ella Macomber Worts. Mr. Worts was for a number of years a member of the New York Game Commission. By a former marriage Mr. Wine had two daughters: Charlotte, Mrs. Gavlak, of Cleveland, Ohio, who has two sons, Joseph and Michael; and Mary, Mrs. Connell, who died in January, 1938, in Toledo, leaving a daughter, Nancy Connell.

As may be inferred from the foregoing, Mr. Wine's hobbies are farming and raising wild turkeys at Winewood Farms.

JOSEPH LEE WRIGHT, M.D.
PHYSICIAN AND SURGEON

Born October 1, 1889, at Keezletown; attended county schools and graduated from Harrisonburg High School; M.D., University of Virginia, 1914; interneship in Martha Jefferson Hospital, Charlottesville; house surgeon and instructor in surgery, U. Va. Hospital; surgeon in World War I at Embarkation Hospital, Camp Stuart, Va.; again on the surgical staff at U. Va.; practicing surgeon in Harrisonburg since 1921; on staff of Rockingham Memorial Hospital; Kiwanian; member of local, state, and national professional societies.

Dr. Wright deservedly holds an honored place in his profession and has a remarkable ancestral background in the same calling. His father, John Frederick Wright (1852-1921), after graduating at Roanoke College in 1873, entered the college of Physicians and Surgeons of Baltimore, where he received his M.D. degree in 1876. For many years he lived near Keezletown, to which place he moved from Augusta County, and carried on a successful practice over a large field in the adjacent communities. His father was a native of England, and five of the latter's uncles, of the name Wright, were surgeons in the British Navy. His maternal grandmother, Mrs. Redner, whose maiden name was Ayler, was a physician, having completed her training in German universities. Dr. John F. Wright's wife was Mary Warren Busick, who was born in Yorktown, Va., but for some years prior to her marriage lived on the Eastern Shore of Maryland and in the city of Baltimore. She died in Keezletown in 1932.

After attending the public schools in his home neighborhood, Joseph L. Wright entered the Harrisonburg High School from which he graduated with the class of 1908. With a view to preparing himself for a career in the field wherein so many of his family had already been distinguished, he matriculated in the medical department of the University of Virginia, in 1909, where he graduated and received his degree of M.D. in 1914. After post-graduate work in New York City hospitals, he returned to the University of Virginia where he was instructor in surgery and house surgeon at the University Hospital until the United States entered the World War early in 1917. He joined up with the University unit, but was soon transferred to Camp Stuart where he served as a surgeon until the end of the conflict. Following the war, he was on the University staff again for several years, then came home when his father suffered a breakdown in health. In 1921 he began practice in Harrisonburg, where he has since remained, establishing an enviable record as a surgeon. He is one of the valued members on the staff of Rockingham Memorial Hospital, which holds high rank among similar institutions of the country. He is a member of various professional societies and participates in appropriate civic and philanthropic activities. Among his other social and fraternal connections, he is a charter member of the city-county Kiwanis Club, which has carried on an effective organization here for the past twenty-odd years.

On November 22, 1924, Dr. Wright married Anne Lewis Blackburn. She is a sister of the late J. Frank Blackburn, who for a number of years preceding his death was clerk of the circuit court of Harrisonburg and Rockingham County. Her father was John W. Blackburn of Grottoes, who took a keen interest in history and genealogy and was possessed of a large store of information concernng events and families in this part of the country. Her mother was Frances Hopkins Harnsberger, a daughter of Capt. Henry Baker Harnsberger, who, in 1869-70 and 1881-82, was a member of the Va. House of Delegates.

HERBERT WILSON WYANT

LAWYER AND BUSINESS MAN

Born January 28, 1889, near Elkton; educated under direction of his father and in William and Mary College; graduate of Washington and Lee University in law; admitted to the bar June 26, 1913; after a year in Texas, he located in Harrisonburg, June 9, 1914; on the Harrisonburg Democratic Committee since 1922; delegate to the Democratic National Convention in St. Louis, 1916; examiner of records and commissioner in chancery since 1917; president of the Harrisonburg Bar Association.

Mr. Wyant has been actively and successfully engaged in the practice of law in Harrisonburg since 1914. From that date J. E. Pifer was associated with him until Mr. Pifer's death in October, 1918. Mr. Wyant is interested also in farming and stock-raising, and is prominent in politics. His grandfather, Alexander E. Wyant, was born on the ancestral place at the foot of the Blue Ridge, and in early life was a teacher. He was a member of the famous 10th Va. Infantry and was killed in the battle of Chancellorsville, May 2, 1863. His wife was Julia Long, also a native of Rockingham. Their son, Alexander E. Wyant, father of Herbert, was born near Elkton, February 16, 1863. He was a farmer and teacher, retiring in 1924 after a service in the schoolroom of 36 years, and is now enjoying a well-earned rest at his home in Elkton. He is a member of the United Brethren Church. He belongs to the Junior Order U. A. M., being secretary and treasurer of the local body. In politics he has been a life-long Democrat. His wife, Sallie A., born near Elkton in 1864, is a daughter of Jesse and Martha Garrison Wyant. Her father, Jesse Wyant, a native of Rockingham, was a farmer and cabinet-maker and lived to the notable age of 95.

Three Wyant brothers of Hesse, Germany, served as British soldiers in the American Revolution, but like many of their fellow countrymen chose to become citizens of the United States. One settled in the Lancaster Valley, Pennsylvania, another in Ohio, and the third in the Shenandoah Valley, becoming the founder of the family to which Herbert Wilson Wyant belongs.

On November 3, 1916, Mr. Wyant married Miss Reine Wise, daughter of Hiram J. and Bessie Ward Wise, of Rockingham, and has a daughter, Herbert Ward, now Mrs. George Haviland Burke of Richmond, Va.

Mr. Wyant maintains various professional and other affiliations. He belongs to the Episcopal Church, the Benevolent and Protective Order of Elks, and his college fraternity, Alpha Tau Omega. During World War I he was a member of the Rockingham legal advisory board. He is now Government Appeal Agent for selective service in Rockingham County. Besides these and other connections already indicated, he has been a member of the Va. Bar Association for 25 years, and is assistant commissioner of accounts for the city and county. His hobbies are fishing and the collecting of antiques. He possesses a keen sense of humor which enables him to find much joy in life and enhances his discernment and judgment. His position in every regard is an enviable one, and his friends, who are legion, have a keen appreciation of his many admirable qualities and take a justifiable pride in his successful achievements. He enjoys a large clientele whereby he has been connected with the most notable activities of the courts.

BURBRIDGE SCOTT YANCEY, M. D.
PHYSICIAN

Born February 3, 1902, in Harrisonburg; attended Harrisonburg schools and Lane High School, Charlottesville, graduating at the latter in 1919; academic student, University of Virginia, 1919-22; M. D., U. Va., 1926; hospital training in U. S. Marine Hospital, Sydenham Hospital, and University of Maryland Hospital, all in Baltimore; student interne, Catawba Sanatorium, Catawba, Va., and Piedmont Sanatorium, Burkeville; in private practice at Chase City, associated with Chase City Hospital, 1928-31; in private practice, internal medicine, at Harrisonburg since 1932; instructor in medicine, R. M. Hospital school of nursing.

Dr. Yancey is a son of Daniel Burbridge and Nannie Rector Reid Yancey. His paternal grandparents were Charles Albert and Julia Portafield Morrison Yancey of Harrisonburg. A sketch of Charles A. Yancey, Esq., appears in Part Two of this work. After Burbridge had gone through the Main Street Graded School and the first two years of high school in Harrisonburg the family moved to Charlottesville, where he completed his high-school work in Lane High School in 1919. Having spent several years in the academic department of the University of Virginia, he, in 1922, entered the medical department of the University where he received the M. D. degree in 1926. For some time he continued his training in Baltimore hospitals and then served as interne in Catawba Sanatorium and Piedmont Sanatorium, as already indicated. Before graduation he served one year (1924) as student assistant in anatomy at the University. After three years of private practice in Chase City, where he was associated with the local hospital, he returned to Harrisonburg, where he has since been successfully engaged in private practice. He was formerly instructor in anatomy in Rockingham Memorial Hospital, and is now instructor in medicine in the school of nursing in the same institution. At Chase City he was president of the Mecklenburg County Medical Society and since locating in Harrisonburg he has served a term as president of the Rockingham Medical Society. At the University he was a member of the Phi Beta Pi fraternity and the Whitehead Society. He was Associate Surgeon (R) of U. S. public health service in the Marine Hospital; from 1928 to 1936 was Captain M. C. of the 116th Va. Infantry; and in 1939 was elected Fellow of the American College of Physicians. He is affiliated with local, state, and national medical societies; is chairman of the Harrisonburg City Board of Health; a member of the Virginia State Pneumonia Commission, and was a member (1930-35) of the military affairs committee of the Medical Society of Virginia. He is also examining physician of the Rockingham County Selective Service Board.

Dr. Yancey has presented numerous papers before medical societies and is the author of several valuable scientific articles that have been published in medical journals. In 1929 he read before the Mecklenburg Medical Society his treatise on Tularemia—case reports—a pioneer study. In 1930 the *Virginia Medical Monthly* published his study of Agranulocytosis Angina. In the same journal, in 1939, appeared his paper on Argyria Following Nasal Packs, which had been read before the Shenandoah Valley Medical Society.

On June 19, 1926, Dr. Yancey married Miss Esther Dodson, born November 8, 1902, daughter of Beverly Sydnor and Mary Ann Dodson of Pittsylvania County, Va. Dr. and Mrs. Yancey have three daughters: Mary Ann, born August 8, 1928; Betty Scott, born October 12, 1930; and Julia Reid, born September 13, 1935.

CHARLES LAYTON YANCEY
LAWYER AND BANKER

Born February 25, 1886, at McGaheysville; attended Oak Hill Academy, McGaheysville; A. B., Randolph-Macon College, 1908; LL. B., Georgetown University, 1912; practiced law at Muskogee, Okla., 1912-17; at Tulsa since March 15, 1917, with offices until recently also in Oklahoma City; has specialized in law of corporations and oil and gas development; active in banking and organizing banks; operator of cattle ranch and dairy farm; owner of numerous real estate developments; member of the Presbyterian Church and active in all civic enterprises; especially interested in promoting commercial aviation.

Mr. Yancey is one of the sons of Rockingham who have won notable success in the great Southwest. His father was Dr. L. B. Yancey and his mother, before marriage, was Virginia Hopkins. His paternal grandparents were Col. Wm. B. Yancey and his second wife, Mary Gibbons. After graduating in law at Georgetown University, in Washington City, he went to Muskogee, Okla., where he practiced five years. Since then he has been located at Tulsa, which, in early days, was termed the "Oil Center of the World." His practice has been devoted mostly to corporation law and those branches pertaining to oil and gas, but he has also been active in banking and has been a director of various banks in the city of Tulsa and Tulsa County. He helped to organize the Fourth National Bank of Tulsa, of which he is a stockholder, a director, and the chief counsel. He organized the Morris Plan Banks of Oklahoma, with branches in Texas and Kansas, as well as in the chief cities of Oklahoma. Besides his headquarters in Tulsa, he did until recently maintain offices in Oklahoma City. He owns and operates a large cattle ranch in eastern Oklahoma and a Grade-A Holstein dairy farm adjacent to Tulsa. Tulsa, when he moved there in 1917, had a population of about 20,000; it is now a city of 175,000. In this city Mr. Yancey has developed a number of business properties of which he is the owner. He has been active in the chamber of commerce, the Salvation Army, the Y. M. C. A., and in the building of airports, taking much interest in the promotion of commercial aviation. As a pilot himself, he flew his own airplane until a few months ago.

In politics Mr. Yancey is nominally a Democrat, but votes independently for those whom he regards as standing for the best principles. He is an active member of the Presbyterian Church and has given much aid to the Salvation Army, helping to build and remodel the Salvation Army Citadel in Tulsa and the S. A. Maternity Hospital near Tulsa. He belongs to the Tulsa Club, the principal social club of the city. For recreation he hunts and fishes, being familiar with the streams and woods from northern Canada to the middle of Old Mexico. He has killed big game, including moose, elk, and deer. In recent years he has devoted much time to fishing and holds the record of landing the second biggest tiger shark (1200 pounds) ever caught along the Gulf Coast of Texas. He keeps good riding horses and is vice-commodore of the Cherokee Yacht Club. The latter is located on "Lake o' the Cherokees," a large lake built by the U. S. Government, about 80 miles from Tulsa.

Mr. Yancey's wife was Miss Eleanor White, married in 1911, a daughter of Thomas S. and Sarah Cameron White of Lexington, Va. Mr. and Mrs. Yancey are the parents of three children: Lois Cameron, born December 25, 1912; Eleanor Virginia, born July 25, 1915 (now deceased); and Tom Spotswood, born November 4, 1918. Tom is now a first lieutenant in a tank destroyer battalion, stationed at present at Camp Bowie, Texas.

PHILO BRADLEY YANCEY
CHEMIST AND INDUSTRIAL MANAGER

Born March 22, 1886, in Harrisonburg; attended Harrisonburg Grade and High School and the University of Virginia, graduating in chemistry in 1906; chemist for the Du Pont Company; chemist and supervisor in plants in the United States and Canada; general manager of Explosives and Ammunitions Division of Canadian Industries, Ltd.; director of Dunlop Rubber Co. of Canada; died April 21, 1942, in Montreal.

Mr. Yancey was a son of John Gibbons Yancey (1853-1914) and his wife, Fannie Bradley, of Harrisonburg. Both the Bradleys and the Yanceys have been prominent in the city and county for generations. Philo Bradley and his brother Nelson, some years prior to the Civil War, started the Bradley Foundry, which is now probably the oldest industrial establishment in Harrisonburg. Mr. Bradley was from New York, and at the outbreak of the war in 1861 he and his family, in a covered wagon, moved back to Aurora. After the war he returned to Harrisonburg and bought up the foundry again. John G. Yancey was a son of Col. William Burbridge Yancey (1803-1858) and his second wife, Mary Gibbons. His older half-brothers, Thomas Layton, Edward Smith, and William Benjamin, were captains in the Confederate Army. Thomas commanded a troop of cavalry that left Harrisonburg for Harper's Ferry on May 24, 1861; Edward also commanded cavalry, his troop, from East Rockingham, being known as the River Rangers; William was captain of Co. E, 10th Va. Vol. Infantry.

Philo Bradley Yancey, having received his early education in the schools of Harrisonburg, entered the University of Virginia where he graduated in 1906, majoring in chemistry. Entering the employ of the Du Pont Company the same year, he served as chemist and supervisor in plants located at different places: Lewisburg, Ala., Gibbstown, N. J., Barksdale, Wis., and Tacoma, Wash. Later he was affiliated with the Canadian Industries, Ltd., of Montreal, Canada, a company associated with the Du Pont Company, serving as manager of plants located at Naniamo, British Columbia, and Nobel, Ontario, this being the largest smokeless powder plant in Canada at the time of World War I. After the war he was located at Montreal, Canada, as general manager of the Explosives and Ammunitions Division of Canadian Industries, Ltd. As already mentioned, he was a director of the Dunlop Rubber Company of Canada.

Mr. Yancey was a member of the Masonic lodge, the Beaconsfield Golf Club, the Winter Club of Montreal, and the Montreal Skeet Club. His favorite hobbies or recreational activities were golf, shooting, and skiing. Several years preceding his death Mr. Yancey purchased extensive tracts of land near Harrisonburg: the Eiler farm on the Keezletown Road, the Harrison place at Peale's Cross Roads, and the two Hinton farms at Massanetta Springs.

On July 18, 1912, Mr. Yancey married (1) Miss Jean Macready of Tacoma, Washington; and on February 22, 1939, (2) Mrs. Jessie Wilson Hendery of Montreal. He has three children: Richard Bradley, born June 17, 1913, now an ensign in the Naval Reserves; John Macready, born November 17, 1915, a lieutenant in the Air Corps; and Jean Gibbons Yancey. He died, as already stated, on April 21, 1942, in Montreal. The body was brought to Harrisonburg and interred in the community mausoleum in Woodbine Cemetery.

EDWARD BURBRIDGE YANCEY
CHEMIST AND INDUSTRIAL OPERATOR

Born January 26, 1888, in Harrisonburg; attended Harrisonburg Grade and High School and the University of Virginia, graduating in chemistry in 1908; chemist for the Du Pont Company; manager of explosives plants in Colorado, Missouri, and Alabama; general manager, Division of Military and Commercial Explosives, Du Pont Company, Wilmington, Del.; director of industrial companies in the United States and Mexico; owner and operator of farms near Harrisonburg.

Mr. Yancey is a son of the late John Gibbons Yancey and his wife, Fannie Bradley. His grandfather, Col. William Burbridge Yancey, married (1) on November 4, 1830, Mary K. Smith, and (2) in May, 1846, Mary Gibbons, daughter of John and Elizabeth Keffer Gibbons. Of the first marriage there were seven children, of the second, three, of whom John Gibbons Yancey, born November 26, 1853, was the youngest. Col. William B. Yancey, a son of Layton Yancey, a lieutenant of dragoons in the Revolution, was a magistrate, and was succeeded by his son William Benjamin (of the first marriage), who was appointed to the office on April 14, 1859. Other items of the Yancey family history are given in the sketch of Mr. Yancey's brother, Philo Bradley Yancey, on pages preceding.

After his preliminary education in the schools of Harrisonburg, Mr. Yancey entered the University of Virginia, majoring in chemistry. He graduated in 1908 and the same year began his connection with the Du Pont Company as chemist. Until 1914 he was employed in chemical research on the nitration of aromatic hydrocarbons and other explosives. The next two years he operated a plant producing T. N. T. explosive shells and bombs. From 1919 to 1923 he was assistant manager of the explosives plant at Gibbstown, N. J.; the next five years, manager of similar plants at Louviers, Colorado, Joplin, Missouri, and Birmingham, Alabama. In 1928-29 he was assistant director of production, Explosives Department, of the Du Pont Company, Wilmington, Delaware; for the next six years he was general manager of the same. Since 1935 he has been general manager of the Military and Commercial Explosives Department of the Du Pont Company at Wilmington. He is a director of the Du Pont Company, Wilmington, the Du Pont Company of Scranton, Pa., and Cia Mexicano de Explosivas S. A., Mexico City, and vice-president and director of the Rio Grande Securities Co. of Wilmington, Delaware.

Mr. Yancey is a 32d degree Mason and a member of the Mystic Shrine, the Wilmington Country Club, the Wilmington Whist Club, the Delaware Turf Club, and the Hickory Mountain Gun Club. His favorite sport is quail shooting, and his hobbies are livestock and farming. In reading he prefers history and biography.

On October 25, 1913, Mr. Yancey married Miss Jessie Willits of Philadelphia, Pa., a daughter of Rear Admiral G. S. Willits, U. S. N. About 1935 Mr. and Mrs. Yancey purchased their first farm on the Keezletown Road, three miles southeast of Harrisonburg. Since then they have acquired several other tracts of land, totaling over 1000 acres, to which they have given the name of Dogwood Hill Farm. The residence on this farm commands a splendid outlook over a large area of the surrounding country. They are developing herds of livestock in connection with general farming.

HOWARD SAMUEL ZIGLER

MASTER FARMER, LEGISLATOR, AND ENTREPRENEUR

Born Jan. 21, 1898, at Broadway; grew up on his father's farm, attending livestock, working in orchards, and farming; attended Mayland Graded School; graduated from Broadway High School, 1917; B. A., Bridgewater College, 1922; special courses in Columbia University; manager, Mutual Cold Storage, Inc., since 1922; president since 1930; in Va. House of Delegates, 1932-40; director, Ruritan National, 1936-42; received Master Farmer of Virginia Award, 1939; an organizer and the first president of the Rockingham Turkey Festival; owner and organizer of the Zigler Packing Co.; a prime mover in establishing the Blue Ridge Labor Camp at Timberville.

Though still a young man, Mr. Zigler's career in agriculture, business, lawmaking, religious, civic, and commercial service has been outstanding. He is a son of Rev. David H. Zigler, a leading minister of the Church of the Brethren, who was a son of Samuel and Annie Miller Zigler. His mother, Sarah Zigler, is a daughter of Samuel Shank, whose wife was a Miss Rhodes. From boyhood he enjoyed the advantages of good schools and profited by practical acquaintance with all phases of farming, stockraising, and horticulture. He has specialized in the growing of apples and peaches, poultry-raising, the packing of fruits and vegetables, and in successful organizations of coöperative marketing. He is public director of the Rockingham Farm Bureau; was one of the organizers and for the first two years president of the Rockingham Marketing Coöperative of Timberville, which in its second year marketed 11 million pounds of poultry. For several years he was a director of the First Natl. Bank of Harrisonburg. In 1939 he was one of four Virginia men to be awarded the title of "Master Farmer" by the *Progressive Farmer*, and the next year he was awarded the Community Service Plaque by the Harrisonburg-Rockingham Chamber of Commerce. The same year (1940) he established the Zigler Packing Co., which cans peaches, apples, tomatoes and their by-products, thus affording a ready local market and effective facilities for distribution. In its second year this company canned over 200,000 bushels of fruit. When, because of the present war, his community was faced with a labor shortage, he negotiated with the Federal Government and took the lead in establishing the Blue Ridge Labor Camp near Timberville. For 15 years he was president of the Rockingham Farm Loan Assn.

As a member of the Church of the Brethren, Mr. Zigler teaches a Bible class; is a director of the Timberville Orphanage and a trustee of Bridgewater College. He is a Boy Scout committeeman and a councilman of the town of Timberville. For eight years he rendered good service in the Virginia House of Delegates and in 1940 was a delegate to the Republican National Convention. While participating in far-reaching activities, he has devoted special attention to home interests and enterprises. In addition to those already indicated, he was one of the organizers and the first president of the Plains District Ruritan Club. When the county's expanding poultry industry required an agency to carry on pathological research, he was largely instrumental in having a state laboratory established in Harrisonburg.

On June 17, 1922, Mr. Zigler married Miss Margaret Smucker, born April 9, 1899, a daughter of Chas. J. Smucker and wife, Sallie Myers, the latter a daughter of Elder Samuel H. Myers, prominent leader in the Church of the Brethren. Mr. and Mrs. Zigler have two children: Charles David, born April 14, 1924, graduate of Timberville High School, 1942, who entered Bridgewater College the same year; enlisted in the U. S. Army in February, 1943; and Sara Virginia, born March 5, 1926, senior in Timberville High School, who will enter Bridgewater College next session.

PART TWO

ACKER, JOHN—Born July 24, 1845, on Linville Creek, son of Peter (1806-1873) and Louisa Barnes Acker (died 1888); in C. S. A.; on December 28, 1875, married Mary June Funk, born Sept. 13, 1851, daughter of Rev. Timothy and Susan Ruebush Funk. Republican; member Va. House of Delegates 1885-86; Va. Senate, 1888-91; delegate to Republican national conventions, 1896, 1904, 1908. Nine children: Claud Elmer; Mary Kate (Mrs. L. O. Bricker); Anna Lovice (Mrs. Charles Keezell); Evelyn May; John William; Harry J.; Preston; Joseph Edward (captain in World War I); and James Sidney.

ALDHIZER, GEORGE STATTON—Born July 4, 1856, at New Hope, Augusta County, son of James Henry (killed at Gettysburg) and Nancy C. Aldhizer. In 1884 he opened a drug store in Broadway, where he spent the remainder of his life as druggist, miller, and banker. He was a prominent Baptist. On November 23, 1879, he married Alice A. Moore. He died September 21, 1941, survived by sons Stuart and Raymond, of Harrisonburg, and three daughters. His eldest son, Henry, died August 10, 1928.

ALEXANDER, R. GLEN—Mr. Alexander is typical of those native sons who, at home and in many other states, have made honorable places for themselves in the progressive business life of the nation. He could tell an interesting story of a long career, dating from September 15, 1886, when he began working in Harrisonburg at $5.00 a week, and of later years when he held lucrative positions with various business firms in different parts of the country. For a number of years he conducted business in Harrisonburg, then after an extended period in other cities returned here for a residence of several years. For two years, 1895 and 1896, he served as master of Rockingham Union Lodge, A. F. & A. M., No. 27, of which he is still an honored member; and he is held in high esteem by his many friends in the city and county. For a number of years past he has made his home in Los Angeles, California, but still retains his affection for the "old home town" and his native state.

ALLEMONG, J. W. F.—Born September 5, 1828, at Stephens City, Frederick County, son of Rev. John and Hannah Payne Allemong; married Sarah C. Hailman, June 7, 1857; moved to Bridgewater in 1863 and there till 1889, mechant, banker, director of wool mill, and operator of carriage works. In 1889 he moved to Salem, Roanoke County, where he died October 29, 1904; survived by a daughter, Mrs. Ella V. Strayer of Harrisonburg, and a son, John Edwin of Roanoke. Mrs. Strayer died February 8, 1943.

AVIS, JAMES L.—Born 1844 in Charles Town, Jefferson County, now West Virginia, son of John, who was deputy sheriff and jailer of John Brown; prominent druggist, Mason, and civic leader in Harrisonburg for many years; died February 3, 1927; survived by son Payne M. of Harrisonburg and daughter, Mrs. Imogen Avis Palmer, who has since died. As a Confederate soldier, Dr. Avis carried the rifle and pistol willed to him by John Brown.

BARBEE, GABRIEL T.—Born about 1825 at Hawsburg, top of the pass in Thornton's Gap, Blue Ridge, now known as Panorama, one of 12 children of Andrew Russell and Nancy Britton Barbee; lived for many years in Bridgewater and died there September 24, 1908; known familiarly as "Colonel Barbee." His brother, William Randolph (1818-1868), and William's son Herbert (1848-1936) were both distinguished sculptors. The "Colonel" was remarkably skilled in wood-carving—his hobby was making canes, which he decorated intricately and beautifully with his pocket-knife, and presented to his friends. He was a typical Old Virginia gentleman. His first Barbee ancestor in this country was Jean, a French soldier under Lafayette, who married Ann Withers, daughter of Colonel Withers of Orlean, near Warrenton.

BASSFORD, KIRBY SMITH (Tommy)—Born March 17, 1867, in Harrisonburg, son of Thomas Woodward (born 1818) and Amanda Secrist Bassford; grandfathers, Oliver C. Bassford (born 1788) and George Secrist; grandmothers, Elizabeth Woodward and Mary Secrist. Junior member of Bassford Bros., contractors and builders, 1892-1916; with Berry Lumber Co. 1923-37; non-com. officer Co. C, 2d Va. Regt., Natl. Guard, 1893-1900; member of various musical organizations 55 years—only living member (1942) of Eshman's Band, organized 1888, and of Rescue Fire Co., 1886; played in concert with John Philip Sousa at the Cotton Exposition in Atlanta, 1895, when Sousa composed "King Cotton" march. In 1876 Mr. Bassford married Clara Regina Cavey, daughter of Joseph and Alice of Woodstock. No children. Mr. Bassford has rendered a valuable service to the community by compiling and publishing two booklets on the history of Harrisonburg.

BAUGH, MISS ADA ELIZABETH—Born near Timberville, daughter of Jacob and Mary Baugh. Jacob's parents came from Germany, where the name was Bach, meaning "brook." They were distant relatives of the famous musician, Sebastian Bach. Mary Baugh was a daughter of Samuel Hinegardner, whose wife was a granddaughter of Benjamin Ralls, one of four brothers who came to Virginia from England. Three of them lived near Richmond, Benjamin in the Shenandoah Valley, where he married. Ada attended local schools, and at later periods the University of Virginia, Madison College, and Columbia University. She has taught at various places in Virginia and New Jersey and has held supervisory positions in Garrett County, Md., and Rockingham County, Va. Has always been active in civic, benevolent, and religious work. She lives in Broadway near her brother Byron, his wife, and daughter Retha. She reared Byron's other daughter, Margaret, now Mrs. J. W. Harbottle.

BAXTER, GEORGE A.—Born July 22, 1771, in Rockingham County; studied under William Graham at Liberty Hall, Rockbridge County; licensed to preach in 1797; traveled as an evangelist in Virginia and Maryland; principal for a short time of New London Academy in Bedford County, Va.; in 1798 became professor of mathematics and natural philosophy in Liberty Hall Academy, and on the death of Mr. Graham became principal. In 1813 Liberty Hall became Washington College, and Mr. Baxter continued as president until 1829. In 1832 he was installed as professor of theology in the seminary of Hampden-Sydney College, and for a short time after the death of J. P. Cushing in 1835 he was president of the college. He died April 14, 1841.

BENNETT, JESSE, M. D.—Born July 10, 1769, in Philadelphia County, Pa.; educated in Philadelphia; came to Rockingham in 1792; April 8, 1793, married Betsy Hog, daughter of Captain Peter, first clerk of Rockingham County; in 1794, with primitive equipment, Dr. Bennett performed a successful Caesarian section on his wife—one of the first in this country. In 1797 he moved to the Ohio Valley, where he died July 13, 1842. Mrs. Bennett lived many years and her daughter (only child) married Dr. Enos Thomas and lived to be 77. For an extended account of Dr. Bennett, see Wayland's "Virginia Valley Records," pages 341-343.

BRADLEY, PHILO—Born February 23, 1829, in Cayuga County, N. Y.; taught school in early life; came to Virginia in 1850 and lived with an older brother Schuyler at Vesuvius, Rockbridge Co., until 1852, when he came to Harrisonburg. Here he and his brother Nelson set up a foundry and plow factory. When Nelson returned to New York, Philo became sole owner until September, 1865, when he sold an interest to Joshua Wilton—until 1878. Later he took his sons, John S. and Schuyler, into partnership and continued to operate the foundry etc. as P. Bradley & Sons. The business is still continued under this name by his grandsons and great-grandsons. In 1869-70 he represented Rockingham County in the Va. House of Delegates; served a number of times on the Harrisonburg town council and was a member of the originial school board of the town under the present public school system; president of the First Natl. Bank, 1884-98; Methodist; Mason; three times master of the local lodge. He married (1) Frances Slater, sister to Wm. A. Slater of Harrisonburg; (2) Annie Ward of Harrisonburg, who was living at his death, March 2, 1908. Children then living: of (1) John S., Schuyler, Delos, Mrs. John G. Yancey, Miss Sue; of (2) Philo, Mrs. Helen Martin of Washington, D. C., and Miss Nannie.

BROWN, COL. EDWARD T.—Born in Gainesville, Ga., 1858; graduate of Davidson College; began the practice of law in Athens, Ga., later moving to Atlanta, where he became wealthy and influential; lieut. colonel on the staff of Governor Chandler. About 1920 Colonel Brown and his son, Major Edward M. Brown, purchased and developed Endless Caverns. They also did much towards having the Valley Turnpike widened and improved. In 1928 Colonel Brown leased Harrison's Cave, now Melrose Caverns. He died in Washington, D. C., March 9, 1933.

BROWN, REV. JOHN—From 1800 to 1850 a leader in the German Reformed Church in Rockingham and adjacent sections;) known in later years as "Father Brown." He was born July 21, 1771, probably in Pennsylvania or Maryland. His wife was Elizabeth, born March 23, 1777; died Dec. 5, 1857. She and her husband are buried at Friedens. In 1818 Father Brown published a book of 419 pages, addressed to the German people of Rockingham and Augusta and neighboring counties; in 1830 one of 72 pages, a brief treatise on the Christian religion. Both volumes were printed in Harrisonburg by Lawrence Wartmann. Father Brown died January 26, 1850.

BRYAN, DANIEL—Born in Rockingham about 1795, son of Major William; brother to Allan C.; named for Daniel Boone, who was probably a great-uncle. When the Boones trekked to North Carolina in 1750 or thereabouts they stopped for some months on Linville Creek, and there Daniel Boone probably met Rebecca Bryan, whom he later married. Daniel Bryan graduated at Washington College, now Washington and Lee University, in 1807; merchant, lawyer, poet; colonel in the War of 1812; postmaster at Alexandria many years; died in D. C. December, 1866. He was the author of several books: 1813, "The Mountain Muse," epic poem on Daniel Boone, printed in Harrisonburg by Davidson & Bourne; 1826, "Appeal for Suffering Genius"; 1830, "Thoughts." Among his other works were "Lay of Gratitude," greeting to Lafayette, and "Education."

BRYAN, MRS. EMMA LYON—Native of Richmond; resident of Harrisonburg after her marriage in 1864 to Pendleton Bryan, son of Allen C.; artist, composer, and author: 1879, "My Sunflower Fan," illustrated by herself and published in *St. Nicholas;* 1892, "A Romance of the Valley of Virginia," 228 pages, a story of the war, 1860-65; printed on Confederate paper. Among her paintings are: 1867, a general view of Harrisonburg; 1886, "Sunrise at Lover's Leap"; 1886, "Where Ashby Fell."

CARR, MRS. MARIA GRAHAM KOONTZ—Born in Harrisonburg in 1812, daughter of Jacob Koontz and wife, Maria Graham. The former was a son of John Koontz of Harrisonburg and Lacey Spring, who built the house at Lacey later occupied by Jacob Nicholas Lincoln. Maria Graham, at age 14—10—24, married Jacob Koontz and died at age 15—9—9, leaving her infant daughter Maria, later Mrs. Wattson Carr. John Graham, Mrs. Carr's grandfather, was one of the early outstanding citizens of Harrisonburg. In 1798 he owned six houses in the town, his own stone dwelling standing at or near the site of the present Joseph Ney store. His son-in-law, Peter Effinger (1790-1844), built the first brick house in Harrisonburg at or near the site of the Rockingham Natl. Bank. Mrs. Carr retained a remarkable memory and late in life wrote in detail her recollections of Harrisonburg in the period between 1818 and 1830, a most valuable and interesting record.

CARR, GEN. CAMILLO CASATTI CADMUS—Born March 3, 1842, in Harrisonburg, son of Dr. Wattson Carr and wife, Maria Graham Koontz. In 1862 left school in Chicago and joined 1st Cav., U. S. Army; made 1st lieut. in June 1864; wounded at Todd's Tavern and Cedar Creek. After the war he served many years in the West against the Indians, rising to rank of brigadier general in 1903. He died July 24, 1914. His wife was Marie C. Camp of D. C. His mother, whose sketch precedes, wrote of early Harrisonburg.

CHRISMAN, MAJOR GEORGE—Born June 2, 1832, in Rockingham, son of Geo. H. and Martha Herring Chrisman; captain of "Chrisman's Infantry," 1861, and of the "Boy Company," cavalry, 1864. On November 13, 1867, he married Lucy Gilmer Grattan. He wrote extensively on farming and stock-raising. In 1898 he, Gen. J. E. Roller, Jas. B. Stephenson, and F. A. Byerly organized a Rockingham County historical society, which did not long continue active.

COLVIN, ROBERT MASON—Born May 13, 1845, in Campbell County, Va., son of Robert (Oct. 31, 1811—Oct. 24, 1881), born in Culpeper County, and wife Lucy Lee Andrew (Nov. 4, 1827—Sept. 1864), born in Campbell County; in 1866 married Lelia Susan Reynolds of Bedford County, who died in 1904; one child, Quita Lee, who died in 1899. "General Colvin" served in Co. E, 11th Va. Inf., 1862-64; was long employed in railroading; prominent in C. S. A. Veteran organizations; active in erecting battlefield markers. He lived in Harrisonburg from about 1883 until his death, July 28, 1938.

COMPTON, GEORGE FRENCH—Long a resident of Harrisonburg; lawyer; later resident in Charlottesville. In 1885 he wrote and had published in the *Rockingham Register* 27 articles on the early history of Rockingham County.

CONRAD, GEORGE OLIVER—Born June 29, 1823, in Harrisonburg, son of George (1785-1850) and Susan Miller (1793-1861) Conrad; the latter a great-granddaughter of Adam Miller, pioneer white settler of the upper Shenandoah Valley; married, Sept. 25, 1850, Diana Smith Yancey (Sept. 15, 1831—Sept. 8, 1895), daughter of Col. Wm. Burbridge Yancey (1803-1858) and Mary Kyle Smith (1804-45). Geo. O. Conrad was a member of the Harrisonburg town council and mayor; president of Harrisonburg Y. M. C. A., 1860; C. S. A. soldier, wounded in action; steward of Harrisonburg Methodist Church, 1869-1906; appointed by Governor O'Ferrall on the board of trustees of Farmville State Normal School. On April 12, 1845, he purchased from Isaac Hardesty the lot southeast of Court Square now (1943) occupied by Friddle's Restaurant, on which he built a house; his later home was Linside, west corner of S. Liberty and Bruce Street. Died January 23, 1907. His sons, Edward Smith and George Newton Conrad, were both distinguished lawyers of Harrisonburg. His father, George Conrad, owned land on the east side of S. Main Street extending from Paul Street to the Port Republic Road, a portion of which is now occupied by Madison College. He also owned a tannery on the west bank of Black's Run, between Bruce and Water Street, now the public parking lot. He bought and occupied the house on the west side of S. Main Street, site of the present Ewing Building. His farm house remains in the rear of the present Elks Home; this for some time was occupied by the Johnstons; it is now the Converse home.

CONRAD, EDWARD SMITH—Born July 24, 1853, in Harrisonburg, son of George Oliver and Diana Smith Yancey Conrad; law student in the University of Virginia, 1873-74; in law practice with Chas. A. Yancey in Harrisonburg till 1880, later with his brother, George N. Conrad; a prominent Mason; an active leader in the Methodist Church; a trustee of Randolph-Macon College from 1885 until his death, August 21, 1916. His wife was Virginia Smith Irick, born in Harrisonburg on May 26, 1855, daughter of A. B. Irick. She graduated at Martha Washington College, Abingdon, Va.; died August 28, 1933. Mr. and Mrs. Conrad had two sons: Dr. Chas. E. Conrad and Laird L. Conrad, lawyer, both of Harrisonburg. Surviving sisters of Mr. Conrad are Mrs. T. O. Jones and Mrs. T. N. Haas.

CONRAD, GEORGE N.—Born August 26, 1869, son of Geo. O. and Diana Smith Yancey Conrad of Harrisonburg; married Emily Pasco, daughter of U. S. Senator Samuel Pasco of Florida and wife Jessie Denham; sons: George D., Sam Pasco, and John; daughters: Jessie, Mrs. Howard K. Gibbons, and Mary Pasco, Mrs. Jas. Stevenson. He was a lawyer; four years in Va. Senate; active in securing State Normal School (now Madison College) at Harrisonburg; an earnest churchman (Methodist); first president of the local Kiwanis Club. At his death, January 21, 1937, he was survived by his wife, children, and sisters: Miss Mary Lynn Conrad, Mrs. T. O. Jones, Mrs. T. N. Haas. His older brother, Edward S., with whom he practiced, died some years earlier, leaving two sons: Dr. Charles E. and Laird L.

CONRAD, MISS MARY LYNN—Daughter of George Oliver and Diana Smith Yancey Conrad of Harrisonburg; active in church and patriotic organizations; author of an illustrated booklet, "Confederate Banners." She died in Harrisonburg several years ago.

COOTES, SAMUEL—Born November 15, 1792; died March 18, 1882. Lived at the mouth of Brock's Gap, northwest of Broadway, village since known as Cootes's Store. Member Va. House of Delegates, 1838, 1842-45. His wife Emily died July 11, 1843, in her 42d year; son Frank left two sons: Harry, colonel U. S. A., and F. Graham, New York artist.

COX, DR. SAMUEL KEENER—Methodist minister, born July 16, 1823, in Baltimore; scholar, orator, author, editor, and educator; a son of Rev. Luther Cox, who also was a Methodist minister. Dr. Cox served his first charge in 1844. In 1859 he founded a female college in Montgomery, Ala., and served as president. In the war (1861-65) he was chaplain of the 23d Alabama Regiment. He was pastor of large churches in Baltimore, Washington, and Charleston, S. C., and was editor of the *Methodist*, denominational journal, to which he contributed many scholarly editorials. In 1888 he came to Harrisonburg where he served as pastor four years; from here he went to Roanoke, and later to Front Royal, Cumberland, Md., Charles Town, W. Va., and Winchester. After he retired he lived in Harrisonburg, where he died on November 27, 1909. His first wife was Augusta Billing of Baltimore, who died many years ago. On December 21, 1892, he married Miss Hannah Bryan Moffett at Walnut Bank, home of her parents, Mr. and Mrs. George A. Moffett, near New Market. She survives. At the centennial celebration of Rockingham Union Lodge No. 27, A. F. & A. M., in October, 1889, Dr. Cox delivered a notable oration which was published in a booklet by the lodge.

CRAVENS, REV. WILLIAM—Born in or near the site of Harrisonburg in 1766. He was junior warden of the Rockingham Union Lodge No. 27, A. F. & A. M., at its first meeting, December 10, 1789. From the records of the order it appears that the lodge met at his house from its organization until the summer of 1796. He became a Methodist preacher, known familiarly as "Billy Cravens," or "Brother Billy." Though eccentric, rude in speech and uncultured, he was zealous and effective in his service. During one of his sermons at Conrad's Store one of his converts was a young man named John Bear, who later became a distinguished preacher in the same denomination. Cravens went to the West; joined the Illinois Conference in 1820; died in October, 1826.

DAVIS, MISS JENNIE YOUNG—Daughter of Charles and Rebecca Cummins Davis of Reedsville, Pa.; came to Harrisonburg in early life. She and her sister Martha were teachers here for many years. During World War I Miss Jennie was recording secretary of the Home Service Committee of the Red Cross for Harrisonburg and Rockingham County, and as such compiled a personal record of each of the 1130 men who went into the armed service of the nation from the city and county. She died in Harrisonburg on March 23, 1937, aged 75. Miss Martha, who died in 1932, was a teacher during her last years in Winthrop College, S. C. She won distinction by her notable work in collecting ballads and folklore.

DAVISSON, ANANIAS—Born February 2, 1780, probably in Maryland or Virginia; printer, compiler, and publisher in Harrisonburg and at Mt. Vernon Forge near Grottoes. His name was written also "Davidson." In 1813, in Harrisonburg, Davidson & Bourne printed Daniel Bryan's epic poem on Daniel Boone in a volume of 252 pages. Davisson compiled and published the famous song-book, "Kentucky Harmony," in Harrisonburg. He died October 21, 1857; buried in the Presbyterian cemetery at Cross Keys. "White Spirituals in the Southern Uplands," by Geo. P. Jackson, Univ. of N. C. Press, 1933, contains extended accounts of Davisson's work.

DEVIER, GILES—Born July 24, 1820, near Bridgewater, son of Allen; died in Harrisonburg, September 3, 1906. In 1868 Giles Devier joined the staff of the *Rockingham Register;* in October, 1875, he succeeded J. H. Wartmann & Co. as proprietor; in 1878 he and D. O. Dechert were proprietors; in 1883, he and John P. Kerr; in 1890, he and A. H. Snyder. His daughter Hortense was for many years a music teacher and organist in Harrisonburg. His daughter Emma, Mrs. Wunder, who died at New Market a few years ago, was one of the charter members of the Harrisonburg Baptist Church, 1869.

DINGLEDINE, WILLIAM JOHNSTON—Born October 21, 1861, in Shenandoah County; son of John B. and ———Zirkle Dingledine. In Harrisonburg bank, 1880-86; in Baltimore and New York, 1886-1900. In 1900 returned to Harrisonburg as first cashier of Rockingham Natl. Bank; on school board. On October 16, 1889, he married Ella J. Black of Baltimore. Children: Raymond C., Gladys, and Wm. Kendall. He died in Harrisonburg, September 6, 1914.

DWYER, JAMES H.—Born February 22, 1838, in New York City; taken in early childhood by his parents to Missouri; came to Virginia during the Civil War in Captain Charles Woodson's company of Missourians, in the Confederate service. In the battle of New Market, May 15, 1864, Woodson's company fought effectively and suffered heavily, many being killed. Dwyer was one of those severely wounded. He, with others, was brought to the Harrisonburg hospital, then in the school building, site of the present Main Street School; thence he was taken to the home of St. Clair Sprinkel, where he recovered. Woodson's men cooperated with McNeill's Rangers in Hardy County, now W. Va., and adjacent sections. Dwyer was one of McNeill's party that went into Cumberland, Md., before daylight on the morning of February 21, 1865, and captured Generals George Crook and B. F. Kelley, who were brought to Harrisonburg and thence taken to Richmond. On April 2, 1867, Dwyer married Mr. Sprinkel's daughter, Ada Catherine. On January 27, 1907, the Harrisonburg Masonic lodge placed his portrait in the lodge room, commemorating his service as secretary for 20 years without ever being absent from a stated communication within that time. About 1915 he erected a marker on the battlefield at New Market in memory of his comrades. He died in February, 1920. Of his 10 children, seven survive: Mrs. Wilmer Chandler, Miss Annie, and Robert S., of Harrisonburg; Helen (Mrs. Hisey) of Staunton; Carrie (Mrs. Kiser) of Luray; Mabel (Mrs. Armstrong) of Annapolis, Md.; and John, of Cumberland, Md.

EARLY, HENRY CLAY—Born May 11, 1855, in Augusta County, son of Noah and Sarah Kidd Early; grandson of Jacob and Annie Wenger Early; on May 25, 1876, married Mary A. Showalter, who died Jan. 17, 1922; children: Fleta Elizabeth, Mrs. John M. Good (March 1, 1877—Dec. 25, 1895); Anna Grace, Mrs. Wm. A. Good (Dec. 25, 1882—Sep. 2, 1903); Crissa, born Nov. 5, 1884; now Mrs. Sam C. Miller of Bridgewater; Noah M., born Nov. 15, 1886; Pearle Virginia, born Aug. 15, 1888; married Brook W. Bontz, Oct. 15, 1907; and Agnes Mae, born Jan. 25, 1895; married Clyde H. Filley, June 21, 1941. Elder Early, Church of the Brethren, was a teacher, farmer, and a preacher of unusual ability; prominent in the councils and work of the denomination; traveled around the world, 1913-14, visiting mission fields in India and China. He was a frequent contributor to the *Gospel Messenger*, official church paper. Married (2) Emma Martin of Lancaster, Pa., Sept. 30, 1922. Died in Hbg., Sept. 1, 1941.

FLORY, GEORGE W.—Born 1870 near Bridgewater, son of Rev. John and Frances Garber Flory; student, 1883-98, and at intervals later, Bridgewater College. Married Abbie McKinney of Maryland; son William R., born March 26, 1897, in Bridgewater; daughter Ollie. Farmer, pastor, and a preacher (Church of the Brethren) of marked ability.

FLORY, JOHN SAMUEL—Born March 29, 1866, near Broadway, son of Daniel and Susannah Wampler Flory; B. L., Mt. Morris College, 1894; B. A., Bridgewater, 1902; Ph. D., University of Virginia, 1907; Raven, Phi Beta Kappa. Teacher in Bridgewater College from 1894; president, 1910-19; teacher, 1919-41; president emeritus. Litt. D., Mt. Morris College, 1922. Author of numerous books and papers on Church of the Brethren history and related subjects; prominent in the councils and educational organizations of the church. In 1897 he married (1) Nannie Coppock of Ohio, who died in 1898; on August 18, 1908, at Covington, Ohio, he married (2) Vinnie Mikesell; children: Susanna May, born May 30, 1909; John S., Jr., September 5, 1910; Robert M., February 21, 1912; Janet C., November 1, 1913; Margaret V., December 24, 1915.

FUNK, JOSEPH—Born March 9, 1777, in Berks Co., Pa., son of Henry and grandson of Henry; married (1) Elizabeth Rhodes (1784-1814); (2) Rachel Britton (1793-1833); five children by first marriage, nine by second. In 1816 Joseph Funk, now known as "Father of Song in Northern Virginia," had his first book, "Choral Music," printed in Harrisonburg. In 1847 he and his sons brought out the 4th edition of his "Genuine Church Music" ("Harmonia Sacra") at Singers' Glen, on their own press, which was in active operation until 1878 or later. Funk and his sons had a school at Singers' Glen; taught singing classes over Rockingham and other counties, and sold their books in many parts of the United States and Canada. Timothy Funk (1824-1909) was the best known of Joseph's sons as a singing teacher; Benjamin edited the diary of Elder John Kline, published at Elgin, Ill., in 1900. Daughter Mary married John Kieffer and was mother of Aldine S. Kieffer. Mary's daughter Lucilla married Ephraim Ruebush; her sons distinguished musicians and music publishers at Dayton. Joseph Funk (Mennonite) died at Singers' Glen, December 24, 1862. Descendants and others are now preparing to erect a monument to him near the house in which he lived at Singers' Glen.

FUNKHOUSER, ABRAM PAUL—Born December 10, 1853, near Dayton, son of Samuel and Elizabeth Paul Funkhouser. A. P. Funkhouser founded Shenandoah Institute at Dayton, now Shenandoah College; was president of Leander Clark College, Iowa, and Lebanon Valley College, Annville, Pa.; superintendent of Rockingham public schools, 1883-86; published the *State Republican* in Harrisonburg; postmaster in Harrisonburg, 1897-1905; author of United Brethren Church in Virginia, published at Dayton, 1921, after the author's death.

FUNKHOUSER, JACOB—Born in Rockingham about 1833; died in July, 1903. He was a prominent citizen and substantial business man; was one of the directors of the Rockingham Natl. Bank, elected when the institution was organized, December 21, 1899. The others were Andrew M. Newman, Jr., Judge Geo. G. Grattan, Capt. A. H. Wilson, and Jesse R. Cover. Mr. Funkhouser compiled a history of the Funkhouser family, a 100-page volume published in Harrisonburg, in 1902.

GAY, DR. SAMUEL—Said to have been a surgeon in Muhlenberg's regiment in the Revolution. In November, 1780, he was granted license to keep a tavern in Harrisonburg. On November 20, 1781, he purchased the lot on the north corner of German (now Liberty) and W. Market Street, on which stands the brick house now occupied by Miss Lizzie Morrison. An old record of the town council shows that he owned a house of the 2d class in Harrisonburg in August, 1798. On May 12, 1810, Dr. Gay and wife Catherine sold the lot purchased in 1781 to Henry McAtey for $800. Born about 1735 in England, a relative of the poet, John Gay; studied medicine in Edinburgh; landowner and constable in Shenandoah County, Va., in 1774; joined the famous Muhlenberg regiment; had children: Lida, who married Samuel Black; Mattalena, Mrs. Michael Lindsay; Catharine, Mrs. Wm. Donavin; Mary, Mrs. Jacob Wyant; Samuel, who married Mary Jane Ireland, daughter of William. Dr. Gay died in Hopkinsville, Ky., in 1811.

GIBBONS, REV. DR. ALEXANDER SEVERNS—Born September 9, 1822, in East Rockingham, son of John (1784-1866) and Jane Elizabeth Keffer (1790-1869) Gibbons; was president of the University of the Pacific in 1852-57 and 1872-79; died March 28, 1912; buried at Oakland, California.

GIBBONS, COL. SIMEON B.—Born May 25, 1833, at Shenandoah Furnace, Page Co., near the Rockingham line; son of Samuel (1802-1870); grandson of Isaac; educated at V. M. I.; located in Harrisonburg; commanded a Harrisonburg company at the execution of John Brown at Charles Town in December, 1859; first commander of the 10th Va. Vol. Inf., regiment made up chiefly of Rockingham men; killed in the battle of McDowell, May 8, 1862. Colonel Gibbons's father, Samuel, was a brother to John (1784-1866), who married Jane Keffer and had 12 children. John lived at Locust Dale, near McGaheysville. One of his sons, Robert Allen (1817-1891), married (1858) Frances Virginia Kemper, and his daughter, Mary Ashby, is the surviving widow of William Lewis Yancey, of whom a biographical sketch appears herein. A son of Robert Allen, William Andrew Gibbons, born 1868, now of Roanoke, is the father of Howard Kemper Gibbons, business manager of Madison College. George Rison Gibbons, prominent business man of Pittsburgh, is a son of John Rison Gibbons (1843-1919) and his wife, Annie A. Felton; John Rison's father was George Rockingham Gibbons (1814-1907), the eldest son of John Gibbons of Locust Dale. Wm. A. Gibbons has prepared and printed a valuable genealogy of the Gibbons-Yancey family, a copy of which has been loaned to the author by Miss Lois R. Yancey of Harrisonburg.

GILBERT, FELIX—A Scot who married a Miss Grant, daughter of Peter. After some time in Spotsylvania County, Va., he settled at the foot of Peaked Mountain, at what is now Peale's Cross Roads, five miles southeast of Harrisonburg. There he had a store, widely patronized. Augusta County records of 1761 mention him. He was regarded as a Tory in the Revolution. Washington passed Gilbert's on Sept. 30, 1784. Soon thereafter Gilbert moved to Wilkes County, Ga. George Rockingham Gilmer, twice governor of Georgia, in his famous book, "Sketches of Some of the First Settlers of Upper Georgia, of the Cherokees, and the Author," tells much of Gilbert and his family.

GILMER, THOMAS MERIWETHER—Born about 1765 at Lethe in East Rockingham, older son of Peachy Ridgway Gilmer and wife, Mary Meriwether; about 1785 married Elizabeth, daughter of Thomas Lewis; moved to a farm on Broad River in northeastern Georgia, where he died in July, 1817. There, on April 11, 1790, was born his son, George Rockingham Gilmer, who married Eliza Frances Grattan of Rockingham County; was a member of Congress and twice governor of Georgia. His chief fame rests upon his book, "Sketches of Some of the First Settlers of Upper Georgia, of the Cherokees, and the Author," first published in or about 1852; reprinted at Americus, Ga., in 1926. In this he gives much interesting history of the Gilmers, Lewises, Grattans, Felix Gilbert, and others, in Rockingham County and in Georgia. Felix Gilbert, after the Revolution, also moved to Georgia.

GRAHAM, JOHN—Born October 1, 1750; died November 30, 1815. Married Margaret Boyd (Dec. 15, 1770—June 7, 1827) on October 7, 1790. These dates are from tombstones. This John Graham (Sr.), according to his granddaughter, Maria Graham Koontz Carr (q. v.), built the first house in Harrisonburg. This must mean after the town was laid out in 1780—the stone house of Thos. Harrison, founder, still here, was probably built by 1755, and his first cabin 10 or 15 years earlier. Records show that John Graham, in 1798, was taxed on six houses: one of the first class, one of the second class, two of the third class, and two of the fourth class. His stone dwelling stood on the site of the Joseph Ney store. He and other members of his family were first buried in the rear, on or near Federal Alley. Their graves are now in Woodbine Cemetery. John Graham gave the land for the stone Presbyterian Church, and aided materially in building it—on the site of the present Masters building, northeast side of E. Market Street.

GRATTAN, JUDGE GEORGE GILMER—Born February 12, 1839; major C. S. A. and adjutant-general of Colquitt's Brigade; on October 18, 1870, married Mary Ella, daughter of Andrew E. and Mary Effinger Heneberger. He was an eminent lawyer and jurist; judge of Rockingham County Court, 1886-1904. Died November 1, 1915. In 1912 Judge Grattan published a valuable account of the battle of Boonsboro Gap, fought in September, 1862.

GRATTAN, PEACHY R.—Born 1801 in Rockingham County; uncle of Judge G. G. Grattan; died in 1881, near Richmond. He was the compiler of the well-known Grattan's Reports.

GRAY, ROBERT—Born in Ireland, November 1, 1781; located in Harrisonburg in 1805. Was a distinguished lawyer. He married Isabella, daughter of Dr. Asher Waterman; built Collicello about 1812; died December 17, 1859. His daughter Harriet was the wife of Dr. Wm. H. Ruffner.

GRAY, COL. ALGERNON SIDNEY—Born in Harrisonburg in 1813, son of Robert Gray; died in Harrisonburg September 29, 1878. He was a lawyer and a militia colonel; was a member of the convention in 1861 and voted against secession. After the war he was a Republican and was marshal of the Western District of Virginia about 8 years.

GWIN, REV. DAVID W.—Born December 6, 1838, at Bridgewater, son of David S. Gwin, merchant. He was a distinguished clergyman, educator, and author; lived in Columbia, S. C.

HAAS, JUDGE TALFOURD NOON—Born February 22, 1864, in Rockbridge County, Va. son of Chas. E. and Isabella R. Hamilton Haas. On February 15, 1900, he married Mrs. Bettie Conrad Logan, mother of Conrad T. and Margaret Logan (Mrs. W. R. Smithey). He lived in Harrisonburg and was judge of circuit court (Rockingham and Page) 21 years, resigning in 1927. He died February 17, 1939, in Bluefield, W. Va., at the home of his daughter Elizabeth(Mrs. A. S. Kemper, Jr.). His son Hamilton, formerly trial justice in Harrisonburg, is now an officer in U. S. armed forces.

HARDESTY, DR. J. R. L.—Son of Isaac of Harrisonburg. In the 1870's he was an eminent surgeon and eye specialist of Wheeling. In 1875, it was reported, the Khedive of Egypt offered him a position at a handsome salary. His father, Isaac Hardesty, was a business man in Harrisonburg for many years; in 1851 master of the Masonic lodge.

HARRIS, HON. JOHN THOMAS—Born May 8, 1823, in Albemarle County, Va., son of Nathan Harris and wife Ann Allan Anderson; admitted to the bar in 1845 and located in Harrisonburg; commonwealth attorney 1852-59; elected M. C., 1859, 1861; judge of 12th judicial district of Virginia, 1866-69; M. C., 1870-80; elector at large on Cleveland ticket, 1888; died in Harrisonburg, October 14, 1899. He, on May 29, 1854, married Virginia M. Miller; children: Anna H. (Mrs. Heard); Emma H. (Mrs. MacQueary); Virginia O. (Mrs. Beall); Graham H.; John T.; Hatton N. T.; Edith; Clement C. Hatton was a surgeon U. S. N.; died 1905; Graham H. and John T. (Oct. 10, 1859—May 13, 1936) were prominent lawyers, the latter with Geo. E. Sipe for many years in Harrisonburg.

HARRISON, DR. GESSNER—Born June 26, 1807, in or near Harrisonburg, son of Dr. Peachy Harrison (Apr. 6, 1777—Apr. 25, 1848). Gessner, M. D., student and distinguished teacher at the University of Virginia, and author of Greek and Latin textbooks; died April 7, 1862. Harrison Hall, Madison College, named for him.

HARRISON, THOMAS—Born about 1704 in Suffolk County, Long Island, N. Y.; died in Harrisonburg, 1785. He married (1) Jane Delahaye; (2) Sarah Davis (?) or Cravens (?); children: Abigail, Jeremiah, Davis, Robert, John, Thomas, Ezekiel, Reuben, Sarah. Had land surveyed on site of Harrisonburg in December 1739; on August 5, 1779, he and Sarah deeded 2 1/2 acres for Rockingham County buildings; laid out Harrisonburg on 50 acres, established a town by act of Assembly, May, 1780. Lived in stone house still standing on Bruce Street, opposite the Methodist Church.

HART, SILAS—Born May 5, 1718, probably in Pennsylvania; died in Rockingham, October 29, 1795. He married Jane Robertson, September 28, 1749, in what is now Rockingham County. Was senior justice when Rockingham County was organized in April, 1778, and was sworn in as first sheriff, but soon resigned because he had been sheriff in Augusta. He was a member of the Linville Creek Baptist Church, organized 1756, and in his will left money to found a theological seminary. This was many years before the Baptists had a theological school in this country. The matter was carried through the courts and the U. S. Supreme Court finally set aside the provision because of lack of definite officials to receive it.

HAWSE, JASPER—Born November 15, 1835, in Hardy County, now W. Va. In 1862 married Mary A. Beery of Edom—14 children, 8 sons and 6 daughters. Teacher in Harrisonburg and elsewhere; superintendent of schools of Rockingham County 1876-83; county surveyor 1887-1903. Died November 30, 1905.

HAY, JAMES, JR.—Born January 28, 1881, in Harrisonburg, son of James Hay, later M. C., and wife Constance Tatum. Married Millicent Larrick of Winchester, July 19, 1922. Journalist and author of books, "The Man Who Forgot" and others. Died May 6, 1936.

HAYS, ELDER DANIEL—Born May 16, 1839, in Hampshire County, now W. Va., son of Kidd and Polly Lyon Hays; on September 3, 1873, married Sarah Myers of Shenandoah County, Va. Attended West Union Academy, Pa., Gettysburg College, and other schools; studied materia medica and related subjects; preacher in the Church of the Brethren and Bible scholar; teacher in Shenandoah and Rockingham schools many years; lived in later life near Broadway; trustee of Bridgewater College and chairman of the faculty one year; contributor to the *Gospel Messenger* and other church papers; author of several books. Died November 3, 1916.

HEATWOLE, BISHOP LEWIS J.—Born December 4, 1852, eldest son of David A. Heatwole and wife Catherine Driver. On November 11, 1875, he married Mary A. Coffman, daughter of Samuel. He was a teacher, astronomer, author; Mennonite bishop; antiquarian—wrote many articles for the local papers on neighborhood traditions; volunteer weather observer at his home near Dale Enterprise from 1885 for more than 40 years. Died December 26, 1932, survived by six children: Mrs. C. M. Grove, Waynesboro; Mrs. E. C. Suter, New Erection; Mrs. D. E. Wenger, Linville; Mrs. Earl Grove, Harrisonburg; Justus B. and Miss Annie L., Dale Enterprise.

HEATWOLE, CORNELIUS JACOB—Born October 20, 1868, near Dale Enterprise, son of David A. and Catherine Driver Heatwole; graduate of Peabody College, Nashville, 1895; B. S., Columbia University, 1908; M. A., 1916; Litt. D., Hampden-Sydney College, 1929; superintendent Morristown, Tenn., schools, 1903-07; dean of educational department State College for Women, Tallahassee, Florida, 1908-09; professor of education State Normal School, Harrisonburg, 1909-17; professor in the University of Georgia, 1917-22; executive secretary and editor, Va. Education Association, 1922-39; died in San Francisco, July 6, 1939; buried in Weaver Church Cemetery, near Dale Enterprise. Dr. Heatwole was a member of the famous "Fence-Corner Council" of 1885 that developed into the Dale Enterprise Literary Society, and was always a prominent figure at the reunions of the "old boys." Some of his early teaching was done in West Central Academy at Mt. Clinton. In 1896 he married Mollie E. Lineweaver, who died in 1906. He married (2), in 1909, Sue Porter of Asheville, N. C., who died in Richmond, December 5, 1937, leaving a daughter, Margaret Porter Heatwole, now Mrs. J. Franklin Lockwood, Jr., whose residence is at 1800 Grove Avenue, Richmond. An extended biography of Dr. Heatwole appeared in the *Virginia Journal of Education*, October, 1939.

HENEBERGER, DR. LUCIEN G.—Born in Harrisonburg, son of Andrew E. (1822-1900), who was a son of Peter (1784-1869). Peter was a silversmith and clockmaker. Dr. Heneberger was surgeon on the *Maine* when it was blown up in Havana harbor in 1898. He died in Harrisonburg in 1917. He was the father of L. Randolph, who died in 1910. Randolph was the father of R. Grymes Heneberger, Harrisonburg city auditor.

HENRY, ARTHUR LEE—Died in Harrisonburg, Feb. 2, 1939, aged 80. Before coming to Harrisonburg he lived on the famous Henry Hill Farm, Manassas battlefield, over which he guided thousands of visitors. His grandmother was killed by shells during the first battle there and is buried in the family graveyard near the Henry House. In Harrisonburg he conducted the Henry Business School, which is now carried on by Mrs. Henry (Elena Page Herrill) and her daughter, Judith Constance.

MEN OF MARK AND REPRESENTATIVE CITIZENS

HERRING, WILLIAM—Born in what is now Rockingham County about 1765, son of Leonard, who was a son of Alexander; on December 28, 1786, married Hannah Robertson, daughter of Peter, of Augusta; master of Rockingham Union Lodge, A. F. & A. M., when it was organized December 10, 1789; was sheriff in 1789 and 1805. He had an uncle, William Herring, who died in1806, who may have been the one who held the offices mentioned. It is uncertain which William Herring it was who died in 1806.

HOG, CAPTAIN PETER—A distinguished captain of Virginia rangers in the French and Indian War. He is said to have been with Washington in the operations between Will's Creek (now Cumberland, Md.) and Fort Duquesne (now Pittsburgh) in the spring and early summer of 1754. In 1756 and 1757 he was in charge of the construction of frontier forts along the border, from a point west of Staunton to the North Carolina line. He was the first clerk of the county court of Rockingham, serving from April 27, 1778, to about January 1, 1782. At the meeting of the court on February 18,1782, he was reported dead and Thomas Lewis was appointed clerk pro tem. His daughter Elizabeth on April 8, 1793, married Dr. Jesse Bennett, the distinguished surgeon, whose biographical sketch appears herein.

HOOKE, ROBERT—On October 16, 1802, Robert Hooke, Sr., deposed in Peter Sipe vs. Mary Gilmer that he was 90 years old and had known a certain walnut tree for 60 years. This would fix his birth year as 1712 and indicate that he located in what is now Rockingham County in or about 1742. With this agrees his deposition at Orange County court, May 22, 1740, proving his importation, in which he stated that he had brought his wife Jean and son William from Ireland to Philadelphia, and thence to Virginia, at his own expense. Chas. E. Kemper says that his home was about a mile south of Cross Keys. He was a large landholder and his descendants became numerous in the region between Cross Keys and Port Republic. In the French and Indian War he succeeded Robert Scott as captain of militia (May 19, 1758), and in 1760 was a magistrate (still in Augusta County). In Rockingham, September court, 1804, his will was proved. In this were named his sons William, Robert, George; daughters Martha, Mary Murry, Esther Belshe, and Jean Read; his grandson, James Murry. Mrs. Audrey Kemper Spence of Wytheville compiled Hooke family data which was published in 1930 in Wayland's "Virginia Valley Records," pages 199-219.

HOUCK, JOSEPH P.—Born April 6, 1839, in Allentown, Pa.; located in the spring of 1866 at Shenandoah Iron Works, Page County, Va., where he remained in successful business 14 years; came with his family in 1880 to Harrisonburg where he was a leading merchant and engaged extensively in other lines of enterprise. He was active in religious, civic, and fraternal organizations. On December 14, 1899, when the Rockingham Union Lodge, No. 27, A. F. & A. M., of which he was an honored member, celebrated the 100th anniversary of the death of George Washington, Mr. Houck presented selections on the Masonic life of Washington. He died June 16, 1908. His son, Joseph T. Houck, was master of the same lodge in 1901 and 1902. His daughter, Mary E. J. Houck, married William B. Dutrow. She died without issue prior to February 26, 1908. His son, Joseph T., succeeded to his father's business enterprises and resides in Harrisonburg.

HULVEY, GEORGE H.—Born April 19, 1844, at Cross Keys; was a Confederate soldier and lost his left arm in the battle of the Wilderness, May 6, 1864. He was a successful teacher and principal of schools, and from 1886 to 1917 was superintendent of the public schools of Rockingham County. In 1914, under his direction, an editorial board composed of his son, Leighton M. Hulvey, Robert L. Eastham, and Robert C. Bowers, compiled and published an illustrated volume of 142 pages giving much interesting information on the character and progress of the county schools from 1886 to 1914. Professor Hulvey was twice married: (1) to Josie R. Bader, November 29, 1874; (2) to Nannie S. Yancey, October 8, 1890. He died about May 1, 1920.

JEFFRIES, THOMAS FAYETTE—Known as "Crippled Fayette" and the "Roaming Invalid." His home was near Keezletown, but he spent most of his time traveling, selling his writings, exhibiting stereoscopic views, etc. His frequent contributions to the *Rockingham Register,* the *Old Commonwealth,* and other periodicals, consisted mainly of travel sketches. He was the author of at least two books: "Nine Years in Bed" (1856), printed by Jos. Funk & Sons, Mountain Valley, and "Invalid's Offering" (date and place of publication unknown). He died in Georgia about 1890.

JONES, GABRIEL—Born May 17, 1724, near Williamsburg, son of John and Elizabeth Jones from Wales. In 1747 he bought land near Kernstown and was king's attorney for Frederick County. In 1751 he bought land on the river below Port Republic, place now known as Bogota, where he died in 1806. He was king's attorney for Augusta until Rockingham was cut off in 1778, when he was appointed deputy attorney of the commonwealth for Rockingham. He was famous as "The Lawyer." The route by which he traveled to Harrisonburg was known for a long time as the "Lawyer Road." On October 16, 1749, he married Margaret Morton, widow of George, and daughter of William Strother. She was a sister to the wives of Thomas Lewis and John Madison; hence, she was an aunt of Bishop James Madison. For an extended account of "The Lawyer," his portrait, and his interesting will, see Wayland's "Historic Homes," pages 221-223.

JONES, GEN. JOHN ROBERT—Born in Harrisonburg in 1828, son of David S. and Harriet Yost Jones; served in Florida in March, 1861, as captain; in April following he enlisted a company of 104 men in Rockingham County and joined Gen. J. E. Johnston at Winchester. His company was shortly made Co. I, 33d Va. Inf., Stonewall Brigade. In August, 1861, he was made lieut. colonel 33d Regt., and in July, 1862, promoted to brigadier general. He was captured at Gettysburg and imprisoned until July, 1865. Following the war he was a dealer in farm implements in Harrisonburg and wrote on agricultural subjects. For eight years or more he was commissioner in chancery for the circuit court. Died April 1, 1901.

JONES, DR. T. O.—Born 1851 in Pendleton County, Va. (now W. Va.), son of John Milton and Phebe Dice Jones; graduated in medicine at the University of Virginia; practiced first in Augusta County; located in Harrisonburg in 1882; was a member of the county board of health and served on the town council of Harrisonburg in a period when many progressive measures were adopted; married, November 19, 1885, Miss Frances Conrad, daughter of George Oliver and Diana Smith Yancey Conrad; died November 22, 1914, survived by a daughter, Corinne, and Mrs. Jones, who still resides in Harrisonburg. A son, Olin C. Jones, died in November, 1913. One of Dr. Jones's brothers was Chas. Pinckney Jones of Monterey, who was for some years rector of the University of Virginia.

KAYLOR, PETER CLINE—Born at Harriston, Augusta County, September 27, 1857, son of Lewis and Elizabeth Cline Kaylor; in 1882 married Lucy Byerly of Rockingham County, who survived at his death, July 29, 1940. Also surviving him were two daughters: Mrs. Harry Whitmire of Pleasant Valley and Mrs. Casper Hinkle of Harrisonburg, and a son, Lupton Kaylor of Harrisonburg; and two brothers, Quincy G. and Wm. Jackson Kaylor. In January 1938, assisted by G. W. Chappelear, he published "Abstracts of Land Grants Surveys, 1761-1791, of Augusta and Rockingham," an 8vo volume of 150 pages. He was an indefatigable antiquarian, and did much to arouse interest in local history and genealogy.

KEEZELL, GEORGE B.—Born near Keezletown, July 20, 1854, son of George and Amanda Fitzallen Peale Keezell; farmer, justice of the peace, county treasurer, and for many years state senator. He died June 22, 1931, and was buried at Keezletown. He was instrumental in having the State Teachers College, now Madison, located at Harrisonburg. His daughter Florence, now Mrs. Fred Simms, was one of the first students; his son, Capt. R. P. Keezell, was distinguished in World War I; his grandfather, George Keezell, founded Keezletown.

KEMPER, DR. ALBERT STRAYER—Born January 28, 1866, son of Dr. George W. Kemper, Jr., and his wife, Margaret C. Strayer. His grandfather, Dr. George W. Kemper, Sr., for many years lived at Madison Hall, southwest edge of Port Republic. This was the home of John Madison, the first clerk of Augusta County and the father of Bishop James Madison. In early June, 1862, in the wind-up of the Valley Campaign, Stonewall Jackson had his headquarters at Madison Hall, though he was an occasional guest at the home of Dr. George W. Kemper, Jr., in the village, and at one or two other places in the vicinity. General Jackson at this time was in and around Port Republic for five or six days. On December 16, 1897, Dr. Albert S. Kemper married Elizabeth Letitia Blackburn. At the time of his death he was survived by Mrs. Kemper and seven children: Mrs. Clyde Payne of Grundy, Va., Mrs. Clayton Lilly of Lynnwood, Mrs. Richard Worthington of South Boston, and Mrs. G. Fred Switzer of Harrisonburg; Albert S. Kemper, Jr., of Bluefield, W. Va., John Blackburn Kemper of Lynnwood, and George Whitfield Kemper also of Lynnwood. Dr. Kemper lived at Bogota, the homestead of Gabriel Jones, the famous lawyer, who entertained General Washington on October 1, 1784. The General had arrived at Thomas Lewis's the evening before, on his way home from a tour in the Ohio Valley. Dr. Kemper died on January 13, 1941. His sister, Frances M. Kemper, was the wife of Gen. William Hugh Young and the mother of Dr. Hugh Hampton Young of Baltimore.

KEMPER, CHARLES E.—Born June 5, 1859, at Meadow View on the Keezletown Road, one and a half miles northeast of Cross Keys, son of Edward Stevens Kemper and wife, Susan Craig. Lawyer in Staunton 10 years. From 1893 to 1911 he held important posts in the U. S. Treasury Department, Washington, D. C., most of that time as Supervising Architect; in 1912 and several years following, in charge of awarding all contracts for public buildings. He has made much research in Valley of Virginia history and has published many valuable articles in the *Virginia Magazine of History and Biography,* Richmond, and other periodicals. He contributed pages 301-331 to "Virginia Valley Records" (1930), by John W. Wayland.

KENNEY, JUDGE JAMES—Born in Harrisonburg March 19, 1821, son of Judge John Kenney (1791-1873) and wife Elizabeth E. Duff. Was captain of Rockingham Rifles, Co. B, 10th Va. Vol. Inf., C. S. A.; judge Rockingham County Court 1870-73. For many years Judge James Kenney kept a valuable diary record of events in Harrisonburg and vicinity.

KIEFFER, ALDINE S.—Born August 1, 1840, in Saline County, Mo., son of John and Mary Funk Kieffer; in 1847 went to Singers' Glen where he lived and worked with his grandfather, Joseph Funk, music teacher and publisher; founded the *Musical Million,* 1869, published at Singers' Glen till 1878, then at Dayton until about 1915; compiled the *Christian Harp, Temple Star,* and other music books; author of "Twilight is Falling" and many other popular and sacred songs; volume of poems, "Hours of Fancy, or Vigil and Vision" (1881), Dayton. In 1878 he and his brother-in-law, Ephraim Ruebush, established the Ruebush-Kieffer Publishing Co. at Dayton. Mr. Kieffer died at Dayton, November 30, 1904. His wife was Josie Hammon of Shenandoah County, married November 16, 1865.

KILMER, WILLIS SHARP—Of Binghampton, N. Y., proprietor of Kilmer's Swamp Root Bitters. In 1923 he leased the George H. Harrison farm between Tenth Legion and New Market; two years later purchased it; named it Court Manor, and on it kept famous race horses, Sun Beau, and others. He remodeled the old mansion and embellished the grounds. Since his death Court Manor has been sold (Jan. 23, 1942) by Mrs. Kilmer to Hugh N. Rakes.

KIMLER, ABRAM C.—Born May 21, 1854, in Smithsburg, Md.; died in Waynesboro, Va., Feb. 26, 1940; graduate of Franklin & Marshall College, 1878; taught at River Bank, Rockingham County, 1878-81; principal at McGaheysville, 1881-89; principal at New Market; president of Shepherd College, Shepherdstown, W. Va.; principal at Waynesboro, 1909-1928. Married in New Market a daughter of Richard Rice; son Richard. At McGaheysville he sent more than a dozen of his pupils to college. At New Market he conducted summer normals.

KLINE, ELDER JOHN—Born June 17, 1797, in Rockingham; was a farmer, preacher, Thomsonian doctor, and philanthropist; an outstanding leader of the Dunker denomination—now Church of the Brethren. For a number of years, between 1840 and 1864, he traveled each year from 4000 to 5000 miles on horseback in Virginia and other states, preaching and attending to church business. His tours to Ohio and other northern states brought him under suspicion and he was assassinated near Broadway, June 15, 1864. For many years he kept a diary, excerpts from which were edited by Benjamin Funk and published in an 8vo volume of 480 pages at Elgin, Ill., in 1900. He is buried at Linville Creek Church, near his home.

KOONTZ, COLONEL JOHN—Mrs. Maria Koontz Carr, who was a daughter of Jacob Koontz and Maria Graham, in her reminiscences of Harrisonburg, says: "My grandfathers Graham and Koontz (both named John) were among the first trustees of Harrisonburg. . . . My grandfather Koontz was a very popular man, and could have held any office he wanted. He went to the legislature for several years (1797-98). When I was about eight years old he was paralyzed. . . . He was elected to the legislature (1822-23) in spite of all this . . . .He had a store before I remember. He bought a farm ten miles N. of Harrisonburg, called Big Spring, and built the house there when I was three years old (1815), which is now occupied by the Lincoln family. He had a fine tan-yard, which was carried on by Isaac Hite, who married Polly Koontz, daughter of Col. John Koontz, sister of my father. He had a large merchant and saw mill near his dwelling. There was also a large log house just above the spring, which was used as a house of entertainment. Mrs. Patten lived there when I first remember; afterwards some of the Lincoln family got it."

The site of this tavern, kept by David Lincoln and known as "Lincoln Inn," has recently been marked by the State Conservation Commission. Parts of the old Koontz-Lincoln house still remain at Lacey Spring.

KYLE, DAVID—Born in 1757 in Ireland; died in Rockingham County, Oct. 25, 1844; his wife Elizabeth died Sep. 24, 1846, aged 77. Both, with several others of the family, are buried in Cross Keys Cemetery. David Kyle was a merchant, had a store at the intersection of the Port Republic and Keezletown roads, near Cross Keys, place now known as Pirkey's Graveyard. Kyle owned the farm of John Stephenson, who obtained a grant of 760 acres in 1741 and was, according to the statement of Hon. Chas. E. Kemper, the earliest settler in the Mill Creek Valley. Later part of this land was purchased by Edward S. and William M. Kemper. David Kyle came to the Valley as a peddler with his pack. When he died he was said to be the richest man in Rockingham County.

LANAHAN, REV. JOHN—Born in Harrisonburg in 1815 of Catholic parents; he at the age of 18 became a Protestant, and in 1838 was licensed as a Methodist preacher. He is described as a master of pulpit eloquence. He had a seat in every general conference from 1856 to 1900. At the general conference of 1868 he was elected as one of the agents of the New York Book Concern, in which capacity he won laurels. He died in Baltimore, December 8, 1903.

LEAKE, WILLIAM GLODOMORE—Born in Albemarle County, 1848; died at Harrisonburg, 1908; by will left the bulk of his estate for a hospital, which was opened (1st unit) in 1912 as the Rockingham Memorial Hospital, at Harrisonburg. In the lobby is a tablet inscribed to him, on which is the statement: "He devoted his life to honest work, and his wealth to relieve human suffering."

LEEDY, COL. ROBERT FRANKLIN—Born July 28, 1863, at Leedy's Pump, a mile southeast of Harrisonburg, son of John (1826-89) and Sarah Ann Mauck. Studied law at U. Va. under John B. Minor; lived at Basic City, then in Luray; member of Va. Gen. Assembly. In 1902 he became captain Va. Volunteers in the Natl. Guard; 1905, lieut. colonel and colonel; 1922 brigadier general on the retired list of Va. Vols. Died some years ago in Luray.

LEWIS, CHARLES HANCE—Born at Lewiston, 3 miles below Port Republic, July 3, 1816, first son of Gen. Saml. Hance Lewis and his first wife, Nancy (Lewis) Lewis; married, about 1841, Ellen, daughter of Hon. John Taylor Lomax of Fredericksburg; children: John Taylor Lomax and Rebecca. Sec'y of the Commonwealth (Va.), 1864-70; U. S. minister to Portugal, 1870-74. Brother to U. S. Sen. John F. Lewis.

LEWIS, JOHN FRANCIS—Born March 1, 1818, at Lewiston, Rockingham County, second son of Gen. Saml. Hance Lewis and first wife, Nancy (Lewis) Lewis; in 1842 married Serena Helen, daughter of Hon. Daniel Sheffey of Staunton; three sons and four daughters. (See Daniel S. Lewis in Part I.) Member of convention at Richmond in 1861, only one east of the Alleghanies who refused to sign the ordinance of secession. Lieut. Governor, 1869-70; U. S. Senator, 1870-75; Lieut. Governor again, 1882-86. Died September 2, 1895.

LEWIS, THOMAS—Born 1718 in Ireland, eldest son of John and Margaret Lynn Lewis, pioneers of Augusta County, Va.; married Jane Strother of Stafford County, Va., January 26, 1749. First surveyor of Augusta County; in 1746-47, one of the surveyors, with Peter Jefferson and others, of the Fairfax Line; kept a journal of the survey, printed in 1925. Located on the Shenandoah River below Port Republic; first surveyor of Rockingham County. Visited at his home (Lynnwood) by General Washington, October, 1784. With Gabriel Jones, his neighbor and brother-in-law, represented Rockingham County in the convention at Richmond (1788) that ratified the Federal Constitution. His daughter Elizabeth married Thomas M. Gilmer, father of George Rockingham Gilmer, governor of Georgia. Died in 1790.

LIGGETT, JACOB N.—Born January 2, 1829, in Harrisonburg, son of Samuel and Romanzy Nicholas Liggett; law graduate, U. Va.; in 1852 married Evelyn Winfield; in 1884, Isabella Spence. On June 24, 1867, he delivered an oration before the Harrisonburg Masonic lodge which the lodge printed. He was a member of the convention in 1868 that drew up the Underwood Constitution, but was expelled by a partisan vote because he did not hesitate to express his unvarnished opinion of the body and its proceedings. Died in Harrisonburg, May 8, 1912.

LILLY, MAJOR GORDON W.—Born in 1860 near McGaheysville; went west with his father when a child; frontiersman and scout; major in U. S. Army; director of a celebrated wild west show; famous as "Pawnee Bill." His wife, May Lilly, expert rider and rifle-shot. She was killed in an auto accident in 1926. In the same accident Pawnee Bill was injured. He died in Oklahoma, February 4, 1942, shortly before his 82d birthday. His uncle, William Lilly, established Lilly postoffice in West Rockingham.

LINCOLN, CAPTAIN ABRAHAM—Born May 13, 1744, in Berks County, Pa., son of John Lincoln and wife Rebecca Flowers Morris; came with his father, "Virginia John," to Linville Creek, now in Rockingham County, probably in 1768; captain of an Augusta County militia company in the Revolution. In the fall of 1781 moved to Kentucky with his wife Barsheba (Herring) and children, one of whom was Thomas, later father of the President; shot from ambush and killed in Kentucky by an Indian about 1786.

LINCOLN, CAPTAIN JACOB—Born 1751, son of "Virginia John"; died 1822. Was a lieutenant in the Revolution; later, captain of militia. He was the only one of "Virginia John's" 5 sons to remain all his life in Rockingham County. Lived on Linville Creek in a brick house still standing. Ancestor of all the Lincolns that have been in Rockingham County since 1820.

LINCOLN, COLONEL ABRAHAM—Born March 15, 1799, on Linville Creek, son of Captain Jacob (1751-1822) and grandson of "Virginia John" (1716-88); farmer, large landowner, and dealer in livestock; colonel of regiment of Va. militia. Married Mary Homan, daughter of John; had 5 daughters. Died June 13, 1851.

LINCOLN, DR. JOHN EDWARD—Born July 22, 1856, at Lacey Spring, son of Abraham (1822-1902) and wife Mary E. Hughes; grandson of David (1781-1849) and wife Catherine Bright; great-grandson of Captain Jacob (1751-1822) and wife Dorcas Robinson. M. D., New York City, 1876. Married Amanda Alice Kline, October 22, 1878; sons: Asa Liggett and Robt. Edson. Lived at Lacey Spring and practiced in Rockingham County 50 years; county health officer. Died in 1931.

LOGAN, JOSEPH TRAVIS—Born July 9, 1834, son of George S. (1803-1853) and Phoebe Travis Rohr (1808-1880) Logan; married, November 8, 1859, Margaret Adelaide H. Haas (1836-1923), daughter of John Haas (1789-1869) of Woodstock and his third wife, Clara Byrd Gore (1797-1852); master of Rockingham Union Lodge, No. 27, A. F. & A. M., 1858-59; deputy grand master, Grand Lodge of Va., in 1861. He officiated at the dedication of the second Masonic temple, west corner of S. Main and Water Street, site now occupied by Hostetter Building, on April 6, 1861, and at the cornerstone-laying of Emmanuel Episcopal Church, June 24, 1868. Was clerk of Rockingham County Court, 1872-85; recording steward, Harrisonburg Methodist Church, 1874-81; trustee and superintendent of the Sundayschool; director of the First Natl. Bank, 1879-81. Joshua Wilton, historian of the lodge, paid him a high tribute as a man and Mason; in F. Johnston's "Memorials of Old Virginia Clerks," pages 350, 351, his efficiency and popularity as deputy and county clerk and in other official positions are recorded. He died Sept. 28, 1885.

LONG, ELDER ISAAC—Born in Rockingham County, September 12, 1818; minister and elder in the Church of the Brethren; married Eliza Saufley, November 24, 1841; had sons: John S., William H., Benjamin F., and Daniel S.; died March 25, 1895; buried at Mill Creek, his home church, in southeast Rockingham. He was a faithful minister 41 years. Under date of Thursday, April 13, 1854, Elder John Kline wrote in his diary: "Council meeting at the Mill Creek meetinghouse. Brother Isaac Long is elected speaker, and Christian Hartman deacon. Brother Isaac Long gives promise of great power in the word. He has a very good voice for both speaking and singing."

Elder Isaac Long's father had the same name and was also a minister in the same denomination. In August and September, 1841, he and Elder Kline spent five weeks together in a preaching tour to Pennsylvania, and Elder Kline termed him an agreeable, cheerful companion, "full of the Spirit, wise in council, clear in judgment." See the Kline Diary, page 138, as published in Elgin, Ill., 1900. Isaac Long, Sr., in his will, proved in Rockingham court, December, 1849, mentions his wife Barbara, sons John, Daniel, Samuel, Isaac, and daughters Frances and Annie (?).

Rev. Isaac S. Long, D.D., now of Baltimore, is a son of William H. and a grandson of Elder Isaac Long. He and his wife, Effie V. Showalter, spent 27 years as missionaries in India.

The writer is under obligation to Dr. C. P. Harshbarger for the dates of birth and death of Elder Isaac Long. The Doctor's wife is a granddaughter of Elder Long.

LOWMAN, MISS FANNIE—Born near Rushville, Rockingham County, in 1831; died in Harrisonburg in November, 1909. A teacher two years in Texas, 30 years in Rockingham County. In 1911 her fellow teachers of Harrisonburg and the county marked her grave in Woodbine Cemetery with a granite monument—the only teacher of the city or county ever so honored. See Wayland's History of Rockingham County, page 294; also "The Public Schools of Rockingham County," by Hulvey, Eastham, and Bowers, pages 102, 103.

LUPTON, JAMES R.—Born December 17, 1854, near Harrisonburg, son of Wm. Isaac and Mary C. Reagan Lupton; married Fannie M. Byerly, daughter of Jacob, December 12, 1879. She died in 1932. In 1934 he married (2) Mrs. Charlena Byerly Bartlett, who died December 13, 1938. Mr. Lupton was related to the Luptons of Frederick County, Va. He did much to establish and promote the Massanetta Springs Conferences. He died March 4, 1941.

McMULLEN, REV. EDGAR WILLIAM—Born near Singers' Glen, February 5, 1863, son of Stephen and Mary J. McMullen; started work as a typesetter in the Funk printing shop at Singers' Glen; taught singing schools and did various kinds of work to earn money for better education; walked to Dayton with weekly supply of food packed by an aunt; took commercial diploma in Shenandoah Collegiate Institute in 1891; graduated, valedictorian, in the classical course in 1893. He was ordained a minister in the United Brethren Church at Churchville, 1891. On August 15, 1895, he married Anna F. Daugherty (1867-1940). His daughter, Edna, born June 19, 1897, is now Mrs. William B. Miller of Harrisonburg. At age 41 Professor McMullen entered Otterbein University, Westerville, Ohio, doing the four-year work for the M. A. degree in three years. After teaching a few years in Rockingham public schools he joined the faculty of Shenandoah College at Dayton, where he taught languages, science, and mathematics until his death, December 11, 1917. His skill and wholesome influence as a Christian teacher elicited warm testimonials from his pupils, many of whom are now distinguished. He was an artist of talent, leaving several finished oil paintings and charcoal sketches.

MADISON, BISHOP JAMES—Born August 27, 1749, son of John Madison, first clerk of Augusta County, and wife Agatha Strother; attended William & Mary College; professor there, 1772-77; took orders in London, 1775; president of the college, 1777-1812; made bishop (first P. E. bishop of Va.) about 1783. Bishop Madison was a relative of Pres. James Madison. In 1779 he married Sarah Tate. He died March 6, 1812. It has been generally stated that Bishop Madison was born at "Madison Hall," Port Republic, but there seems to be some question about this. John Madison settled at "Madison Hall" at an early date, which has not been ascertained. Madison's Run and Madison's Cave are both in the vicinity.

MAPHIS, CHARLES GILMORE—Born February 12, 1865, near Edinburg, son of John Miley and Elizabeth Coffelt Maphis; died in Charlottesville, May 15, 1938. He was a professor in the University of Virginia and for many years a distinguished educator of the state. From 1887 to 1890 he was principal of Harrisonburg High School. On October 14, 1890, he married Bessie Dold of Harrisonburg, who survives him. A son, Edwin W., was living at the University in 1927.

MARSHALL, JAMES W.—Familiarly known as Judge Marshall; nicknamed "Cyclone Jim" because of his eloquence, stentorian voice, and vigorous gestures; born near New Hope, Augusta Co., March 30, 1843, eldest son of Mansfield and Sarah Parsons Marshall. When he was a child his parents moved to the vicinity of Ottobine and Paul's Mill, Rockingham. James for some years owned a farm a few miles north of Harrisonburg, where he was an occasional visitor in later life. After serving as a C. S. A. soldier he attended Roanoke College; then studied law; was a member of the Va. legislature and in Congress two terms; was successful in defense cases before juries and a favorite orator at C. S. A. veterans' reunions. One of his choice stories was to the effect that one day during the war his mother received word that he had been killed in the battle of Seven Pines. "Seven Pines, did you say?" "Yes." "I don't believe it! If there were seven pines I know that Jim was behind one of them." He married Jennie Grant of Ronceverte, W. Va.; died at his home in Newcastle, county-seat of Craig County, Va., in 1911; was survived by a brother John and a sister, Mrs. James R. Price of Harrisonburg, and two sons, John and Hugh. His friends and admirers erected a monument to him at Newcastle on which is engraved a saying he often repeated: "I have made more people laugh than cry."

MARTZ, COL. D. H. LEE—Born near Lacey Spring, March 23, 1837, son of Hiram; on November 14, 1860, married Mary Nicholas Carter of Nelson County, Va. His son, Edward C., was born December 28, 1868; was a prominent lawyer of Harrisonburg; a daughter was Mrs. G. Richard Berlin of Bridgewater. Early in the war of 1861-65 D. H. Lee Martz succeeded Chas. A. Sprinkel as captain of the Valley Guards, Co. G, 10th Va. Vol. Inf., C. S. A. Later he commanded the regiment. For many years preceding his death in Harrisonburg, Oct. 20, 1914, he was circuit court clerk. In 1912 he prepared a history of his regiment for the history of Rockingham that was published that year.

MASSEY, JOHN E.—Born April 2, 1819, in Spotsylvania County, Va., youngest of the seven children of Benjamin and Elizabeth Chewning Massey; lawyer and Baptist preacher. On August 30, 1847, he married Margaret Ann Kable, daughter of John, of Kabletown, Jefferson County, now West Virginia. From about 1844 to 1854 he lived in Rockingham County, seven years in Harrisonburg. In later years Mr. Massey was distinguished in the political and educational life of Virginia, as state auditor, lieut.-governor, and superintendent of public instruction. In the Readjuster years he was the most effective stump speaker in Virginia. He lived at Ash Lawn, the old home of James Monroe, near Charlottesville, where he died April 24, 1901. His autobiography was edited and published by Elizabeth H. Hancock in a 12mo volume of 312 pages in 1909. It is a valuable contribution to Virginia history.

MAUZY, RICHARD—Born June 17, 1824, at McGaheysville, son of Col. Joseph Mauzy. From 1860 to 1895 he was owner and editor of the *Staunton Spectator*, an outstanding weekly newspaper. In 1911 he published a history of the Mauzy family. He was also a contributor to Wayland's History of Rockingham (1912).

MAY, GEORGE ELLIOTT—Born Dec. 26, 1869, at Port Republic, his present home, son of James Henry and Regina Pforr May; grandson of Adam and Nancy Raines May; married Beatrice Glenna Worley of Danville in 1900; living children: George E. May, Jr., of Chester, Pa., and Mrs. Wm. H. Merrill, Jr., of Baltimore. He has written many newspapers articles and has had extended correspondence with British Army officers on the American Civil War; has prepared and read to schools papers on subjects as widely diverse as the battle of Port Republic and "What to Read." For many years has collected materials for a history of Port Republic and environs, which he has ready for publication. Among his collections are old patents and deeds for land, one for site of a church and graveyard deeded by John Carthrae to the Methodist Society in 1793; day-books, account books, ledgers, including the day-book (1809-18) of James Burgess who moved to Port from Harrisonburg; account books and day-books of William S. Downs, 1855-94; account book of Joseph Graham, 1821-26; of Dr. Geo. W. Kemper, 1841-72. He has also copies of the class books of the M. E. Church at Port—all that are now known—one of 1812-13, another of 1833-40.

MILLER, ADAM—Born probably at Schreisheim, Germany, about 1700. Early in life he came to Lancaster County, Pa., with his wife and an unmarried sister. Later, in Williamsburg, Va., he heard of the Shenandoah Valley from some of the men who had been with Spotswood in 1716 and crossed the Blue Ridge to spy out the land, which pleased him. In 1726 or 1727 he seems to have located land in what is now known as the Page Valley. This gives him the distinction, so far as now known, of being the first white settler in the upper Valley. In 1741 he purchased 820 acres in what is now Rockingham, including the great lithia spring below Elkton, and was living thereon in 1764 when he sold 280 acres of his tract to his son-in-law, Jacob Bear. The spring has long been known as the Bear Lithia Spring. In the field near by are the gravestones of Jacob Bear (1724-1780), Barbara Bear (1726-1791), and Jacob Bear (1765-1827). Records show that Adam Miller was a soldier in the French and Indian War. His homestead is a short distance below (northeast of) Elkton. His grave is supposed to be at St. Peter's Lutheran Church, on the northwest side of the river, near Shenandoah City.

MOFFETT, ANDERSON—A pioneer Baptist preacher, born in Fauquier County, Va., August 28, 1746; married Barbara Hupp, daughter of Casper. She died in Rockingham County, November 9, 1848, aged 90. In the days of persecution, Elder Moffett spent some time in Culpeper jail. He lived for a number of years in Shenandoah County, between Mt. Jackson and New Market, then settled in the lower edge of the "Plains," in Rockingham County, near the line of Shenandoah County, where he died, May 14, 1835, and is buried. On his tombstone it is stated that he was a Baptist minister upwards of 70 years.

MOFFETT, DR. S. H.—For many years, beginning prior to the Civil War or about that time, Dr. Moffett was a prominent citizen of Rockingham. During the war he was a director on the board of the Western State Hospital in Staunton. From 1874 to 1877 he represented Rockingham County in the state senate in Richmond, where he was an influential figure. In 1879 the Moffett liquor law of Virginia was adopted in Texas, and the Moffett bellpunch register was ordered from Virginia in large quantities. The *Rockingham Register* of November 17, 1881, and August 7, 1896, contained interesting accounts of Dr. Moffett as a politician and statesman. Mrs. Myra Moffett Wunder of Strasburg, Va., has much information concerning the Moffett family, members of which were distinguished in different fields.

MYERS, JOSEPH G.—Born September 2, 1852, on Linville Creek, son of Rudolph (1821-1896) and Evaline Cromer (1830-1900) Myers; from age of four to 54 he lived on Beaver Creek; later, near Harrisonburg. After some years on the farm, he took up surveying and worked in West Virginia and Maryland, as well as in Virginia. For 12 years or more he was county surveyor for Rockingham, and from 1916 to 1924 was county treasurer. On January 13, 1880, he married Mary Graham (1856-1938), daughter of David (1817-1905) and Sarah Curran (1819-1906) Graham. He died at his home near Harrisonburg, April 29, 1931, and was buried in Mossy Creek Cemetery. His son, William G., is city engineer of Harrisonburg; his other son, Arthur R., is county surveyor of Rockingham.

NALLE, COLONEL WILLIAM—Of East Rockingham. In October, 1774, he commanded a company in Dunmore's War, said to have been in the battle of Point Pleasant; in April, 1778, he was one of the first justices of Rockingham County; and on April 27, 1781, he was sworn in as lieut. colonel of Rockingham militia. Noll and Null are probably different spellings of the same name. Enrolled in Colonel Nalle's company of volunteers in 1774 were Lieut. Martin Nalle and privates Jacob and John Null. Among others with names familiar in East Rockingham were Jacob Pence, Robert Rains, and Adam Hansburger.

NEFF, DR. JOHN H.—Born in 1842 in Shenandoah County, son of Daniel (1810-76) and Elizabeth Garber Neff; died in Charlottesville, March 18, 1912. For many years he was a leading physician of Harrisonburg; member of schools board, etc. In 1885 he lived on German (now Liberty) Street; later in a brick house that stood on the south corner of S. Main Street and Newman Avenue. On November 1, 1883, he married Brownie Morrison; had a daughter and several sons, one of whom was the distinguished Dr. John H. Neff of U. Va. Hospital staff. Daniel Neff was a son of John (1776-1852), who was a son of Francis (who died in 1812), who was a son of Dr. John Henry (who died in 1784). Dr. John Henry Neff took up land on Rude's Hill in 1750 and 1756.

NEY, ISAAC—Born March 28, 1871, in Harrisonburg, oldest son of Baruch Ney and his first wife; associated with his father and brothers in the firm of B. Ney & Sons and president of the company from 1914 until his death, November 25, 1941. His wife was Salina Wise, daughter of Adolph. She survives with four sons: Sylvan, Bernard, Leonard, and Dr. Ronald Ney, all of Harrisonburg. Mr. Ney was a member of the Hebrew Friendship Congregation of Harrisonburg, the Kiwanis Club (charter member), the Elks, and other organizations. He was one of the organizers of the Harrisonburg Loan & Thrift Corporation and other business enterprises. He was active in the promotion of good roads and had a wide acquaintance—was probably able to call more people by name than any other man in the city. Although burdened with many business affairs, he never seemed in a hurry, and always took time to talk with his friends whenever and wherever he met them.

NEY, JOSEPH—Born in Germany, January 7, 1850; came to America in 1869; was first in Rutland, Vermont, then in New York City; came in 1872 to Harrisonburg where he worked a year in the store of his older brother, Baruch Ney; then, after a year in Iowa, he returned to Harrisonburg and opened a confectionery store in the old Spotswood Building. Shortly afterwards he began selling dry goods in the Sprinkel Building, site of the present Brock Building. In 1890 he moved his store to the next building northeast where he continued until his death, April 6, 1916. On March 25, 1875, he married Regina Rosenfield (Aug. 1, 1853—July 11, 1930) of Baltimore. Alfred and Eddie Ney were two of his seven children. His sons were associated with him and carried on the business after his death. Eddie died not long ago. A grandson, Dr. Joseph Ney, is a successful physician of Harrisonburg.

O'FERRALL, GOV. CHARLES TRIPLETT—Born October 21, 1841, in what is now Berkeley County, W. Va.; died in Richmond, September 22, 1905. He was a colonel of cavalry, C. S. A.; located in Harrisonburg 1869— lived there until elected governor. Member Va. House of Delegates, 1871-72; judge Rockingham County Court, 1874-80; M. C., 1881-93; governor of Virginia, 1894-97; author of "Forty Years of Active Service" (1904). His mother was Jane Laurens, born in Fauquier County, 1817; spent her later life in Bridgewater, dying there in May, 1891; buried in Woodbine Cemetery, Harrisonburg. In 1862 Col. O'Ferrall married (1) Annie McLain; in 1891 (2), Jennie Knight Danforth. On June 13, 1942, his portrait was placed in the circuit court room in Harrisonburg, with appropriate exercises.

OTT, LEWIS PHILIP—Born in Woodstock, son of William and Eliza Hariman Ott; died in Harrisonburg in March, 1939, aged 90. He came to Harrisonburg in 1865; in 1874 married Fannie Dulaney, who died in 1935. His son, E. Dulaney Ott, is a prominent lawyer of Harrisonburg. His brother, Luther H. Ott, for many years was a leading druggist of Harrisonburg, his store being located on the east side of Main Street, opposite the First National Bank.

PALMER, JOHN WALLER—Born October 6, 1827, at Port Republic, where he spent his life; son of Robert Waller Palmer and wife, Sarah Harrison Austin; his grandfather, James Palmer, was a Revolutionary soldier. John W. studied law, history, English, the classics, and mathematics; merchant; postmaster for many years; extensive property owner; humanitarian and community leader. For a number of years was on the Rockingham County board of supervisors, instrumental in building new jail and improving the court house. In 1861-65 directed transportation of troops and supplies in Port Republic area; friend of Stonewall Jackson and entertained him at Port Republic several times. Methodist, Oddfellow, Republican; member of Loyal Temperance Legion. Died at Graham, Va., June 26, 1919. His 1st wife, who died May 24, 1867, was Annie Maria Eddins, daughter of Major Eddins of Port; 2d wife, who died July 5, 1918, was Mary Catherine Funkhouser of Edinburg. Children living 1942: Annie Laura (Mrs. M. B. Stickley), Silver Springs, Md., of 1st wife; of 2d: Olin Austin, author of note, Baltimore; Virginia Harrison (Mrs. M. D. Hinton), Dayton; Nellie Neff (Mrs. D. R. Mays), Laurel, Md.; Albert Ballard, lawyer and member of N. C. Senate, Concord, N. C.; Carroll Harrison, Methodist minister, Gaithersburg, Md. Deceased children of 1st wife: Mary Catherine, Chas. Minor, Robt. Vernon, Viola Maria; of 2d wife, John Waller Palmer, Jr.

PAUL, JUDGE JOHN—Born near Ottobine, Rockingham County, June 30, 1839, son of Peter and Maria Whitmore Paul; married Katherine S. Green of Front Royal, 1872; commonwealth attorney Rockingham County, 1871-77; M. C., 1880-82; U. S. judge, western district of Virginia, 1883-1901; died November 1, 1901. At the laying of the cornerstone for the new court house in 1896 Judge Paul delivered a notable address, reviewing the history of Rockingham County. This address was printed. His son, John Paul, Jr., born in Harrisonburg December 9, 1883, was member Va. Senate, 1912-16, 1919-22; captain in World War I; M. C., 1921-23; and has been U. S. judge, western district of Virginia, since January 1932.

PENNYBACKER, SENATOR ISAAC SAMUELS—Born September 3, 1805, at Pine Forge, Shenandoah County, son of Benjamin (1760-1820) and Sarah Samuels (1768-1825) Pennybacker; 10th of 13 children. Married Sarah A. Dyer (1816-1891), daughter of Zebulon of Pendleton County; lived in Harrisonburg; M. C., 1837-39; later, judge of U. S. District Court and a regent of the Smithsonian Institution; U. S. Senator from Virginia, 1845-47; died in Washington, D. C., January 12, 1847. His son, John Dyer Pennybacker (1833-1904), was a member of the Virginia Senate from Rockingham, 1859-63. His other sons were Isaac S., Jr., and J. Edmund.

PENNYBACKER, KATE ABIGAIL—Born May 30, 1868, on Linville Creek, second daughter of John Dyer Pennybacker (1833-1904) and his wife, Mary Elizabeth Lincoln (1827-1905), who was a daughter of Col. Abraham Lincoln (1799-1851) and his wife, Mary Homan (1802-1874). Mary E. Lincoln first married Dr. Richard S. Maupin, who died December 7, 1855. Miss Kate Pennybacker never married. She lived on one of the old Lincoln farms (that formerly belonged to the Bryans) on Linville Creek, and was the genealogist and conserver of family traditions for the Lincolns, Pennybackers, and related lines. She died in Rockingham Memorial Hospital at Harrisonburg, December 17, 1938, and was buried in the Lincoln family graveyard on Linville Creek. She had a sister Mary Lee, born August 24, 1866, and a brother, John George, born November 18, 1870, both of whom died some years ago.

PRICE, JAMES R.—Born August 26, 1847, in Monroe County, now W. Va., son of Rev. Addison H. and Mary Cox Price; distant relative of Rev. W. T. Price, well known in Rockingham for many years; C. S. A. soldier in 10th Va. Vol. Inf.; married Mary Marshall, daughter of Mansfield and a sister of James W. ("Cyclone Jim") Marshall; farmer near Harrisonburg; merchant in Dayton and Roanoke. Returning to Rockingham, he lived at the southwest end of Harrisonburg, where he died in 1925, survived by his wife and children: Mrs. J. M. Cultice of Harrisonburg; W. Edgar Price of Charlotte, N. C.; Oscar R. Price of Baltimore; R. Marshall Price of Miami, Fla.; and C. Grattan Price of Harrisonburg.

PRICE, JOSEPH, M. D.—Born January 1, 1853, near Tenth Legion; M. D., University of Pennsylvania, 1877; a leading surgeon of Philadelphia, 1885-1900; president of the American Association of Obstetricians and Gynecologists in 1895; died June 6, 1911. For an extended account of Dr. Price and his brothers, see Wayland's "Virginia Valley Records," pages 344, 345.

REED, REV. LEMUEL S.—A Methodist minister who, on December 11, 1866, married as his second wife Mrs. Robert M. Kyle of Harrisonburg, who was born Mary Catherine Byrd, daughter of Abraham and Rebecca Samuels Byrd. For a number of years Rev. Mr. Reed and his wife (Mary Byrd Kyle Reed) made their home on East Market Street in Harrisonburg, at the place now well known as Stoneleigh Inn, and here they were visited occasionally by his son, Dr. Walter Reed, who had been born in Gloucester County, Va., September 13, 1851, and had graduated in medicine at the University of Virginia in 1869. In April, 1876, Dr. Reed and his wife spent about a month in Harrisonburg. He then went west to his army assignment. His wife remained until October, when she followed him.

REHERD, JAMES E.—Born 1846 in Harrisonburg, son of William and Annie Keller Reherd; Confederate cavalryman; operator of sawmills; progressive farmer and successful business man and banker; a patron of Rockingham Memorial Hospital. Died in Harrisonburg, September 14, 1940. For a number of years he was president of The National Bank, Harrisonburg, and for several years preceding his death was believed to be the oldest bank president in the United States.

ROLLER, COL. OLIVER B.—Born May 5, 1854, near Mt. Crawford, son of Peter S. and Frances Allebaugh Roller; a younger brother of Gen. John Edwin Roller; graduated 1876 at V. M. I.; studied law at the University of Virginia and admitted to the bar in 1878. He had come to Harrisonburg in July, 1876, and in March, 1877, was elected first captain of the Harrisonburg Guards; lieut. colonel in the Spanish-American War, 1898; was a number of times mayor of Harrisonburg. Colonel Roller was the senior member of the law firm of O. B. Roller & Martz, Edward C. Martz being his partner.

ROSENBERGER, GEORGE W.—Lived at Rosendale, on Smith Creek, where he was born, February 22, 1823. On October 16, 1845, he married Barbara Ann Kagey, granddaughter of John, the "Good Man." Mr. Rosenberger was a successful business man and farmer, and was one of the first in Rockingham County to develop improved breeds of livestock. He had eight children, one of whom is Arthur Russell Rosenberger of Harrisonburg, whose biography appears in Part I of this book.

RUEBUSH, GEORGE—Born August 7, 1811; died August 11, 1893; eldest of 12 children of John, Jr. (Aug. 8, 1782—Feb. 6, 1874), whose mother, Mary Keller Ruebush, widow of John, Sr., came from York County, Pa., with her sons and daughters and settled near Friedens Church, Rockingham County. George and wife Catherine Cook (July 20, 1813—Aug. 12, 1878), lived near Greenville, Augusta County, Va. Mary was a German Reformed; John, Jr., joined the United Brethren. He married Mary Huffman, daughter of George, grandaughter of Valentine, and lived near Stover's Shop, Augusta County. James Addison Ruebush (1852—Aug. 21, 1892), son of George, in early life lived and worked with his uncle, Ephraim Ruebush, at Singers' Glen, in the music publishing business. He married Sallie Esther Whitmore (July 9, 1852—March 2, 1942). His only child is a son, Glenn, q. v., page 306).

RUFFNER, WILLIAM H.—Born February 11, 1824, at Lexington, where his father, Dr. Henry Ruffner, was president of Washington College, now Washington and Lee University; on September 3, 1850, he married Harriet A. Gray of Harrisonburg; lived here for the next 12 years or more. In 1861 Mrs. Ruffner was corresponding secretary of the Rockingham Soldiers Aid Society. Dr. Ruffner was a Presbyterian minister, a noted geologist, and a distinguished educator. He organized the new public school system of Virginia in 1869-70 and was state superintendent of schools from 1870-82. He drafted the plan for Virginia Polytechnic Institute and the state normal school at Farmville, of which he was the first president, 1884-87. He died November 24, 1908, at the home of his daughter, Mrs. R. E. Campbell, in Asheville, N. C.; buried in Lexington.

SALYARDS, JOSEPH—Born in 1808 near Front Royal; died August 10, 1885, in New Market. He was an eminent scholar, largely self-educated, and was for many years the most distinguished teacher in the Shenandoah Valley. He taught in Harrisonburg and other places in Rockingham, as well as at New Market and other places in Shenandoah and Page. His epic poem, "Idothea," has received wide recognition.

SCHOLL, CAPTAIN PETER—Lived on Smith Creek a short distance south of where the town of New Market now stands. Thomas Lewis, Peter Jefferson, and others who surveyed the Fairfax Line camped at Scholl's place the night of September 29, 1746, as Lewis records in his journal. According to Waddell, Augusta County historian, Scholl, as early as 1742, was one of the 12 militia captains of Augusta, and in 1745 was one of the first magistrates. Valentine Sevier, father of John (who was later governor of Tennessee), is said to have been a member of Scholl's company in 1742. On May 20, 1765, land for Rader's Church, near Timberville, was deeded to Scholl as trustee for the Presbyterians (German Reformed) and Michael Neice as trustee for the Lutherans.

SCOTT, THOMAS—In August, 1798, Thomas Scott was president of the Harrisonburg town council; S. McWilliams was clerk, pro. tem.; Asher Waterman, John Koontz, and Frederick Spangler were the other members. At that time Mr. Scott was taxed with two houses, one of the first class, one of the second class. The one of the first class was probably the stone house that stood until a few years ago on the south corner of N. Main and Elizabeth Street, site of the present Charles Store. Mrs. Carr, in her description of Harrisonburg houses in or about 1820, coming south on the east side of N. Main Street, says: "The next house was a stone one built and owned by Mr. Thomas Scott. He lived with his daughter, Mrs. Henry Welsh, until he died. . . . S. of old Mr. Scott's house and adjoining it was a frame building used as a store by Mr. Scott."

SEVIER, GENERAL JOHN—Born September 23, 1745, between Broadway and New Market, son of Valentine and Joanna Goade Sevier; married Sarah Hawkins in 1761; founder of New Market; owned property in Woodstock; moved to East Tennessee in 1773, where he became famous as "Nolichucky Jack." His second wife was "Bonny Kate" Sherrill. He died September 24, 1815. In Knoxville he is honored with a tall monument, bearing a long inscription, part of which is as follows:
"Pioneer, soldier, statesman, and one of the founders of the Republic; Governor of the State of Franklin; six times Governor of Tennessee; four times elected to Congress; the typical pioneer who conquered the wilderness and fashioned the State; a projector and hero of King's Mountain; thirty-five battles, thirty-five victories; his Indian war-cry, 'Here they are! come on, boys, come on!' "

SHACKLETT, SAMUEL—Born, probably in Fauquier County, Va., May 31, 1804, son of Edward Shacklett and Elizabeth Rector; married (1) Maria Graham Henry (daughter of Samuel and Sarah Stuart Henry), who died August 17, 1870, aged 59; (2) Sarah Long, who was born July 16, 1825, and died June 2, 1893. Mr. Shacklett died June 30, 1886. Of his first marriage there were two children: Henry and Frances. Frances married Col. Simeon B. Gibbons, but lived only six months after her marriage. Henry married Ellen Glasscock. His daughter, Margaret Rector Shacklett, was the first wife of Gen. John E. Roller. Samuel lived upstairs in the large brick house at the northeastern corner of Court Square and had his store in the rooms now occupied by the Fletcher drugstore. Turner Washington Shacklett, family historian, says: "Of Uncle Samuel, too, I have a good recollection. He looked very much like the pictures we see of Henry Clay and was a successful merchant in Harrisonburg, Rockingham Co. Va., who was succeeded by his son Henry, who also successfully conducted the business for many years."

SHOWALTER, ANTHONY JOHNSON—Born May 1, 1858, in Rockingham, son of John A. and Susanna Miller Showalter; studied music and methods of teaching in America and Europe; married (1) Callie Walser of Giddings, Texas, November, 1881; (2) Mrs. Eleanor Dorsey, born Gillen, of Washington, June, 1912. He was a distinguished teacher, composer, compiler, and publisher; president of the A. J. Showalter Co., music publishers, of Dalton, Ga., Texarkana, and Chattanooga. His most popular composition is the gospel song, "Leaning on the Everlasting Arms," said to have been published in more than 1000 music books and translated into nearly every language where Christianity is known. Professor Showalter died September 15, 1924. He was a brother to Professor J. Henry Showalter, whose biography appears in Part I of this book.

SHOWALTER, WILLIAM JOSEPH—Born July 10, 1878, at Dale Enterprise, son of David Bowman and Susan Catherine Swope Showalter; student in Bridgewater College, 1894-96; Sc. D., Pennsylvania College, 1921; LL. D., Bridgewater, 1930. Teacher in public schools, 1896-98; newspaper reporter and editor in Harrisonburg, 1898-1901; journalist and correspondent in Washington City, 1902-07; writer for Haskin Syndicate, 1907-13; editor of Harrisonburg and Staunton newspapers, 1913-15; on the staff of the *National Geographic Magazine,* Washington, from 1914 till his death, October 13, 1935. He traveled widely over many countries of the world, and wrote numerous illuminating articles for the *National Geographic Magazine* and other periodicals; was decorated Order of Bolivar by the government of Venezuela in 1912 for his writings on South America. On November 12, 1902, he married Effie Caldwell Coyner of Waynesboro, Va. No children.

SIPE, COLONEL EMANUEL—Born July 5, 1830, in Rockingham County; prior to 1861 he was lieut. colonel of the 116th Va. Militia; in the war, 1861-65, he was first captain of Co. H, 12th Va. Cavalry and later colonel of the 7th Va. Cavalry, C. S. A. Both before and after the war he was a prominent merchant and man of public affairs. He died September 23, 1901. His son, William H. Sipe (November 12, 1858—January 9, 1939), was a leading merchant at Lilly and Bridgewater, a county supervisor, trustee of Bridgewater College, and president for 20 years of the Planters Bank of Bridgewater. His biography appears in Part I of this book.

SLATER, VERNE R.—Born in Harrisonburg, April 3, 1871, son of William A. and Sarah E. Slater. After working for William Loeb & Co. and B. Bloom, merchants, he in 1905 formed a partnership with Charles E. Frazier and operated a store handling men's clothing and haberdashery. Mr. Slater, the surviving partner, closed out the store in 1927 and went into the coal business. For 21 years he was a member of the Harrisonburg town and city council, and had numerous connections in fraternal and benevolent organizations. In 1902 he married Miss Ray Levy, who survives him. He died January 11, 1934.

SMITH, ABRAHAM—A son of Captain John Smith. Abraham Smith was a captain of militia in Augusta in 1756. He took part in the French and Indian War and in 1757 was a prisoner in the French dominions. In 1758 he was court-martialed, but was acquitted, his accuser being punished. In 1776 he was a colonel of militia; in 1778 one of the first justices of Rockingham County, and county lieutenant. He presided over the county court, composed of 13 justices, at the first session, April 27, 1778, and signed the minutes. The first courts were held at Smithland, two miles northeast of Harrisonburg, at the home of Daniel Smith, who was probably Abraham's brother. Abraham owned a large estate at the foot of North Mountain, on or near North River, which descended to his son Henry.

SMITH, JUDGE DANIEL—Born at or near Harrisonburg in 1779, son of John and Margaret Davis Smith; grandson of Daniel Smith, of Smithland, one of the first county justices. Judge Daniel married Frances Strother Duff, June 10, 1809; children: Margaret, Elizabeth, Lucius, Frances, Marie, John Daniel; died November 8, 1850. In 1805 he was a member of the Va. House of Delegates; from 1804 to 1811 he was commonwealth's attorney for Rockingham; on April 10, 1811, he was appointed a judge of the general court, and from that date until his death was judge of the circuit superior court for Rockingham. He lived at Waverly, near Dayton, site now occupied by Shrum's brickyard. His portrait hangs in the circuit court room in Harrisonburg.

SNAPP, ROBERT J.—Born July 17, 1865, near Romney, W. Va., son of Rev. Silas R. Snapp, Methodist minister, and wife, Sarah V. Smith, daughter of Stephen. Robert J. finished his high-school education at Port Republic, where his father was stationed at the time. In 1884 he entered the employ of the Shenandoah Valley (now Norfolk & Western) Railway Co., learned telegraphy, and at various times later was operator and agent at Stanley, Buchanan, Buena Vista, and Elkton—at the last place for many years. He is a member of the Elkton Methodist Church, a past master of the Masonic lodge, and has served as town councilman and mayor. He is much interested in local history, and was one of the original promoters of the successful campaign for the Shenandoah National Park.

SNYDER, ADOLPH HELLER—Born October 22, 1863, in Woodstock, son of Rev. J. A. Snyder, Lutheran minister, and wife, Theresa Heller; from 1878 to 1882 a pupil under Joseph Salyards; graduate of Roanoke College, 1883; student in Mt. Airy Theological Seminary, Philadelphia, 1884; teacher in Wichita, Kansas; editor of newspapers in Strasburg, Woodstock, and Harrisonburg. He was editor of the *Rockingham Register* in Harrisonburg from 1889 until his death, January 10, 1910, and owner from 1900 to 1903. He was town recorder for Harrisonburg for a number of years, and in November, 1909, was elected to the Va. House of Delegates. His failing health prevented his going to Richmond. At the time of his death he was chairman of the Harrisonburg school board, and through his paper and otherwise he aided the movement for locating the new normal school, now Madison College, at Harrisonburg. On November 26, 1890, he married Anne Wierman of Shenandoah County. Of the marriage were born four children: Fred, Paul, Katherine, and Anne.

SNYDER, ROBERT HENRY—Born February 11, 1843, in Rockingham, son of Harry Gilmer and Elizabeth Snyder. After early years in school he became a skilled wood-worker. In 1861 he enlisted at New Market in Co. E, 11th Va. Cavalry, and was later a member of Rosser's famous "Laurel Brigade." While recovering from wounds he and his friend, John C. Morrison, repaired guns for the Confederacy. After the war he opened shops in Harrisonburg and made wagons, coaches, and carriages, employing a number of helpers. He was typical of the skilled mechanics, numerous in those days, among whom were some of the Sprinkels, Bassfords, Reherds, and many others. On February 11, 1868, he married Elizabeth Ann Liskey, daughter of George Abner and Eveline Miller Liskey. The latter's grandfather, Rev. Alexander Miller, Presbyterian minister, located near the site of Dayton in 1753, and preached at different places, among them "Old Erection," at the head of the present Silver Lake. Robert Henry and Elizabeth Snyder had seven children: one died in infancy; Mrs. Cora V. Dovel and Mrs. Ella G. Coffman, some years ago; surviving are Mrs. Laura A. Jones and Mrs. Annie Guyer Lyons of Washington, Lewis B. Snyder of Cincinnati, and Miss Maude R. Snyder of Harrisonburg. Mr. Snyder died September 5, 1883, from an accident suffered at Washington, Rappahannock County. For 31 years (1887-1918) Mrs. Snyder and her daughter Maude kept the toll gate on the Valley Pike just south of Harrisonburg, at the mouth of the Port Republic Road. This was a famous landmark that will be remembered by older residents.

SPIRO, MORRIS—Born September 26, 1872, in Lithuania; came to America in early life. With rabbinical education, he chose an industrial and mechanical career and became a skilled worker in railway shops. In 1906 he came to Harrisonburg as foreman in the shops and construction work of the Southern Railway, holding this position until a short time before his death, June 28, 1940. Mr. Spiro was an enthusiastic Mason, ever alert to every enterprise for the amelioration of human suffering and the care of orphan children. For years he was the untiring and efficient leader of the Red Cross organization of the city and county. He is survived by his wife, who was Sadie Miller, daughter of Abel, and a daughter, Celia Ann, who is a graduate of Madison College and a teacher.

SPRINKEL, CAPTAIN CHARLES A.—Born 1834 in Harrisonburg, son of Nelson Sprinkel; in 1861 (and possibly before) he was superintendent of Rockingham County public schools, B. F. Lincoln, Madison West, Geo. W. Kemper, Arch'd Hopkins, Jno. Q. Winfield, and Jacob Caplinger being among the 23 other commissioners. In the same year he was captain of the Valley Guards, Co. G, 10th Va. Vol. Inf. This company two years earlier had formed a part of the militia force at Charles Town in attendance upon the trial and execution of John Brown and his associates. For some years prior to 1868 he carried on a mercantile business in Harrisonburg and in 1870 was a census enumerator. From 1871 to 1881 he was local agent for the B. & O. Railroad, and afterward, until the time of his death, was a dealer in farming implements and other machinery, having his son, Walter N. Sprinkel, associated with him. The latter is now of Hanover, Va. Surviving, also, are his daughter, Mrs. James M. Warren, and his son, Dr. Carter Sprinkel, both of Harrisonburg. Captain Sprinkel died February 13, 1910. His wife was Sallie Carter (1837-1910).

STAPLES, JUNIUS CLAY—Born in Fluvanna County, Va., in October, 1846; C. S. A. soldier; came about 1870 to Harrisonburg where he was a prominent business man and owner of real estate until his death, May 29, 1931; was a mainstay of the Harrisonburg Baptist Church for many years; from 1894 to 1897 he was moderator of the Augusta Baptist Association, and from 1898 to 1901 was treasurer of the same. Mr. Staples' first wife, Emma Scott Devier, had 10 children, seven of whom, four sons and three daughters, were living in 1931; his second wife, Lilah Roberts of Georgia, survives, without children. Two sons, Ralph and J. Kemper, are well known in Harrisonburg.

STRAYER, JULIET LYLE—Born November 12, 1826, daughter of Abraham and Martha Reid Smith of Rockingham; died in Harrisonburg, August 31, 1893. She was the wife of Crawford C. Strayer, lived in Harrisonburg over 40 years, and for about 25 years was president of the Ladies' Memorial Association. At the entrance to the soldiers' section of Woodbine Cemetery is a tablet with this inscription: "To the Memory of Mrs. Juliet Lyle Strayer, Founder and for Many Years President of the Ladies Memorial Association."

TAYLOR, DAVID A.—Born at Broadway, June 24, 1866, son of Edwin and Mary Burkholder Taylor; the latter a daughter of Abraham Burkholder; began his career as a printer at Dale Enterprise with Abraham Blosser, publisher of the *Watchful Pilgrim;* then worked on the various weeklies in Harrisonburg; next 13 years with the Ruebush-Kieffer Co. in Dayton. During 1909 he was editor and publisher of the *Times,* at Buena Vista, Va. Going to Washington, he was employed for 30 years in the Government Printing Office, from which he retired 10 years ago, after having spent more than 50 years in the printing business. He and R. B. Smythe, well known among Harrisonburg printers and publishers, were associates in their earlier careers. Since his retirement Mr. Taylor has done some writing, mostly poetry, in which he has decided talent. His verse has appeared in a number of anthologies and in various magazines. His wife's maiden name was Maggie D. Byrd, daughter of Levi S. Byrd. His address (January, 1943) is 1121 Morse Street, N. E., Washington, D. C.

TAYLOR, PROFESSOR JOHN W.—Born in 1836 on the west bank of the Shenandoah River, East Rockingham, opposite the town of Shenandoah, son of Zachary Taylor (Scotch-Irish) and Nancy Eppard (German); began teaching at age 17 or 18; later attended Richmond College and Randolph-Macon; M. A., Randolph-Macon, 1860; was principal of the male academy in Harrisonburg; in 1865 opened his school at Lacey Spring where he taught for more than 40 years. His wife was Virginia C. Lincoln (August 2, 1850—March 6, 1923), daughter of Jacob Nicholas Lincoln.

TUTWILER, HENRY—Born in Harrisonburg in 1807, son of the postmaster and glove-maker, Henry Tutwiler; first M. A. of the University of Virginia. He and Gessner Harrison, also of Harrisonburg, were in the University with Edgar Allan Poe. Tutwiler was a distinguished educator of Alabama; his daughter Julia was outstanding among Alabama women. Henry died in 1884.

WAMPLER, ISAAC SAMUEL—Born March 15, 1866, near Harrisonburg, son of Samuel H. and Mary Good Wampler; attended public schools, Shenandoah Normal, and Bridgewater College; student at Peabody, Nashville, Tenn., 1889-91; in 1891, with his brother, D. B. Wampler and others, founded West Central Academy at Mt. Clinton, where he was principal 11 years, conducting summer schools at various places. From 1902 to 1907 he studied at Washington and Lee University (B. A., 1906, M. A., 1907). In 1907 he returned to Peabody as a teacher. In 1908 he became president of the Peabody Alumni Association, as such doing outstanding work. In 1911 he was elected Alumni Secretary and Fiscal Agent and as such served widely and efficiently until 1918. From 1918 to 1938 he was superintendent of the state school for the blind at Nashville. His wife, Mabel Glenn McCue of Staunton, has been an efficient and inspiring helpmeet. Of his general alumni directory, published in 1910, President Bruce R. Payne spoke in highest terms, repeatedly speaking of it as a "million dollar book." Professor and Mrs. Wampler live at 1313 18th Avenue, South, Nashville.

WARTMANN, LAWRENCE—The most distinguished early printer of Harrisonburg. He was born in 1774, probably in Pennsylvania or Maryland; died in Harrisonburg, April 11, 1840. His grave is in the old Methodist Cemetery, adjoining the Church of the Brethren, on the hill, site of the first Methodist church in Harrisonburg. The upper half of his tombstone was broken off some years ago and has since been carried away. In 1812 Wartmann was working with the Henkels in New Market, superintendent of their printery. By 1816 he was established in Harrisonburg, for in that year he printed here Joseph Funk's "Choral Music," a book of 88 pages. In 1822 he established the weekly newspaper, the *Rockingham Register,* which he and his sons and others continued for nearly 100 years. His son, J. H. Wartmann, seems to have been the leading printer among his sons; Henry T. was much interested in music. In 1879 Henry T. moved to Citra, Florida, where he died, February 27, 1905. The address of his daughter, Miss Byrd Wartmann, is 701 Sanchez Street, South Ocala, Florida. Lawrence Wartman (1774-1840) was probably a son of Rev. Lawrence Wartmann, a Lutheran minister who was preaching in the Valley in 1758. His name appears also as "Rev. H. Wartmann."

WATERMAN, DR. ASHER—Said to have been a surgeon in the Revolution and with Washington on that Christmas-night crossing of the Delaware. On November 10, 1791, he, a member of Staunton Lodge, No. 13, visited the new Masonic lodge in Harrisonburg. He was such a visitor several times between 1791 and June 1792, and on June 14, 1792, he was admitted to membership in this lodge; hence we assume that he took up his residence in Harrisonburg about that time. He served as master of the Harrisonburg lodge in 1794, 1797, 1809, 1814, and 1822. In 1797 he was one of the town trustees. His wife, married August 30, 1787, was Sarah Lockhart of Augusta County. He had sons Albert G. and Augustus; daughters, Annie and Isabella. The former married Charles Douglas, the latter, Robert Gray. In 1795 he owned 93,000 acres of land in West Rockingham and what is now Pendleton County, W. Va., as shown by a contemporary map. He built and lived in a stone house which still remains at the southwest side of Court Square.

WATERMAN, A. G.—In 1910 Mr. A. G. Waterman of New York City, scion of an old Rockingham family, gave three acres at the northern edge of Harrisonburg, on which the Waterman School was opened the next year, September 15, 1911.

WAYLAND, JOHN WALTER—Born December 8, 1872, at Woodlawn, Shenandoah County, son of John Wesley and Anna Kagey Wayland; attended a one-room school and later taught three years in Shenandoah public schools; B. A., Bridgewater College, 1899; Ph. D., University of Virginia, 1907; LL. D., Bridgewater, 1936; came to Harrisonburg in 1909, as one of the first faculty of the State Normal School, now Madison College; in active service on this faculty until the summer of 1931; taught at various times in Bridgewater College, the University of Virginia, the Jefferson School for Boys, at Charlottesville, and the University of Tennessee. Raven, Phi Beta Kappa, Delta Sigma Rho; Baptist; Mason. Married Mattie V. Fry of Bridgewater, June 8, 1898; sons Francis Fry and John Walter. Has had published about 30 books, among them "A History of Rockingham County" (1912), "How to Teach American History" (1914), "A History of Virginia for Boys and Girls" (1920), "Ethics and Citizenship" (1923), "A History of Shenandoah County" (1927), "Virginia Valley Records" (1930), "World History" (1932), with C. J. H. Hayes and Parker T. Moon, "Historic Homes of Northern Virginia and the Eastern Panhandle of West Virginia" (1937), and "Stonewall Jackson's Way" (1940). Wrote the words of the song "Old Virginia," set to music by Will H. Ruebush.

WHITMORE, PETER—Born February 6, 1806; died October 25, 1861; son of Abraham, who bought a farm and mill on Beaver Creek in 1813, which, after deaths of himself and wife, was sold to the husband of his youngest daughter, Maria Whitmore Paul. Abraham's father, Michael Whitmore, came from Lancaster County, Pa., and settled on Cook's Creek, between Harrisonburg and Dayton. Peter was a Mennonite; was buried at Bank Church, on Dry River, with his second wife, Cynthia Deputy (July 21, 1812—April 26, 1879), and his sons, John B. and Benjamin D., who served in Co. H, 10th Va. Vol. Inf., C. S. A. Peter's daughter, Sallie Esther Whitmore, married James Addison Ruebush and was the mother of Glenn, q. v., page 306.

WILSON, REV. BENJAMIN F.—The portrait and biography of Dr. Wilson appear in Part I of this book. Below we reproduce several unique tributes from several of his friends. For these tributes we are indebted to Mr. A. R. Rosenberger of Harrisonburg, who, some years ago, had them printed on an attractive card which he has distributed as a souvenir.

> My heart is heavy laden,
> My eyes are filled with tears,
> This world has lost a nobleman,
> My friend of many years.
>
> He filled this life with sunshine,
> By kind words, acts, and deeds;
> He always saw the flowers,
> Where others saw but weeds.
>
> Of course, the world is sadder,
> He had friends everywhere;
> But heaven is so much brighter.
> With Dr. Wilson there.
> —Carroll Menefee, 1932.

The following was added by Mr. Rosenberger:
"Henry Ney told me, not long ago, that some one came to him soon after Rev. Dr. B. F. Wilson's death and said to him: 'Why, they tell me that Dr. Wilson died poor, had nothing, left nothing.' Henry Ney replied: 'To the contrary, in my opinion Dr. Wilson died one of the richest men that ever died in Harrisonburg—left more, and took more with him, than anyone I ever knew.'

"I think the above a very fine sermon within itself, well worth reading and thinking about often, which I do. Knowing Dr. Wilson, and the unselfish, commendable life he lived, enables one more fully to understand and appreciate the beautiful truth of what Mr. Ney stated in his reply on that occasion."

WILTON, JOSHUA—Born in Ontario, Canada, August 19, 1843; in 1865 came to Harrisonburg with Philo Bradley, who was returning after an earlier residence here; in 1868 opened his hardware store which he and his sons operated for many years. He served on the town council, was for some years president of the First National Bank, and in 1870 was master of the Masonic lodge. In 1889, when the lodge celebrated its centennial, he, with James H. Dwyer and Edward S. Conrad, prepared a valuable history of the lodge, which was printed. He was a prominent Episcopalian, and about 1911 wrote a very interesting account of the Episcopal Church in Rockingham and Harrisonburg, most of which was printed in the history of the county which appeared in 1912. Mr. Wilton died in Richmond, November 17, 1928, at the home of his daughter Hattie (Mrs. R. Coleman Rice), and was interred in Harrisonburg on November 20. His wife, Mary E. C. Christie, married June 10, 1873, died some years ago. Besides his daughter, he was survived by sons Ernest C. and Harold H. His son Claude had died in 1927.

WINFIELD, CAPTAIN JOHN Q.—Born June 20, 1822, at Mt. Jackson, son of Dr. Richard and Katherine Salvage Winfield; spent most of his life in and near Broadway; in 1852 married Sallie Neff of Cootes's Store. In 1859 he raised and in 1861 and 1862 commanded the Brock's Gap Rifles, a cavalry company which served with distinction under Turner Ashby. When Ashby was promoted Winfield was mentioned as his successor, but retired on account of poor health. He died at Broadway, July 29, 1892, survived by his son Charles R. and his daughter Paulina S.

WINFIELD, PAULINA S.—Daughter of Captain John Q. Winfield. Miss Winfield has collected a rich store of materials from tradition and local history, and has been a contributor for many years to leading magazines. She edited her father's war-time letters which were published in 1930, pages 231-299, in Wayland's "Virginia Valley Records." Appended to these letters is a muster roll of the Brock's Gap Rifles, Co. B, 7th Va. Cavalry, C. S. A.

YANCEY, CAPTAIN WILLIAM BENJAMIN—Born December 31, 1837, son of Col. William Burbridge (1803-1858) and Mary K. Smith Yancey, who died April 16, 1845. On February 16, 1860, Captain William Benjamin married Victoria Winsborough. In the war, 1861-65, he commanded the Peaked Mountain Grays, one of the companies of the 10th Va. Vol. Inf., until he was severely wounded in 1864. He died September 1, 1913.

YANCEY, CHARLES A.—Born February 19, 1839, on the farm of his father, Col. Wm. Burbridge Yancey, in East Rockingham; attended Prof. White's school at Mossy Creek and the University of Virginia; lieut. of infantry in 1861, later served in the 6th Regt. Va. Cav., in a company commanded by his brother, Capt. E. S. Yancey, and Capt. Mark Kemper; lawyer in Harrisonburg. His wife, married January 24, 1867, was Julia P. Morrison of Cumberland, Md. His mother was Mary K. Smith; his paternal grandfather was Layton Yancey, a soldier of the Revolution, whose wife was Fanny, daughter of Thomas Lewis, the first surveyor of Augusta and of Rockingham. Charles A. Yancey died on Sunday, November 14, 1880. It was stated in the *Rockingham Register* of November 18 that his funeral was one of the largest ever known in Harrisonburg. Pallbearers were members of the bar and prominent business men: C. E. Haas, F. A. Daingerfield, W. B. Compton, Robert Johnston, L. H. Ott, B. B. Botts, Chas. T. O'Ferrall, and J. Samuel Harnsberger. In resolutions of respect, presented by Col. O'Ferrall, a high tribute was paid to his professional character and fine personal qualities.

YANCEY, WILLIAM LEWIS—Born November 24, 1860, son of Capt. William Benjamin Yancey, C. S. A., and his wife, Victoria Julia Winsborough; grandson of Col. William Burbridge and Mary Kyle Smith Yancey; great-grandson of Col. Layton and Frances Lewis Yancey; the latter a daughter of Thomas and Jane Strother Lewis. On October 27, 1885, he married Mary Ashby Gibbons, daughter of Robert Allen (1817-1891) and Frances Virginia Kemper (1830-1912) Gibbons; children: Kemper Winsborough, Mary Virginia, William Burbridge, Lois Rodham, Robert Gibbons, Charlotte, Ruth, who died in infancy, and Mildred Lewis, who died in 1921. Kemper W., now of Richmond, married Edith Stafford of Texas and has daughters Mary Elizabeth and Laura; Mary Virginia married Dr. Noland McKenzie Canter of Harrisonburg and has sons: Noland McKenzie, Jr., Harry Yancey, and Gibbons Hall; Col. William Burbridge, U. S. A., married Elizabeth Faw of Staunton and has children: Ann Elizabeth, captain WAACS; Mildred Mason, who married Capt. Richard Brown and has a daughter, Elizabeth Yancey; and twins (of Col. Wm. B.), William B. and Mary G.; Capt. Robert Gibbons, U. S. A., married Margaret Hunter of Raleigh, N. C., and has children, Robert, Jr., and Margaret H.; Charlotte married James Hillyer Boice, now of Lynchburg, and has children: Charlotte, James Hillyer, Jr., and William Grant. William Lewis Yancey was a popular and successful lawyer of Harrisonburg, where he died on July 31, 1901.

YOUNT, WALTER BOWMAN—Born June 22, 1859, son of Daniel and Margaret Bowman Yount; graduate of Juniata College, Natl. School of Elocution and Oratory, Philadelphia, and Illinois Wesleyan University; student six years at the University of Virginia; Ph. B. (Wesleyan), 1903; D. D. (Blue Ridge College), 1913; D. D. (Bridgewater), 1930. From 1892 to 1910 he was president of Bridgewater College; later taught in Western Maryland College, Westminister; died at Westminister, January 6, 1932. He married (1) Minnie B. Andes of Rockingham; (2) Emma Eller of Botetourt County, Va., who survives him and lives at Westminster, Md. Of the first marriage there are two sons: Karl Edwin, born February 27, 1897, at Bridgewater, and Dee Andes, born September 16, 1899, also a native of Bridgewater. Karl is in business in Baltimore (address, 1107 Longwood Street); Dee is an electrical engineer, address 215 Lighthouse Avenue, Richmond, Staten Island, N. Y.

GENERAL INDEX

"Abstracts of Land Grants" 409
Acker, Peter 25 388
Adams, Ward B. 319
"Adventures in Christian Living" 261
Alaska 45 77 226
Alexandria, Va. 174 175 205
Allebaugh, Frances 425
Allebaugh, Maria 33
American Legion 68 69 84 85
Anderson, Elizabeth 247
Andover, Mass. 99
Andrews, F. Genevieve 313
Angell, Bob 133
Antiques collected 337
Apple orchards 146 293 360 361
Appomattox, Va. 311
Armentrout, Virginia 345
Arnold, Susana 47
Arthur, Bessie Wilson 293 367
Ashby, Gen. Turner 25 437
"Ashlawn" 418
Assassination in 1864 411
Astronomer and antiquarian 404
Atlanta, Ga. 174 391
Aubrey, Capt. George W. 59
Augusta *Herald* 97
Augusta Military Academy 43 64 65
Aviation 178 179 356 357 379
Avis, Capt. John 389
Bach, Sebastian 390
Baltimore Convention of 1912 97
Baltimore Polytechnic Institute 90 91
Baltimore Sun 97
Bands organized 247
Barbee, Wm. Randolph 389
Bare, Bertha B. 315
Basic City, Va. 102 103 412
Bavaria 227
Bear, David 91
Bear Lithia Spring 419
Beauregard, Gen. P. G. T. 299
Beaver Creek School 256 257 346
Beery, Noah W. 199 323
Bell, Ida F. 109 111 113
Bellaire, Ohio 36
Berkeley Springs, W. Va. 350
Berlin's printery 222
Berryville, Va. 96 97
Bertram, Judge H. W. 177
Bethany Biblical Seminary 31 50 51

Big Lick 169
"Big Spring," Harrisonburg 289
"Big Spring," Lacey 411
"Biography of Gospel Song and Hymn writers" 162 163
"Biography, the Literature of Personality" 206 207
Blackburn, Elizabeth L. 409
Blackburn, John W. 329 373
Black Rock Springs 215
Blacksburg, Va. 204 313
Blackstone College 156 157
Bliss, James 348 349
Blosser, Peter 39 41
Blosser family 39 41
Blue and Gray Division 106
Blue Ridge College 46 184 185 193
Blue Ridge Labor Camp 95 385
"Blue Water" 171
"Bogota" 408 409
Bohemia 227
Book of Martyrs 305
Books and manuscripts 303 305
Books on education 161
Books on local history 435
Boone, Daniel 392 396
Boone's Creek 46 47
Boonsboro Gap battle 402
Boston University 51
Botts, Hon. John M. 233
Bower, James R. 99
Bowman, George, pioneer 45
Bowman, Dr. Samuel J. 47
"Boy Company, The" 393
Bradley, Nelson 381 391
Bradley Foundry 52-56
Bragg, Hon. Thomas 293
Branner, Dr. John C. 189
Branum, Leona 39
Brethren Publishing House 51
Bridgewater, Va. 141 193 295 297 353
Bridgewater College 46 47 51 76 77 161 183 185 202 257 259 308 309 439
Brittany, France 182 183
Broadway, Va. 24 25 172 173 314 315 384
Brock's Gap Rifles 25
"Brother Billy" 396
Brown, Major E. M. 301 391
Brown University 51 99

General Index

Brubaker, F. John 255
Brunk, Christian H. 61 355
Brunk, Elder John 353
Bryan, Pendleton 392
Bryan, Rebecca 392
Bryan, Major William 392
Bryan, Wm. Jennings 133
Bryan & Stratton 282 283 285
Bucher, Elder George 31
"Builder, The" 121
Bureau of Reclamation 241
Burkholder, Elizabeth 275
"Burning, The" 361
Burns, Mary L. 53 55 57
Burns, Sylvia G. 309
Burtner, Ada 351
Burtner, George P. 123
Byrd, Sen. Harry F. 97 241 343
Byerly, Capt. Frank A. 267 393
Cabell, P. H. 299
Cabinet-makers 102 103 375
Caesarian section 390
Callender, Rev. S. N. 71 251
Calvert, Judge George R. 349
Calvert, Major John S. 349
Camden, N. J. 182 183
Campbell, Lucille 121
Cambridge University 307
Camp Dix 369
Camp Lee 61 183 219 307 369
Camp Lee newspaper 365
Camp Meigs 313
Camp Sevier 306 307
Camp Sherman 173
Camp Stuart 373
Case, C. C. 163
Catawba College 154 155
Catawba Sanatorium 376 377
Catholic Univ. of America 50 51
Cave, Adaline M. 319
Cayuga County, N. Y. 53 391
"Challenge of the Market-place, The" 275
Chappelear, Prof. G. W. 409
Charleston, S. C. 205 367
Charles Town, W. Va. 53 55 213 389 432
Charlottesville, Va. 174 175 376 377 417 418
Chase City, Va. 121 377
Chateau Thierry 173
"Cherry Grove" (home) 171
Cherry Grove, Va. 319 320

Chesapeake-Western Railway 68 69
Childress, Rev. W. L. 351
China, missionaries to 367
Choral Club of Singers' Glen 351
"Choral Music" 434
Chrisman, William J. 129
"Chrisman's Infantry" 393
"Christian Harp, The" 410
Christie, George S. 55
Churchville, Va. 182
Clarke Courier 96 97
Clark University 202 308 309
Clary, J. O. A. 289
Clay, Henry 428
Cleveland, Col. Ben 75
Click, Lizzie M. 151
Clifton Forge, Va. 233
Cline, Elder John A. 257
Cline, Elder Joseph M. 261
Clinedinst, Anna 349
Clockmakers 139 405
Clower, Julia 133
"Cockade City, The" 293
Coffman, Bishop John 353
Cole, Virginia Garber 335
College Station, Texas 135
"Collicello" 402
Columbia University 120 169 242 368 384
Columbus, Ga. 49
Commonwealth Club 291
Community service plaque 385
Concert-Goer, The 349
Concord, Mass. 99
Concord, Va. 310 311
"Confederate Banners" 395
Conrad, Capt. Stephen 85
Conservation and irrigation 240 241
"Conservation Sermonettes" 77
Contractors and builders 289 295 297 357 389
Converse, Rev. Amasa 91
Converse College 113 366
"Converse's Index" 91
Cook, Roy Bird 223
Cootes's Store 26 27 395
Cornell University 193
Court Manor 410
Cox, Gen. Creed F. 95
Coyner, Effie C. 428
Craney Island 69
Craun, Eva 51

GENERAL INDEX 443

Crickenberger, Aphelia 269
"Crippled Fayette" 407
Crook, Gen. George 397
Cross Keys, Va. 327 330 331 406
Cross Keys Cemetery 396 412
Crowell, Gen. Benedict 85
Crowne, Col. William 97
Crozer Theological Seminary 46 47 152 153
Culpeper Jail 420
Cumberland, Md. 351
"Cyclone Jim" 417 424
Daily Independent 324 325
Daily News 206 241 324 325
Daily News-Record 96 97 238 239 241 324 325
Daily Times 233 241
Dairy products 181 314 315 357
Dale Enterprise 177 178 357
Dale Enterprise Literary Society 60 61 341 405
Daleville College 30 184 185
Dana's Musical Institute 162 166 167
Davidson & Bourne 392 396
Davidson College 369
Davis, Arlene V. 255
Davis, Dr. E. D. 64 65
Davis, Frances 57
Davis, Richard S. 89
Davis, Col. Zimmerman 205
Dayton, Ohio 132 133
Dayton, Va. 72 73
Dean Bible Class 98 99 107
DeBard, Louisa 85
Delaney, Blanche 313
Denbigh, Va. 316
Denver, Colo. 226 227
Dewey, Admiral George 1115
Diamond ring awarded 319
Diary of John Kline 399 411 415
Dickinson College 171
Dockery, N. C. 142 143
Dogwood Hill Farm 235
Dold, Bessie 417
Dorsey, Capt. Eli 119
Drake University 44
Driver, Bertie E. 127
Duff, Margaret A. 311
Duke University 49 152 153
Dunsmore Business College 24 172 173
Dupuy, John 337
Earl of Essex 119

Early, Rebecca 149
Eastern Mennonite School 178 179 316 317
Eastman Business College 234 235
East Side Highway 311 329
Ecuador 47
Edinburg, Va. 63 417
Edom, Va. 32 33 135 338
"Eighteenth Century Novel, The" 203
Electric hatcheries 209 317
Elizabeth Furnace 138 139
Elkton, Va. 93 133 229 311 375
Elon College 305
Emerson College 148
Emory and Henry College 95 197
Emory University 49
Endless Caverns 391
"England's Attitude toward the Monroe Doctrine" 275
English Journal, The 243
Eshman's Band 389
Essary, J. Fred 97
Eversole, John 139
Fairfax, Va. 28 29
Fairfax Line, The 153 313 427
Fansler, Effie R. 41
Farm Bureau of Rockingham 25 327
Farmville State Teachers College 48 49 71 120 121
Farrar, J. Clough 367
"Father Brown" 391
"Father of Song" 303 351 399
Fawley, Pauline E. 33
Federal Building in Harrisonburg 343
"Fence Corner Council" 405
Ferrisburg, Vt. 98 99
Filler, Rev. Samuel 143
Firebaugh, Robert D. 201
Fire Company No. 3 347
First brick house in Harrisonburg 392
First M.A. of U. Va. 433
Fishburne Military Academy 170
Fitzgerald, Harriet L. 279
Flat Rock 153 368 369
Fletcher, Abner K. 221
Fletcher, Mary M. 155
Fletcher, Virginia 221
Flory, Annie R. 193 195 197
Flory, Daniel C. 259
Fluvanna County, Va. 74 75
Flying field at Harrisonburg 178 179
Flynn, Elijah H. 165

GENERAL INDEX

Flynn, Hanora 130 224 225
"Forerunners" 199 335
Forestville, Va. 125 173 189 313 368
Fort Belvoir 65
"Fort Egypt" 199
Fort Defiance, Va. 144 145
"Fort Hoover" 59
Fort Myer 241 293 306 307 339
Fort Seybert, W. Va. 67
Fort Worth, Texas 165
"Forty Years of Active Service" 422
Frank, Berdie 285
Friedens Church 217 391
Front Royal, Va. 176 177 331
Fulton, Capt. Samuel M. 95
Funk, Benjamin 399 411
Funk, Rev. Timothy 388 399
Funk genealogy 303 305
Funkhouser, A. Paul 305 353 399
Funkhouser, History 399
Furniture merchant (pioneer) 102 103
"Gadsden Treaty, The" 152
Gainesville, Ga. 391
Garber, Annie E. 43
Garber, Rev. John 153
Garber's Academy 146 147
Garber's Church 39 151
Garden Club of Virginia 89
Gay, Dr. Samuel 129 400
Geil, Barbara A. 33
George Peabody College 49
Georgetown University 158 159 238 239 378
George Washington University 171 184 185 205
Gettysburg, Pa. 362 408
Gillian, Annie 87
Gilmer's book, 401
Glass, Sen. Carter 97
Glasscock, Micajah 299
Glen Choral Club 351
Glendale High School 307
Glens Falls, N. Y. 99
Good, Prof. M. A. 245
Good, Mrs. S. G. 63
"Good Man, The" 301 425
Good's Mill, Va. 30 134 135
"Good Neighbor" motorcades 107
Gordonsville, Va. 55 75
Gore, Isaac 243
Gospel Messenger 404
Graham, David 420

Grandle, Maggie R. 319
Grant for a third term 233
"Grattan's Reports" 402
Green Island Seed Farm 363
Greenmount 274
Greensboro, N. C. 319
Greenwood, W. C. 101
Grottoes, Va. 328 329
Guest, Edgar 127
Hagerdon, Elizabeth 275
Hagerstown, Md. 47 100 101 127 169
Hall, Bernice 61
Hall, Col. James 299
Hampden-Sydney College 90 91 293 390
Hampton, Gen. Wade 221
Hampton Legion 367
Handler, Evelyn E. 37
Hannah, Miss Belle 27
Harman Hills, W. Va. 166 167
Harman's School of Music 166 167
"Harmonia Sacra" 399
Harper, Bettie R. 287
Harrison, Nathaniel 177
Harrison, Nebr. 85
Harrison genealogy 174 175 177
Harrison Hall 403
Harrisonburg 281 285 338 339 343
Harrisonburg in 1820 392
Harrisonburg in 1867 392
Harrisonburg in 1885 393
Harrisonburg band 110 111
Harrisonburg Board of Trade 347
Harrisonburg city engineer 128 129
Harrisonburg, first brick house 392
Harrisonburg schools 55 206 207 220 221 235 417
Harrison's Cave 391
Harriston, Va. 214 216 409
Harshbarger, Dr. C. P. 415
Harvard University 60 61 157 206 366
Haverford College 98 99
Hays, Prof. Daniel 127 149
"Heart of the Crimson Cross" 184 185
Hebron Seminary 264 265
Hedrick, Rev. Joseph M. 183
Heinze, Victor 349
Henkel, Christina 167
Henry House, The 405
"Heroic Lives" 261
Herrill, Elena P. 405
Highland Recorder 324 325
Highways of N. C. 129

General Index 445

Hillsville, Va. 97
Hinegardner, Ida F. 197
Historian-General for U. C. Veterans, 274
Historical pageant 235
Historical works 175 305 389
"Historic Homes" 175 408
"History of Jewish Rationalism" 37
Hite, Lucy Winfield 149
Hoenshel, Elmer U. 135
Hoffman, Edna 45
Hog, Betsy 390
Hog, Captain Peter 390 406
Hollingsworth family 69
Hollins College 74 75 348 349
Holstein herd 33
Hood College 299
Hoover, Flora 47
Hoover, Hon. Herbert 191
Hoover family 193
Hopkins, Capt. John 201
Hopkins homestead 129
Horace Mann School 242
Horn, Mary E. 339
Horses and cattle 210 211 213
Horticulture 42 43 147 189 195 361 363 385
Hotchkiss, Major Jed 371
"Hours of Fancy" 410
Houston, Rev. William 175
Houston, Miss. 165
Howe, John W. 302
"How to Do Research in Education" 160
Huffman, Emily F. 45
Huffman, Frances 229
Huguenot ancestors 299 336 337 359
Humphrey, Hon. Wm. E. 244 245
Huntington, W. Va. 222 223
Hupp, Casper 420
Hylton, Ann 47
"Idothea" 426
Inglewood Seminary 75
Improved livestock 95 301
India, missionaries to 31 415
Indiana University 308
Indian Road, The 219
"Infant of the Regiment" 299
Irick, Virginia S. 87 394
Iron works 138 139 407
Irwin, Clarence P. 237
Island Ford, Va. 177 359
Jackson, Dr. George P. 305 396
Jackson, Stonewall 409

Jarman, Miletus M. 243
Jefferson, Thomas 35
Jewelers in Harrisonburg 108 109
"John Carlisle Kilgo" 153
Johns Hopkins University 61 90 91 274
Johnston, Gen. Joseph E. 408
Johnston, Judge Robert 207
Johnston-Willis Hospital 49 61
Johnstown Flood 177
Jones, Hon. Charles P. 408
Jones, Gen. J. R. 55
Journal of Educational Research 161
Juniata College 46 48 49 182
Kagey, Rev. John 301
Kagey, Noah I. 269
Kavanaugh Hotel, 212 **213**
Kaylor, Lewis W. 215
Kaylor's Mill, Va. 214
Kaylor's Park 214 215 217
Keezletown, Va. 122 218 219 372 373 408
Keezletown Road 219 383 412
Kelley, Gen. B. F. 397
Kelley, John E. 225
Kemper, Elizabeth 343
Kenney, Judge James 207 410
Kenney house in Harrisonburg 103 105 410
Kent, Frank R. 97
Kent, Ohio 319
"Kentucky Harmony" 396
Kerfoot, Cornelia M. 205
Kidd, Orina W. 153
Kieffer, Lucilla 305
Kieffer genealogy 303
Killed by an Indian 63 414
Kilmarnock, Va. 171
Kingfisher, Okla. 44 45
King's attorney 408
"King's Mountain Men" 305
Kirby, Rev. R. J. 323
Kirkpatrick, Wm. J. 163
Knupp, Mary 315
Koiner, Elizabeth 287
Koogler, John R. 241
Koontz, Col. John 392 411
Kyger's Shop 231
Lacey Spring 65 67 187 411 414
Ladies' Memorial Association 432
Laird, David 219
Lake Junaluska 49
"Lake o' the Cherokees" 379

General Index

Lambert, Emma V. 247
Lambert, Vernie E. 125
Land grants 409
"Land of the Sky" 143
Lane High School 376 377
Langley Field 85
Latham, R. H. 277
"Laurel Brigade" 25
"Lawyer, The" 408
"Lawyer Road" 123 408
Lay, Judge John F. 91
Leake, W. W. 131
Ledger-Dispatch 241
Lee, Gen. Robert E. 281
Leedy's Pump 412
"Lethe" 359 401
Levy, Anna 37
Levy, Ray 429
Lewis, John (pioneer) 413
Lewis, Sen. John F. 233
Lewis, Gen. Samuel H. 215 412 413
Lewiston, Va. 412 413
Lexington, Va. 379
Libby Prison 59
Liberty Hall Academy 390
Lilly, Va. 322 323 413 429
Limerick, Ireland 131 224
Lincoln, B. F. 432
Lincoln, David 411 414
"Lincoln Inn" 411
Lincoln lands 25 414
Lincoln Memorial University 185
Linganore, Md. 92 93
Linville, William 315
Linville Creek 315
Linville-Edom School 33
Lipscomb, Judge H. S. 97
Liskey, Harvey 235
Liskey, Robert D. 59
Livestock improved 33 95 211 217 255 425
Lockwood, Mrs. J. Franklin 405
Loewner, Emanuel 227
Logansport, Ind. 118 119
Lomax, John T. 412
Long, Ina E. 35
Long, Sarah 428
Loose, Rev. E. P. 207
Los Angeles, Calif. 158 159 388
Lost in the Blue Ridge 215
Louisville, Ky. 90 191
Lumber merchants 267 295 297

Lupton, Stella 287
Lupton family 287 416
Luray, Va. 199 326 334 335 412
Lurty, Capt. W. S. 55
Lynchburg, Va. 61 87 91
Lynnwood, Va. 232
Lyon, Mona L. 85
MacDonald, Norine J. 171
McComb, Gen. William 75
McConnell, Dr. John P. 337
McDowell Academy 220
McDowell battle 141 400
McGaheysville 28 29 231 247 295 358 378
McGarr, Judge E. G. 163
McKellar, Suelle 341
McLaughlin, Lizzie E. 347
McLeod, John H. 223
McNeill's Rangers 397
McPherson, Kans. 141
McPherson College 190 191
Madison, Bishop James 409 417
Madison, President James 417
Madison College 74 75 90 91 169 207 221
"Madison Hall" 286 287 409 417
Madison Quarterly 243
Madison's Cave 417
Manakin Town 337
"Man Who Forgot, The" 404
"Maplewood" 168
Marks, Mrs. Myra McC. 275
Marksville, Va. 326 327
Marshall, Mansfield 291 417
Martha Washington College 394
Martz-Harrison home 174 175
Mary Baldwin College 81 123
Mason, Walt 127
Masonic Lodge in Harrisonburg 63
Massanetta Springs 222 290
Massanetta Sprngs Conferences 367 416
Massanutten Academy 154 155
"Master Farmer" 384 385
Matheny, W. H. 325
Mauck, Pearl 253
Maupin, Dr. Richard S. 424
Maury, Matthew Fontaine 371
May, Ola 197
Mayo Clinic 159
Meadville, Pa. 71 114 115
Medical College of Virginia 34 267 308 309 368

General Index

Medical journals 87
Meigs, Lieut. John R. 361
Melrose Caverns 391
"Memorials of Old Virginia Clerks" 415
Mencken, H. L. 97
Mercer County, Pa. 114 115
Merck Company 311 338
"Methodist Meeting House, The" 153
Meuse-Argonne Offensive 69 83 307
Miami University 161
Middlebrook, Va. 154
Middle River Church 151
Middleton, Helen 43
Miller, Adam 329 335 359 419
Miller, Elsie R. 339
Miller, G. Edward 353
Miller, John W. 263
Miller, Rev. Martin P. 257 259
Minister to Portugal 412
Minor, John B. 412
Mitchell, Prof. B. B. 286 287
Mitchell, Rev. M. D. 53
Moffett, Anderson 153
Moffett, Hannah Bryan 395
Mohler, John N. 145
Monroe, James 418
Montague, Mrs. R. T. 27
Monterey, Va. 248 249 324 325
Montreal, Canada 380 381
Moon, Lottie 75
Moore, Margaret 345
Morgan, Maisie L. 113
Morris Plan Bank 171 379
Morrison, Brownie 279 421
Morton, Margaret 408
Mosby, Col. John S. 345
Moscow, Va. 294-297
Mossy Creek, Va. 139 190 191 371
Mossy Creek Cemetery 420
"Mountain Muse, The" 392
Mount Vernon Association 290
Mt. Carmel School 73
Mt. Crawford, Va. 209 216 217
Mt. Crawford Military Academy 266 267
Mt. Sidney, Va. 136 150 261 269
Musical Courier 349
Musical Million 302 303 305 410
Music books 162 163 320 321 399
Music contest, national 167
Music schools 162 166 167 321 399
Music teachers 78 162 302 320 399
Myers, Benj. Allen 277

Myers, Dr. J. Sidwell 205
Myers, Elder Samuel H. 147 385
Myers, Dr. Weldon T. 277
Nashville, Tenn. 191
National Geographic Magazine 313 428
Neff, Dr. John Henry (pioneer) 279
New Erection Church 138 139
New London Academy 390
Newman, Caroline Lee 55
New Market, Va. 62 63 183 300 302
New Market battle 397
New Market Music School 162 321
New Market Polytechnic Institute 34 62
News-Virginian 328 329
Niederstetten, Germany 280
Noble Center School 49
Nokesville, Va. 30 31 264 265
"Nolichucky Jack" 427
Norfolk, Va. 240 241
Norfolk & Western Railway 139 169
North Carolina Highway Engineer 128 129
Northwestern University 50 51 77 101 357
Nourse, James 205
Oak Hill Academy 26 230 231 378
O'Ferrall, Gov. Charles T. 394 422 438
Ohio State University 304
"Oil Center of the World" 379
Oil paintings 281 416
Old Commonwealth 407
Oldest bank president 425
Old Folks Singings 163
Omaha *Bee* 97
Omohundro, Mamie 343
Oslo, Norway 51
Ouachita College 74
Overlock, Frances C. 123
Oxford University 305
Page County pioneers 335
Page Valley 229
Parnassus, Va. 145
Parsons, W. Va. 167
Pasco, Sen. Samuel 395
Patterson, Washington 337
Paul, Abram 353
Paul, Capt. John 241
Paul's address on Rockingham 423
Paul's Summit School 352 353
"Pawnee Bill" 413
Payne, Dr. Will 353
Peabody Conservatory 257

448　　　　　　　　GENERAL INDEX

Peabody Normal College 135 257 289
Peabody scholarships 257 289
Peale, Amanda F. 409
Pennypacker, Samuel W. 305
Perkins, Col. Joseph P. 75
Pershing, Gen. John J. 307
Petersburg, Va. 292 293
Philadelphia 354 355 390
Photographers of Harrisonburg 85 99
Pierce, Lyman L. 183
Pirkey, Elias 145
Pirkey's Graveyard 412
"Plains, The" 127 153 420
Pleasants, Julia Page 291
Poems of Dr. Fahrney 127
"Poet Laureate of the U. B. Church" 351
Point Pleasant battle 421
Pop Geers 213
Port Republic 273 329 419 423
Port Republic battlefield 215
Port Republic bridge 217
Port Republic history 419
Portsmouth, Ohio 130 131
Poultry industry 38-41 43 73 95 189 209 353 355 385
Poultry specialist 136 137
Powell's Fort 63
Powhatan County, Va. 337
"Practice Leaves" 74 243
Pratt Institute 169
Preacher 70 years 420
Price, Elizabeth B. 117
Prince Edward County, Va. 337
Princeton Seminary 366
Princeton University 197
Prince William Academy 149
Progressive Farmer 385
"Psalms, Hymns, and Spiritual Songs" 320 321
Quaker minister 99
Queen welcomed 229
Quiller-Couch, Sir Arthur 307
Rader's Lutheran Church 43
Ramsey, Virginia 345
Randolph-Macon Academy, Bedford 88 121
Randolph-Macon Academy, Front Royal 55 255
Randolph-Macon College, 89 121 243 355 378
Randolph-Macon Monthly 243
Randolph-Macon Woman's College 87 169
Rappahannock County 251 253
Raven Society 171 203
Rawley Springs 211 213
Readjuster orator 418
Rector, John 299
Red Cross 195 196 367
Reed, Dr. Walter 425
Regimental Band, 4th Ga. 246 247
Revere House 225
Revolutionary soldiers 217 223 301 303 375 414 429
Rhodes, J. B. D. 305 323
Richest man in Rockingham 412
Richmond, Va. 60 61 308 309 312 313
Richmond College 26 27
Rickard, W. H. 347
Rickard & Voorhees 233
Riggin, Frances 57
Rion-Bowman Post, V. F. W. 107 173
"River Bend" 168-170
"River Rangers" 381
"Roaming Invalid" 407
Roanoke, Va. 133 169 235 263 388
Roanoke College 46 116 169 373
Roanoke County, Va. 117
Rockingham Farm Bureau 25 327
Rockingham Public Library 47 169 206 207 243
Rockingham Memorial Hospital 47 67 87 192 193 291 373 412
Rockingham Outlook 305
Rockingham Register 289 393 396 407 420 430 434
Rockingham schools 276 277 416
Rockingham Union Lodge, A. F. & A. M. 396 406 435
Rocky Mount, Va. 116
Roller, Caroline 343 345
Root, Fred W. 320 321
Rosemary Mont 335
"Rosendale" 301 425
Rosenfeld, Bertha 281
Rosser, Gen. Thomas L. 25
Rude's Hill 279 421
Ruebush-Kieffer Co. 303 305
Rural electrification 95 151 245
Salem, Va. 388
Sangerville, Va. 264 265
Saum, John R. 133
Saur, Christoph 305
Schools of Rockingham 276 277 407

General Index 449

Scott, Capt. Robert 406
Scott, Col. Thomas 337
Scott's Ford, Va. 273
Sculptors 389
Sebrell, Thomas E. 69
Seedsmen 353 362 363 365
Sellers, Dr. J. S. 64 65
"Settlers by the Long Grey Trail" 174 175
Seven-Mile Ford, Va. 340
Seven Pines battle 417
Shackelford, W. C. 95
Shacklett family historian 428
Shaffer, Francis M. 237
Shakespeare Pageant 75
Shamokin, Pa. 164 165
Shands, Capt. E. A. 211
Shank, Jacob L. 357
Sheffey, Daniel 233
Shenandoah Camp for Boys 108 109
Shenandoah College 59 167 172 291 303 399
Shenandoah Iron Works 407
Shenandoah National Park 97 329 337
Shenandoah Valley Academy 91 336
Shenandoah Valley Inc. 283 337
Shendun, Va. 145
Shepherd College 411
Shepherdstown, W. Va. 34 101
Sherman, Daisy G. 65
Sherman, Rev. H. H. 53
Sherman, Sarah 343
Shirley, Henry G. 97
Shoup, Capt. J. C. 25
Showalter, John A. 321
Showalter, Ottie F. 277
Sidwell Friends' School 205
Silliman College 350 351
Silver Lake 51 81 331 353
Simms, Mrs. Fred 409
Singers' Glen 189 271 303 305 351 399 416
Sioux City, Iowa 288 289
Sipe, Col. Emanuel 305
Skipper (magazine) 341
Slater, Frances 53 55
Slemp, Hon. C. B. 97
Smith, Olive M. 49
"Smithland" 429
Smucker, Charles J. 385
Smythe, R. B. 325 433
Snapp, Rev. Silas R. 329
Sousa, John Philip 247 389

South Bend High School 308
South Chard, England 99
Southern Literary Messenger 337
Sparkling Springs 103
Sparta, Va. 322
Spartanburg, S. C. 113 277 366
Spilman, Louis 329
Spirit of the Valley 101 232 233
Spring Creek, Va. 256 259 346
Sprinkel, Capt. C. A. 281 432
"Star of Bethlehem" 162 163
State Republican 399
Staunton, Va. 79 233
Staunton Spectator. 418
Stephens City, Va. 388
Still College 264 265
St. Nicholas 392
Stoneleigh Inn 425
Stonewall Brigade 408
Stonewall Brigade Band 126 127
Stonewall Jackson 35 371 409
St. Peter's Lutheran Church 229 419
Strasburg, Va. 82 83 331 345
Strayer, Mrs. Ella V. 388
Strickler, Eld. Reuben T. 199
Strother, Jane 89 413
Strother, William 243 408
Stuart's Draft, Va. 77 138 145 354
Sublett, Frank L. 283 336
Sun Beau 410
"Sunrise at Lover's Leap" 392
Surgeon on the *Maine* 405
Surgeons five 373
Surgeons of Rockingham 35 117 137 279 368 373 405 409 425
Surveyor of 1822 139
Suter, John R. 39
Swisher, Lola 105
Switzer, John A. 343 345
Switzer, Valentine 345
Swope, Elizabeth 347
Swope, Susan C. 428
Taft, Chief Justice 275
Tanneries in Virginia 93
Taylor's Academy 187 433
Tazewell County, Va. 171
"Telephone Spirit" 231
"Temple Star" 410
Tenth Legion, Va. 35 174 333 424
"Tenth Legion Tithables" 335
Texas historical societies 164 165
Theological seminary proposed 404

Thomas, Rev. Daniel 309
Thomas, Elder Jacob 257 347
Thomas, Susan 309
Thompson, Wm. B. 349
Thomsonian doctor 411
Thrasher, Col. Paul M. 323
Timber Ridge School 244
Timberville, Va. 127 149 189 193 195 249
Times-Dispatch 341
Todd's Tavern 393
Toledo, Ohio 370 371
Trucking business 179
Tucker, George R. 351
Tulsa, Okla. 171 379
Turkey drives 139
Turkey Festival 65 85 95 149 173 229 239
Turley, Giles 109
Turner, Dr. J. H. 331
Twenty sermons in one day 31
Tyerman, Ambrose S. 187
Tyerman, Bertha G. 35
Tyerman, Margaret R. 187
Tyree, Josiah S. 27
Umbarger, Martha E. 119
Underwood Constitution 413
University of Chicago 49 161
  Cincinnati 160 161
  Colorado 227
  Maryland 65 127 143 333
  Michigan 161
  New Mexico 353
  North Carolina 197 255
  Pennsylvania 152 257
  Pittsburgh 197
  Texas 165
  Virginia 57 61 67 77 171 203 359
  West Virginia 197
  Wisconsin 161
University of Virginia Hospitaal 278 279
Unseld, B. C. 162 321
U. S. Geological Survey 170 171
Valparaiso University 182
Vance, Col. Samuel 289
Vaughan, Ethel 195
V. F. W. work 106 107
"Vineyard Farm" 275
Virginia Academy of Science 46 309
Virginia Craftsmen, Inc. 63 195 337
"Virginia John" 25 414
Virginia Journal of Education 243 307 405
Virginia Lee Literary Society 197
Virginia Magazine of History and Biography 410
Virginia Medical Monthly. 87 377
Virginia Military Institute 219 299 425
Virginia-Pilot 97
Virginia Polytechnic Institute 32 49 57 71 194 198 341 371 426
Virginia State Fair 136 137
Virginia Teacher 206 243
"Virginia Valley Records" 390 406 424
Wagner, Sadie W. 245
Walking from Texas 25
Wampler, Prof. Isaac S. 201 271
Wampler, Letitia J. 273
Warm Springs Turnpike 53
Warren, Mrs. James M. 432
Warrenton, Va. 204
Wartman, Harvey 289
Warwick, Mary Byrd 117
Warwick Castle 75
Washington, Gen. George 401 409 413
Washington and Lee University 55 94 123 201 220 344
Watauga Country 47
Watchful Pilgrim 41 433
Waterman School 63 435
Watson, Dr. Thomas L. 171
Watts, Dr. Stephen H. 279
Waynesboro, Va. 125 145
Weaver's Church School 39 41 234
Wenger, Lucy B. 317
West, Madison 432
West Central Academy 32 60 79 201 271 434
Western, Rena B. 151
Westhampton College 207
West Milton, Ohio 320 321
Whitehead Society 377
"White Spirituals" 305 396
Widow Tea's 125
Wildcat Division 307
Wildlife Federation 76 77
Wild turkey farm 371
Wilkinson, Lucia G. 359
William and Mary College 29 43 249 417
Williams, Hon. R. Gray 97
Willits, R. Admiral G. S. 383
Wilmington, Del. 382 383
Wilson, Capt. A. H. 93 399

General Index

Wilson, Rev. John L. 367
Wilson, Hon. William L. 55
Wilson, Hon. Woodrow 35 45
Winchester, Mass. 259
Winchester, Va. 198 199
Wine, Jacob 141
Winewood Farms 370 371
Winfield, Capt. John Q. 25 432 437
Winsborough, Frances M. 247
Winston-Salem 358 359
Winthrop College 396
Wise, Kattie 281 283 285
Wise, Laura W. 101
Wise, Leopold 281 285
Withers, Ann 389
World's S. S. Convention 51
World War I record 396
Wood, Capt. John I. 177
Woodberry Forest School 101
Woodson, R. Lee 113

Woodson's Missourians 397
Woodstock, Va. 155 237
Worrell, Major C. C. 341
Wright, Dr. John F. 373
Wunder, Mrs. Myra M. 420
Wyant, Alexander E. 375
Wyoming, Ohio 161
Yale Divinity School 50
Yale University 307
Yancey, Capt. Edward S. 381
Yancey, John G. 381 383
Yancey, Capt. Thomas L. 381
Yancey, Col. Wm. Burbridge 379 381 394 437
Y. M. C. A. in 1860 394
Yost, Harriet 408
Young, Dr. Hugh H. 409
Zigler, Rev. David H. 385
Zigler Packing Co. 385

www.ingramcontent.com/pod-product-compliance
Lightning Source LLC
Chambersburg PA
CBHW071223290426
44108CB00013B/1277